Charles John Abbey

The English Church and its Bishops 1700-1800

Vol. I

Charles John Abbey

The English Church and its Bishops 1700-1800
Vol. I

ISBN/EAN: 9783743373587

Manufactured in Europe, USA, Canada, Australia, Japa

Cover: Foto ©Lupo / pixelio.de

Manufactured and distributed by brebook publishing software (www.brebook.com)

Charles John Abbey

The English Church and its Bishops 1700-1800

THE
ENGLISH CHURCH

AND ITS BISHOPS

1700—1800

BY

CHARLES J. ABBEY

RECTOR OF CHECKENDON : LATE FELLOW OF UNIVERSITY COLLEGE, OXFORD
AND JOINT-AUTHOR OF 'THE ENGLISH CHURCH IN THE EIGHTEENTH CENTURY'

IN TWO VOLUMES

VOL. I.

LONDON
LONGMANS, GREEN, AND CO.
1887

All rights reserved

PREFACE.

CERTAIN phases of life and thought in the English Church of the eighteenth century were discussed with some fulness in a book published a few years ago, and now about to be republished in a shorter form by Canon Overton and myself.[1] But the subject was there treated in what might almost be called a series of essays, leaving many important questions wholly, or nearly wholly, untouched, and expressing only on particular points the individual opinion of each author. Thus the work itself, and the great amount of unexhausted material which I had collected, often served to remind me that one of us might do well to take up the subject in a more continuous manner.

When, however, I began my present task, I had not the least intention of anything more than to illustrate the history of the English Church in that century by sketches from the lives of its prelates. But the undertaking grew upon my hands. When I had finished the chapter relating to the Episcopate of Queen Anne's reign, I thought I would supplement it with a general survey of

[1] *The English Church in the Eighteenth Century.* 2 vols. 1878. Longmans.

the Church life of that period. Presently I found that this general survey was becoming a connected history, and I felt grave doubts whether I were not spoiling two subjects by attempting to unite them in one. On further consideration I resolved to continue my work in its double character. After all, there may be some advantages in combining the history of a period in a Church's life with sketches of its principal officers.

I have carefully avoided more than very occasional repetition from the previous work. The entirely different form in which that book was written has made it generally easy to escape treading in my own or my former coadjutor's footsteps. There are only two subjects, and they collateral ones—'Sacred Poetry,' and 'Church Fabrics and Church Services'—which I have thought it necessary on this occasion to pass almost entirely by.

CONTENTS

OF

THE FIRST VOLUME.

CHAPTER I.

THE ENGLISH CHURCH, 1700–14.

	PAGE
Influences of the Revolution of 1688 upon English religious life	1
The war with Louis XIV. one of Roman Catholics and Protestants	2
Protestant feeling	3
Alliance with foreign Protestantism	4
Jurors and Nonjurors	5
Jacobites and High Tories	6
Party spirit	8
'Church in danger'	9
The Sacheverell prosecution	10
Convocation	12
Nonconformity	14
Failure of the late Comprehension Scheme	15
The sacramental test	17
Occasional Conformity	18
Purpose of the Schism Act	22
Growth of free-thought; Locke	24
Toland	25
Mysteries in religion	26
Shaftesbury	28
Disinterested virtue	30
Archbishop King on the origin of evil	31
'Whatever is, is right'	31
Mandeville	32
Deistical attacks on the clergy	33

	PAGE
Cry of 'Priestcraft'	35
Arianism of Emlyn, Clarke, and Whiston	36
Dodwell and lay baptism	39
Materiality of the soul	41
Theological literature	42
The Essayists	43
Contest against irreligion	45
Societies for the reformation of manners	46
Religious associations	50
Foundation of the Christian Knowledge Society	54
Cheap theological literature	55
Parochial and diocesan libraries	56
Activity of the Christian Knowledge Society	58
Education of the poor; charity schools	59
Catechising	61
Dissenters' efforts in the cause of education	61
Education in the upper and middle classes	62
The universities	64
The poor clergy	68
Politics at Oxford and Cambridge	69
Female education	73
Revival of missionary enterprise	74
Missionary spirit of the early colonists	75
Intolerance in the colonies	77
New England Society for the Propagation of the Gospel	78
Virginia	79
General condition of the English Church in America at end of seventeenth century	80
Commissaries to Bishop of London	82
T. Bray in America	83
Formation of the Society for the Propagation of the Gospel	85
Proposals to send bishops to America	87
Co-operation with Danish missions in India	89
Negroes and slavery	90
The Society's missionaries in America	91

CHAPTER II.

ENGLISH BISHOPS, 1700–14.

The Episcopate high in estimation	92
Bishops and clergy	93
Tenison	94
Wake	96

	PAGE
Sharp	103
Compton	106
Robinson	109
Burnet	110
Patrick	115
Moore	116
Fowler	119
Fleetwood	120
Cumberland	122
Kidder	123
Lloyd	124
Trelawney	128
Hough	129
Hooper	131
Bull	133
Beveridge	135
Wilson	138
Atterbury	142
Spratt	149
Hall	151
Williams; Blackhall	153
Dawes	154
Trimnell	155
Ironside	156
Talbot	157
Mew	158
Smith; Nicholson	159
Manningham	160
Stratford; Bisse	161
Gardiner; Humphreys; Beaw; Tyler	162
Welsh bishops; Otley	163
Jones; Watson	164
Crewe	164
Nonjuring bishops	166
Frampton	167
Lloyd	169
Ken	170
Bishops of the Revolution of 1688	172
Honour paid to the bishops	176
The bishops in Parliament	179
Differences with their clergy	181

CHAPTER III.

THE ENGLISH CHURCH, 1714–60.

	PAGE
Abatement of previous controversies	183
Jacobitism	185
Nonjurors	187
Convocation	193
Divine right and passive obedience	201
Church in danger	202
The Protestant interest	203
Church comprehension	205
Schism and occasional Conformity Acts	208
The sacramental test	209
Condition of Nonconformity	210
Friendly relations between Churchmen and Dissenters	213
Growth of tolerance in the educated classes	213
The Jew Bill	214
Popular horror of Popery	216
Feeling towards Rome	218
Subscription to the Articles	220
Proposals for revision of the Liturgy	224
Deism	226
Deistical writings	227
Decline of Deism	229
Scepticism and unbelief	230
Popular interest in theological questions	232
Free-thinking	233
Liberty of thought	235
Biblical inspiration	237
The atonement	238
Future punishments	239
Evidence of miracles	242
Evidence of prophecy	244
'Christianity as old as creation'	247
The religion of nature	248
Nature and revelation	251
'Christianity not founded on argument'	252
Reactionary influences of Deism	254
Wesley on external evidences	255
The Methodist movement	257
Greatness of the work	258
Wesley's expectations	259
The preachers and their audiences	260

Wesley's zeal and activity	261
Field preaching	264
Methodist discipline	266
The message preached	267
Wesley on orthodoxy	268
Small success among the educated classes	269
Wesley on the depravity of human nature	271
Wesley on his state before conversion	273
Wesley on childhood	275
Wesley on Calvinistic reprobation	278
Wesley on conversion	279
Wesley on the new birth	281
Wesley on perfection	282
Bodily agitations	284
Opposition to his theology	286
Impossibility of most sober Churchmen adopting Methodism	288
The English Church and Methodism	289
Weak ground taken by most of its contemporary opponents	290
Union with Methodism	291
William Law	293
His theology of redemption	295
The fall and the restoration	296
John Byrom	298
Henry Brooke	299
Moravianism and the English Church	301
The Wesleys and the Moravians	303
Increasing estrangement	305
Ingham; Gambold; Okely	307
The Hutchinsonians	309
Character of the clergy	312
Absenteeism and pluralities	317
Clerical poverty	319
The universities	320
The public schools	328
Grammar schools	330
Academies	331
Elementary education	332
Charity and industrial schools	334
Dame schools	335
Charitable institutions	337
Societies for reformation of manners	342
Work of the Christian Knowledge Society	345
Missions in South India	347
Work of the Society for the Propagation of the Gospel	348
Bishop Berkeley's scheme	349

	PAGE
Oglethorpe in Georgia	349
The Wesleys in America	353
Whitefield's preaching in America	355
The English Church in the southern States	358
S. Johnson and Connecticut	360
Bishops for America	362
The English Church in the northern colonies	365

CHAPTER IV.

THE ENGLISH EPISCOPATE, 1714–1800.

Deterioration early in George I.'s reign	367
Successors of King William's bishops	370
Walpole and Church patronage	371
The bishops in disfavour	372
Archbishop Blackburn	374
Imputations against bishops	376
Queen Caroline's influence	378
Her theological opinions	381
Her interest in Church matters	382
The bishops and Methodism	384
Eighteenth century bishops in England	397

CHAPTER I.

THE ENGLISH CHURCH. 1700–1714.

BOTH religiously and politically, the late Revolution was, throughout Queen Anne's reign, in one or another of its bearings, and by action or reaction, the great predominating influence of the time. The affairs of Church and State were hence most intimately connected. So far as the quenched fire of the civil wars had left any heat of zeal in the hearts of the people, it had been kindled into new life by the dangers which threatened alike the liberties and the Protestantism of England in the reign of James. There had been a struggle which had touched, not indeed the deeper strings of religious feeling, but a great deal of strongly rooted religious sentiment, and very many of those prejudices and antipathies which always play so large a part on the surface of religious life. These feelings were intensified rather than quieted during the remaining years of William, and throughout the reign of the queen who succeeded him.

A great war was raging, but, so far from diverting the minds of the people from their interest in Church questions, it did but strengthen it. In the eyes of most Englishmen, the strife which Marlborough was conducting in the Low Countries was a kind of crusade, and Ramillies and Blenheim were the victories of a religious cause. The one idea which inspired William with a fervour which was otherwise foreign to his nature, was that he headed the Protestant interest in Europe, and that through his agency, and under his leading, the tide of Roman reaction should be turned. Until the Peace of Utrecht in 1713 brought, amid varied feelings, an end to the war, 'the point of discourse which seldom' (says the 'Tatler') 'escapes a knot of true-born Englishmen,' was not so much what it would have been in later or in earlier days, whether English would prevail or French, but 'whether the Protestants would not be too strong for the Papists.'[1]

A similar war was being carried on in legislature, and in controversy, and in popular opinion at home. It was as though the nation, having narrowly escaped from a great danger, could scarcely feel that it was safe. Roman Catholics were all but outlawed. No doubt feeling had somewhat abated since the crisis of the Revolution, when Romanists had been forbidden even to set foot in Westminster Hall,[2] and when, in some towns, the houses of any who were suspected of being 'Popishly affected' were attacked and rifled.[3] But still the very name of Popery was 'a strangely madding cry.'[4] Nor was it only a cry, as Roman Catholics knew to their cost. Bill after Bill, in the reigns alike of William and of Anne, was levelled against them. Toleration was for Protestants only. Somers was a liberal and high-minded statesman; but under his lengthened rule the penal code against Romanists was made far more severe than ever it had been under Elizabeth or her successors. Their priests were to be banished, and if they returned were to be hanged. Twenty pounds were to be given for the discovery of a priest. If a Papist would not tell where he last heard mass he was to go to prison for a year. No Papist was to keep a school, and no one, except under heavy penalties, might send a child to be so educated

---

[1] *Tatler*, No. 155.   [2] Calamy's *Life*, i. 625.
[3] Prideaux, *Life and Letters*, 17.   [4] South's *Works*, iv. 207.

abroad. No Papist might be guardian to a child; and if the child of a Papist became a Protestant any part of his father's estate might, by order of Chancery, be applied to his use.[1] Such and such like were the laws which the wisest legislation of the day, with the full consent of public opinion, thought desirable for England and for Ireland. If a certain connivance existed in regard of the illicit practices referred to, there were those who angrily argued that such relaxation of laws 'may seem to proceed from benignity of nature, which the gospel that inclines to mercy does indeed justify and encourage, but has nothing in it of the masculine dictates of our most holy religion, but is indeed nothing but feminine weakness where this tenderness of disposition is carried to such dangerous excess of indulgence.'[2] Better ' expel the whole sect from the British dominions, and once and for all clear the nation of these monsters.'[3] Not a voice, unless it might be from one of their own body, was raised in their defence. On this point at least all were nearly agreed. High Churchman, Low Churchman, or Dissenter, orthodox or Latitudinarian, Whig or Tory, Arian, Deist, or infidel—nearly all men at this period seem to have considered the Romanist (unless, as in the case of Pope, love or admiration might except an individual) an outcast from ordinary sympathies. Not even among the highest of High Churchmen among the ranks of Jacobites and Nonjurors[1] was there a single divine of any note whatever, who could be justly charged by any reasonable man with any leaning toward the detested doctrines of the general foe. The

[1] From various enactments of William and Anne quoted in Campbell's *Lives of the Chancellors*, iv. 227.

[2] W. Scot's *Short and Easy Way*, 2nd ed. 1713. Somers' *Tracts*, xiii. 473.

[3] *Id.* 466.

[1] It was at a somewhat later date, when the persistent Nonjurors had become more widely alienated, that Leslie could say, 'I am grieved that so many of the handful show inclinations to Popery.'—Leslie's *Works*, i. 424.

fiercest campaigns are brightened by some gleams of generous feeling towards opponents. In this instance an exceptional respect was reserved for two or three distinguished Gallican divines. As Marlborough protected the estates of Fenelon, and sent him waggons of grain,[1] so also in England the controversialists, the pamphleteers, and essayists recognised in him, as in Bossuet and Pascal, a noble enemy, and rarely mentioned any of those three names without a tribute of honour, which their general tone made the more emphatic. A little later and we shall find Archbishop Wake entering into a remarkable correspondence with the champions of Gallican liberties.

For the same reason that Rome was under a universal ban, there was a strong feeling of friendship toward foreign Protestants. On this point the consent of opinion was not quite so universal. Churchmen, both as individuals and in Convocation, were not minded to be too closely identified with churches which had neither bishops nor liturgy. Those who were dissatisfied with the Revolution, or who (as was the case with many) were content with it, but had little love for William, and less for the Dutchmen who came over with him, were strongly disinclined to fraternise overmuch with co-religionists in Holland. Insular prejudice could not always restrain a self-satisfied sneer at the poverty-stricken, wooden-shoed hosts [2] who sought a refuge on English shores. Commercial jealousy had not always a warm greeting for the industrious artisans of the Cevennes and the Palatinate. The suspicious horror of fanaticism, which was a strongly marked feature of the time, could ill bear with the rapturous extravagances of the French Camisards. But all such counter-influences made for the time little head against the current which was everywhere strongly flowing in favour of all who were against Rome.

[1] Alison's *Life of Marlborough*, ii. 199.   [2] De Foe's *Works*, xx. 19.

The refugees found, on the whole, a very hospitable reception. Bills were introduced into Parliament for their naturalisation. Immense sums were collected for their benefit in churches and chapels. English bishops and divines were in frequent communication with the leaders of reformed churches abroad. The clergy in Convocation expressed 'their readiness to maintain and cherish such a fraternal correspondence with them as may strengthen the interest of the reformed religion against the common enemy.'[1] All Churchmen and all Englishmen were gratified at the respectful deference which was paid to their Church by oppressed Protestants abroad, and felt a pride in knowing that their country was at the head of the whole Protestant confederacy.

Another marked feature in the history of those fourteen years also arose directly out of the Revolution and the events that led to it. Nonjurors and Jacobites entered very largely into public thought and conversation. The most important part of the history of the Nonjuror secession is contained within this period. In 1701 King James died, and it seemed for the moment quite possible that this might end the schism. Men who felt that they could not be absolved from the allegiance which they owed personally to the late king might reasonably hold that no such paramount obligation bound them to his son. Many were at first inclined to take this view. But their hesitation was soon brought to an end, and the schism strengthened and enlarged, by the Abjuration Act, which followed in the next year at the very close of William's life. They no longer had any choice, when they were compelled not only to vow allegiance to the ruler of the realm, but also to repudiate the claims of the young prince, and to acknowledge William as king, not in fact only, but by right. It was a harassing and perplexing time, not so much for the existing Nonjurors,

[1] Quoted in Anderson's *Colon. Church,* iii. 50.

whose determination was henceforth sealed, but for many conscientious men who had taken the oath before, but must now either decline to do so, or be troubled with doubts and scruples, which would be all the more embarrassing because they could be so variously answered. Anne, however, succeeded; and in her time, Stuart as she was, and almost a Jacobite, and quite disposed to lighten the burden of the oath, difficulties were for the time quieted, and even Nonjurors could serve their queen in peace. A few years later, in **1710**, Ken was left the one survivor of the dispossessed bishops, and he had definitely resigned all claim to the canonical obedience which Nonjuring clergymen considered to be his by right. Thereupon the moderate Nonjurors, though they could not take the oaths, returned to the communion of the National Church. The remainder, who loved to call themselves the faithful remnant, now dwindled into a 'handful,' and, though their remaining history is in some respects an interesting one, passed out of connexion with the main stream of our national and ecclesiastical history.

Jacobitism, during the reign of Queen Anne, entered into the thoughts of English Churchmen, and, it may be added, of statesmen also, to a degree which was far from wholesome. The extent to which it prevailed is no easy question to decide. There was a considerable party of professed and known Jacobites, who took little pains to cast more than the thinnest of veils over opinions which would not bring them into serious risk under a queen who in heart was not greatly averse to the succession of her brother. Some were Nonjurors; some had had no occasion to take the oath of abjuration; many, with more or less want of scrupulousness, had taken the oath with explanations, understandings, or reserves. But the acknowledged Jacobites could only for the time wait and hope, correspond among themselves and with their friends abroad, rise conspicuously from their hassocks during the State prayers, and drink innumerable bumpers to the health of their absent master. A far larger party, and much more nearly connected with current interests alike in Church and State, was made up of men who were not avowed Jacobites, and who did not for the most part even in their own hearts consider themselves disaffected subjects, but were still so nearly on the verge, that a slight turn in the course of events might decide them to rally round the Pretender's banner. During the reign of Anne, and especially in her last four years, Tory and Jacobite merged into one another by the most imperceptible gradations. John Wesley was very indignant at his father and his elder brother being called Jacobites.[1] They were no more Jacobites, said he, than they were Turks. If they were called by that name, even among their intimate associates, it was only because people did not distinguish between Jacobite and Tory. 'Both my father and all his sons have always praised God for the happy Revolution.' In fact, a man might be not only a high Tory, but even a Nonjuror, and yet in no respect a Jacobite. Just as Ken or Turner had joined in expressing the public gratitude for the deliverance which had been effected through William, so now also it was quite possible for a Nonjuror to prefer, under the name of a prolonged interregnum, the Protestant succession. On the other hand, Tories who had taken the oaths, and were wholly faithful to Queen Anne, were being continually drawn on by the principles they loudly advocated to the very brink of Jacobitism. Non-resistance, passive obedience, the divine right of kings, and January the Thirtieth sermons kept the minds of a large proportion of the clergy,

---

[1] The question, as argued between J. Wesley and Badcock, is related in Nichols' *Lit. An.*, v. 247.

and many others besides, in just the ferment which Jacobites could most desire, but which was very unfavourable to the tranquil performance of their spiritual duties. It is probable that, for twenty years after the Revolution, Tories and High Churchmen were in most cases really friends, though in a somewhat cold and listless way, to the new dynasty and the Act of Succession. But when the reaction had at last fairly set in, when the prospect was already near of a German and a Lutheran on the English throne, the temporal head of the English Church; when the prosecution of Sacheverell had excited Tory passion to a frenzied pitch—it is quite likely that Hickes was right in his assertion that 'the main body of the clergy were Jacobites in heart.'[1] Indeed, the whole country was at that crisis so nearly divided in opinion, that it was only the sudden death of Anne, and the unprepared condition of the Jacobites, which, under Providence, enabled George the First to assume his place without the expected struggle.

In speaking of the relations between the bishops of Queen Anne's reign and their clergy, there will be occasion to make some mention of the extreme violence of party. The Revolution had, indeed, been almost bloodless, but it might seem that the passions which had not been expended in civil warfare could not rest without finding some sufficient vent in violent animosities, bitter recriminations, and party cries which rang through the nation like battle shouts. Moderate men might protest. But, unfortunately, 'moderation' was itself one of the foremost passwords in the strife. The one party held the word in more abhorrence than any other in the language; while, on the other hand, it was as likely as not that the 'moderate' man was among the very ringleaders of his faction. Unfortunately the Church was dragged into the fray, and was made the central and most prominent

[1] Q. by J. H. Overton in *The E. Ch. in the 18th Century*, i. 85.

figure. It could not be helped. Burnet and Hough, Kettlewell and Frampton, and many another good Churchman on either side, might lament that the terms High Church and Low Church had ever been invented. But had it not been so, some other titles would have sprung up instead. For all the questions of the day had a religious as well as a political side, and touched the vital as well as the external interests of the Church, no less than of the State. Doubtless Churchmen were much in fault in permitting excited feelings and exaggerated fears to carry them so far beyond the bounds of calmer reason. Yet he would have been but a cold and lukewarm member of his communion, who could look on with dispassionate indifference amid the clamours that surrounded him, unless, indeed, he possessed some superhuman faculty of foreseeing that the anxieties which filled the minds of this party or of that would alike be falsified, and that the real danger in prospect was altogether of a different kind from what men anticipated—not Rome, and not Geneva, but a dull and sluggish level which had no part in either.

This intensity of mixed Church and political feeling came to its height in 1709. Reaction against the principles of the Revolution had long been gaining in strength, and was fast reaching its height. The clergy were getting into a ferment of excitement. Fear lest the Church should be betrayed into the hands of Presbyterians, jealous fears lest the bishops themselves should prove false to their own cause, anger that their voice in Convocation could not be more fully heard, and all other supposed dangers of the Church, were working five-sixths of the country clergy into a state of angry discontent. Their influence was great in the parishes, and a large majority of the squires shared their feelings. There were other causes of dissatisfaction. Trade was dull, distress frequent, and the war, however glorious, was a very heavy burden to bear. Everything was ripe for a Tory and High Church outburst. Then, when all was thus prepared for it, came that singular episode of history—the sermon and trial of Dr. Sacheverell, and the triumphal progress which followed his virtual acquittal. The story has been often told, and the reader need be here only reminded of the principal circumstances of it. In 1709 he preached before the Lord Mayor a Fifth of November sermon, the subject of which was 'Perils among False Brethren,' and its drift a vigorous declamation on the absolute duty of non-resistance to the supreme power, and a bitter tirade upon the Whig and Low Church principles which came in with the Revolution. It was published immediately afterwards, but would have quickly passed into oblivion had not the Government made what Lord Campbell truly calls the preposterous mistake of instituting a State prosecution against the preacher. Godolphin and the other ministers were well aware that opinions fatal to the principles of the new constitution had reached a dangerous height, and were determined to make an example. Accordingly, all the resources of the law, all the paraphernalia of power, were put in action, and Dr. Sacheverell was formally arraigned in Westminster Hall. Nevertheless, the prosecution was essentially weak. He had not denied the legality of the Revolution, for he had declared that it had not been a case of resistance. For the rest, he had but said in vehement and excited language what had once been the all but universally accepted doctrine of the most honoured Anglican theologians. Day after day the impeachment pursued its lengthened course, engrossing the attention of the whole country, and each day popular feeling expressed itself more unmistakably and tumultuously in favour of the victim, as he was considered, of Whig oppression. As for the sermon, the unworthy cause of all this uproar, ' 40,000 copies were sold in a few months, and it acquired more celebrity than any production of Milton or Dryden.'[1] It was, indeed, ordered to be burnt by the hangman, but in the good company of a decree, passed in 1683 by the University of Oxford, which had exalted the doctrine of passive obedience, and had then been considered a loyal and meritorious act.[2] The doctor was suspended for three years, but within a week of the giving of this sentence the queen herself gave him the rich living of St. Andrew's, Holborn, and he was in the highway of becoming a bishop. Then another living in Shropshire was given to him, and he passed through the country like a victorious hero. 'Often a thousand gentlemen on horseback escorted him; magistrates welcomed him into their corporation; at Bridgenorth 4,000 horse met him, and as many on foot, with white favours edged in gold, and gilt laurel leaves in their hats.'[3] It must be added that his victory was consummated by the downfall of the Whig Government.

Thus ended the Sacheverell prosecution. It was, however, but the culminating point of the hot party strife which, throughout the greater part of Queen Anne's reign, was raging all over the country. For it pervaded the whole kingdom. In both Houses of Parliament, in both Houses of Convocation, in street and coffee-house, in town society and in country coteries, among all classes and in all callings, in squib, in pamphlet, and in treatise, the combat of High and Low, Whig and Tory, raged on with the utmost vehemence. It reached even the lowest of the people.

> Black tinkers bawl aloud ' to settle
> Church privilege!' for mending kettle.
> The oyster wenches lock their fish up,
> And cry, ' No Presbyterian bishop!'

---

[1] Campbell's *Lives of the Chancellors*, iv. 204.
[2] Perry's *Church Hist.*, iii. 221.   [3] Noble's *Cont. of Grainger*, i. 130.

> The mousetrap men lay save-alls by,
> And 'gainst ' Low Church men ' loudly cry.
> Some cry for ' penal laws,' instead
> Of ' pudding-pies and gingerbread ; '
> And some for ' brooms, old boots and shoes,'
> Roar out, ' God bless our Commons' house ! '
> Masons, instead of building houses,
> To ' build the Church ' would starve their spouses.[1]

Swift truly said that this rancour of party faction was poisoning the national life.[2] And it penetrated also into domestic life. ' Scarce anywhere,' wrote Thoresby in 1710, ' without unhappy disputes even among nearest relations about these wretched distinctions betwixt High and Low Church.'[3]

One of its results involved a very long-lasting injury to the English Church. Under all ordinary circumstances it is obviously a most desirable thing that a church should have its deliberative council, in which representative members should consult for its increased welfare and efficiency. In a national church all ecclesiastical legislation is ultimately vested in the voice of the nation itself, constitutionally expressed in Parliament. But Parliament is ill fitted for investigating the details of church work, and therefore without its own ecclesiastical council a church will be deprived of a very valuable part of its organisation. The two Houses of Convocation are very imperfectly representative of the Church, especially in their entire absence of the lay element; but they are its ancient and constitutional organs, and however much this composition might be improved, they are fully competent to do great service by their deliberations. That passionate strife of party in Queen Anne's reign had the unhappy consequence of silencing the voice of

---

[1] J. Hughes' *Poems*, ' Imitation of Hudibras.'
[2] Swift's *Works*, viii. 279.   [3] Thoresby's *Diary*, i. 69.

Convocation for nearly a hundred and fifty years. Moreover, there must have been many good Churchmen who, weary of this long contention, must have heard with satisfaction and relief that such miserable disorder was no longer to be continued.

Under the Stuarts of the seventeenth century Convocation had met occasionally, and with long prorogations. In 1689 it had assembled to discuss the important questions of revision and comprehension, only to be prorogued again after it had become thoroughly apparent that feeling in the Lower House was far too hot to allow of any calm debate. Archbishop Tillotson had hoped that the meeting of Convocation might promote his favourite measure. He quickly found out how irretrievably it had wrecked it. For eleven years the Synod remained in abeyance. It met again in 1701, but its history for the next seventeen years was a very unedifying one. The long and learned controversy as to its natures and powers was by no means satisfactory—the one party arguing for an independence which was impracticable and impossible, while the other side seemed indifferent whether Convocation should exist at all. As for the debates themselves, there were, no doubt, a few useful questions discussed; but far the greater time was occupied in the Lower House with altercations which only brought discredit on the Church, or with passing upon recent publications censures which were in some cases—as in their proceedings upon Burnet's book on the Articles—mere outbursts of party feeling, and which, in other cases, only brought into more prominent notice the opinions which they condemned.

The excited feeling and intemperate spirit of the Lower House was the more regrettable because in the latter part of Queen Anne's reign there was a definite inclination in Parliament to acknowledge in a more marked manner than hitherto the services which Convocation might render in preparing Church questions for the consideration of the legislative houses. In reference to the Bill for building fifty-two new churches in and about London the Commons passed a resolution—'That they would receive all such information as should be offered in this case by the Lower House of Convocation; and would have a particular regard to such applications as should at any time be made to them by the clergy in Convocation assembled, according to the ancient usage, together with the Parliament.'[1] Such co-operation, particularly if the representative character of Convocation could have been further strengthened, might have had a very beneficial effect upon the organised labours of the Church, and the religious activities of the country in general. If such hopes were entertained, they were at all events quickly thwarted. Convocation turned from useful toils to its futile, but, as it seemed, its favourite task of censuring unorthodoxy. When, in the beginning of the next reign, these efforts were directed against opinions which, however unpalatable they might be to a large section of Churchmen, were still undoubtedly permissible within the border of the National Church, it was preparing its own doom.

All the questions which the Revolution had brought uppermost in men's minds involved that of how to deal with Nonconformity. An excellent beginning had been made, in 1689, in the Act of Toleration. But the matter could not stop here. There must be either advance or retrogression. For a time, all Low Churchmen, many High Churchmen, and many moderate Dissenters looked hopefully to 'a comprehension.' If possible, it seemed a natural and fit measure in presence of the dreaded enemy, at a crisis when, both in England and abroad, one national church stood indisputably in the van and forefront of the

[1] Quoted in Perry, iii. 251.

whole Protestant interest. Comprehension involved revision of the formularies. These two considerations occupied, therefore, no little attention, both among politicians and Churchmen, in the last decade of the seventeenth century. But the state of feeling which alone rendered the measure possible soon passed away, and before the new century began, the hopes and fears which the project had excited, and the zealous labours which its promoters had spent upon it, had already passed into history. It was vividly remembered, and frequently spoken of, but no longer as a practical matter which had any interest for the Church of England as a whole. The High Church party had utterly withdrawn from it. The Earl of Nottingham, who in 1689 had introduced the measure, was now the leader of a powerful body of high Tories who railed at the very mention of it. The invective[1] which Sacheverell heaped upon it as 'latitudinarian' and 'heterogeneous,' as 'absurd, contradictory, and self-inconsistent,' gave fresh zest to his famous sermon. Yet many, even among those who did not rank among the Low Churchmen of the day, looked back with regret to the failure of the scheme. The 'Athenian Oracle'—a thoroughly Church paper, prefaced by Samuel Wesley—discussing in 1706, and again in 1708, the question whether 'a comprehension, or the uniting of Conformists and Nonconformists, be not necessary for the reforming of England,' gave its answer strongly in the affirmative. One reason which is there insisted upon is, that till then 'we see not how the ancient Church discipline, so much desired, and the loss thereof so much lamented, can ever be renewed.'[2] Archbishop Sharp, said Thoresby in 1702, 'has spoke to me with deep concern of a disappointment for which all good Christians have the

---

[1] Sermon of Nov. 5, 1709, p. 15.
[2] *Ath. Oracle*, i. 301-2, and ii. 353.

deeper cause for sorrow, because we are positively told that in all probability it would have brought in two-thirds of the Dissenters of England.'[1] On the occasion of Sacheverell's impeachment in 1710, Archbishop Wake made a remarkable speech on the subject in the House of Lords. 'The person,' he said, 'who first conceived this supposed design against our Church was the late Most Reverend Dr. Sancroft, then Archbishop of Canterbury. ... It was visible to all the nation that the more moderate Dissenters were generally so well satisfied with that stand all our divines had made against Popery ... as to express an unusual readiness to come to terms. ... The design was, in short, this: to improve, and if possible enforce, our discipline; to review and enlarge our Liturgy, by correcting of some things, by adding of others, and (if it should be thought advisable by authority when this matter should come to be considered, first in Convocation and then in Parliament) by leaving some few ceremonies, confessed to be indifferent in their nature, as not to be necessarily observed by those who made a scruple of them. ... How would our excellent Liturgy have been the worse if a few doubtful expressions had been changed for plainer and clearer; and a passage or two, which, however capable of a just defence, yet in many cases seem harsh to some even of our own communion, had either been wholly left at liberty in such cases to be omitted altogether, or been so qualified as to remove all exception against them? ... if some of the occasional offices had been enlarged, and new ones added; if, for instance, there had been a greater variety of prayers, psalms, and lessons, appointed by authority, instead of the composition of private persons, now necessarily to be used for the visitation of the sick, and new forms composed for the use of prisoners for debt or crimes?'[2]

[1] Thoresby's *Diary*, i. 399.   [2] *Parliamentary History*, vi. 870-1.

The whole speech is reported with more than usual care, and appears to have been listened to with much attention. No time, however, could have been more unfavourable to any practical issue from it than the year of Sacheverell's trial. The general feeling of that time would be far better represented by the words of a magazine writer, who denounced as 'the most fatal enemies of the Church of England those who pretend to enlarge her borders when they resolve to tear out her vitals, and with fine healing comprehensive designs would overrun her with confusion that they might erect their own idols upon her ruins.'[1] Or, as another writer expressed it, 'the notion is first for a comprehension, and that prepares us for a Presbyterian government; and if that once get up, down goes episcopacy, down goes comprehension.'[2] For a few more years the subject was often discussed, but only in a speculative way, and by about 1720 it had sunk almost wholly into rest.

So far from entertaining any thought of comprehension, the party, which in Queen Anne's reign was becoming continually more dominant, was bent on marking out with greater rigidness than before the external bounds which separated the Established Church from Nonconformity. The sacramental test had been imposed in 1673 against the Romanists, who were being placed by Charles II. in posts of important trust. The Dissenters had given their full concurrence to the measure. They disliked it in its bearings upon themselves, but considered it necessary for the security of the country. In the earlier part of Elizabeth's reign, English Roman Catholics had been frequently in the habit of joining with their brethren of the National Church in acts of worship, and had not scrupled even to communicate with them.

[1] The *Scourge*, May 27, 1717.
[2] E. Hart's *Preservative against Comprehension*, 1718.

But the Council of Trent strictly forbade this occasional conformity; and it was obvious, therefore, in 1673 that a sacramental test would effectually exclude Romanists from office. Its intrinsic evils do not appear at the time to have been even thought of, and, strange to say, were not keenly or generally felt for many generations afterwards. Dissenters were gratified at seeing its immediate effect in the resignation of the Duke of York and the breaking up of the Cabal ministry, and, so far as their own position was concerned, did not just then feel its burden oppressively. Most of their communities were in a depressed condition, and felt it no great hardship to be debarred from offices to which they did not aspire. The Presbyterians numbered many men of position and influence; but their relations with the Established Church were very amicable, and their most eminent ministers had generally advocated and practised the custom of attending from time to time at the celebration of the Holy Communion in the parish churches. Bates and Baxter had been especially prominent in holding this view.[1] So it continued, not only while the struggle with Rome lasted, but as long as the sense of partnership in danger was still strong. To kneel side by side in the holy rite seemed to cement the feeling of a common Protestantism as well as of a common Christianity. To some the narrower of the two bonds seems to have been the one chiefly thought of. 'Many,' said a writer of 1705, 'joined in constant communion with us, and some of them communicated with us occasionally, thinking that all Protestants, too long divided among themselves, should join together against the common enemy.'[2] The custom seems to have prevailed widely; so much so as to have had a distinct effect in weakening Nonconformity and strengthening the National

---

[1] Calamy's *Life*, i. 475; Thoresby's *Diary*, i. 324.
[2] *Occ. Thoughts on the Memorial of the Ch. of E.*, 1705.

Church. But shortly before the end of the seventeenth century, and still more in the reign of Anne, the aspect of the matter became a good deal changed. High Churchmen, and Tories in general, had become far more alive to points on which they differed from Dissenters than to those on which they were at one with them. They also professed to believe, or rather had actually frightened themselves into the belief, that the Church was falling into a serious danger of becoming as Presbyterian on this side of the Tweed as on the other.[1] The habit, therefore, of occasional conformity offended and alarmed them as tending to level the barriers which protected them. Moreover, it had now become fully apparent that the regulations of the Test Act put a different colour upon occasional conformity from what it would otherwise have worn. A slur had been thrown upon it which was hard for an honourable man to bear. If a Dissenter received the sacrament from an Anglican clergyman, he could still say, and perhaps with perfect truth, that he did so because it did him good to feel that minor differences did not separate him from the communion of his fellow-Christians, or that he had been baptized into the universal Church and had a right, therefore, to communicate with all true churches.[2] But, however sincerely he might say this, he knew that he might also be open to the reproach of conforming for the time in order to qualify for office. English Churchmen, to their shame, could, without remonstrance, see this continually done by members of their own communion. 'I was early,' writes Swift, 'with the Secretary (Bolingbroke), but he was gone

---

[1] The Act of Union, in 1706, was to many persons in either country a cause of much alarm, lest episcopacy might be endangered in England, or Presbyterianism in Scotland (Calamy's *Life*, ii. 60). In the debate in the House of Lords, Feb. 8, 1707, Bishop Hooper thought the former probable, Bishop Talbot the latter (*Parl. H.*, vi. 568-76; the *Scourge*, Nos. 38 and 42).

[2] J. Humphrey, in Thoresby's *Diary*, Aug. 23, 1798, i. 324.

to his devotions and to receive the sacrament. Several rakes did the same. It was not for piety, but for employment, according to Act of Parliament.'[1] But those who were almost blind to such profanity on the part of irreligious men of their own communion, spoke of occasional conformity as if it outraged conscientious feeling. It is 'a shifting practice,'[2] said they, which makes men knaves and hypocrites;[3] and when, in 1703, a Bill was brought forward to put a stop to occasional conformity, it was very commonly called by the term Sir John Pakington had applied to it in Parliament, 'a Bill to prevent hypocrisy.'[4] Such an expression would have been far more applicable to a Bill for the abolition of the test. But this they would have looked upon with the most unfeigned horror. For the test, as they said with unwearied repetition, was 'the barrier of the Church of England,' and 'the chief bulwark of the Protestant interest.'[5] Abolish the test, and there was scarce a national church remaining.[6] No wise Government could dare to entrust office to men who might be only waiting to betray the country's liberties to Rome, or its ecclesiastical constitution to Scotland or to Dutchmen. It was on this ground that occasional conformity was so fiercely attacked as an evasion of the test, and one that defeated its very object. There were many, on the other hand, who defended both the test and occasional conformity by one and the same argument. The test would admit moderate Dissenters, who would not object to conform thus

---

[1] Swift to Stella, quoted in Lecky's *England in the Eighteenth Century*, i. 255.

[2] Wall's 'Dissuasive from Schism,' in Wordsworth's *Christian Institutes*, iii. 487.

[3] *A Brief Defence*, &c., 1706; Brokesby's *Life of Dodwell*, 436.

[4] *Parliam. Hist.*, vi., 154, Nov. 11, 1703; Rogers' *Letter to the Lords*, i. 1704.

[5] Nicolson's *Letters on Various Subjects*, sect. 9, 1717, 473, &c.

[6] Swift's 'Letter concerning the Sacr. Test,' 1708; *Works*, viii. 360.

far, and whose adhesion to the Government would be strength rather than weakness to the common cause, while it would exclude the Romanist and the fanatic, the over-rigid and the narrow-minded.[1] This was the Whig view; for there were but few as yet even among them who were prepared to dispense with the test altogether. The Tories, who filled the House of Commons when the Bill against Occasional Conformity was introduced in 1702 and 1703, would be content with nothing short of the utter exclusion of all Nonconformists. But when the Act, loaded with pains and penalties, and containing some singularly unjust provisions, had been passed on to the House of Lords, it was found impossible to carry it through. After many attempts to come to an agreement, and a crowded and excited conference of the two Houses in the Painted Chamber, the Bill was thrown out by what was practically a majority of one. Great was the resentment of the Tories, and hot their indignation against the bishops, for a majority of the Episcopal bench had voted against the measure.[2] Now, more than ever, the Whig bishops were branded by the more violent of the opposite party as Dissenters and Presbyterians, traitors to their order and enemies of the Church. One more unsuccessful effort was made the next year to force the Act through, in a somewhat modified form, by 'tacking' it to an important money Bill. After this the question remained at rest until 1711, when the Whigs, finding they could not regain power without the Earl of Nottingham's support, consented to let the measure

[1] *A Brief Defence*, &c., 1706.
[2] The non-contents among the bishops, including three proxies, were Tenison, Lloyd, Burnet, Patrick, Hough, Moore, Cumberland, Fowler, Hall, Talbot, Williams, Gardiner, Humphrey, and Evans. The contents, also including three proxies, were Sharp, Compton, Trelawney, Stratford, Crewe, Sprat, Mew, Jones, and Beaw (*Parl. Hist.*, vi. 163). Prince George of Denmark, himself a Lutheran and occasional Conformist (as, in fact, King William had been), voted for the Bill.

pass. It was repealed, together with the Schism Act, in 1718.[1]

There can be no doubt that in Anne's reign the prevailing party were resolutely bent upon a policy towards Nonconformists which can hardly be called by any milder name than persecution. Tories and High Churchmen would not by any means have allowed that they were offending against the law of toleration so far as it had already been accepted. No doubt much was said that was bigoted and prejudiced in the extreme. But though the remark sounds rather paradoxical, their conduct was to a great extent actuated by the very same principle which had led many of them, ten or fifteen years before, to advocate comprehension. The ruling idea then had been the great desirability, if not absolute need, of presenting a united front against all assailants. It was so still. There had been no success in the attempt to frame a healing measure of peace, which might attract all moderate Dissenters by gentle means of persuasion. The idea now was to compel them to come in, or at all events, if that were not possible, to make their position outside a chill and uncomfortable one. Dissent was at this period unaggressive and depressed,[2] content with the limited toleration it had secured, and quite disinclined to favour uncompromising champions like De Foe. Bishop Trimnell could dwell with truth upon ' the number of men of sobriety and learning among the Dissenters who have been admitted to orders in our church.'[3] Their numbers were enfeebled; they had lost

---

[1] The bishops who advocated repeal were Hough, Talbot, Trimnell, Willis, Gibson, Hoadly, Kennet, and Bradford. Proxies, Fleetwood and Blackbourne. Those who opposed it were Wake, Dawes, Trelawney, Robinson, Atterbury, Wynne, Potter, Manningham, and Chandler (Nicholson's *Letters*, Dec. 20, 1718; 485).

[2] Skeats's *Hist. of the Free Churches*, 264.

[3] *Parl. Hist.*, vii. 880; March 14, 1710. Many authors have remarked on the distinguished Churchmen, such as Leighton, Tillotson, S. Wesley, Butler,

their principal leaders; they were excluded from the universities; their social standing had become lowered; they stood apart from most of the social and literary life of the age; they retained much of the strictness of the old Puritanism, but none of its vigour. Toleration and the mild attitude of liberal Churchmen had greatly diminished their hostility to the National Church.[1] Nottingham, with all the Tories and High Churchmen who followed his lead, cherished a sanguine, and perhaps not an ungrounded hope that Nonconformists might yet be reduced to an inconsiderable and unconsidered remnant. Many, without absolutely avowing themselves hostile to the Toleration Act, would gladly have pared it down to the very minimum of indulgence. A large proportion of them, towards the end of Anne's reign, were eagerly in favour of any measure which might impose new restraints upon Nonconformity, and yet further check its growth. Hence the odious provisions of Bolingbroke's Schism Act, which in the last year of Queen Anne passed the Commons by an immense majority, and the Lords by the help of twelve newly created Tory peers.[2] It aimed at dealing a fatal blow on Nonconformity through the demolition of its nurseries. The public and private schools of Dissenters were to be all closed, and no one might be a tutor or teacher who had not subscribed to a declaration of conformity, received the sacrament according to the usage of the English Church, and obtained a licence from the diocesan. Happily the Bill remained a dead letter, and not long afterwards was repealed. There was no later attempt to stop Nonconformity by force.

Secker, Bishop Maddox, Abp. Hort of Tuam, &c., who had been brought up as Nonconformists. J. Taylor, *Wesley and Methodism*, 18; Mrs. Oliphant, *Hist. Sketches of the Reign of George II.*, 8; Hunt's *Relig. Thought in E.*, iii. 224.

[1] Skeats, as above, 245-8.

[2] Campbell's *Lives of the Chancellors*, iv. 338. A protest against the Bill was signed by twenty-eight temporal peers and five bishops—Wake, Moore, Fleetwood, Evans, and Tyler (*Parl. Hist.*, vi. 1354).

For the first fourteen or fifteen years of the century controversial activity was generally occupied with one or another of those semi-political, semi-ecclesiastical questions which the Revolution, and the events leading up to it, had brought into especial prominence. Questions bearing on Romanism on the one hand, on Protestant Nonconformity on the other, the need of a Protestant unity, the danger which might be threatening Church or State, the principles on which rested the authority of princes and the duty of subjects, questions between Jacobites and Hanoverians, Jurors and Nonjurors, the rights of the Church in relation to the State, the prerogatives of Convocation, and above all (the main and leading division, on one side or another of which men ranged themselves, according to their views on these and kindred subjects) questions between Tory and High Churchman on the one hand, Whig and Low Churchman on the other—such points of difference, vehemently and even passionately discussed, were quite enough to exercise all who were polemically inclined.

But meanwhile matters of great theological importance were beginning to demand the attention of every reflecting man. The Reformation had long ago released the mind from a slavish subservience to authority. But the liberty of thought and right of reasoning upon which it was based had never been realised. At length, after a century and a half had nearly exhausted the various ecclesiastical controversies which were the direct consequence of the separation from the Roman unity, and which could not be settled without prolonged and lamentable strife, reason essayed its strength in testing doctrines which hitherto had been held for the most part too sacred for such investigations. For a time such inquiries remained almost entirely in the hands of learned men. But in the later years of the seventeenth century Locke's famous essay had popularised philosophy, and taught educated men of every class to exercise with a new freedom the power which reason gave them. His 'Reasonableness of Christianity' opened a new era in religious thought. His example was followed for good and evil. 'Freethinking' was henceforth liberally used and abused; often by those who were not unqualified for such liberty, often by those who would have been wiser and better men had they remained more modestly under some wholesome restraint of authority. No one can read the pages of the 'Tatler,' and other popular essayists of the time, without coming upon many a satire on the ignorance and pretentiousness of the fashionable freethinking. Meanwhile, through many hard encounters, through many saddening doubts and many painful struggles, and through a long period in which reason laboured wearily on, without seeking aid from any emotional or spiritual faculty, Christianity began the great task of completing what the Reformation had begun, and establishing itself as firmly upon the reasoned convictions of humanity as it already had upon the will and feelings of those who were conscious of its power.

Without going further back to the influence on the popular mind of Hobbes and Herbert of Cherbury, it will be enough in this brief sketch to refer to the effect in the early years of the eighteenth century of the 'Christianity not Mysterious,' published in 1696 by John Toland. The author —a young Irishman, whose considerable talents were obscured by inordinate self-conceit—fell into no small disgrace by his publication. He had been tabooed in society; had become so poor as to be at a loss for a daily meal; his book had been declared by Convocation impious, heretical, and immoral, and burnt under order of Parliament by the common hangman, and he had escaped imprisonment only by a hasty flight. Hearne called him 'an ingenious man, but of vile principles.'¹ The outcry against him might seem at first sight unaccountable. For he professed² to defend Christianity; he declared his faith in the Christian Creed; he said that he believed in miracles, that he repudiated Socinianism, that he vindicated revelation, but that he wished to divert men's minds from speculation to practice. All this might be sincere or not, for in a later work he openly claimed a liberty of holding one thing 'in pectore et privato consessu, aliud in foro et publica concione;' and in his last treatise, the 'Pantheisticon,' he showed much levity in treating questions of the most serious import. In 'Christianity not Mysterious' even his main thesis is so far explained as to leave little but harmless paradox. The real cause of offence chiefly lay in his utter contempt for authority, and his repudiation of all evidence but that of simple reason. Above all, though he acknowledged that there were, in a sense, mysteries in faith no less than in nature, it was felt that the very title of his work, and all that it implied, tended to strip religion of the very elements that are holiest and most impressive in it, and to fall in with some of the worst characteristics of the 'freethinking' of the day.³ There was some ground for the attempts made, not only by Deists, such as Toland and Chubb, but by many defenders of Christianity, to explain away the mysteries of faith, and to make all plain and reasonable. For ages there had been far too much of that 'indolent retreat upon the mystery of divine revelation,'⁴ which excuses itself from

¹ Reliq. Hearnianæ, iii. 164.

² My knowledge of most of Toland's and of several other Deistical writings is chiefly derived at second hand from Schlosser's *History of the Eighteenth Century*; Dorner's *Hist. of Prot. Theology*; Overton's 'Deists,' in *The E. Ch. of the Eighteenth Cent.*; Hunt's *Religious Thought in England*; Cairns' *Unbelief in the Eighteenth Cent.*; and Pattison's paper in *Essays and Reviews*. But I have read some of the Deists.

³ Chubb's *Works*, vol. iv., 'Enquiry into the Foundation of Religion,' 40, 92.

⁴ Dorner's *Prot. Theol.*, ii. 256.

exercising the reason on things divine, and seeking to penetrate intelligently into the things of God. Such a temper of mind leads rather to superstitious credulity than to thoughtful faith. But even the orthodox rationalisers of the eighteenth century far outran the mark on the other side. Everywhere the specious argument was to be heard, 'Let us fix our eyes on the practical and moral precepts of the gospel; these it most concerns us to know; these, therefore, let us study. Such is the frailty of our nature, such is the strength and number of our temptations to evil, that in reducing the gospel moralities to practice we shall find full employment; and by attending to them, rather than to those high mysterious doctrines which you are pressing upon us, we shall best prepare to appear before God.'[1] Sound reason and Christian morality—what can be better? But pure reason is one only of the senses by which we attain to spiritual knowledge, and Christian morality needs the support of solemn worship and reverent adoration; it dwells upon the unseen, the infinite, the eternal, things which eye hath not seen nor ear heard—it cannot afford to be deprived of hopes, and intuitions, and aspirations which no logician's skill can classify; it blends with the emotions; above all, it craves for that divine breath of the Spirit which is, indeed, the life of the soul, but which, no less than the bodily life, eludes the search of reason. A religion grounded upon reason, and nurtured on holy laws and fair examples, however much it may be fortified by sanctions of future rewards and punishments, needs other and more subtle elements to redeem souls from sin, and to be indeed a very gospel of salvation. But at the very beginning of the eighteenth century theology in England opened, as it were, on Toland's text of 'Christianity not Mysterious,' and scarcely got away from it until the end. The treatise

[1] Wilberforce's *Practical View*, 131.

did not immediately elicit any answer of great importance. To the vast gratification of Toland's vanity, it had caused, in the concluding years of the preceding century, a warm debate between Locke and Stillingfleet. Two Irish divines of some distinction—Archbishop Synge and Peter Browne—wrote against him; and among the English replies were one by Samuel Clarke, and one by Norris of Bemerton, whose poetical mind, deeply imbued with a profound and reflective mysticism, must have revolted from Toland's whole train of thought with a more than ordinary abhorrence. But for several generations to come almost every theological writer of eminence seems to have had in mind, if not Toland's arguments, at all events the subject of them. Many laboured to show how 'there are not so many mysteries as the Deists say,'[1] and that revelation has made most things plain. Others, as Butler in his 'Analogy,' William Law in his 'Spirit of Love,' and, more indirectly, Berkeley in the spiritual and transcendental philosophy which has made his name famous, preferred rather to show how mystery is essential to religion, and that we do well ' to keep ourselves in an attitude of faith and expectation until we shall receive that light which we may hope hereafter to have.'[2] Warburton's words on the subject should be quoted for their sound common sense: 'Of the dark parts of revelation there are two sorts: one which may be cleared up by the studious application of well-employed talents; the other which will always reside within the shadow of God's throne, where it would be impiety to intrude.'[3]

The Earl of Shaftesbury's 'Characteristics' were published in 1708. He was a Deist in the wider sense of the word as it was then understood, for he assailed all positive

---

[1] Bp. Watson's *Life*, i. 415.
[2] Bp. Thirlwall's *Lit. Remains*, 251.
[3] Quoted in a note by Angus on Part II. ch. iv. of Butler's *Analogy*.

doctrine.[1] But he did so covertly, and with his favourite weapon of half-disguised mockery. Above all other things he detested enthusiasm, 'that greatest incendiary of the earth,' which 'overthrows established churches, violates the most lawful rites, and, in a word, confounds all things divine and human.'[2] It was not he who would be a martyr for any opinion he might hold. He praised, therefore, the 'established rites of worship,' as 'decent, innocent, and pure;' and even expatiated on 'the true zeal and good disposition, and wholesome reflections' with which, at the beginning of the new year, he received the sacrament, 'it being in a manner our duty, at least for example's sake, on the account of our stations in Parliament.'[3] Let fanatics endanger their comfort, and raise needless commotion by openly assailing 'holy rites and records by law established;'[4] for his own part, he remembered that if men could not speak their mind seriously, they could yet do so ironically —'it is the persecuting spirit that has raised the bantering one.'[5] After all, there was nothing like raillery and humour for revealing truth and laying bare imposture. It was a fiercer test than persecution, as Socrates had long since found.[6] We can easily understand how much harm could be done with such arms by an able and witty man in Shaftesbury's station, who feared little from the deficiency of religion, but everything from its abuse.[7]

Yet one could have greatly desired that Shaftesbury, gifted with a more serious feeling of the gravity and responsibilities of human life, could have been a defender of the Christian faith in those days, and not its assailant. For his philosophy was essentially pure and lofty, just at the very points where it touched most intimately upon

---

[1] *E.g. Characteristics*, P. III. § 3.
[2] *Letter to his Brother*, Jan. 19, 1702.   [3] *Id.*
[4] *Charact.*, P. III. 3.   [5] *Id.*, P. II. § 4.   [6] *Id.*, P. I. § 4.
[7] Schlosser's *Hist. of the Eighteenth Cent.*, i. 31.

morals and religion. It is very probable that, like Chubb and some other of the Deists, his mind had revolted from 'the amazingly selfish views of religion held by many Christians,'[1] who seemed to resolve the highest aims of life into a mere personal desire to escape punishment and to gain reward. No doubt such objections lie somewhat on the surface; practically it would be found that a Christian life, even where it supposes itself to be mainly actuated by those lower motives, is yet stronger to overcome selfishness than any other known power. Nevertheless, where such incentives are made over-prominent, Christianity sinks below its ideal, and takes a lower character; and in Shaftesbury's age the tendency was very strong to make expedience, interpreted in its better sense, the motive power of Christian action. Whether Shaftesbury felt this or not, at all events he based his entire system of philosophy upon the very same ground as that taken by many of the best and saintliest of men. Like Tauler, like Guyon, like Jeremy Taylor,[2] like Fenelon, like William Law, and in the very spirit of the apostle's words, which tell that 'Charity seeketh not her own,' he made disinterested virtue the true principle of all high morality. He was not so blind as to deny the efficacy of hope and fear in stirring lethargic spirits; and in one place he is so far unfaithful to his general teaching as to say 'it is the height of wisdom, no doubt, to be rightly selfish.'[3] But, on the whole, he was

---

[1] Chubb's *Works*, iii. 23.

[2] There is a story in Jeremy Taylor how Ivo, on an embassy to St. Louis, met a grave, sad woman with fire and water. 'My purpose is with fire to burn paradise, and with water to quench the fires of hell, that men may serve God without the incentives of hope and fear and purely for the love of God.'—Quoted in Vaughan's *Mystics*, ii. 165. Lavington accused J. Wesley of inconsistency in saying, 'I now declare both that all true love is disinterested, and that there is no one caution in all the Bible against the selfish love of God.' —Lavington's *Enthus. of Methodists*, P. II. § 31.

[3] Quoted in Mackintosh's 'Progress of Eth. Philos.,' *Works*, 44.

never so much in earnest as when he was attacking, with all the vigour of his polished wit, the prudential maxims which, by their undue predominance, depressed both the religion and the philosophy of his age. It might have been well if this part of Shaftesbury's mind had impressed itself more upon his contemporaries, and had done more than it did to neutralise the effects of his scornful and flippant scepticism. The question did no doubt attract more than a passing attention[1] in the first decade of the century, but it was chiefly owing to a controversy which arose in 1706 between the two most advanced champions of the High and Low Church parties. Atterbury, preaching upon 1 Cor. xv. 19, had declared that without the hope of a future life Christians would be miserable. Hoadly, arguing as Shaftesbury might have done had he written in a religious sense, contended that 'virtue is the imitation of God, and therefore must be the happiness of man. The chief happiness of a reasonable creature must consist in living as reason directs, whether he lives one day or to eternity.'[2]

The origin and meaning of evil have probably claimed some share in the thought of every reflecting person since man became a reasonable being. But in the first half of the last century it occupied more than a usual share in general attention. The able work of Archbishop King, of Dublin, on the origin of evil, published in Latin in 1702, could have interested only learned men; and Shaftesbury's speculations on the subject would have passed comparatively unnoticed unless they had found a popular interpreter. But the easy and careless optimism with which he held the creed that 'whatever is, is right,' gained the ear of all educated Englishmen in the verses of their favourite

[1] At a later date the question was discussed to some extent by Berkeley and Butler, and more definitely by W. Law in his answer to Mandeville; also by Balguy and others.
[2] Hoadly's *Works*, i. 55.

poet. All literary men knew something of Shaftesbury, but in polite society every one quoted Pope. The influence this exercised on the popular mind was not beneficial. It is well to believe that goodness overrules the universe—that evil is temporary and finite, but good eternal; and to acknowledge practically, as a steadfast truth, that he who follows goodness follows what is always and necessarily best, and meanwhile to confess our ignorance and to wait. But the facile carelessness with which the philosopher and his disciple descanted with flowing pen upon problems full of deep and spiritual mystery fell in far too well with the growing indifference of the age, and tended not to faith and reverence, but rather to blur the distinctness of good and evil, and to confuse their bounds. In fact, a very few years later, in 1714, Mandeville published four or five hundred lines of verse—his 'Fable of the Bees'—with the distinct purpose of showing that humanity could spare its vices even less than its virtues, for that

>Vice is beneficial found
>When it's by justice lopt and bound.[1]

The verses, being cleverly written and easily circulated, had many readers and many answers, among which was one which is sometimes considered the ablest production of William Law. Long after, in 1750, we find John Wesley writing, 'Some (I hope but a few) do cordially believe that "private vices are public benefits." I myself heard this in Cork when I was there last.'[2]

The earlier works of two other Deists, Collins and Tindal, come in Queen Anne's reign. But their more distinctive productions belong to a rather later date, for even Collins's 'Discourse on Freethinking' did not appear till 1713; and his 'Essay on the Use of Reason,' 1707, is almost identical

---

[1] Mandeville's *F. of the Bees*, 424-5.   [2] J. Wesley's *Works*, 9, 86.

in general purport with Toland's 'Christianity not Mysterious.' But early in the century, that storm of bitter invective which the Deists in general showered upon the clergy began in full force under the leadership of Tindal, in his 'Rights of the Church vindicated against Romish and all other Priests,' 1706, and of Collins in his 'Priestcraft in Perfection,' 1709. If this outcry had been directed against the high sacerdotal claims maintained by many of the clergy, it would have become intelligible enough from an opponent's point of view. But the Deists as a body were very far indeed from limiting their attack to any such bounds. There was scarcely one of them who did not speak of the clerical order in general as enemies to whom no quarter was to be given. The object of the clergy, said Howard, was 'to preserve themselves in the authority they have gotten,' and for this, 'they invented two great assistances, Mystery and Persecution; by Mystery to prevent the use of understanding, and by Persecution to keep back any that should attempt to break out of the brutal pound.'[1] 'Natural religion,' said Toland, 'was easy first, and plain,' but then came priests, that 'worst of plagues,' that 'scourge of men,' and then 'tales made it mystery, offerings made it gain.'[2] They came, said Tindal, with their 'thousand sophistical and knavish methods of defending their opinions,' and 'burning with implacable hatred,' ever eager 'to gratify their insupportable itch of tyrannising.' 'It is manifest,' said Collins, 'that all priests, except' (as he cautiously adds) 'the orthodox, are hired to lead men into mistakes.' 'Besides, they who have an interest to enlarge their sect, and keep it united, know that nothing tends so much to its increase and union as the toleration

---

[1] Sir R. Howard's *Hist. of Religion as managed by Priestcraft*, pref.
[2] Toland's *Letters to Serena* and *Tribe of Levi*. Qu. in *Q. Rev.* No. 231, 65, whence also most of the quotations immediately following are borrowed.

of vice and wickedness to as great a degree as they can conveniently.' They 'all,' said Mandeville, 'passed muster that could hide their sloth, lust, avarice, and pride.' 'I am transported,' said Woolston, 'with the forethought of the happiness of mankind upon the extinction of ecclesiastical vermin out of God's house, when the world will return to its paradisaical state of nature, religion, and liberty, when we shall be all taught of God, and have no need of a foolish and contentious priest.' 'The generality,' said Morgan, 'of the clergy of all denominations, from the very beginning, have been continually palming upon us false coin under the authority of God.' 'As the clergy,' said Chubb, 'were set on increasing their wealth and power at all hazards, they have introduced such doctrines and . . . . superstitious practices as have rendered the Gospel of none effect.' 'If the mysteries,' said Annet, 'of the spiritual craftsmen were exposed by reason, no man would buy their merchandise any more.' It may be judged from such samples how savage and indiscriminate was the onslaught which eighteenth-century Deism made upon the general body of the Christian ministry. There is something almost absurd in such denunciations when we consider who and what the English clergy were. Their general opinions and habits as a body were, no doubt, open to criticism, but it was mainly to such kind of criticism as might be brought against them by the zealous missionaries of the Methodist revival. Such imputations as those which have been quoted fell very flat upon the average opinion of Englishmen, who saw in their parochial clergy a kindly and, for the most part, a high-principled order of men, who preached excellent morality and fair doctrine in rather dry but not too lengthy sermons, and who lived among them as friends, with common daily interests not widely separated from their own. Had the Church been really corrupt, the declamations of the Deists might have had no less effect than those which rang through Europe before the Reformation, and through Paris before the Revolution. As it was, there was much truth in the allegory which one of Collins's writings suggested to Berkeley. The view presented to his imagination was a formidable one indeed. 'But, as I drew near, the terror of the appearance vanished; and the castle I found to be only a church, whose steeple with its clock and bell-ropes was mistaken for a tower filled with racks and halters. The terrible giants in black shrunk into a few innocent clergymen.'[1] Still, such reiterated charges did not altogether fail to make some impression. The cry of 'Priestcraft' was taken up by a few pamphleteers, and was very often to be heard among those who had adopted 'freethinking' opinions. And though the Deists fought upon this point, as well as upon others, a losing battle, they seem to have succeeded in creating an unacknowledged feeling of alarm, and in making the nation more than usually sensitive of any influence which could by any possibility be called priestly usurpation. In the early years of the century, and above all about the time when the High Church hero of the day was 'making his pilgrimage through England with trumpet and drum,' it is likely enough that the minds of some of the weaker-headed of the clergy were a little turned with novel anticipations of ecclesiastical power. But from the very beginning of the next reign, and markedly in the middle and latter part of the century, there appears to have been a timidity of action which fell in only too easily with the general disinclination to any effort which went beyond the ordinary routine. There were those both of the clergy and laity who discountenanced all nascent enterprise in the

[1] *Guardian*, No. 39.

Church on the express ground that it might revive the charge of the clergy being athirst for authority and power.

Apart from all these attacks upon the clergy, many of the questions raised in their earlier works by Collins and Tindal merged into that general one of the authority of the Church which, just at the end of Queen Anne's reign, was starting upon its tedious and involved course under the name of the 'Bangorian controversy.' It will have to be touched upon a little later.

The great doctrinal questions which Deism had already started in the works of Hobbes and Herbert of Cherbury were almost at rest during the first thirteen years of the eighteenth century. But meanwhile another theological controversy was being actively carried on in that singular resuscitation of the old Arianism originated by Emlyn, Whiston, and Clarke. John Emlyn, an Irish Presbyterian minister of English birth, was deposed from his clerical charge and prosecuted both in Dublin and London in 1703. William Whiston—a man full of learned and eccentric fancies, of whom it is but just to say that he pressed his theories and followed what he conceived was true without the very remotest thought of consequences— was deprived of his professorship and expelled from Cambridge in 1710. Two years later, Samuel Clarke published the work upon the Trinity which brought upon him the censures of Convocation. These three were entirely independent one of another, and their views did not entirely accord.[1] But they agreed in this, that they held a position by themselves, apart from orthodox Christians, Deists, or Unitarians. They were by no means Deists. Whiston wrote against Collins; and Clarke's discourse on Natural Religion, in answer to

---

[1] Whiston approximated more closely than the others to the Arians of the fourth century. Burnet called him 'partly Apollinarist, partly Arian, for he thought that the *νοῦς*, or word, was all the soul that acted in our Saviour's body.'—*Own Times*, p. 867.

Hobbes, Spinoza, and others, was pronounced by Bishop Smalridge to be 'the best book on these subjects that had been written in any language.' Neither were they Unitarians. Some of Emlyn's friends tried hard to make him one, but he answered that he could never doubt of the preexistence of our Saviour as the Word of God, or that God created the material world through Him. Their Arianism came in as a rather singular break, separating Petavius and the other Socinians, against whom Bishop Bull wrote in 1685, from those who in the latter half of the last century followed the teaching of Lardner, Priestley, and Belsham. 'It is remarkable,' said the last-mentioned writer, in a letter to Dr. Parr (March 23, 1819), 'that Unitarianism, or rather Socinianism, after having made so conspicuous a figure in the latter half of the seventeenth century, should have been totally silent for the first half of the eighteenth century.' He goes on to say that one reason for this was that 'Dr. Clarke, Mr. Emlyn, Mr. Whiston, and other learned men, at the commencement of the eighteenth century, so powerfully advocated the doctrine of Arianism that for a time it put every (Socinian) hypothesis out of countenance. And when I first began to inquire fifty years ago, an advocate for the proper Unitarian doctrine was hardly to be found. Dr. Lardner, indeed, who appeared to have been an early and a pure Unitarian, whose well-known maxim it was that "the pride of Arianism should have a fall," . . . did not venture to publish his book till thirty years after it was written, so that when genuine Unitarianism came to be received, avowed, and defended by Mr. Lindsey, Dr. Priestley, and others, it excited as great astonishment and horror as if it had never been heard of before. And, indeed, in the simple form in which they professed it, it differed almost as much from Socinianism as it did from Athanasianism.'[1] But

[1] Parr's *Works*, viii. 154-55.

though Arianism was neither Deistical nor Unitarian, neither, on the other hand, did it ever find an acknowledged place within the widest latitude conceded by the National Church. There were many who strove hard to secure such admission. Bishop Robinson had occasion to write a circular letter to the London clergy warning them not to adopt an Arian innovation in the doxologies;[1] and the case of the Arian subscription, or the claim to sign the articles in an Arian sense, was a question which at one time created much alarm and perplexity. This sort of intermediate position which Clarke and Whiston held made it seem to the Churchmen of their day especially formidable. There were many who began to fear that all English Christianity was in danger of being undermined by doctrines which would lead on to Unitarianism. In the exaggerated language which was then common in such publications, a pamphleteer of 1697 had declared that 'all the Arminians are joined in a confederacy with the Socinians; . . . that is to say, almost all the Church of England, a moiety of the Presbyterians, nine parts in ten out of Quakers.'[2] Another pamphleteer of 1704 had pronounced, on similar grounds, that 'Arminianism was a shoeing-horn to draw on Socinianism, and that draws after it Deism.'[3] By Arminianism they meant, generally speaking, that rational school of Christian theology which the Cambridge Platonists and Tillotson had headed. And it must be acknowledged that there was a certain modicum of reason in their fear. The charge often brought against Tillotson and Burnet of being Socinians was utterly absurd. But Socinianism, and, to a still greater extent (as being a few shades nearer to orthodox Churchmanship), Arianism like that of Clarke, seemed, to some

[1] Waterland's *Works*, i. 64.
[2] *An Apology for the Parliament, &c.*, 1697.
[3] *The Principles of the Reformation on Ch. Commun.*, 1704.

who had been shaken by Deist arguments, a sort of refuge midway between rational Churchmanship and the bare and negative form of Christianity—if it could pretend to that name at all—which the Deists held. Often it was but a temporary shelter where they waited for a while until they went onward on their way. The position, however, seemed the more tenable, because Dr. Clarke remained to the end of his life a clergyman of the English Church. His explanations before the Upper House of Convocation, although not very satisfactory, had yet been accepted; and a year or two later it was only through his own refusal that he was not made a bishop.[1]

A great number of writers contended against the new Arianism: Waterland and Bennet, Potter, Smalbroke and Gastrell, Atterbury, Hickes and R. Nelson, Gale, Berryman, Thirlby, and others. Among the many answers to Whiston which appeared in 1712 was one by the Earl of Nottingham, leader of the Tory party, which went through nine editions. The University of Oxford returned him solemn thanks in full Convocation, and Whiston condescendingly remarked of it that 'my Lord Nottingham's answer is no ill one for an English temporal peer, and that his Lordship justly deserves very great commendations on this account.'[2]

In 1706, Henry Dodwell, a Nonjuror, whose profound erudition, simple-hearted piety, and kindliness of temperament[3] won the love and honour even of those who listened with wonder at the extraordinary theories which he was accustomed to take up, published a work in which he maintained that immortality was a special gift of God to those only who had been baptised into the communion of

---

[1] *Diary of Mary, Countess Cowper*, 1714-18.
[2] Calamy's *Life and Times*, ii. 527, and Rutt's note.
[3] Brokesby's *Life of Dodwell*, pp. 518-42.

the Church, and that no baptism was valid except such as was administered through the hands of lawfully, that is to say of episcopally, ordained clergy. Probably no human being but himself accepted to its full extent this amazing hypothesis. But there were many who were by no means inclined to let the opinions of so good and learned a man as to the validity of lay baptism fall silently to the ground. The Nonjurors especially had every disposition to magnify their office. A small and dwindling communion, they were apt to give a very exaggerated importance to the tenet for which they had suffered, or even to hold that they alone were the one orthodox remnant of the whole vast Catholic Church. They could not, indeed, affirm that apostacy from the sacred doctrine of Non-resistance had altogether unchurched their Anglican brethren. But at the least they stood upon a level higher beyond comparison than Dissenters in England or Presbyterians in Scotland, who could hardly, by a great stretch in charity, be called a Church at all. Holding such views, many of them hastened to support Dodwell in his proposition that lay or Presbyterian baptism was no true sacrament. Hickes and Wagstaffe, Brett and Laurence [1] all published to this effect. The time was just then very favourable to a wide acceptance of such a view, for polemical and party feeling was at its height, and Tories and High Churchmen were maintaining that Presbyterians were conspiring with Latitudinarians to subvert the constitution of the English Church. A number of the more extreme members of the High Church party proclaimed their adherence to it, and the matter began to get so much discussed,[2] that the bishops thought it desirable to publish a collective declaration, first against the irregularity of baptism by lay persons, and then showing that 'primitive

[1] Lathbury's *Nonjurors*, pp. 381 86; Nichols' *Lit. An.*, vi. 227.
[2] Kennet's *Life*, p. 111.

and Anglican usage disallowed the reiteration of baptism.'[1] Three or four, however, of the bishops, headed by Sharp,[2] declined to sign, not from any difference in view, but for fear it might encourage irregularities, and the Lower House of Convocation thereupon refused to consider the question. From the writings that appeared on either side two ingenious 'ad hominem' arguments are worth mentioning. Wagstaffe declared that they who could defend the deposition of kings and the validity of lay baptism must needs be ripe for perversion, since these were wholly Romish doctrines.[3] Fleetwood recommended Nonjurors and Jacobites above all other men to reconsider their opinions, as Charles I. himself, he said, was baptised by Presbyterian hands.[4]

Dodwell's singular speculations gave fresh vigour to a wholly different controversy which had been started two or three years before. In 1702, Dr. Coward, a physician, had published a book in which he argued that the doctrine of the soul being immaterial and immortal was erroneous and contrary to the Christian teaching. Several treatises were published in answer to it, and Coward defended his theory in a second book, which gave such grave offence, that in 1704, after examination by a committee of the House of Commons, it was advertised in the most effectual manner possible by being burned by the hangman in the Palace Yard. There could be no such outcry against Dodwell, for, however fanciful might be the conclusions to which he sometimes arrived, no one could ever doubt the simple earnestness of his piety. He found, however, a very uncongenial ally in Collins; while the Nonjuror and the Deist alike had their opinions ably contested in the clear

---

[1] Burnet's *Own Times*, p. 888; Calamy, ii. 237.
[2] Sharp's *Life*, i. 375; ii. 27.   [3] Wagstaffe's *Works*, p. 306.
[4] Fleetwood's *Works*, p. 551. This, however, was fully proved to be not the case.

and solid reasonings of Samuel Clarke. The opponents of Christianity long found what they considered a useful weapon in this view of the materiality of the soul; and in the pages of the 'Guardian' and other popular essayists many a shaft of ridicule was aimed at the 'pineal gland,' where some materialistic writer had affirmed that the soul was to be discovered.

Theological literature was enriched during Queen Anne's reign with several valuable contributions. Among these may be mentioned Daniel Whitby's 'Paraphrase and Commentary on the New Testament,' 1703, a work highly spoken of by divines of almost every denomination; the 'Christian Institutes' of Francis Gastrell, afterwards Bishop of Chester, a digest of the Bible in its own words under different heads, published in 1709, and frequently reprinted at later dates; Joseph Bingham's learned 'Origines Ecclesiasticæ,' or 'The Antiquities of the Christian Church,' of which the first of the nine volumes was published in 1708; Bishop Bull's last work ('Primitiva Traditio,' &c.), on 'The Divinity of our Lord,' 1703; Samuel Clarke's 'Discourse on the Being and Attributes of God,' 1705-6, a book which has deservedly passed through many editions; various treatises on the Prayer Book and Articles &c. by T. Bennett, 1709-11; the 'Codex Juris Eccl. Anglicanæ,' 1711, of Edmund Gibson, afterwards Bishop of London, a standard work upon the laws of the English Church; the 'Discourse upon Church Government,' by Potter, afterwards Archbishop of Canterbury, in 1707; the English Ecclesiastical History of Jeremy Collier, the Nonjuror, of which the first volume appeared in 1708 and the other in 1714; two learned dissertations on the Septuagint Version, 1705 and 1710, by Ernest Grabe, an accession to the English Church from the ranks of Lutheranism; William Derham's 'Physico-Theology,' interesting as one of the earlier efforts to bring

natural science into connection with theology, in 1713; the
'De Origine Mali' of William King, Archbishop of Dublin,
in 1702; and the 'History of the Apostles' Creed,' published
the same year by Peter King, afterwards Lord Chancellor.
It may be added that Burnet completed the 'History of his
own Times'[1] in 1708; and that Berkeley's 'Principles of
Human Knowledge' and his 'Dialogues between Hylas and
Philonous' appeared, the one in 1710, the other in 1713.
Two productions of a devotional kind have yet to be
mentioned: Robert Nelson's 'Festivals and Fasts,' published
in 1703; and in the first year of the century those hymns
which seem likely to remain and live so long as the world
lasts—the Morning and Evening Hymns, together with one
for midnight, by Bishop Ken.

Neither can we pass over that long and famous series
of short essays which began in 1709 with the 'Tatler,' was
continued with still more brilliant success by the 'Spectator,'
and was carried on with diminished lustre by similar
periodicals through a great part of the century. Doubtless
they are chiefly notable in the history of general literature.
'They made,' as it has been truly said, 'a people of readers,
of thinkers, and of writers, and they gave a new direction
to the literature of Europe.'[1] Not only were they circulated
in the British Islands, to the extent, on some occasions, of
20,000 copies in a day, but on the Continent also they were
often translated and very largely imitated. The French
had their 'Babillard,' the Dutch their 'Spectator,' the
Germans their 'Guardian.' This last had already begun
to succeed, but the sale became still more rapid and general
when translations were inserted from the English 'Spectator.'[2]
But their influence was far from being only literary and
educational. They had a very definite bearing on the morals
and Christianity of the country. 'It is incredible,' says a

[1] *Quarterly Rev.*, i. 399. [2] *Id.*

contemporary writer, speaking of the 'Spectator,' 'to conceive what effect his writings have had upon the town; how many thousand follies they have banished or given a check to; how much countenance they have given to virtue and religion. His writings have set our wits and men of letters on a new way of thinking. . . . Every one writes and thinks more justly.'[1] Their whole tendency was to purify taste, to exhibit virtue as beautiful, and wherever they touched upon religion to inculcate its dignity and attractiveness. They did not aim at anything more serious and profound than this. They did not, and could not, without ruin to their designs, intrude upon the province of the preacher, but as Christian essayists, touching with kindly but high-minded satire the follies and errors of the day, they did their duty well. It was no light advantage to the cause of Christianity that at so many thousand breakfast-tables [2] these wholesome and instructive papers should be daily served; and that no English man or woman who had any pretension to education should remain wholly uninfluenced by a wit that never descended below the level of high Christian principle. Nor was it a trifling gain to the English Church that these popular writers should have been so loyal to her observances, her ritual, her liturgy, her clergy; never more anxious to show their reverence and respect than when they sought to point out and to amend her blemishes.

In the early part of the century there was much more

[1] *Present State of Wit*, &c., 1711. Quoted by Overton in *The English Church of the Eighteenth Century*, i. 659.

[2] Even in 1712 we find the Evangelical writer, James Hervey, writing to his sister: 'I once thought I should make less use of the *Spectator* than you; but now I believe the reverse of this is true; for we read one or more of these elegant and instructive papers every morning at breakfast. They are served up with tea, according to their original design. We reckon our report imperfect without a little of Mr. Addison's or Mr. Steele's company.' *Works*, i. 225.

stir and activity in the practical work of the English Church than was to be found in it at a somewhat later date. There can be no doubt that a great need had arisen for good men to use their best efforts to meet the evils of the times. There can also be no doubt that the excitement of party contests absorbed a vast deal of the energy which might better have been expended in active pastoral labour. Still this period may be contrasted not unfavourably with the time before and after. The 'decay of religion,' the 'profligacy,' the 'general corruption,' the 'universal degeneracy,' which in every variety of term was so continually deplored by every successive writer for ninety years or more from about the beginning of James II.'s reign, was battled against not without energy, and not without some success, in Queen Anne's time. For some years before her accession most religious and earnest people seem to have awakened with a feeling of dismay to what they saw around them. After the Restoration, the anti-Puritan reaction had been not only so strong, but so universal that the dangers of a sudden release from the strait and rigorous formalities of the Puritan rule were by no means fully appreciated. But it soon became apparent enough to all who were alive to such considerations, that liberty had to a grievous extent become licence, alike in action and in thought. The coarse selfishness of Hobbes's philosophy was eagerly adopted by many who were only too ready to popularise it in its most injurious sense. A corrupt and venal court, a thoroughly ignoble administration of public affairs, and a sense of insecurity and instability both in Church and State, all tended to increase the evil. He must be strangely blind to accumulated evidence who can doubt that irreligion and immorality had gained formidable ground. In the early years of the eighteenth century this was talked about more than ever. But there were two special reasons for this;

expressed their cordial approval. It is a testimony to a good deal of sound moral feeling amid much that was corrupt, that Archbishop Sharp, writing about these societies in a tone of not more than qualified approval, could yet say in their favour that 'the nation was much set on them.'[1]

The object of these societies was mainly to co-operate with the law in checking all such forms of immorality as could be brought under legal penalties. They endeavoured to close profligate houses; they brought actions against vendors of vicious books and prints, against shopkeepers and publicans who persisted, after notice, in trading during the hours of divine service on Sunday, against cheats and impostors, and against persons who were guilty of gross cruelty to animals; they tried to reform the stage, and to stop unlawful plays, games, and lotteries.[2] In 1724 the society had prosecuted, since its foundation, no less than 91,899 persons for these and similar offences against public morality.[3]

These efforts met, however, with a good deal of vehement opposition. After the first enthusiasm of the movement had somewhat spent itself, the system became very dependent on informers, and these could only be got under promises of secrecy.[4] There was no little outcry against these men, as 'meddling' and 'pragmatical,' 'hypocrites' and 'rogues.'[5] The rich were too powerful, it was said, to be meddled with, or fee'd the officers, and poor men made off and left their families on the parish. Others asked in anger whether these 'knight reformers' were not trying to bring in Puritanism or Presbytery. 'It is only too

---

[1] Nicolson's *Letter*, p. 157.

[2] Bisset's *Plain English Sermon for Ref. of Manners*, 1704, p. 19; *The Athenian Oracle*, 1715, iii. 44, &c.

[3] Malcolm's *Manners &c. of London*, i. 140.

[4] Johnson's *Clergyman's Vade Mecum*, 1709, i. 271.

[5] Bisset, p. 22, *Ath. Oracle*, iii. 161.

plain,' wrote another, 'that our societies' zeal tends chiefly towards the fatal revolt of Forty-one.'[1] The more straitlaced and exclusive of the High Churchmen—and they were many—looked with great suspicion at a movement in which not unfrequently Churchmen and Dissenters acted side by side. 'It was all part of the conspiracy,' they muttered, 'to undermine the Church, and make us Whigs and Presbyterians.' They were, in Sacheverell's estimation, 'odious and factious' coalitions.[2] These prejudices were inflamed by the unwise action of some of the more advanced of what we should now call the Broad Church clergy. They did well to urge the co-operation of good men of all opinions in the great cause of Christian morality; but, in the excited state of Church feeling which prevailed throughout the reign of Anne, they did more harm than good to the object for which they were contending, when they proposed that they and some of the Nonconformist ministers should interchange pulpits in a series of mutual lectures. Nicolson, afterwards Bishop of Carlisle, had much correspondence with leading Churchmen on this subject. Sharp, Archbishop of York, answered him that he hardly knew how to give directions in the matter. Personally, he did not like these 'confederacies,' as of doubtful legality and possible issues; but, still, many of the bishops were warmly in favour of them; nor did he wish to discourage societies started with so excellent an object. On the whole, his opinion was, that any clergymen of the English Church who preached in meeting-houses, or permitted Dissenters to lecture in their churches, must be admonished to forbear such practices; that on other points no existing societies must be disturbed or discouraged; that it was advisable for such societies to be constituted on Church principles; and that 'more good

[1] *Plain English made Plain*, 1704, pref.
[2] Woodward on the *Societies*, 1711, p. 6.

expressed their cordial approval. It is a testimony to a good deal of sound moral feeling amid much that was corrupt, that Archbishop Sharp, writing about these societies in a tone of not more than qualified approval, could yet say in their favour that 'the nation was much set on them.'[1]

The object of these societies was mainly to co-operate with the law in checking all such forms of immorality as could be brought under legal penalties. They endeavoured to close profligate houses; they brought actions against vendors of vicious books and prints, against shopkeepers and publicans who persisted, after notice, in trading during the hours of divine service on Sunday, against cheats and impostors, and against persons who were guilty of gross cruelty to animals; they tried to reform the stage, and to stop unlawful plays, games, and lotteries.[2] In 1724 the society had prosecuted, since its foundation, no less than 91,899 persons for these and similar offences against public morality.[3]

These efforts met, however, with a good deal of vehement opposition. After the first enthusiasm of the movement had somewhat spent itself, the system became very dependent on informers, and these could only be got under promises of secrecy.[4] There was no little outcry against these men, as 'meddling' and 'pragmatical,' 'hypocrites' and 'rogues.'[5] The rich were too powerful, it was said, to be meddled with, or fee'd the officers, and poor men made off and left their families on the parish. Others asked in anger whether these 'knight reformers' were not trying to bring in Puritanism or Presbytery. 'It is only too

[1] Nicolson's *Letter*, p. 157.
[2] Bisset's *Plain English Sermon for Ref. of Manners*, 1704, p. 19; *The Athenian Oracle*, 1715, iii. 44, &c.
[3] Malcolm's *Manners &c. of London*, i. 110.
[4] Johnson's *Clergyman's Vade Mecum*, 1709, i. 271.
[5] Bisset, p. 22, *Ath. Oracle*, iii. 164.

plain,' wrote another, ' that our societies' zeal tends chiefly towards the fatal revolt of Forty-one.'[1] The more straitlaced and exclusive of the High Churchmen—and they were many—looked with great suspicion at a movement in which not unfrequently Churchmen and Dissenters acted side by side. 'It was all part of the conspiracy,' they muttered, ' to undermine the Church, and make us Whigs and Presbyterians.' They were, in Sacheverell's estimation, ' odious and factious ' coalitions.[2] These prejudices were inflamed by the unwise action of some of the more advanced of what we should now call the Broad Church clergy. They did well to urge the co-operation of good men of all opinions in the great cause of Christian morality; but, in the excited state of Church feeling which prevailed throughout the reign of Anne, they did more harm than good to the object for which they were contending, when they proposed that they and some of the Nonconformist ministers should interchange pulpits in a series of mutual lectures. Nicolson, afterwards Bishop of Carlisle, had much correspondence with leading Churchmen on this subject. Sharp, Archbishop of York, answered him that he hardly knew how to give directions in the matter. Personally, he did not like these ' confederacies,' as of doubtful legality and possible issues; but, still, many of the bishops were warmly in favour of them; nor did he wish to discourage societies started with so excellent an object. On the whole, his opinion was, that any clergymen of the English Church who preached in meeting-houses, or permitted Dissenters to lecture in their churches, must be admonished to forbear such practices; that on other points no existing societies must be disturbed or discouraged; that it was advisable for such societies to be constituted on Church principles; and that ' more good

[1] *Plain English made Plain*, 1704, pref.
[2] Woodward on the *Societies*, 1711, p. 6.

might be expected from a zealous carrying out of all pastoral duties than by informing against offenders, although this also was likely to be beneficial.'[1]

The Societies for the Reformation of Manners were but part of a more extensive organisation which had been set on foot in James II.'s time, and had been largely developed afterwards. One is almost inclined to say that the Church of England has throughout its history had no greater benefactor among its kings than this monarch. His whole heart was bent upon subverting it; he only succeeded in calling forth its energies, and rooting it in the affection of the people. He thought to Romanise it, and did but elicit an opposition which united Churchmen into one, made the cause of Rome hopeless in the island for generations, and strengthened the Protestant cause throughout Europe. He hoped to inflame the mutual jealousies of Churchmen and Dissenters, but his efforts abated animosities, weakened Nonconformity, and arrayed the most influential Nonconformists almost on the side of the Church. In intention he disgraced its bishops, and found that he had made those bishops the most popular men in his whole domain. He did the Church of England a far greater service still. He awoke, by the gravity of the crisis which his hostility brought about, an earnestness of religious life among many Churchmen which gave promise of making the National Church worthy of the high place it had taken in popular favour. Less followed from it than might have been hoped for. The movement did not become deep enough or wide enough to cope very successfully with the counter influences of the time. Still, the religious revival which began before the Revolution continued for some thirty years to show abundant signs of healthy activity. The form it took was chiefly that of association. 'In King James's reign,' says Burnet, 'the

[1] Nicolson's *Letters*, pp. 149-77; *Life of Abp. Sharp*, i. 177-88.

fear of Popery was so strong, as well as just, that many in and about London began to meet often together, both for devotion and for their further instruction. Things of that kind had been formerly practised only among the Puritans and Dissenters; but these were of the Church, and came to their ministers to be assisted with forms of prayer and other directions; they were chiefly conducted by Dr. Beveridge and Dr. Horneck. After the Revolution these services grew more numerous, and for a greater encouragement to devotion, they got such collections to be made as maintained many clergymen to read prayers in so many places, and at so many different hours, that devout persons might have that comfort at every hour of the day; there were constant sacraments every Lord's Day in many churches; there were both greater numbers, and greater appearances of devotion at prayer and sacraments than had been observed in the memory of man. These societies resolved to inform the magistrates of swearers, drunkards, profaners of the Lord's Day, and of lewd houses; and they threw in the part of the fine, given by law to informers, into a stock of charity. . . . Other societies set themselves to raise charity schools for teaching poor children, for clothing them and binding them out to trades; many books were printed, and sent over the nation by them, to be freely distributed: these were called Societies for Propagating Christian Knowledge. By this means some thousands of children are now well educated and carefully looked after. In many places of the nation the clergy met often together, to confer about matters of religion and learning, and they got libraries to be raised for their common use. At last a corporation was created by the late king for propagating the Gospel among infidels, for settling schools in our plantations, for furnishing the clergy that were sent thither, and for sending missionaries among such of our plantations as were not able to provide one for themselves. It was a glorious conclusion of a reign that was begun with preserving our religion, thus to create a corporation for propagating it to the remoter parts of the earth and among infidels. There were very liberal subscriptions made to it by many of the bishops and clergy, who set about it with great love and zeal. Upon the Queen's accession to the crown they had all possible assurances of her favour and protection, of which, upon every application, they received very eminent marks.'[1]

These words of a contemporary historian give an excellent general idea of what was alike the most interesting and the most cheering feature in the Church life of the period between 1690 and 1730. It only remains to fill up the sketch.

Antony Horneck had gained great influence as a preacher at the Savoy. It was no easy matter to get through the crowd to the church, and strangers were astonished at the number of communicants. Few men, we are told, were so frequently applied to in difficulties and cases of conscience.[2] His societies were composed of young men who had been confirmed, and had resolved upon a holy and serious life. Apprentices were not admitted, and no member was to be received without the consent of the directing minister. They met on a stated day once a week, a fine of 3d. being imposed for absence without cause. The Church prayers were read; a psalm might be sung; religious discourse was optional; controversy was strictly forbidden; the practical divinity was to be chosen by the clergyman. Each member paid 6d. every time to the alms-box, and on Whit Tuesday a steward was appointed and the money distributed among the poor. Such as left the society were required to pay a fine of five shillings. The rules of life commended to all members called upon them to love one another, to speak

[1] Burnet's *Own Times*, p. 709. [2] Kidder's *Life of Horneck*, 1698, p. 41.

evil of no man, to wrong no man, to pray, if possible, seven times a day, to keep close to the Church of England, to be peaceable and helpful, to examine themselves at night, to give all their due, to obey their spiritual superiors.[1] They were called upon to communicate regularly, and were recommended to 'admonish and watch over one another, and to fortify each other against those temptations which assault them from the world and their own corruption. . . . And these persons, knowing each other's manner of life, and their peculiar frailties and temptations, partly by their familiar conversation and partly from their own inward experience, can much better inspect, admonish, and guard each other than the most faithful minister usually can.'[2] Such were these societies, which so rapidly increased under the management of many zealous clergymen, and with the active encouragement of the bishop and archbishop, that before long there were forty-two of them in London and Westminster, and many others in all parts of England and Ireland.[3] The wide and general interest taken in them is well shown by the fact that Woodward's 'Account of the Religious Societies in London' passed through six editions in a few years.[4] One permanent result of their influence was the establishment of a number of additional services and lectures. In Paterson's account, published in 1714, of the London Churches, mention is constantly made of regular weekly services, services in preparation for Holy Communion, and weekly or monthly lectures, 'kept up (as it is said in each case) by a religious society.'[5]

Out of the movement thus originated sprang the two

[1] Kidder's *Horneck*, p. 15.
[2] Woodward's *Account*, p. 75. (Qu. from Wedgwood's *Life of J. Wesley* p. 155.)
[3] Perry's *Church History*, pp. 3, 90.
[4] Anderson's *Hist. of the Colon. Church*, ii. 577.
[5] Paterson's *Pietas Londinensis*, passim.

great Church Societies for the Promotion of Christian Knowledge, and for the Propagation of the Gospel in Foreign Parts.

The first meeting of the Christian Knowledge Society was held in March 1698–99. It consisted of only five persons. The main originator of it was a clergyman, Dr. Thomas Bray, who is truly described as 'a person most eminent and exemplary in his age for a truly apostolic zeal as the projector and promoter of almost every scheme for the propagation and the improvement of Christianity.'[1] With him were associated four distinguished laymen, Lord Guildford, Sir Humphrey Mackworth, Mr. Justice Hook, and Colonel Maynard Colchester. They met for the furtherance of three definite objects : (1) The education of the poor. (2) The care of the colonies. (3) The printing and circulating books of sound Christian doctrine. Such was the beginning of this great organisation. Its first numbers rapidly increased, and from the very first High Churchmen and Low Churchmen took an equal interest in its welfare. At a time when party spirit was at its highest, the council-room of this society steadily maintained its position as a quiet place of refuge from all such differences, where the one object was to extend the usefulness of the Church of England as a whole in contending with sin, ignorance, and unbelief. Nonjurors, such as Nelson, Mapletoft, and Wheeler, consulted there with one accord not only with their High Church brethren in the National Church, but with Burnet and Fowler and all the most eminent members of the Whig and Low Church party. So, also, William Whiston remained an active member until his views became too widely divergent from those of the English Church for intimate co-operation to be any longer possible. And when, in 1710, he did withdraw, he declared

---

[1] *An Account of the Designs, &c. of the late Dr. T. Bray*, p. 1.

'his heart was entirely with them in their brave, and religious, and charitable, and Christian undertakings,'[1] and trusted he might still in a private capacity be of service to them.

The society had a great variety of business to discuss in their weekly and often daily meetings. Its action was of course greatly coloured by the designs of its principal founder, and Dr. Bray was a man of versatile energy in different forms of Church work. The ability of his catechetical lectures had commended him to Bishop Compton as well fitted by his powers of instruction and organisation to be his commissary in Maryland. One of the first things which Bray's missionary and colonial experiences brought home to his mind was the great need of providing the poorer clergy both on the plantations and at home with the means of keeping up some theological knowledge. The necessity seemed to him so urgent that it took perhaps the leading place in the three great enterprises to which he devoted himself, and for which he invoked the aid of the society that was soon to arise—education, missionary effort, and cheap theological literature. Even the Bible was still an expensive book, and often full of inaccuracies[2] from being printed on the Continent. Works of general and theological literature were not very accessible to men who, like the majority of the clergy, were in straitened circumstances. 'Booksellers' shops in the provincial towns of England were very rare; so that there was not one even in Birmingham, in which town old Mr. Johnson used to open a shop every market day.'[3] A poor clergyman found 'a grievous impossibility of buying books,' and his scanty shelves might be seen 'furnished with such valuable pieces as "The Pearl of Eloquence," "Spencer's Similitudes, or Things

---

[1] Whiston's *Memoirs*, p. 175.   [2] Perry, iii. 91.
[3] Boswell's *Johnson*, i. 12.

New and Old," rare helps all for matter and sense; old Burgersdccius, for method and ranging; some German system for a general view; here and there a classic for the use of interlarding; a few sticht sermons by way of imitating, and an old Genevan Bible with an useful concordance at the end on't, to crown and complete all.'[1] In America, where the episcopal clergy were recruited for the most part from the poorest of their class at home, Dr. Bray found it still more difficult for them to maintain a tolerable standard of learning and theological knowledge. He evidently felt the need to be a very urgent one. For he first represented the case to the bishops, and begged them to use their aid and influence in procuring parochial libraries for the use of the missionaries, and in 1696 published an earnest appeal on the same subject. 'It was from the colonies,' he said, 'that our citizens and merchants have had in great measure their prodigious wealth, and thither the countryman and the tradesman vend their manufactures and commodities. All ranks gained great advantages from the foreign plantations. They ought to repay something to their chief well-being. It was a discredit to our country and to religion that no persuasion of men on earth had been so cold and wanting to promote this as we had been. Yet we professed great zeal for the Protestant religion, and our merchants were very generous, pious, and charitable ones. The slackness must be for want of application.'[2] He then pressed the need of establishing libraries in every deanery, at some market towns, with a larger and more general one in every province, and buying books which even poor clergy could not properly do without, and thus to raise the general character of the clergy for learning and education. He added full

---

[1] *Hardships of the Inferior Clergy: A Letter to John, Bishop of London,* 1722, pp. 102, 112.

[2] Dr. Bray's *Bibliotheca Parochiana,* 1696, preface.

details of the measures which he wished to adopt, and two interesting lists—one fuller, the other more compressed—of the books which such libraries should contain.[1] His proposals related in the first instance only to the colonies, and met with such success that not in Maryland only, but in other of the American colonies, in some of the West Indies, and in the factories in Africa, such libraries were established, and their preservation secured by votes of legislation.

After leaving America early in the eighteenth century he actively engaged in the same work at home. A very considerable amount was raised by subscriptions of gentry and clergymen, and libraries formed—for the preservation of which an Act was passed in the seventh year of Queen Anne—in many parts of England. Bray hoped that one might soon be established in every rural deanery.[2]

An appeal published by him in 1697, under the name of 'An Essay towards Promoting all Necessary and Useful Knowledge,' already foreshadowed in its title the formation next year of that great society, of which, as we have seen, he was the principal originator. After it was established, all the benevolent designs which had occupied the thoughts of him and of his fellow-labourers quickly took larger proportions and a wider range; but, among the many excellent men who were now united with him in the operations of the society, he was still for twenty or thirty years the presiding spirit. Great as was their activity in their multifarious work, there was scarcely a single branch of it in which they were not more or less directed by Dr. Bray's wide knowledge of such subjects, and by his personal exertions. There was no man in England—with the exception, in some particulars, of General Oglethorpe—who was so versed in the details of

---

[1] Dr. Bray's *Bibliotheca Parochiana*, pp. 63-65.
[2] *The Designs of the Associates of the late Dr. Bray*, p. 5; T. Bray's *Essay towards Promoting*, &c., pp. 2-10.

schools, missions, and clerical libraries. He also took a great interest in the improvement of prisons.

The society was very active. It made the Bible a cheap book; it published Prayer-books, books of devotions, innumerable plain and practical tracts, reprints from approved divines, and new works on religious subjects by the best contemporary writers. It placed in a convenient, popular form arguments intended to confirm faith against the attack of Deism and unbelief. It printed works for the clergy, for missionaries, for parochial libraries. It translated the Prayer-book into Welsh, and sent to the Isle of Man the first books that had yet been written in the native Manx. It sent printing-presses to the American colonies and to the West Indies. It endeavoured to set new Christian influences at work among mercantile sailors, in seaport towns, among bargemen. It communicated with Admiral Benbow and Sir J. Rooke about improving the state of religion in the army and the navy. It did its utmost to co-operate with the excellent men who were introducing improvements and reforms in prisons and in workhouses. It maintained correspondence with fellow-workers among Protestants abroad. It encouraged the inclination shown among some of the foreign Protestant churches to adopt the English liturgy. It received, at a general meeting, Ziegenbalg, the head of the Danish mission to Tranquebar, gave him a free passage out, and translated his report. It was active in the establishment of charity schools, and invited German teachers from Halle to assist in the improvement of catechetical teaching. It responded to an appeal of the Archbishop of Gotcham, in Armenia, in getting works of piety printed for him in the language of his country. It appointed a committee to report upon the condition of the stage, and printed for distribution among ladies and others some grave words of Archbishop Tillotson on the 'weighty reproach which plays, as they are now ordered among us, are to the age and nation.'[1] It forwarded the various objects of the societies for the reformation of manners; it passed a vote of thanks to Sir J. Phillips for his bold refusal of a challenge;—in a word, it aimed at nothing less than to diffuse throughout society an improved Christian tone, and, as far as was in its power, to unite and concentrate the efforts of all who were honestly seeking to purify the national life.

The education of the poor had ranked first among the special objects for which the Christian Knowledge Society had been formed. Its members, both in their individual and corporate capacity, co-operated vigorously with many other diligent workers in the good cause. Their efforts were rewarded with much success. 'The charity schools,' Steele wrote in 1712, 'which have been erected of late years are the greatest instances of public spirit which the age has produced.'[2] Addison, a year after, wrote still more enthusiastically of them. 'I have always,' he said, 'looked on this institution of charity schools—which of late years has so universally prevailed through the whole nation—as the glory of the age we live in, and the most proper means that can be made use of to recover it out of its present degeneracy and depravation of manners. It seems to promise us an honest and virtuous posterity. There will be few in the next generation who will not at least be able to write and read, and have not had an early tincture of religion.' Better, he exclaimed, than all the pomps of a Roman triumph, and more pleasing, both to God and man, had been the spectacle of that great multitude of children who, on the recent day of thanksgiving, had lined the Strand, and joined together in their hymn of praise. For his own part, he could not but hope that the signal

[1] Serm. on Eph. iv. 29; *Works*, ix. 114. [2] *Spectator*, No. 294.

victories with which the English arms had been crowned were in some measure blessings upon that national charity which had been so conspicuous of late.[1] Some of those who bear the most well-known and most honoured names among the Churchmen of that period were particularly zealous in this form of benevolence. Bishop Bull, writing in 1708 a circular letter to his clergy, begged them to use their best efforts to promote the erection of charity schools in every parish. He referred to their great success in London, and reminded them that there was no charity so good as that of religious education.[2] Robert Nelson was a most active promoter of these institutions, and at his death left most of his property to them.[3] Bishop Ken could not but rejoice at their growth; it was the carrying out of a work in which he himself had been zealously interested in earlier days.[4] Bishop Wilson, from the very beginning of his episcopate in the Isle of Man, introduced them into his diocese, and made attendance at them a principal feature in his system of discipline.[5] The important position which the Christian Knowledge Society rapidly obtained, and the leading part which it took in this general movement, is clearly recognised in a memorial presented to it in 1710, 'for the setting up of charity schools universally in all parishes of England and Wales.'[6] About the same time Dean Swift was pleading for a no less universal extension of the elements of education in Ireland. 'It is in the power of the lawgivers,' he wrote, 'to found a school in every parish of the kingdom for teaching the meaner and poorer sort of children to speak and to read the English tongue, and to provide a reasonable maintenance for the teachers. . . . And, indeed, considering how small a tax would suffice for

[1] *Guardian*, No. 105.   [2] Nelson's *Life of Bull*, p. 380.
[3] Nichols' *Lit. An.*, iv. 189.   [4] Bowler's *Life of Ken*, p. 98.
[5] Cruttwell's *Life of Wilson*, p. 72.   [6] Whiston's *Memoirs*, p. 153.

such a work, it is a public scandal that such a thing should never have been endeavoured, or, perhaps, as much as thought upon.'[1]

In the general absence of any completer system of religious and secular education for the poor, it was natural that earnest Churchmen should feel very strongly the great importance of frequent and regular catechising. They could not, indeed, on this point speak more emphatically than Hammond and Hall, and other eminent divines of the preceding generation had done. 'I have spent,' said the last-mentioned prelate, 'the greater half of my life in the station of our holy service; I thank God, not unpainfully, nor unprofitably. But there is no one thing of which I repent so much, as not to have bestowed more hours in this public exercise of catechism, in regard whereof I would quarrel with my very sermons.'[2] In the beginning of the eighteenth, as at the end of the seventeenth century, laments at the frequent disuse of catechising in favour of the afternoon sermon alternate with commendations of the older practice, and exhortations to continue it.[3]

Although the Church of England in Queen Anne's time was, on the whole, by no means inactive in the cause of education, greater proportionate efforts were being made by Dissenters. Notwithstanding their depressed condition, their schools were numerous and successful. They joined heartily in the movement for erecting charity schools; in some country towns and villages they occupied the ground which the indifference of Churchmen had left unfilled, and provided almost the only means of education which the

---

[1] 'On the Cause of the Wretched Condition of Ireland,' Swift's *Works*, viii. 7.   [2] *Q. Rev.* xix. 28.

[3] *Life of Kettlewell*, pp. 24, 91; *Life of Bull*, p. 359; Sherlock on *Religious Assemblies*, ii. 145, 196; Tillotson's *Works*, ii. 127; Moss's Sermon, p. 51; Frampton, in Lathbury's *Nonjurors*, p. 211; Wake, in Nichols' *Lit. An.*, i. 415 Dean Stanhope, in *id.* iv. 170; Fleetwood's *Works*, p. 472, &c.

place afforded. Some of their ablest men devoted themselves especially to the work of tuition, and established seminaries of such high repute that Churchmen of position and influence were sometimes tempted to send their sons to be educated there.[1] Some eminent men, the most well-known of whom were Secker, Archbishop of Canterbury, and Butler, author of the 'Analogy,' owed their early training to these schools. Such efforts aroused in the minds of those who professed a great zeal for the Church a most unworthy spirit of jealousy and alarm. In the height of the Tory reaction a successful cry was raised that the Nonconformist schools were imperilling the principles of monarchy and episcopacy. The Schism Act was the result—a disgraceful Bill. It remained on the statute-book for only four years, and was held in abeyance even from the first. But had its provisions been enforced, every Dissenting school would have been closed; and, in a country which professed toleration, all means of education would have been proscribed within its borders to those who could not consent that their children should be brought up in the doctrines of the National Church.

The education of the upper and middle classes was by no means in a satisfactory state. 'I am come to the determination,' said Swift, 'that education is always the worse in proportion to the wealth and grandeur of the parents.'[2] It had been so, he added, ever since the Restoration, and there was but little improvement. Out of fifteen thousand families of lords and estated gentlemen, he supposed not

---

[1] Thus Samuel Wesley, arguing in 1704 against the toleration of Dissenting academies, says, 'He'll hardly be able to persuade the world that it has been no injury to the universities to drain away such considerable numbers—several of the nobility, and many of the gentry—who would have sought their education there, had they not been intercepted by these sucking academies' (S. Wesley's *Reply to S. Palmer's Defence of the Dissenters' Education*, 1704, pp. 14, 15).

[2] 'Essay on Modern Education,' *Works*, ix. 160.

more than one in thirty were tolerably educated.¹ Locke, who was perhaps somewhat prejudiced on the subject, declared that the public schools were seminaries of every pernicious principle; and Dean Prideaux lamented that as the discipline of families was neglected and broken, so also it had grown loose in schools.² The clergy at this time were, as a rule, too poor to give their sons a learned education;³ and the comparative absence of this element had a bad effect both on the upper schools and on the universities. The rod, sternly and severely used, was still the great engine of discipline, upon which schoolmasters almost exclusively relied. 'He used to beat us unmercifully,' said Dr. Johnson of his master at Lichfield;⁴ though he records this appreciatively and with gratitude, declaring that without it he should have done nothing. We may perhaps pause, therefore, before we ask with Eachard, in the generation immediately preceding, 'How can a boy care about his master, when he hah measured out unto him, very early in the morning, fifteen or twenty well laid-on lashes for letting a syllable slip too soon, or hanging too long upon it?'⁵

Meanwhile, among many other intimations that the Church was not altogether asleep to the higher interests of her public-school boys, we find Ken writing prayers and his Morning and Evening Hymns for the lads at Winchester; Fleetwood preaching earnestly in the Eton Chapel;⁶ Robert Nelson endeavouring to introduce some Christian authors into the school curriculum;⁷ and Archbishop Sharp interesting himself greatly in the grammar schools of his diocese.⁸ It should be added that Bishop Berkeley spoke,

---

¹ Swift's *Works*, 'On the Contempt of the Clergy,' ix. 271.
² Prideaux's *Life and Letters*, p. 195.
³ Swift's *Works*, ix. 270; Eachard, p. 125.   ⁴ Boswell's *Johnson*, i. 19.
⁵ Eachard on the *Condition of the Clergy*, p. 7.
⁶ Fleetwood's *Works*, p. 115.   ⁷ Teale's *Life of Nelson*, p. 322.
⁸ *Life of Sharp*, i. 219.

in 1713,[1] of the feeling prevalent in public schools in a favourable tone, which contrasts strongly with that used by Locke and Swift.

Lord Campbell, speaking of Oxford in 1701, says that 'Jacobite politics were the chief business of the place, and hard drinking its chief recreation;'[2] and though the saying is a hard one, its general truth cannot be gainsaid. Swift inveighs against the want of discipline in the universities, the idleness and the drinking,[3] but is angry at the 'scandalous reflection on them for infecting the youth of the nation with arbitrary and Jacobite principles.'[4] Whiston, in 1698, speaks of the hard drinking at Cambridge.[5] The Vice-Provost of King's College told Calamy, a few years earlier, that 'the Cambridge youth were grown more corrupt than ever.'[6] An anonymous writer, in 1700, asserts that the university had grown so degenerate, 'that the gentry of England begin to bethink themselves of academies and other ways of education for their sons, to avoid a place where only poverty, and the want of opportunity to be vicious, can secure from vice.'[7] Toland would doubtless have declaimed fiercely against the 'bigotry and narrowness' of Oxford, even if the training received there had been ever so excellent: there was more weight in his reproach of its 'ignorance, idleness, and want of discipline.'[8] 'The heads of houses,' said Hearne, in his diary for 1716, are 'generally great epicures, and very illiterate.'[9] A writer in the 'Tatler' in 1710, having been a Fellow in one of the universities, grows 'weary of that inactive life, and resolves to be doing good in his generation.'[10]

[1] *Guardian*, No. 62.   [2] Campbell's *Lives of the Chancellors*, iv. 619.
[3] 'Argument against abol. Christianity,' *Works*, viii. 92.
[4] 'Sentiments of a Ch. of E. Man,' *id.* viii. 258.
[5] Whiston's *Memoirs*, i. 128.   [6] Calamy's *Autobiog.*, i. 137.
[7] *Growth of Leisure: a Collection*, p. 157.
[8] Toland's *State Anatomy of Great Britain*, 1707, p. 39.
[9] *Reliquiæ Hearnianæ*, ii. 30.   [10] *Tatler*, No. 220.

At Cambridge, however, there was in Queen Anne's reign a remarkable but temporary revival of educational activity under the auspices of Bentley. In 1699, by the unanimous recommendation of a commission of bishops, he had been appointed head of Trinity College. The reformation effected by his energy and example may best be told in his own words. 'I found the college,' he said, 'filled, for the most part, with ignorant, drunken, lewd fellows and scholars; but in the course of about nine years (wherein I had chosen forty new fellows, and had quite a new race of scholars) we were grown to that deserved fame for discipline, learning, numbers of gentry, improvements of revenue, of public buildings, as chapel, lodge, astronomical observatory, chymical laboratory, that we became the envy not only of our own, but of the other university. . . . We were grown like an university within ourselves, having within our own walls better instruments and lectures for experimental philosophy, chymistry, &c., than Leyden, Utrecht, or any university could show. By the example of our college, the whole youth of the university took a new spring of industry. Oriental learning was cultivated; mathematics was brought to that height that the questions disputed in the schools were quite of another sort than was heard there before. And the public press (which had lately been projected and founded solely by myself, and purchased and endowed solely by my friends) was full of bound books in several languages and sciences.'[1] This was indeed a great work for one man to have accomplished, and one that does him no less honour than the profound scholarship for which he was unique among his contemporaries. But even at that date he speaks with harsh, but perhaps not unmerited, censure of the cabals which were being raised up 'among

---

[1] Bentley to Bateman, Dec. 12, 1712; Bentley's *Correspondence*, vol. ii.

the drunkards,' and it would appear that the improved state of things quickly fell off after Bentley's time. At Oxford there was no such movement. The foundation of Worcester College in 1714 was perhaps the only visible sign of its having any share whatever in the reviving practical energy which, in Queen Anne's reign, Churchmen were showing elsewhere. There were learned men, besides and after Bentley, at both universities. Ambrose Bonwicke [1] was not the only example, in the generation just before Wesley, of deep and fervent piety in a student. Nor were there wanting a few conscientious and laborious tutors. But, apart from the exceptional movement described, even Cambridge was far from being what it was when Cudworth and Henry More were among its teachers. Still less was Oxford any longer the Oxford of Hales and Chillingworth. The universities were angry with Le Clerc for proclaiming his opinion, in 1699, that literature was declining in them; and it might be true in individual instances that religion and learning nowhere met so well together as in their venerable cloisters. But it was for the most part clear enough that, for a long period from the end of the seventeenth century, Oxford without any break, and Cambridge with one bright interval, were in a condition unworthy of themselves and greatly in need of reform. Without such reform, said Prideaux in 1715, 'it is, humanly speaking, impossible that the Church of Christ can be well supported against its adversaries.' [2] It was needful, he said, both in study and discipline. Among other changes, elections should be by merit only, and limitation to founders' kin should be done away. Whiston and Robert Nelson, two very different minds, were both agreed in an earnest wish that more could be done by the universities in behalf of candidates for Holy

[1] Nichols' *Lit. An.*, v. 118–36.
[2] *Life and Letters of H. Prideaux*, pp. 197, 215.

Orders.¹ An alteration, however, of some importance was gradually introduced by custom about this time of receiving undergraduates at a later average age than heretofore throughout the preceding century. Sixteen had been the common age, and some went up much younger still. William Wotton, a boy of extraordinary attainments, entered at St. Katherine Hall before he was yet thirteen.² But throughout the eighteenth century, and even at its beginning, although a mere lad might sometimes seek and obtain matriculation, the ordinary standard of age was becoming much the same as now.

In one of the magazines of that time we read, 'In other places they bow to men's fortunes, but in the universities to their understandings.'³ The position of sizars and poor scholars was a strange commentary on this remark, for they were still little better than 'porters and serving-men.'⁴ Even as late as Goldsmith's time, about 1745, the 'sizars wore red caps, and were compelled to perform derogatory offices such as sweeping part of the courts in the morning, carrying up the dishes from the kitchen to the fellows' dinner-table, and waiting in the hall till that body had dined.'⁵ In olden times there had been no anomaly in this custom. When Oxford and Cambridge were almost the sole seats of learning and education in England, and all ages and conditions resorted thither for teaching which could not elsewhere be obtained, it was reasonable to admit to the benefits of a learned foundation those who were willing, for such a recompense, to act as servitors to the brotherhood. Even at the beginning of the eighteenth century it might be said that the occasion for that class of servant scholars had not wholly passed

---

¹ Whiston's *Memoirs*, i. 69; Nelson's *Life of Bull*, pp. 16–18.
² Nichols' *Lit. An.*, iv. 258.   ³ *Tatler*, No. 47.
⁴ *Growth of Deism*, pp. 452–61; Eachard's *Grounds and Occasions*, &c., p. 20.
⁵ Prior's *Life of Goldsmith*, i. 59.

away. As in the previous generation, of which Eachard wrote, there were still, though in continually decreasing numbers, many benefices in the Church of twenty or thirty pounds a year, which could only be filled by men who were willing to join to the sacred duties of their calling the coarsest drudgery of a petty farmer. It is certain that there were some clergymen of education and character whose high qualities were superior to all the terrible disadvantages of their position, and who could labour in their villager's smock, or drive their produce to market, without disparagement to the respect and esteem in which they were held alike by their richer and by their yet poorer neighbours.[1] This, however, was by no means the case always, and the existence of poverty-stricken cures was strongly felt to be an evil which greatly needed amending.[2] Such poverty-stricken benefices were sometimes filled from quite the lower orders. Eachard tells us, in his own strain of compassionate humour, what was often the earlier history of these

[1] See, for instance, at a later date in the century, the warm panegyric of a clergyman, not indeed quite so poorly off as those referred to, but still supporting a family on an income of only 50*l.* a year. He managed the little farm, and his wife the dairy; he brewed, and she baked; but 'the best people in the county were fond of visiting them,' and he was 'almost worshipped by the parishioners, who found in him their clergyman, doctor, lawyer, friend, and cheerful companion' (*The World*, 1753, May 24, No. 21; compare the Parson Adams and the Parson Trulliber of Fielding).

[2] Though it should scarcely be relegated to a note, mention may here be made of the generous restitution to the Church by its attached friend, Queen Anne (1703), of Firstfruits and Tenths. The preamble to the Confirmation of this gift, in an Act establishing the Corporation known as the Governors of Queen Anne's Bounty, dwells upon the need referred to in the text. It states that no sufficient settled provision has yet been made for the Clergy in many parts of the realm. 'By reason whereof divers mean and stipendiary preachers are in many places entertained to serve the cures and officiate there, who, depending for necessary maintenance upon the goodwill and liking of their hearers, have been, and are, thereby under temptation of too much complying and suiting their doctrines and teaching to the humours rather than to the good of their hearers, which hath been a great occasion of faction and schism and contempt of the ministry' (Quoted in *Annals of England*, iii. 180, note).

peasant priests. The boy had been at school at 'the little house by the churchyard only intended for poor parish children,' but whose master was very ambitious to send now and then a promising pupil to Oxford or to Cambridge. So if the lad 'can sing over very tunably three or four stanzas of Lilly's poetry, be very quick and ready to tell what's Latin for all the instruments in his father's shop, if he knows a spondee from a dactyl—"A forward boy! a pregnant child! ten thousand pities but that he should prove a scholar! away to the university he must go." Then a little logic, a little ethics, and God knows a very little of everything else, and the next time you meet him is in the pulpit.' How should he learn much at the university, when he goes to it with so little preparation, and when his chief business, 'so long as his name stands airing as a servitor on the college tables, shall be to buy eggs and butter, bed-making, chamber-sweeping, and water-fetching'?[1]

The Oxford of Queen Anne's reign was much less prominent as a learned and educational body than as a High Church and semi-Jacobite one. Nor can this be said of Oxford only. Bishop Patrick spoke in the House of Lords of the 'heat and passion' in both universities, both sending out

[1] Condensed from Eachard as above. Babington has quite clearly shown that Macaulay was misled in his account of the condition of the clergy by trusting too much to Eachard and to those who borrowed from him. That author was not only speaking of exceptional cases, but was also carried away by his love of jest and humour (Mr. Macaulay's *Character of the Clergy considered*, by Churchill Babington, 1849). But it is none the less certain that up to at least the middle of the eighteenth century many of the clergy were in a condition of miserable poverty. (*Miseries and Hardships of the Inferior Clergy*, 1722; *The Clergyman's Advocate*, 1711; Swift on the 'Contempt of the Clergy,' *Works*, vol. ix., and 'Letter to a Young Clergyman,' *Works*, vol. iii., and on the 'Irish Clergy Bill,' 1731, vol. viii.; Mackay's *Journey through England*, 1724; pref. to Burnet's *Four Discourses*, 1694; *Guardian*, No. 65; *Free Thoughts on the Pretended Dignity of the Clergy*, 1700; Secker's *First Charge*, 1738; Fielding's *Joseph Andrews*, 1742, &c.)

men 'to bring fury into the parishes, to the great disturbance of public charity.' It was shameful, he said, to see in the Cambridge election of 1705 the mobs of students bellowing out, 'No fanatic, No occasional conformity.'[1] Burnet, speaking of the same year, describes the manner in which 'the universities were inflamed with tragical apprehensions of the danger the Church was in,' and of the vehemence with which they sought to spread these feelings throughout the nation.[2] Indeed, there was never any lack of enthusiasm when some question came forward which involved a condemnation of heresy or Dissent, or the support of any champion of High Church orthodoxy. To condemn Sherlock's book on the Trinity as ' impious and heretical '[3]— to refuse a degree to a suspected Arian—to return to the Earl of Nottingham 'solemn thanks for his most noble defence of Christian faith' against Whiston[4]—to hold a meeting 'for the relief of Mr. Wesley, to the great mortification of the fanatics'[5]—to thank Atterbury for his defence of Convocation, or to express indignation against Nicolson for his resistance to Atterbury[6]—to rejoice in the triumph of Sacheverell—of such kind were the occasions when Oxford most awakened to life and action. Cambridge was not very strongly Jacobite; and when George I., in the year after his accession, visited that university, there was nothing but ringing of bells, and ' King George for ever!'[7] 'What will Oxford say?' the writer naturally continues. Oxford had been in a ferment of Jacobite

---

[1] *Parliamentary History*, vi. 496.
[2] Burnet's *History of his own Times*, 778.
[3] *Apology for Parliament*, 1697, p. 74.
[4] *Life of Calamy*, ii. 528.
[5] *Reliquiæ Hearnianæ*, i. 41, Sept. 1705. The elder Wesley had been a sufferer in his parish from his hot zeal against Dissent.
[6] Nicolson's *Letters on Various Subjects*, 1704, p. 274.
[7] Wilkins to Gibson, in *id.*, p. 465.

excitement, especially in the year after Queen Anne's death. John Byrom writes to a friend, on May 3, 1715, that, owing to the disturbed feeling, the Vice-Chancellor had forbidden the coffee-houses taking in any other paper but the 'Daily Courant,' 'Evening Post,' and 'Gazette,' and that the written news-letters were all banished. The abjuration, he continued, had not yet been put to them, but everybody was talking of it. He himself could not make up his mind; sometimes he thought that it was lawful, sometimes that it was unlawful.[1] A little later in the same month the university and city were almost in a state of insurrection. 'Last night,' writes Hearne on May 29, ' a good part of the Presbyterian meeting-house was pulled down. To-day—though Sunday—there is great rejoicing and illumination. The people run up and down, crying, "King James the Third! the true king! No usurper! The Duke of Ormond!" &c., every one toasting to a new restoration. In the evening a good part of the Quaker and Anabaptists' houses were pulled down.'[2] Angry letters ensued from Townshend to Dr. Charlett, Pro-Vice-Chancellor, and on June 10 Hearne writes that rejoicings on this 'his Majesty's birthday' were carefully stopped by the Pro-Vice-Chancellor and the proctors. Ormond, the Chancellor of Oxford, had been attainted; but the university, making no secret of their sympathy, had elected his brother in his stead, and conferred their honorary degrees only on Nonjurors or high Tories. The Government took at first no very serious notice of the agitation at Oxford, and an undergraduate wrote to his friend in London, 'Here we fear nothing, but drink James's health every day.' But in the autumn, news having arrived that Jacobite officers were being sheltered there, and that several heads of Houses and

---

[1] *Remains of John Byrom*, i. 31.   [2] *Reliquiæ Hearnianæ*, ii. 40.

other leading members of the university were plotting treason in concert with the disaffected at Bristol, a troop of dragoons was sent to maintain order.[1] As it was just at this time that the King bought and presented to the University of Cambridge Bishop Moore's library, the coincidence gave rise to two epigrams. The first was—

> The King to Oxford sent a troop of horse,
> For there they own no argument but force;
> To Cambridge, books the generous monarch sent,
> For there they own no force but argument.

The retort was—

> The King, observing with judicious eyes
> The state of both his universities,
> To one he sent a regiment—for why?
> That learned body wanted loyalty:
> To the other he sent books, as well discerning
> How much that loyal body wanted learning.[2]

After speaking of the vehemence of Church and Tory feeling at Oxford, it is just to add that Calamy has spoken warmly of the courtesy with which he, though a Presbyterian, was received during his year's stay there in 1692. He found the Dissenters commonly ill spoken of, and 'was often argued with about consorting with such an unsociable sort of people,' but was himself 'treated with all imaginable civility,' and every facility was given him for attending public lectures and academical exercises.[3] It is noticeable, also, that the same strict conservative spirit which made the universities a stronghold of Jacobitism and the staunchest High-Churchmanship, still—at all events in theory—maintained a position which, in the Middle Ages, had been of great service to the cause of liberty of thought—that in

---

[1] Mahon's *History*, chap. v.   [2] Note to *Life of Calamy*, ii. 306.
[3] Calamy, i. 224.

a seat of learning all intellectual argument was entitled to a hearing. The disputations, which had once done so much for sifting truth, still kept up a rather shadowy existence. 'Those,' writes Addison, 'who have been present at public disputes in the universities know that it is usual to maintain heresies for argument's sake. I have heard a man, a most impudent Socinian for half an hour, who has been a most orthodox divine all his life after.'[1]

Swift, in one of his latest letters, speaks of a great improvement in the education of ladies.[2] He had spoken of it earlier as 'shamefully' bad.[3] Lady Mary Wortley received in Queen Anne's time a learned education; but she speaks also of the very careless teaching which was all that most women of her station could obtain, and of the false notions and absurd superstitions with which her governess had filled her head.[4] In 1713 we find a paper in the 'Guardian' by Addison, in which he wonders that learning should be thought no proper ingredient in the education of a woman of quality or fortune. He was concerned, he said, when he went into a great house, 'where, perhaps, there is not a single person that can spell, unless it be by chance the butler, or one of the footmen.' If women were married to men of education, their husbands were generally but strangers to them. Why should not domestic employments be varied by other diversions, and more intelligent interests than cards, gossip, and ogling?[5]

The educational work undertaken at the opening of the eighteenth century by the newly started Society for the Promotion of Christian Knowledge has led on to more general remarks on the state at that time of schools and

[1] *Spectator*, No. 556, June 18, 1714.
[2] Swift, quoted by Lecky, *England in Eighteenth Century*, i. 519.
[3] Swift's *Works*, ix. 269.
[4] Oliphant's *Hist. Sketches in Reign of George II.*, i. 211.
[5] *Guardian*, No. 155.

colleges. We now return to another vast field of Christian enterprise to which the Church of England was beginning to awaken.

When Dryden, full of his new zeal for Popery, published in 1687 'The Hind and the Panther,' he taunted the English Church with an inert self-content which had no care of extending itself beyond the single limits of the British Islands. 'In her own labyrinth she lives confined,' and 'to foreign lands no sound of her has come.' In one respect there was no longer any force in this reproach. Ever since the Revolution, the Church of England had held a high position abroad. Protestants in every part of Europe looked to it with honour and respect, not unmixed with envy, as to the champion of their common cause. To the Roman Catholic powers, on the other hand, it was a source of no little anxiety; and, although there was never a likelihood of its being actually transplanted to any part of the Continent, there seemed at one time much probability of its having a great influence upon the constitution of other churches. In Prussia, especially, there was a strong inclination among many leading Lutherans to approximate more closely to it; and in France, if the Gallican movement had continued unchecked, there would probably have been a sympathy with the tone of Reformation in England somewhat corresponding to that which is felt in our own day by the 'Old Catholics.'

But until very near the close of the seventeenth century real missionary effort had for some time seemed almost dead in England. The colonies were increasing in population and importance, but among those who were interested in them there was now none of that warm ardour of Christian enterprise which inspirited some of the early founders.[1] When Newfoundland was first colonised in 1578,

[1] Anderson's *English Church in the Colonies*, i.

one of the captains of the expedition spoke of the glorious opportunity, which these new discoveries had given, to sow the seed of eternal life in those lands of heathenism. 'The carriage of God's Word into those very mighty and vast countrys' was a matter of so excellent a nature as should make men well advised how they handled it; and motive should 'be derived from a vertuous and heroicall minde, preferring chiefly the honour of God, compassion of poore infidels, captived by the devill, and the advancement of their honest and well-disposed countreymen.' Heriot wrote with the same consciousness of Christian obligation when Virginia was founded in 1587; and when Raleigh, two years after, gave his patent to Sir T. Smith and others, he made a donation of 100*l*. 'for the propagation of the Christian religion in Virginia.' The Virginian charter of 1606 dwelt emphatically upon the Christian duties of the colonists. 'Remember,' said Crashaw, in his sermon at the Temple, 'thou art a general of Christian men, therefore principally look to religion.' When Lord de la Warr, Captain-General, came in 1610, his first act on landing was to fall upon his knees, and before all the people to make a long and silent prayer. In 1619 alms were collected throughout the country by royal letters for the erecting of churches and schools in the plantations, and for the education of the children of the barbarians. Dr. King, the Bishop of London, by himself collected a thousand pounds for the teaching of Indian children. Drake, Bishop of Bath and Wells, spoke very strongly in 1616 of the guilt that rested on Christian states if they were not very careful to bring the heathen into participation of the Gospel, and declared that, were it not for his age, he would himself go and carry that knowledge to the Indians of America. Ferrar, a principal member of the Virginian Council, took orders in 1626, and was greatly inclined to devote the rest of his life to the conversion of the natives. Into his hands were put the last of George Herbert's manuscripts, in which occur the words—

Religion stands tiptoe in our land,
Ready to pass to the American strand.[1]

Doubtless many of the early colonists were mere self-seeking adventurers, but there were not a few whose feelings accorded with the spirit of the prayer made for morning and evening in Virginia when that colony was entrusted to Dale in 1614 : 'Seeing thou hast honoured us to choose us out to bear Thy name unto the Gentiles, we therefore beseech Thee to bless us and this our plantation, which we and our nation have begun in Thy fear and to Thy glory.'[2] It was to this colony, then chiefly directed by the genial and tolerant spirit of the Ferrars, that the Pilgrim Fathers, under their good pastor Robinson, would have steered the *Mayflower*, had not Providence marked them out for other designs. These first New England settlers had been Nonconformists from the Church of England from the time that their leader had given up his benefice near Yarmouth. But this was not the case with the Massachusetts colony in 1625. There was no less warmth of religious zeal in these men, nor were their opinions widely different, only they had not, when they left the English shores, seceded from the National Church, and they believed themselves to be more faithful members of it than those who molested them for their Puritan sentiments. Their parting address ' to the rest of their brethren

---

[1] Anderson, i. 365. The passage continues,—

' When Seine shall swallow Tiber, and the Thames
By letting in both pollute her streams,
Then shall religion to America flee :
They have their times of gospel, even as we.'

It is quoted and commented on by Tillotson in one of his sermons *Works*, x. 41.

[2] Anderson, *Append.*, i. 474.

in and of the Church of England' breathes a spirit of attachment to it which, under wiser treatment, might easily have been made lasting. 'We esteem it,' they said, 'our honour to call the Church of England, from whence we arise, our dear mother, and cannot part from our native country, where she specially resideth, without much sadness of heart and many tears in our eyes; ever acknowledging that such hope and part as we have obtained in the common salvation we have received in her bosom, and sucked it from her breast. We leave it not, therefore, as loathing that milk wherewith we were nourished; but, blessing God for the parentage and education, as members of the same body, shall always rejoice in her good, and unfeignedly grieve for any sorrow that shall ever betide her; and while we have breath, sincerely desire and endeavour the continuance and abundance of her welfare, with the enlargement of her bounds in the kingdom of Christ Jesus.' [1]

However genuine such expressions of affection may have been at first, the connection of the English Church with the New England colonies was practically broken off from their very commencement.[2] Uniformity was the law of the time, alike among Churchmen and Puritans. At home, and, to the best of his power, in America also, Laud was bent on exacting a strict and literal adherence to every tenet, canon, and rubric; the young colonies of New England, on their side, made use of their new-born freedom to insist upon a no less rigorous conformity to their own favourite usages. It is very doubtful whether the wisest judgment could at this time have framed any concordat by which

[1] Dr. Wilson's *Pilgrim Fathers*, chap. xv.
[2] 'It is remarkable that, with the exception of the Plymouth settlers, all the first New England colonists, up to their leaving England, were members of the Established Church there. . . . But on arriving in America they immediately proceeded to the founding of an ecclesiastical economy upon the Independent plan' (Baird's *Religion in America*, p. 183).

High Churchmen and Puritans could have worshipped within the bounds of the same Church; still more hopeless was it where neither party entertained the very thought of toleration.

The device on the seal of the Massachusetts Company had been an Indian, with the label 'Come over and help us.' There were some among the Puritan settlers, both in the Massachusetts and in the Plymouth colony, who nobly responded to such a call. The name of Elliot, 'the Apostle of the Indians,' will never be forgotten. His labours among them began about 1646, and by 1674 there were no less than fourteen towns of 'praying Indians,'[1] all under his supervision, within the bounds of the Massachusetts jurisdiction. Mayhews and Bourne were other successful workers in the same field. The New England Society for the Propagation of the Gospel was founded by an ordinance of the Long Parliament in 1669. General contributions were made in its behalf through England and Wales. The universities issued public letters, and an appeal for its support was also circulated through the army.[2] After the Restoration its powers were renewed under a new charter, obtained chiefly through the efforts of Robert Boyle, who was himself an earnest Churchman.[3]

But by this time the English Church was practically extinct in New England. The political franchise was confined to members of the tolerated churches, and for many years no Anglican clergyman was ever allowed to land. It was only after 1686 that, by what was considered a despotic interference on the part of the Governor at Boston, the rule was in that single instance broken through.

Even in Virginia, where the English Church had been fenced round with enactments no less rigid in its favour

---

[1] Anderson, i. 390; T. Smith's *Progress of Missionary Societies*, intr., xii.
[2] Anderson, i. 391.   [3] Anderson, i. 680-82.

than those which had been made against it in New England, its condition had become, long before the end of the seventeenth century, very unsatisfactory. The intolerance of the laws in that settlement had been greatly abated by the tolerant spirit in which they were for the most part administered. Puritans, therefore, and other Nonconformists, to whom the colony might have seemed absolutely closed, frequently found there a comfortable home. The Church, however, was not strong, even among those who guarded it most jealously. It had been made irksome to many by stringent laws, which made attendance at its services compulsory under heavy penalties[1]—regulations which were the more distasteful because there were a great number in the colony who had scarce other thought than to seek abroad an opening which careless or dissolute ways had closed to them at home. The clergy were few and scattered, for though the province had been carefully mapped out into parishes, and provision made for endowment, little care had been taken to provide men for the newly founded benefices. Of those who did come, many were such as would by no means advance the best interests of a church. There were a few excellent clergymen in Virginia, but many of a very inferior kind.

In the utter absence of any system of direction and organisation, a clerk whose character or incapacity precluded him from employment at home might generally find an opening in the plantations. A bishop was greatly needed, but none was sent. Laud had at one time wished to maintain, by force if necessary, a bishop in New England. He would have done better to direct his care to the southern colony.[2] In Clarendon's administration Alexander Murray was actually nominated as Bishop of Virginia. But difficulties,

[1] Keith, quoted by Anderson, i. 661.   [2] Anderson, ii. 23.

especially one which arose out of a plan for providing for the endowment out of the customs, had put an end to the design.[1]

One among many evil effects of the absence of a bishop was the contention which arose in almost all the parishes as to the government of the Church. The practical direction of ecclesiastical affairs was for the most part vested nominally in the Governor; but the townships, bent upon keeping the control entirely in their own hands, would allow of no regularly inducted ministers, but appointed them only from year to year. Holding, therefore, their livings on a most precarious footing, and entirely at the mercy of ignorant vestries, the clergy often found their position intolerable, and few remained who could look for a more independent standing elsewhere.[2]

In general it may be said that towards the end of the seventeenth century the Church of England was most inadequately and miserably represented in most of the foreign plantations. The English traders in Aleppo, and some other places in the Levant, had proved themselves worthy Churchmen, and had provided themselves with an unbroken succession of active and learned clergymen. But in America, the West Indies, and India, there had been for the most part a neglect and indifference which strangely contrasted with the zeal of some of the earliest settlers. For the space of nearly twenty years from the date of the first Carolina Charter (1662-63), not a clergyman of the English Church was sent to that province;[3] and in Newfoundland, although there were already several thousand settlers, there was no public exercise of religion except at St. John's, where there was a clergyman, but no regular provision for his subsistence.[4] Too often the Church history of a colony had been an unhappy record of high purposes miserably

---

[1] Anderson, ii. 569. [2] Anderson, ii. 543, 591, 605.
[3] Anderson, ii. 529. [4] Anderson, i. 616.

disappointed, of neglect of those within, and oppression to those without—carelessness and intolerance combined,—of a few earnest men struggling almost helplessly against difficulties such as could hardly fail to depress their spirits and dull their energy. As for the coloured races, there was throughout the Western continent very little left of the old earnest wish to convert them to Christianity. At the Savoy Conference, in 1661, the office for adult baptism had been added to the liturgy, mainly with a view to the baptism of natives in the plantations, and at the same time that prayer for all conditions of men which asks that God's saving health may be made known unto all nations. But the colonists were now occupied with designs which led them a very different way. Greed of land was involving them in wars with their Indian neighbours, and the negro slave trade was being pushed with intense eagerness. In Charles the Second's time it was said in favour of the planters that they had at their cost brought above 100,000 negroes from Africa.[1] The degrading effect of this trade was strongly marked both in America and the Indies. There was no wish to improve the condition of these poor aliens, whose only function was to be profitable instruments of labour. In the Romish organisation, the Church had sufficient power to insist, to some extent, upon the baptism and instruction of the blacks; but elsewhere the planters in most cases systematically and successfully opposed all such attempts. Godwyn, a clergyman in Barbadoes, met with very rough treatment in his advocacy of the negro cause.[2]

When Compton became Bishop of London in 1675, he found, it is said, that there were scarce four ministers of the Church of England in the whole continent of America.[3] His

---

[1] Anderson, ii. 473.   [2] Anderson, ii. 497.
[3] *An Account of the S.P.G. Society.* By order, 1706, p. 12. The authority is good, or I should have suspected exaggeration.

appointment to that see may be held to mark the rise of a quickened sense of religious responsibility in regard of the colonies. Ecclesiastical jurisdiction abroad was, at his instance, given to him and his successors, and he at once sent out a commissary to furnish him with as full reports as possible of the condition of the English Church in the American colonies. James Blair, formerly of the Scotch Episcopal Church, was the first of these commissaries. Although rather too apt to mix in political contentions, he did good service. Through his exertion an educational institution was founded in Virginia, and provided with a charter and privileges. It was named William and Mary College, and might have been of great service in supplying candidates for the ministry, but was unfortunately burnt down very soon after its erection.[1] Meanwhile, at Oxford, Sir Leolyne Jenkins founded in 1685 two fellowships at Jesus College, the holders of which were to go as clergymen to sea or the plantations.[2] Robert Boyle died in 1691. In the absence as yet of any active missionary agency in his own Church, he left money to the New England Society for the propagation of the gospel, and for the relief of poor Indian converts. He also left directions that his Boyle preachers should assist in the cause.[3] As an early member of the East Indian Committee he had been very urgent to stimulate the company ' to promote the honour and worship of God by the conversion of the poor infidels in those places where, by His blessing, they had so much advanced their worldly interests.'[4] After Boyle's death, Prideaux, then tutor of Christ Church, his friend and coadjutor, continued to press the appeal for churches, schools, and training colleges in India, and especially for good men. In a letter to Archbishop Tenison in 1695 he spoke of the millions of souls there ' to

---

[1] *Account*, &c., 27. [2] *Id.*, 7; and Anderson, ii. 497.
[3] *Account*, &c., 9. [4] Anderson, iii. 702.

whom no care has yet been extended, to the reproach of the Church and nation, not savage and wild as in the Western plantations, but civilised, polite, ingenious, and docile.'[1] The Dutch, he added, supported thirty or forty missionaries, and had converted many hundred thousands.[2] In Ceylon alone they had a college with 80,000 Christianised Indians.[3] For some thirty years Prideaux continued the warm advocate of Christian effort in India, and it is to be noticed that he specially insisted on the absolute necessity of bishops and seminaries in India itself.[4]

In 1695, Bishop Compton sent as his commissary to America Thomas Bray, of whose benevolent activity at home and abroad mention has been already made. It has been told how the important movement which gave rise to the Christian Knowledge Society originated in Bray's early American experiences. The libraries and societies which he formed in Virginia for the benefit of the missionaries were the germ of a work which was soon to be widely developed, and with great results. He returned to England the next year, and with unwearying energy, by his writings, by personal solicitations, by appeals to the citizens of London, by conference with the bishops, by petitions to Parliament, and by engaging the warm interest of Queen Mary and the Princess of Denmark, he promoted with much success the cause he had at heart. An attempt however, to obtain a Parliament grant eventually failed, though it had been recommended by a committee of the House. After seeing the Christian Knowledge Society fairly launched by his own and others' exertion in 1698–9, he went

---

[1] Prideaux's *Life and Letters*, 151.
[2] In the seventeenth century, at a time when missionary zeal was generally very slack in other Protestant countries, the Dutch Church was very active in sending the gospel, not only to their own settlements, but to the East generally (Braunius, *La véritable Religion des Hollandois*, 1675, quoted in Fabricius, *Salutaris Lux Evangelii*, 1731, p. 587).
[3] Prideaux, *Life*, &c., 160. [4] *Id.*, 168, 186.

again to America. His special object on this occasion was the establishment of the English Church in Maryland, a design which, after much opposition, was carried out with more zeal than wisdom or liberality. Neither religion generally nor the interests of the English Church gained by a law which required that the Book of Common Prayer should be used in every place of public worship within the province.[1]

Coming back to England, Bray published, early in 1701, an interesting 'Memorial on the State of Religion in America,' addressed to the Archbishop of Canterbury. Virginia was under the ecclesiastical superintendence of Commissary Blair, who was well supported by the Governor, a great patron of religion and learning. A college was being founded there. In North Carolina there were two settlements, a hundred miles apart; each wanted a missionary. In South Carolina the Church was thriving, but at least three more clergy were needed. In Maryland the endowment was as yet very insufficient, but the people had built themselves churches. The Pennsylvanians had one Church of England minister, well esteemed, and they wished for more. The Jerseys had as yet none, but he thought there would be reception for six. New York had one; there was room for at least two more. In Indiana the French were making great progress, and some English missionaries were much required. In Long Island there were nine churches, but no minister. In Rhode Island the Quaker neglect for outward teaching had caused great irreligion. There was a church there, and room for at least two ministers. Bermuda was in great poverty. It had one clergyman, who barely subsisted, but ought to have three at least. New England was under Independents. 'My design is not to intermeddle where Christianity under

[1] Anderson, ii. 633.

any form has obtained possession, but to represent rather the deplorable state of the English colonies where they have been in a manner abandoned to atheism.'[1] Of Newfoundland he said, 'A colony very profitable to England, and where there are many thousand souls. Can any one believe that there neither was, nor is, any preaching, prayer, or sacrament, or any ministerial and divine offices?'[2] He concluded by urging the necessity of sending out to America at least forty missionaries, good, experienced, active, and well-informed men. In three or four years the people would subscribe for their own spiritual needs, as they had done in Pennsylvania and Carolina. For his own part, he had already expended at his own charge above a thousand pounds, the greater part of his little fortune; nor would his efforts be wanting for the future, and he would gladly accompany the missionaries who should be sent.

The immediate result of Dr. Bray's report was the formation of a new society; for it was already obvious that the one recently constituted for the Promotion of Christian Knowledge was too overburdened with business to be able to undertake the further responsibility of providing clergy for the service of the English Church abroad. Bray, Tenison, and Compton procured the charter which incorporated the Society for the Propagation of the Gospel in Foreign Parts. It was dated June 16, 1701. Its preamble set forth how 'in many of our plantations, colonies, and factories beyond the sea the provision for ministers is very mean, . . . whence many of our loving subjects do want the administration of God's Word and sacraments, and seem to be abandoned to atheism and infidelity, and divers Romish priests and Jesuits pervert them to Popish superstition and idolatry; . . . and whereas we think it our duty, as much as in us lies, to promote the glory of

---

[1] Bray's *Memorial*, &c., p. 9.   [2] *Id.*, 10.

God by the instruction of our people in the Christian religion,' it was desirable therefore to form a Corporation to carry out this end, and to encourage charity.[1] The archbishop and 93 others by name were incorporated into the society. Most of the bishops gave their willing support, but Patrick's special zeal seems to have been the cause of the Bishops of Ely being constituted members by charter.[2] Generally speaking, its supporters were nearly the same as those who had set on foot the elder society. Among its lay members were R. Nelson, and Melmoth, Philipps and Mackworth, Lord Colchester and Lord Guildford. Evelyn took much interest in its colonial work, and subscribed 10*l.* a year to its funds. Another lay member was Sir John Chardin, who not only gave the society 1,000*l.*, but did much during his extensive travels to promote its interests. General Codrington, eminent alike as a soldier and a scholar, left, in **1710**, his Barbadoes estates to the society, who built in that island the college which bears his name.[3] A Dutch gentleman bequeathed Dr. Bray 900*l.* for the teaching of negroes. The queen, in **1711**, authorised a collection for the society, from house to house, throughout the diocese of London.[4] Archbishop Tenison, at his death in **1715**, left the society 1,000*l.* to promote the appointment of two bishops, one for the continent of Europe, the other for America.[5] Bishop Kennet made it a valuable gift of every book and map which he could get relating to the colonies;[6] he also published a narrative of its proceedings. Nor was assistance wanting in America itself. In the State of Vermont reservations of land were made by the Governor in favour of the society.[7] In the south, some of the

---

[1] *A Collection of Papers printed by Order of the S.P.G.*, 1702, p. 15.
[2] Anderson, iii. 128.   [3] Anderson, ii. 694.
[4] Malcolm's *Manners and Customs of London*, i. 19.
[5] Calamy's *Life and Times*, ii. 335.
[6] Anderson, iii. 149.   [7] Caswall's *American Church*, 130.

planters warmly seconded its efforts, and began to bestir themselves in building churches, and otherwise repairing the evil effects of long neglect. The extended character of this neglect became more apparent with every year of effort. Brokesby, in a letter to R. Nelson in 1708, cites from the reports which were received as to the great declension of religion, except perhaps in New England,[1] the small provision made for religious teaching, the vast parishes, funds long wasted or embezzled, ministers hired by the year, and held perfectly in subjection, negroes openly treated like brute beasts, efforts to promote Christianity treated of as ridiculous. Like other Churchmen interested in the work, he too was urgent on the need of sending bishops, not only to confirm and ordain, but to keep order, control, and administer. One only might suffice at present, but he hoped that one day Canterbury might be a patriarchate over many sees.[2] The society did not neglect this need. A committee was formed to submit the case to the Attorney-General, and the report of 1706 expressed a hope of speedy success.[3] In fact, preparations were already made for endowing, from lands ceded to the English by the treaty of Utrecht, four bishoprics in America.[4] But just before the intention was carried out Queen Anne died, and the scheme was allowed to drop. New England was vehemently opposed to the introduction of bishops into America. The Puritan and Congregational element there was so entirely predominant, and the memory so alive of former persecutions, and of the dread excited by Laud's ill-judged proposals, that the idea and very name of prelacy

[1] Which also shared to some extent in the religious apathy which had begun to gain ground (Baird's *Religion in America*, 214-30).
[2] F. Brokesby's Letter to Nelson, *Proposals towards promoting the Gospel in our Plantations*, 1708, pp. 14-21. [3] *Account*, &c., 1706, p. 82.
[4] Caswall's *America and Am. Church*, 131; Beardsley's *Life, &c., of S. Johnson of Connecticut*, 15.

was scarcely less odious [1] than it had been to Scotch Covenanters. There was also a growing democratic feeling against the title and dignity of bishops, and a notion that their presence would be unfavourable to the liberty of the people. Even as early as the first year of the eighteenth century it was several times declared that the independence desired by the colonies was notorious.[2] New England opinion ought not to have interfered with a measure which was essential to the welfare of the Church in the southern States. Nor would it have done, had the Church movement which marked the earlier years of the century continued. After that time the interests of the Colonial Church were hindered quite as much from the indifference as from the timidity of English ministries.

In the charter of the Society for the Propagation of the Gospel nothing had been said about missionary labours among the heathen. What was urgently needed in the colonies and foreign factories seemed in itself more than enough to overtax the power of the new society. Perhaps, also, the hope of evangelising the heathen world seemed to the relaxed energies of the Church a too overwhelming conception for immediate practical exertions. The taunt constantly levelled by Roman Catholics against Protestant remissness in this respect[3] had commonly met with the answer that such labours could do no great good, there being so little prospect of success to men not endowed with supernatural gifts.[4] But when a missionary spirit was once fairly aroused, it was not likely to be satisfied with any lesser

---

[1] Baird's *Religion in America*, p. 183.

[2] Caswall's *American Church and Union*, p. 73.

[3] 'Criminatio est non infrequens in Rom. Eccles. hominum scriptis, curam propagandi evangelii parum cordi esse nostratibus, Protestantiumque principes ac respublicas nihil minus curare quam ut operâ, copiis et laboribus ipsorum Religionis Christianae lux ad nationes a Christi nomine alienas proferatur' (Fabricius, *Salut. Lux Evang.*, 586).

[4] *Id.* Even in 1775 Bishop Barrington speaks of this as a common objection.

hope. The very first report of the society bore on its front 'Go, teach all nations,' and strongly urged the duty which lay upon the Church of bearing the Gospel to those who were wholly ignorant of it. In the first year after its incorporation missions were sent to the American Indians, a good example which the New England Congregationalists at once confessed, and began quickly to follow.[1] There were great difficulties in these attempts. 'The Indians cannot believe,' one of the missionaries reported, 'that we wish them a place in heaven when we deny them a place in earth.'[2] In India the work began by association with the Danish missionaries on the Coromandel Coast, and was set on foot, not so much by the Society for the Propagation of the Gospel, as by that for the Promotion of Christian Knowledge. The Danish mission had been sent to Tranquebar in 1705 by King Frederic of Denmark, and was under the direction of Ziegenbalg, an earnest and efficient missionary. Their report, two or three years later, was translated into English by the chaplain to Prince George of Denmark, and attracted a good deal of attention. We are told how John Wesley's mother found the account in her husband's study, and was deeply touched by the story of their zeal.[3] Subscriptions were collected, a printing-press sent, with a version of the Portuguese Testament; sympathising letters were written, help given from Madras; and intelligence being received that they would gladly welcome English missionaries, preparations were made to carry out their wish. It was the beginning of much successful work, which, after Ziegenbalg's death, was worthily carried on by Schulz, and afterwards, for nearly fifty years, with still greater results, by Schwartz.[4]

---

[1] *Account, &c., of the S.P.G.*, 1706, p. 57.
[2] *Account, &c., of the S.P.G.*, 1706, p. 53. [3] Anderson, iii. 89.
[4] *Account of the Success of the Danish Missionaries*, dedicated to the S.P.G., about 1719; also Anderson, iii. 89–111, and Smith's *History of the Missionary Societies*, intr. xii.

It seems curious to note that the Society for the Propagation of the Gospel was, from its very early years, a considerable proprietor of slaves. But as yet no scruple of conscience on the score of slaveholding was felt, even by the most benevolent of mankind. Penn had always been a slaveholder. Lord Cowper, kindly and liberal in other respects, was as indifferent to the natural rights of negroes as he was to those of Roman Catholics.[1] Locke's proposed constitution for Carolina contained an article that 'every freeman shall have absolute power and authority over his negro slaves.' The society, therefore, acted up to the very highest level of its age in confining its efforts simply to the instruction of the negro, and the amelioration of his general condition. 'We are now,' said Bishop Fleetwood, in a sermon before the society, 'by the munificence of a truly honourable gentleman (General Codrington), ourselves become the patrons of at least 300 slaves, who are to cultivate and be maintained upon the two plantations he hath left to the society for the promoting of learning and religion. . . . The servants of this society shall be assuredly the Lord's freemen, whatever else their condition shall be in this world; and yet I hope even that will be changed a great deal for the better.[2] The papers published by the society in its first year contained full directions for the instruction of the negroes on their plantations at Barbadoes;[3] and both in the West Indies and on the mainland their chaplains and missionaries did excellent work, both in direct labours among the blacks, and by infusing among the planters a higher sense of the responsibilities which attached to masters. But as a

---

[1] Campbell's *Lives of the Chancellors,* iv. p. 339.

[2] Sermon before the S.P.G., 1711; Fleetwood's *Works,* p. 504. The euphemisms 'patrons' and 'servants,' and 'whatever else their condition shall be,' are remarkable testimonies to an almost unconscious repugnance to the idea of slavery.

[3] *Collection of Papers,* &c., 1702. pp. 29–31.

necessary condition of success in these efforts, they made it a special aim to remove a prevalent and noteworthy impression that the baptism of a negro impaired his owner's proprietary rights.[1]

There is some variation of account as to the general character of the early missionaries of the society. Kennet spoke of them in a somewhat disparaging tone, asserting that some of the clergy took to colonial work as a refuge from poverty or scandal, and that others contended unduly for rites and ceremonies, power and privileges.[2] The latter allegation, as coming from the mouth of a very Low Churchman, must be accepted accordingly. In the last part of what he says he may have been correct enough, for some of the most efficient agents of the society were among the highest of the High Churchmen of Queen Anne's reign. Such was Talbot, afterwards a confessed Jacobite and Nonjuror;[3] and such was Hewitson, the commissary who succeeded Bray, a rigid High Churchman of deep and ascetic piety, a loved and intimate friend of Bishop Wilson.[4] The former and more important imputation seems also to have been correct in regard of some few missionaries in the southern States. Careful as the society was in its requirements from those who entered into its service, it was sometimes imposed upon; and when such a man was once away from England, in a vast province, destitute alike of superintendence and organisation, it was easy for him to fall in, without much fear of rebuke, with the lax manners that surrounded him. But the missionaries in general obtained a very good report. Lord Cornbury wrote of 'their great zeal, exemplary piety, and unwearied diligence;' and Colonel Heathcote, in 1705, said that 'all agree as to their good character.'[5]

[1] *An Account of the S.P.G.*, 1760, 59.
[2] Anderson, iii. 149; Kennet's *Life*, 123.   [3] Anderson, ii. 722.
[4] Cruttwell's *Life of Wilson*, 13.   [5] *Account*, &c., p. 23.

CHAPTER II.

ENGLISH BISHOPS. 1700–1714.

At the beginning of the eighteenth century the English episcopate stood high in public reputation. This was partly owing to causes independent of the personal character of the bishops. In Queen Anne's reign the National Church was undoubtedly very popular; nor was its general popularity at all diminished by the heat and vigour with which ecclesiastical as well as political partisanship was at this time manifested. High was divided against Low, and Low against High, angrily and noisily, in every grade of society. But High and Low, Whig and Tory, all professed to honour and uphold the Church; and when the faction cry of 'Church in danger' was raised, the one party was not more keen in its defence than the other in urging that it was too secure in the love of the people to be in any peril, and that they themselves were truer friends of the ecclesiastical establishment than those who claimed to be its peculiar supporters. The Puritan movement had in England utterly worn itself out; and there was but a very insignificant minority that desired either to overthrow the Anglican Church, or to revert to any form of government for it than that of bishops. Fear of Rome was still in the ascendency—not without reason, for the conflict which had brought about the Revolution was still very recent; and if the danger had been exaggerated, it had still been serious.

All acknowledged that the Church of England headed the Protestant interest, and that its strength and prosperity were essential to the safety of the cause. Its writers had conducted the late controversy with ability and success, while the firmness of the seven bishops had created an enthusiasm in the nation, and brought the struggle to a crisis. Nonconformity had decreased alike in power and in hostility to a quite extraordinary degree. As for the Presbyterians, who were at this time the most numerous and influential section of the Dissenting body, they might almost be considered as half Churchmen. Plans for comprehension had failed; but their leaders lived on the most friendly terms with deans and bishops, and as a body they might generally be reckoned among the defenders of the Church rather than among its assailants.

Because the Church, as an institution, was at this time highly popular, it does not follow that the clergy as a body stood correspondingly high in popular estimation. This opens a question upon which opinions may very easily differ. It is equally easy to quote from the pamphlets and general literature of the day passages in which they are spoken of in a tone of considerable sarcasm and contempt, and others which seem to imply that they were held in no little respect and esteem. The general truth is that a large proportion of them were drawn from a lower stratum of society than is now the case, and that they were, in many cases, comparatively illiterate in mind and uncultivated in tastes. Their poverty often reduced them to eke out their income by occupations somewhat derogatory to the dignity of their office. Add that they were constantly bigoted and illiberal, and it will be readily understood that they were a ready butt for the raillery of fine gentlemen and freethinkers about town. On the other hand, their general morality was high and their religion genuine. The country people liked them all the better for the familiar manner in which they mingled with their social life; and in education and refinement they were at all events more than equal to most of the country squires. In the towns there were a number of clergy who commanded a very high position, not only for their piety, activity, and their eloquence, but also for learning and practical ability; the cathedral foundations supported many men of culture and marked attainments; and even in the country there was always a fair sprinkling of parish priests who would have done honour to any church or period.

It is, however, certain that there was at that time a far wider gap than there has been in later times between the episcopate and the general body of the clergy. There can be but one opinion as to the high estimation in which, throughout the early years of the last century, the bishops were held. No doubt several of the most popular prelates on the bench were very bad Churchmen in the eyes of a majority of the clergy. But the High Church element was still represented by two or three very distinguished men; and, in speaking of the position which the episcopate held in general esteem, we must not forget that it owed a part of its lustre to Ken, and other Nonjuring bishops who were yet living, in seclusion indeed, but not forgotten. A brief record of the more prominent occupants of the different sees in the first and second decades of the century will show very clearly that the high places of the English Church were filled in a more than usual proportion by men of very high repute. The list of bishops in Queen Anne's reign is a distinctly stronger one than it was, as a whole, through many subsequent years.

Tenison was primate for the first fifteen years of the century (1694–1715).[1] He had been one of that distinguished

[1] And Lincoln, 1691–94.

company of contemporary London[1] preachers of whom Macaulay remarks that ten of the twelve became bishops, and four of them archbishops. His excellences, it must be allowed, were not of the brilliant kind.[2] James the Second had dubbed him 'that dull man,'[3] and the epithet was not by any means forgotten.[4] His admirers praised his 'steadiness,' which perhaps meant much the same thing. He had succeeded Tillotson, and the extraordinary and what seemed the ever-growing reputation of his predecessor rather eclipsed his humbler virtues. But he was a man of great worth; and when in 1697 he was advanced from Lincoln to Canterbury, Garth, in the rather affected style of the age, told with delight how 'good Tenison's celestial piety at last had raised him to the sacred see.'[5] For the rest, it may be added that he had taken an active part in the controversy with Rome; that shortly before his consecration he joined the seven bishops when they drew up at Lambeth the declaration which led to their imprisonment; that he was a leading member of the commission for revising the Prayer-book;[6] that he had acted as first of the Lords Justiciary during the king's absence in 1695; that Whiston said of his collect after the great storm of 1703, that it expressed the deepest and most touching sense of the divine attributes of any composition he had ever seen;[7] that, to use Calamy's words, he was 'even more honoured and respected by the Dissenters than by many of the Established Church;'[8] and,

---

[1] Both at Cambridge in the time of the plague, and at St. Martin-in-the-Fields, he had been a devoted parish priest.

[2] Mackay described him as 'a plain, good, heavy man, tall, with fair complexion' (Noble's *Cont. of Grainger*, i. 27).

[3] *Life of Ken*, by a Layman, ii. 655.

[4] 'A very dull man,' said Swift, 'who had a horror of anything like levity in the clergy, especially of whist' (*Works*, x. 231).

[5] Garth's *Poems*, British Poets, vii. 92.

[6] Birch's *Tillotson*, 125.   [7] Whiston's *Memoirs*, i. 132.

[8] Calamy's *Life*, ii. 334.

lastly, that he was very anxious that a bishop should be appointed for America, and another for Englishmen on the Continent, and that he left to the Society for the Propagation of the Gospel one thousand pounds to be applied for these purposes.[1]

William Wake succeeded Tenison. He had been Bishop of Lincoln from 1705, and held the primacy from 1715 to 1737. In Charles the Second's[2] reign he was already a well-known preacher at Gray's Inn. In James the Second's time he had distinguished himself by the skill with which he had conducted the argument with Bossuet.[3] In the first four years of the eighteenth century, when much vehement discussion had arisen as to the rights and powers of Convocation, he had proved himself more than a match for the wit and eloquence of Atterbury. His work on the Authority of Christian Princes had shown a complete mastery of the question, and gained for him great applause among all who dreaded—not without excellent cause—a Convocation of the clergy possessed of the large and almost independent powers which its advocates were claiming.

Wake's wide sympathies, and his elevated sense of the duties and capacities of a National Church, make his archiepiscopate an interesting one. His own views were those of a moderate High Churchman, heartily attached to the tenets and constitution of his Church, and greatly valuing all such bonds of affinity as connect it with that early post-

---

[1] Calamy's *Life*, ii. 334; and Anderson's *Church in the Colonies*, ii. 630.

[2] In the civil war, the Wakes had taken an ardently Royalist side. The archbishop's father, Colonel Wake, had been (as we are told) eighteen times imprisoned, and twice condemned to be hanged for his loyalty. His grandfather, the Rev. W. Wake, had been imprisoned nineteen times. His uncle, the Rev. E. Wake, had been imprisoned twenty times, was once wounded in the head by a gun-shot, and once nearly poisoned. (Noble's *Grainger*, iii. 67.) The elder branch were baronets.

[3] Hunt's *Relig. Thought in England*, iii. 70.

apostolical era which he had made an especial study.¹ On some points, as on remembrance in prayer of the blest departed,² he was doubtless more in accord with the spirit of the second than of his own century. But the main and predominating element of his thought on all ecclesiastical subjects was the conviction that the fundamentals, upon which almost all Christians are agreed, ought so to overrule all lesser differences as to leave little excuse for violating to any serious extent the general unity of the Church.³ He therefore took great interest in all that might tend to bring more nearly together Christians of varying opinions, while he resented, almost with intolerance, whatever seemed likely to set and harden the existing differences. It was with great concern that he had watched the failure of the hopes which had been entertained of bringing a large proportion of the Dissenters into the pale of the National Church. At the time of the Sacheverell trial, long after the schemes of comprehension had been finally given up, he recurred to the subject in the House of Lords with eloquence and pathos.⁴ On the other hand, he advocated the intolerant clauses of the Occasional Conformity, Schism, and Quakers Bills,⁵ not so much from any change of front—as he was charged with at the time—as because he thought there were no such differences between Churchmen and Nonconformists as could justify the latter in standing apart. He particularly valued union in external worship as one of the best methods of healing uncharitable dissensions;⁶ and,

---

¹ He published, in 1695, an edition of the Apostolical Fathers, with preliminary dissertations.

² His published views on this subject are quoted in Blackburne's *Intermediate State*, p. 161.

³ Wake's Sermon on Rom. xv. 5–7, quoted in *Athenian Oracle*, ii. 353; and frequently in his letters attached to Maclaine's 5th vol. of Mosheim's *History*.   ⁴ *Parliamentary History*, vi. 870–71.

⁵ *Id.*, vii. 570, 946; Nicolson's *Letters*, p. 485.

⁶ Maclaine's Mosheim's *History*, v. 120.

since at that time Dissent was visibly and markedly decreasing, he began to cherish a hope that, notwithstanding the failure of the comprehension measure, a time was yet at hand when the National Church would unquestionably be the Church of the whole nation.

The same craving for unity led Wake to keep up constant communications with the Protestant churches of the Continent. 'It may be affirmed that no prelate since the Reformation had so extensive a correspondence with the Protestants abroad, and none could have a more friendly one.'[1] His name was well known and his influence frequently felt among the leading Lutheran, Reformed, and Moravian pastors of Berne and Geneva, Nismes and Piedmont, Prussia, Denmark, and Holland, Hungary and Lithuania. One of his special correspondents was Turretin, the 'second founder of the Genevan Church,' who did much to tone down the harsh Supralapsarianism of Calvin and Beza, and to bring about a closer union between Lutheran and Reformed.[2] The archbishop's special object in these letters was not only to express his earnest sympathy in the work of bringing the Protestant churches more nearly together, but also to counsel with him on the question of subscription to the Helvetic confession. His own opinion was that although such subscriptions were unfortunately a necessary safeguard, great care should be taken that the use of them be not needlessly multiplied, and that learned men should by no means be interfered with in the private exercise of their judgment on difficult questions.[3]

[1] Maclaine's Mosheim, v. 143.
[2] H. B. Wilson, in *Oxford Essays*, 1857, p. 98. Turretin was much favoured by Frederic I. of Prussia, and frequently corresponded with the Cardinals Quirini and Passionei (*id.*, 102).
[3] 'Id solum caveatur, ne multiplicentur hujusmodi subscriptiones absque necessitate, neque stricte nimio inquiratur in privatas hominum eruditorum sententias ; modo suis opinionibus frui pacifice velint.' (Wake to Turretin, App. No. xxii. to Mosheim, vol. v.)

About the same time, Jablouski, a principal leader of the Polish Lutherans, was consulting him[1] on the possibility of any sort of union or common action between the Roman and Evangelical Churches. Wake replied that in his own opinion the pride, the tyranny, the pretensions of the Romans were such as would prove an absolute bar to any such attempts. The respective Churches could only treat on terms of perfect equality.[2] Then, and then only, could be discussed the fundamentals on which they were agreed, how far on other points a concordat could be come to or mutual toleration admitted, and whether a liturgy could be framed which would admit of united worship. Unless such preliminaries were firmly insisted upon and willingly accepted, all conciliatory advances could end in nothing but failure, or concessions in which truth would suffer.[3] But whatever Jablouski and his coadjutors might attempt, he had perfect confidence not only in the wisdom and learning with which he would carry on his endeavours after peace, but also in his firmness and love of truth.

Impossible as Wake held it to have any negotiations with the Papacy, he was himself engaged for three years (1717–20) in an active correspondence with some eminent Gallican Churchmen. His controversy with Bossuet, conducted as it had been with mutual respect and moderation, had made him feel very strongly that a large party of intellectual and high-minded French Churchmen were pre-

[1] 'The two questions were: "An de unione Evangelicorum cum Ecclesiâ Romanâ agendum sit; (vel) An omnis de eâ re tractatio tanquam periculosa et fallax omnino sit evitanda." Id., No. xxv.

[2] 'Neque tamen sic intelligi vellem, quasi omnem omnino de pace tractatum etiam cum Pontificiis refugiendum putarem. Tractemus, si libet: sed, ut decet, cum æqualibus. . . . Christiani sunt illi? et nos Christiani. Catholici? et nos Catholici. Errare nos possumus; etiam illi possunt errare. Liberi sunt illi a dominio nostro? neque nos ullâ in re subditi sumus.' Id.

[3] 'Absque hujusmodi stipulatione præmissâ frustra cum iis tractabimus: nisi sub pacis conciliandæ prætextu veritati renuntiare decreverimus.' Id.

pared, and even anxious, to minimise those parts of the Roman system which are most repugnant to Protestant thought. For the action of the Papal Court had at that time greatly alienated Gallicans. The Papal bull entitled 'Unigenitus'—issued by Clement II. in 1713—had marked with the stigma of heresy the mild and reasonable views which had been adopted by the doctors of the Sorbonne, and by those who loved and admired Cardinal de Noailles, Archbishop of Paris.[1] The Jesuits seemed victorious, and the Jansenists prostrate. But it yet seemed possible to some of the defeated party to regain their footing. They talked of a general council, and some even considered whether it might not be practicable to assert a Gallican independence. In 1717, Beauvoir, chaplain to the Earl of Stair, ambassador at Paris, after conversation with the Syndic of the Sorbonne and some others, wrote to the English primate upon this subject. Wake at once replied, and a long series of communications followed, conducted on the French side by Du Pin, De Girardin, and Beauvoir; while De Noailles, though greatly interested in the discussion, kept almost entirely in the background. But the correspondence, full though it was of earnestness and good-will, soon betrayed the essential hopelessness of the project. The Sorbonne theologians were at one with the English archbishop while they dwelt upon revision and reformation, upon separating things which are necessary from things which are not, and of Papal decisions being by no sort of necessity articles of faith. Yet even they could not refrain from the expression of a hope—conceived completely in the spirit of Rome—that the English, secured against dependence, might yet return into the bosom of the Church with even greater zeal than once, from fear of tyranny, they had fled from it.

[1] Mosheim, v. 78–79.

Such an idea was of course utterly alien to Wake's thoughts; nor throughout the correspondence did he ever make any admission which was in any way unworthy of an English archbishop. He chiefly contented himself with expressing a fervent desire that, as a general council could not be expected, the Gallican Church would throw off the Papal yoke in a national council. 'O that you would assert your claims with an authority worthy of the Church of your great Empire—a Church subject by no right, divine or human, to any other church, to any other man; but which has within itself the right of settling its own affairs, and of governing, under its own laws and sanctions and under its own most Christian king, the people committed to its charge!' If this were done, then might follow fellowship and concord with other national churches, and if not uniformity, at least a peacefully allowed diversity of sentiments.[1]

The Duke Regent and Henry appeared to favour the correspondence, and let it run on. But the Jesuits spread the alarm of a coalition of De Noailles and the Jansenists with the heretics. They got their way. Gerardin was severely reprimanded and threatened with the Bastille, and the Gallican liberties were repressed more vigorously than ever. But Wake's letters, when once divulged, were much read and talked of in Paris, and, it is said, much admired.[2] There were those in England who charged him with 'going to the very verge of Popery,'[3] or who treated the whole project with ridicule.[4] No one, however, who really read the letters could do otherwise than respect the spirit in which their author wrote them. Wake also had some communications with the Patriarch of Jerusalem, who wrote

---

[1] Mosheim, v. App. No. iv.   [2] Mosheim, v. 138.
[3] F. Blackburne, in Nichols' *Anecdotes*, iii. 12.
[4] Warburton, in Doddridge's *Correspondence*, iv. 17.

to him on the subject of the overtures to the Greek Church made by the Scotch Nonjurors. He appears to have acted in the matter with kindness and good judgment.[1]

Wake was greatly disturbed in George the First's time by the inclination evidently shown in high quarters to favour not only the extreme Low party, headed by Hoadly, but also those who, like Clarke and Whiston, had impugned the doctrine of the Trinity. Nor did he hesitate to imply that the unorthodoxy of the Low Churchmen of that time was intricately associated with the new Arianism. 'Some of our bishops,' he said, 'are labouring to pull down the Church in which they minister, and to introduce such licentiousness as would overthrow the grace of the Holy Spirit, the divinity of Christ, and all other fundamental articles of our religion.'[2] In this the archbishop was carried into injustice by his fears. The views of Hoadly, to whom he was chiefly referring,[3] were unquestionably injurious to the sanctity of religion, and to depth of spiritual feelings, and, as such, were favourable to the growth of different forms of Arianism. But he never laid himself open to a charge such as that which Wake has made, and would certainly have earnestly repudiated it. None the less, not English Churchmen only, but Christians generally, had good cause to be anxious. The tendencies which were too plainly visible were not to be stemmed by measures such as the Bill against Arianism, which Wake and the Earl of Nottingham endeavoured to bring in. They would contend best against an easy-going and commonplace religion, who could best instil by preaching and by example a higher appreciation alike of Christian doctrine and of the dignity and earnestness of life.

[1] Lathbury's *Nonjurors*, p. 358.
[2] Quoted in Mrs. Thomson's *Memoirs of Lady Sundon*, p. 79.
[3] Also, no doubt, to Bishop Talbot.

This sketch of Archbishop Wake may properly close with a peaceful picture, occurring in one of his letters to Courayer, when he was now fast advancing into old age. 'For myself, I live almost a monastic life. I have a numerous family, and I keep it under the best regulation I can. We have the service of God within ourselves, and that in public in my chapel and house, four times a day. We live orderly and peaceably together; and though the necessity of business draws a great number of persons to me, yet I reduce even that as much as possible to certain times, and then eat openly with my friends two days in the week. To the Court I seldom go, save when obliged to attend my duty, either in the public or Cabinet councils; and when in Parliament time, I am rather faulty in not going so often as I should to it than in attending constantly upon it; so that I use my best endeavours to live clear of the world, and die by degrees to it. My age and infirmities (being now ready to enter on my seventieth year) admonish me to look upon myself as a citizen of another and better country, and ready to go from hence to it. Your prayer for a happy passage to it will be a reasonable and friendly help, added to my own. In return, I shall not be wanting to wish you all happiness in your longer pilgrimage upon earth. And though we go by somewhat different paths, yet as we do in effect pursue the same road, so I trust we shall meet together at our journey's end.'[1]

John Sharp was Archbishop of York between 1691 and 1714. It may be truly said of him that he represented one of the highest types of an English Churchman. His father was a Puritan, in much favour with Fairfax; his mother a zealous Royalist and hearty Churchwoman. At Cambridge he had studied under that noble-minded

[1] Quoted by Mrs. Thomson, in *Mem of L. Sundon*, from the *Biogr. Britann.*

Christian Platonist, Henry More. Under these varied influences he grew up a devout,[1] learned, liberal-minded man. He was an excellent preacher, noted especially for the zeal, pathos, and vivacity of his delivery.[2] His interests were versatile, for he was not only a theologian and a Hebraist, but was very fond of Greek and English poetry, kept up his early studies in philosophy, chemistry, and botany, was a famous numismatist, and an able antiquary.[3] He had been an exemplary parish priest,[4] and when bishop, his cathedral was acknowledged to be under better management than any other in England.[5] Himself a High Churchman, especially in the latter part of his episcopate, and a warm friend to the Nonjurors, many of whom he persuaded to return to Conformity,[6] he had been also Tillotson's 'dear and fast friend;'[7] and Baxter, Calamy, and Firmin had been among his intimate companions. His uncompromising language in the pulpit had cost him his suspension in the reign of James the Second, and his views on many Church matters[8] were very decided. But he was full of kindness and charity to those who differed from him, and there was undoubtedly no other Churchman in England who had

---

[1] He kept the anniversary of June 24, 1688, as his spiritual birthday, as he beginning of a more uninterrupted service of God (*Life*, by his Son, ii. 67).

[2] Calamy's *Life*, i. 168; *Life of Kettlewell*, 69; *Life of Sharp*, by his Son, i. 37; Thoresby's *Diary*, i. 224.

[3] Nicolson spoke of him as 'the greatest master of antiquities in the kingdom' (Nicolson's *Letters*, p. 117).

[4] 'His labours were unwearied, and such efficacy accompanied the word preached that St. Giles was greatly reformed' (J. Dunton, 1702, quoted in note to Nicolson's *Letters*, p. 48).

[5] Nichols, *Lit. An.*, i. 10; Browne Willis, *Cathedrals*, i. 63. He was exceedingly beloved and admired at York (Noble's *Cont. of Grainger*, i. 75).

[6] *Life*, by his Son, i. 268; Secretan's *Life of Nelson*, pp. 78 79.

[7] *Life of Sharp*, by his Son, i. 29.

[8] Among his distinctively High Church opinions may be mentioned his preference for King Edward's Prayer Book, and his regret at the omission of the Prayer of Oblation in the Communion Service (*Life*, by his Son, i. 355; Secretan, p. 178).

so large and varied a circle of attached friends. High and Low Churchmen, Nonjurors,[1] Latitudinarians, and even Arians, Scotch Episcopalians,[2] foreign Protestants, English Nonconformists,[3] scholars, philosophers, and antiquarians, all might be sure of a kind and generous reception from the Archbishop of York. He had unpardonably offended Swift by representing him as not a Christian, and standing in the way of his advancement;[4] but with that exception it may be truly said, in Robert Nelson's words, that 'he filled the archiepiscopal see with universal applause.'[5]

Like Wake, and many other principal Churchmen of his day, Sharp was very desirous of seeing the English Church strengthened and the Protestant interest consolidated by a closer union with sympathisers on the Continent. Towards the end of the first decade of the eighteenth century there appeared to be very reasonable grounds for hoping that the Prussian Protestants, both Lutheran and Reformed, might be induced to restore a regular episcopate, and to introduce a liturgy closely akin to the English one. Frederic I. at one time took great interest in the subject. The English

---

[1] *Cf.* Whiston of him: 'That very good, that very honest man, that excellent preacher, and great friend to Mr. Clarke and myself' (Whiston's *Memoirs of S. Clarke*, p. 10).

[2] 'Many of whom owed much to his sympathetic liberality' (*Life*, by his Son, ii. 67). 'He was as much the patron and friend of the Scotch Episcopal clergy as if they had been in his province, and they as readily applied to him as if he were their primate' (*id.*, i. 384).

[3] 'In public life his later opposition to Dissenters contrasted strongly with his earlier attitude. This was owing partly to the very changed circumstances of the times, and partly to the influence of his friend and old patron the Earl of Nottingham' (Thoresby's *Diary*, i. 437). He spoke, voted, or protested against all his old Whig friends in the debates upon Occasional Conformity, upon Dissenting Seminaries, and upon the question of the Church in Danger, and the Sacheverell case (*Parl. Hist.*, vi. 163, 493, 498, 880).

[4] Nichols' *Lit. An.*, i. 9, 10.

[5] Nelson's *Life of Bull*, 238. Thoresby also speaks of him as 'universally beloved' (*Diary*, i. 224).

Church system seemed to him to supply a promising basis for promoting an object on which his heart was much set, as a thing greatly to be desired—an assimilation between the two great sections of the Protestant Church in Germany. He therefore caused the English liturgy to be translated into German, and meditated the introduction of it into his own chapel and the Cathedral Church, and requested Ursinus, to whom he had some time previously given the name of 'Bishop,' to consult with the Archbishop of Canterbury on the general subject. Either the letter was not delivered, or Tenison was neglectful and dilatory, and Frederic, feeling somewhat rebuffed and offended, took for a time no further step. But two or three years later, in 1710, the discussion was again opened. Frederic desired some of his principal divines to write their thoughts separately on the subject, and to forward the packet to Archbishop Sharp.[1] Sharp was greatly interested, and wrote at once in terms of warm approval. The letters that followed, chiefly[2] between him and Jablouski, the king's chaplain, show that the scheme received much serious consideration. It was submitted before the Prussian king in council, and Secretary St. John wrote to the English ambassador at Berlin to express the queen's approval of so 'laudable a design.' Frederic's interest had cooled, but he was still not unfavourable to the project, and if he had lived longer some practical results might possibly have followed. But he died in 1713, and Sharp the year after. It need hardly be said that the succeeding King of Prussia, Frederic William, was one of the last men in the world to trouble himself about ideas of Church union.

Compton, a son of the second Earl of Northampton, was Bishop, first of Oxford (1674-75), and then of London,

[1] *Life of Sharp*, pp. 410-49.
[2] Robinson, Grabe, Smalridge, and others consulted with the archbishop.

(1675–1713). He was sometimes, on account of a well-known episode in his history, called by the irreverent nickname of Jack Boots. At the time of the Restoration he had been a cornet of horse. He entered into holy orders soon after that date; but in 1688, when he was a bishop of fourteen years' standing, the excitement of the Revolution, and the danger of his pupil, the Princess Anne, so roused the soldier in him that he resumed his military dress, and, with swords and pistols by his side, escorted his charge to Northampton. 'In a little while,' adds Burnet, 'a small army was formed about her, who chose to be commanded by the Bishop of London, of which he too easily accepted.'[1] Kettlewell, in great disgust, immediately rased his name from the Dedication of all the unsold copies of his 'Christian Obedience.'[2] Apart from this ill-judged episode in his episcopal life, Compton wore the rochet with much credit. It may be easily said that, through William and Mary's reign, he was too much of a politician. But it was a time when religious and political interests were inseparably mingled, and when it was quite impossible for any man of warm feeling not to be the keen supporter of a party. Compton had a generous and ardent temper, and was so vehement a supporter of Reformed principles, that although all English Churchmen at this period, High and Low alike, were emphatically staunch in their support, he was sometimes called pre-eminently 'the Protestant Bishop.' He had vigorously opposed James, and had been suspended from his bishopric for two years by the irritated king. He was the only spiritual peer who signed the invitation to the Prince of Orange to come over in defence of the Protestant cause; though it must also be added that when called to account for it by James, he condescended to an equivocation[3]

---

[1] Burnet's *Own Times*, p. 502. [2] *Life of Kettlewell*, p. 19.
[3] Macaulay, chap. ix.

very unworthy of a good and courageous man. No one was
more active than he in endeavouring to gain over Dissenters
by a wide comprehension; none more zealous in labouring
to gain the sympathy and co-operation of Protestants
abroad. There was much truth in Ken's remonstrances
with him [1] upon the dangerous concessions he was too ready
to make in order to attain these objects. He must not,
however, be regarded as in any way disloyal to his own
Church. The ruling principle of his action was a feeling,
in the first place, of the paramount necessity of Protestant
unity; and secondly, that separation of English Protestants
from the National Church might be made both needless and
inexcusable. In Queen Anne's reign, when the danger and
the hope had alike passed by, it was not necessarily through
any change in Compton's own principles that he became in
general estimation almost a High Churchman.[2] It may be
said of him in conclusion that he was not a learned man,
but was diligent in his profession, active in preaching and
confirming throughout his diocese,[3] and that he had done
very signal services to his country in the care with which he
had fulfilled his important office as preceptor to the two
royal princesses, Mary and Anne.

It is rather curious that the last English bishop who
appeared in arms and took the command of troops should
have been succeeded by the last bishop who in England has

---

[1] *Life of Ken*, by a Layman, i. 167.

[2] As in his speech on the Dangers of the Church (*Parl. Hist.*, vi. 491).
In the Occasional Conformity debate he deserted the Low Church party,
and voted with the Tories (*id.*, p. 163). His opposition to the prosecution of
Sacheverell (*Parl. Protests*, pp. 175, 181) was of course no argument that
he agreed with him.

[3] 'He had a method of passing every summer in some new part of his
diocese, riding out every day to visit the churches and parsonage-
houses. . . . His *Episcopalia* give one the impression of a man well versed
in practical work, and also a man of firmness and independent judgment'
(Overton's *Life in the English Church* (1660-1713), p. 67).

held a high diplomatic appointment, and been, in a specific and individual capacity, a chief officer of State. On Compton's death Robinson was promoted to the see of London (1713–1726). He had been for a number of years in Sweden, first as chaplain, then as ambassador. In 1710 he was made Bishop of Bristol; in 1711, Lord Privy Seal; and in 1713, Plenipotentiary at Utrecht. The treaty is generally allowed to have been a dishonourable one, abandoning as it did for little or no compensation the immense vantage-ground which English victories had won. But at the time there was a large party who hailed it with delight. Allowance being made for the somewhat fulsome strain customary at that time in the dedication of books, there were very many of Robinson's contemporaries who would have assented to the following words of praise: 'The great services you have done to your country by the happy conclusion of a welcome peace, after vast expenses of blood and money seemed insufficient to procure it, have rendered your lordship the darling of all well-wishers to peace.'[1] At all events, it was more creditable to an episcopal negotiator to err on the side of conciliation, than to have continued a war, not plainly needful, for the sake of renewed glory and greater advantages. But many spoke of his abilities with extreme contempt,[2] and he was undoubtedly overrated by the Earl of Oxford, who had a very high opinion of his capacity and knowledge.[3] Personally he is described as a little brown man, of grave and venerable appearance,[4] in deportment and everything else a Swede, of good sense, and very careful in his business,[5] good-humoured and charitable,[6]

---

[1] Dedic. to Paterson's *Pictas Londinensis*, 1714.
[2] Calamy's *Life*, ii. 270.   [3] Noble's *Cont. of Grainger*, i. 79.
[4] Stoughton's *England under Queen Anne*, p. 121.
[5] Mackay, in note to Nicolson's *Letters*, p. 121.
[6] Among other kind deeds, he was, in 1718, a considerable benefactor to Oriel College.

and strictly religious,[1] but not very competent as the
bishop of an important diocese. He assisted Archbishop
Sharp in his efforts to restore episcopacy in Sweden;[2] and,
on account of his strenuous opposition to Whiston, Waterland spoke warmly 'of his truly primitive zeal against the
adversaries of our common faith.'[3] There is an anecdote
of Queen Caroline's anger at his wishing to wait upon her
to explain what she did not comprehend, and to satisfy her
in any doubts and scruples. 'Send him away civilly,' she
said; 'but he is very impertinent to suppose that I, who
refused to be Empress for the sake of the Protestant religion,
do not understand it fully.'[4]

Everybody who knows anything at all of the period of
the Revolution of 1689, and the years that immediately
preceded and followed it, must of necessity be more or
less familiar with the life and character of Burnet, Bishop
of Salisbury from 1689 to 1715. His character was a
strongly marked one, and his life insatiably active. His
faults lie prominently on the surface. He was petulant
and self-conceited, a great admirer of his own abilities, and
very unable to appreciate the virtues and abilities of those
who differed from him. He was a thorough-going partisan,
often a bitter, and always a formidable one, detested therefore and feared, above all his contemporaries, by his
political and ecclesiastical opponents. Moreover (to take
Seward's words), he was 'a great gossip, and very inquisitive,
often very ill-judged and impertinent in his questions.'[5]
There were many, both in his own and later days, who would

---

[1] Noble's *Cont. of Grainger*, i. 79.
[2] Anderson's *Colonial Church*, iii. 49.
[3] Van Mildert's preface to Waterland's *Works*, i. 67.
[4] Countess Cowper's *Diary*, p. 41.
[5] Seward's *Anecdotes*, ii. 188. Noble tells of him that he was extra-
vagantly fond of smoking, and had a hole made in his broad-brimmed hat
to put his long pipe through while he wrote (*Cont. of Grainger*, i. 31).

believe nothing that was good of him. Hearne gives with a very genuine relish some of the wonderful stories of which he was the subject; 'how,' for instance, 'the Bishop of Sarum has received 5,000 lbs. for voting for Occasional Conformity, and that he is to receive 30,000 lbs. more, and the revenue of his bishopric during life, whenever Presbytery shall be established in England, which he endeavours to have effected.'[1] Yet a little later, 'People say Burnet has offered S. Wesley 25 or 26 lbs. not to speak in private or otherwise against the Presbyterians and the rest of the Whiggs.'[2] Again, three years afterwards, 'he hopes the Bishop of Sarum is no great friend to Popery, but by his "Exposition on the Articles" one would think he was half channelled over.'[3] It was a pleasant and unexpected surprise to Thoresby, going from among his High Church friends, to find out how much there was to admire in Burnet. 'And what was the best of all was his pious and excellent converse; for notwithstanding the censures of a malignant world, he is doubtless an admirable, holy, and good man, and has one of the best regulated houses in the world.'[4] Burnet had indeed many unmistakable faults, but he had many admirable qualities, some of which were at first appearance rather inconsistent with his foibles. Apart from his inveterate self-sufficiency, his failings were mainly in language and in manner; his better qualities were far more deeply rooted. Much that he said might seem to argue a small-minded, illiberal man, but in thought and action he was tolerant, both from kindness of feeling and from strong conviction. No one could gainsay his

---

[1] *Reliquiæ Hearnianæ*, p. 38.   [2] *Id.*, p. 41.   [3] *Id.*, p. 170.

[4] Thoresby's *Diary*, ii. 67. It would appear that his family worship was somewhat tediously protracted. 'It was said that to the over-long religious exercises in the house of his father the bishop, W. Burnet, Governor of New York, attributed a distaste in after life to religious worship' (Lady Sundon's *Diary*, i. 170).

beneficent activity in all the pastoral duties of his office. In his early manhood, as a Scotch clergyman under the Bishop of Edinburgh, he had won the warmest affection of his parishioners;[1] and he alone, as it was said, of all the Scotch clergy had influence enough to establish firmly in his church the use of the English liturgy. At Salisbury he was no less indefatigable, and his favourite[2] published work, that on 'the Pastoral Care,' was the genuine expression of his own practice. He was a powerful and attractive preacher. Many readers will remember how Macaulay describes that 'he was often interrupted by the deep hum of his audience; and when, after preaching out the hourglass, he held it up in his hand, the congregation clamorously encouraged him to go on till the sand had run out once more.'[3] He greatly desired to remove abuses from the Church. In his diocese he checked non-residence to the best of his power;[4] and if he could have persuaded the Lords to accept his Bill,[5] he would have done much to restrain that system of pluralities which throughout the eighteenth century was one of the most glaring abuses of the Church. Upon all political and ecclesiastical questions he was a Liberal to the very core. In Scotland, encouraged by the constant support of Archbishop Leighton, whom he loved as 'of the most angelical rank of men,' but amid the vituperation of extreme men on either side, he had laboured hard, but in vain, to find some term of accommodation between Presbyterians and Episcopalians. In England he exercised all his energies in a somewhat similar work, and,

[1] Grub's *Eccles. Hist. of Scotland*, iii. 223.
[2] 'Of all the tracts of which I wrote, it is that in which I rejoice the most' (Burnet's *Own Times*, p. 906). It was a book which made a strong impression on the mind of the distinguished evangelical leader, John Scott (Stoughton's *Religion under Queen Anne*, p. 102).
[3] Macaulay's *Hist.*, chap. vii. [4] Whiston's *Memoirs*, p. 41.
[5] Prideaux's *Life*, pp. 80 82.

in one most important respect, with far greater success. He could not, indeed, carry out his cherished hopes of a comprehension of Presbyterians. But more than any one man besides, he was influential in averting a yet worse schism than that of the Nonjurors by keeping loyal to the unity of the English Church that great Whig party whom the Sacheverells of their day would have hopelessly estranged. With High Churchmen, as such, he had no sympathy. It was not that any of their theological tenets were obnoxious to him. For though his mind was formed on a wholly different mould from theirs, he would have been the last man of his age to impose restrictions on Christian thought. While yet quite a young man he had become well acquainted, during his stay at the English universities, in London, and on the Continent, with men of very different modes of thought, and many different forms of religion, in all of which he 'found men of such real piety and virtue, that he became fixed in that strong principle of thinking well of those who differed from him,[1] and of invincible abhorrence of all persecution on account of religious dissensions.' Much of the High Churchmanship which came most in Burnet's way was in direct antagonism to his most cherished convictions. He saw and knew comparatively little of that pure and noble type of High Churchmen who were well represented in his time by such men as Ken and Frampton and Kettlewell, by Bull, Beveridge, and Wilson, by Robert Nelson and Brokesby, by Bray and Oglethorpe. But a noisier and more intolerant crowd of so-called High Churchmen were his constant opponents, ever clamouring against what he believed to be the best interests of the Church and true religion, ever pursuing him with unsparing and merciless invective. He had been proscribed and outlawed in

[1] This was no doubt Burnet's principle, but scarcely his practice. He found it very difficult to speak well of those who differed from him.

the time of James; in Queen Anne's reign he was at one time in hourly fear that his house would be gutted by a senseless mob who imagined themselves champions of the Church.¹ He was firmly persuaded that if the opinions against which he was contending recovered an unchecked ascendency, they would undo whatever good the Revolution had effected, and bring back some of the worst evils of the past. Such being his view, he threw himself into the struggle, without too much consideration whether his arguments were always fair, or his judgments discriminating. Yet there was great injustice in the charge brought against him of hypocrisy in his behaviour to the Nonjurors, of being, as one of their poets said, 'an artful enemy, but seeming friend.'² In the House of Lords he had earnestly pleaded for moderation and forbearance in the matter of the oaths,³ and in his own diocese he was scrupulously considerate to the ejected clergy, as was specially instanced in the permission he gave them to nominate their successors.

Burnet died early in 1715, his last few years being spent in a comparative retirement from the world, more congenial to the declining years of a religious man than the busy restlessness of his previous life. Among his later services to the Church had been one which was wholly independent of party. He had suggested to William and Mary the boon they would confer upon the Church by the surrender, for the augmentation of poor livings, of the considerable fund arising from clerical tenths and firstfruits, which at the Reformation had passed from the Pope to the Crown. The proposal had been favourably received, and if King William had lived longer, might probably have been granted by him. Burnet did not fail to keep it before the notice of

---

¹ Thoresby's *Diary*, ii. 233. ² Harte's *Poems*, 'Macarius.'
³ *Parliamentary History*, vi. 263.

Queen Anne, and to his great satisfaction she generously consented to its being carried out.

The name of Simon Patrick, Bishop of Ely, is still well remembered, on account of the Commentary on Holy Scripture of which he was the author. In his own day he was universally esteemed. Nearly forty years before the eighteenth century began, his election to the Provostship of Queen's College, Oxford, against the king's mandamus had brought upon that body a storm of royal indignation, and the expulsion not only of the head of the college, but of the majority of the Fellows. Afterwards, as rector of St. Paul's, Covent Garden, he gained reputation as one of the great London preachers, and the affection of his parishioners by his unremitting attentions to them through the terrible time of the Great Plague.[1] In King James's reign he took a zealous part in the controversy with Rome. On one occasion he argued against the Roman Catholic deputies before the king in person, until James, discomfited at Patrick's address, dismissed the disputants with the remark 'that he never heard a bad cause so well, nor a good one so ill defended.'[2] In conjunction with Tillotson, Stillingfleet, Tenison, and other of the London clergy, he joined with the seven bishops in the famous Lambeth Declaration.[3] Immediately after William's accession he was made Bishop, first of Chichester (1689-91), soon afterwards of Ely (1691-1707). Comprehension of Dissenters, which soon became a subject of consideration among Churchmen, was a question on which his opinion entirely altered. He was at one time strongly averse to the scheme, and published an argument against it. But frequent conversation on the

---

[1] He was at all times a most energetic parish clergyman. 'Four services were held every day in his church, and his offertories were enormous' (Overton's *Life in the E. Ch.* (1660-1714), p. 78.

[2] Bentham's *History of Ely*, append. p. 113.   [3] *Life of Ken*, p. 108.

subject with Archbishop Sancroft and Sharp both of whom for a time favoured the movement—led him to feel that such union might be desirable, and he gave his best efforts to promote it.[1] He was on the commission for revising the Prayer Book, and, being supposed to have a special faculty for composing prayers,[2] was entrusted with the duty of remodelling the collects to the taste of the age. Happily the Church was saved from the somewhat prolix effusions[3] of this most worthy prelate. Patrick was interested in the Church societies which at the end of the seventeenth and early part of the eighteenth centuries sprang up in London and other chief towns, rich in deep religious feeling and earnest Christian work. He could not, however, persuade himself to join their prayer meetings. 'You know,' he wrote to a friend, 'how much averse I am naturally to such things, and that I can breathe out my soul better alone or with a friend than in much company. But tell me the time, and I will sequester myself from all employments, and do the same in my privacy.'[4] In the two venerable societies which had their origin in the genuine but temporary revival of that period, Patrick took a very leading part. Burnet and he were the first bishops to join the five founders of the Christian Knowledge Society in 1698. He was no less active and interested in the early proceedings of the Society for the Propagation of the Gospel in 1701.[5]

John Moore, Bishop of Norwich from 1691 to 1707, and

---

[1] Though he returned to his former opinion as to the impossibility of any such union (Noble's *Cont. of Grainger*, i. 37), his voice was always raised on the side of moderation. He especially protested, at the time of the Occasional Conformity Bill, against 'the heat and passion of the universities' (*Parliam. Hist.*, vi. 496).

[2] Birch's *Tillotson*, p. 125.

[3] Of which Macaulay gives specimens in a note in his 14th chapter.

[4] Chamberlain's *Selected Letters*, p. 110.

[5] Anderson's *Colonial Church*, iii. 118.

then of Ely, after Patrick's death, till 1714, is to be mentioned chiefly as a learned man himself, and a great patron of learning in others. He was the most noted collector of books in England.[1] His library, which Burnet describes as 'a most invaluable treasure, both of printed books and manuscripts, beyond what one could think the life and labour of one man could have compassed,'[2] was purchased after his death by George the First,[3] and presented by him to the University of Cambridge. Many a story was told, in truth or jest, of his eagerness to get a rare book, and how he would beg them from his clergy, either paying them in return with sermons or books, or with the exclamation to the more ignorant of them, 'Quid illiterati cum libris?'[4] It was even whispered that it was not quite safe to trust him with a valuable author, and that on one occasion warning was sent to a librarian to be on the lookout, 'for the Bishop of Ely was coming.'[5]

Be this as it may, he is spoken of in the most loving and admiring terms by Samuel Clarke, who had not yet broached his Arian opinions, but had already gained great note as a philosopher and theologian, especially by his Boyle lectures on the Being and Attributes of God. Clarke was for some time his chaplain, and after his death published his sermons and wrote his life. He was a man, he says, of piety and virtue, full of kindness to the poor, zealous in promoting the interests of his country and the Protestant religion, a laborious and constant preacher, and very just and skilful in determining practical cases and questions of divinity.

---

[1] Blomfield's *History of Norwich*, p. 390.
[2] Burnet on the *Reformation*, part iii. p. 46; quoted in Calamy, ii. 307.
[3] His library contained 6,725 volumes in folio, 8,200 in quarto, and 11,040 in octavo (Noble's *Grainger*, i. 89). It was bought for 6,000 guineas (Van Mildert's Introd. to Waterland's *Life*, p. 14).
[4] Bentham's *History of Ely*, supplement, p. 113.
[5] Note to Burnet's *Own Times*, p. 569.

From his judgment and sound learning, the world, he adds, had reason to expect from him many excellent and useful works, had not his continued application to the duties of his office, and his perpetual readiness to help learned men, left him very little time for his private studies.[1]

In politics he was a Whig, and in Parliament voted consistently upon that side on all ecclesiastical questions.[2]

In Edward Fowler, Bishop of Gloucester (1691-1714), we again come to one of the most distinguished Whig prelates of his age. A Presbyterian by early training, the son of one of the ejected ministers, he had felt some hesitation about conforming at the time of the Restoration, and a few years later had been suspended for disobedience to the canons of the Church. He was laughed at in later days for having scarcely overcome his old Puritan antipathy to painted windows.[3] But in the time of James he was, as a leading London clergyman, one of the boldest and most able defenders of the English Church, both against the encroachments of the king, and against the theology of Rome. In personal character genial,[4] tolerant, and of exemplary worth, he was an ardent defender of civil liberty, and a powerful supporter of the rights and authority of reason. Many attacks were made upon him as (to use his own expression) 'a person with the long name,' a Latitudinarian.[5] But in his dialogue between Philalethes and Theophilus[6] he ably defended himself against the opprobrium conveyed in that term. He eloquently expounded the

---

[1] Quoted in Noble's *Grainger*, i. 89.
[2] *Parliamentary Hist.*, vi. 163, 886; vii. 1356, &c.
[3] *Life of Ken*, by a Layman, p. 763.
[4] Warm-tempered, said Skelton of him, but full of kindness.
[5] Noble's *Cont. of Grainger*, ii. 87.
[6] He also wrote a special treatise on the *Principles and Practices of certain Moderate Divines abusively called Latitudinarians*.

deep and earnest Christianity of such men as H. More and
Whicherly, Smith and Cudworth. 'I have been,' said he,
'as constant a hearer of them as any man, but never was
my judgment more convinced, my will persuaded, nor my
affections wrought upon, by any sermon than by theirs. I
found that in their discourses generally they handled those
subjects that were weightiest and of most necessary importance; I mean such as have the greatest respect unto
reformation of men's lives, and purification of their souls.
Nor had I ever so lively an idea of the divine nature, which
is the most powerful incentive to obedience to the divine
will, nor so clear a sense of the excellency of the Christian
religion, the reasonableness of its precepts, the nobleness
and generosity of its design, as, through the blessing of
God, I have obtained from these men.'[1] One of Fowler's
works gave rise to a very sharp encounter between him and
John Bunyan, neither of whom—after the manner of good
men in those days—spared hard words. Bunyan declared
that his 'Design of Christianity' was all 'Popery, Socinianism, and Quakerism.' Fowler answered it by 'Dirt
wiped out; or, a Manifest Discovery of the Gross Ignorance,
Erroneousness, and most Unchristian and Wicked Spirit
of one John Bunyan, Lay Preacher at Bedford.'[2] It may be
remarked in the last place of Bishop Fowler that he was a
firm believer in ghosts, witches, fairies, and such other
supernatural potencies. This, however, was by no means
inconsistent in that age with a profound reverence for the
divine gift of reason.[3] He simply believed, as Henry More
and Glanville did, that the existence of such agents rested
on clear testimony, and he studied them as he would any
other established phenomena.[4]

[1] Hunt's *Relig. Thought in England,* ii. 131.
[2] *Gentleman's Mag.* for 1732, p. 1002.
[3] He was one of the principal leaders of the 'reasonable' school, in which the eighteenth century abounded. [4] Hunt, ii. 170

William Fleetwood was Bishop of St. Asaph from 1706, and of Ely from 1714 to his death in 1723. It is creditable to Queen Anne that although he was in politics an ardent and uncompromising Whig, he was appointed to his first bishopric by her express nomination, and that even while he was under the hot displeasure of a High Church ministry she never ceased to esteem him very highly.[1] But he was a good Churchman, and thought by many to be the most gifted preacher of his age. He was also much consulted on perplexed questions and wounds of conscience. For he had a clear and judicial mind, and 'a peculiar talent in making things plain and easy which seemed to many difficult and disturbing.'[2] The event of his life by which he is now most remembered is that which affords a familiar example of the futility and folly of banning by vote of censure obnoxious political opinions. Towards the end of the queen's reign, shortly before the peace of Utrecht, Fleetwood published four of his sermons preached on State occasions. In the preface he spoke of an inalienable right which Christianity had left inviolate, by which a free people are entitled to defend their liberties against oppression or injustice. And speaking of the high anticipations which he had cherished at the time of the queen's accession, he lamented the spirit of discord that had gone forth 'to spoil for a time this beautiful and pleasing prospect, and to give us in its stead I know not what—our enemies will tell the rest with pleasure.' The Government were furious at what they declared to be an open insult, and it was at first proposed to impeach the author.[3] Eventually the Commons resolved, by a vote of 119 to 54, that the preface was malicious and factious, and sentenced it to be

---

[1] She used to call him distinctively 'my bishop' (Noble's *Cont. of Grainger*, ii. 98).

[2] Pref. to Fleetwood's *Works*, viii-ix.

[3] Campbell's *Lives of the Chancellors*, iv. 590.

burnt by the common hangman.[1] The result might have been foreseen. Every one called for the proscribed pamphlet, and read it with avidity. The 'Spectator' published it in full for its morning paper,[2] and, as Fleetwood remarked with some glee in a letter to Burnet, 'has conveyed 14,000 of them into the people's hands that would otherwise have never seen or heard of it.'[3] This preface contained a sentence, simple and natural enough in itself, but which, from the whole having attracted so much interest, impressed itself upon the public memory as words well befitting an English Churchman. 'I would be transmitted,' said Fleetwood, '(for the little share of time such names as mine can live), under the character of one who loved his country, and would be thought a good Englishman as well as a good clergyman.' Fleetwood was what few men of his time were, consistently tolerant, and was particularly indignant at the cruel provisions of the Schism Act. 'If it was not persecution,' he said, 'he knew not what was. The way to judge of such matters was to bring the case home to ourselves, and to suppose that others believe themselves to be as much in the right as we do.'[4] That he carried out his mild, forbearing principles into the actions of his own life is evident from the love and esteem in which he was held among his clergy,[5] who, as a body, differed widely from his views. There is some excellent matter in his pastoral charges, and they are quoted by Napleton[6] as useful to students for holy orders as late in the century as 1795—an unusually long life for such ephemeral productions. In addition to his theological works, the principal of which is the Essay on Miracles, Fleetwood published, shortly before

[1] *Parliam. Hist.*, vii. 1154. [2] *Spectator*, No. 384.
[3] *Parl. Hist.*, vii. 1158 (note).
[4] Pref. to Fleetwood's *Works*, x.
[5] Bentham's *History of Ely*, supplement, p. 115.
[6] Napleton's *Advice to a Student*, p. 32.

he was made bishop, a valuable work on the history of money and prices in England.

Whiston speaks of Richard Cumberland, Bishop of Peterborough from 1690 to 1718, as 'that truly great and good man,'[1] a high encomium from one who was apt to be somewhat meagre in his praise. The term 'great' is scarcely appropriate; but he was undoubtedly a very good and an exceedingly learned[2] man, and his abilities, though sometimes too much wasted on obscure subjects, were of a very commanding order. Hallam speaks in the highest terms of his work upon 'The Laws of Nature.' He speaks of him as 'the first Christian writer who sought to establish systematically the principle of moral right independently of revelation,' and describes his book as 'an epoch in the history of ethical philosophy.' 'His mind,' he added, 'liberal and comprehensive as well as acute, had been forcibly impressed with the discoveries of his own age, both in mathematical science, and in what is now more strictly called physiology. From this armoury he chose his weapons, and employed them in some instances with great capacity and depth of thought.'[3] He was a man of strong feelings, and his anxious fear of what might result from James's attempts to restore Romanism in England had thrown him into a melancholy which ended in serious illness. William recognised his merits, and appointed him to a bishopric when he was

---

[1] Whiston's *Memoirs*, p. 250.

[2] 'Languages, divinity, history, physics, mathematics, and indeed every branch of learning and science, were understood by him' (Noble's *Cont. of Grainger*, i. 89).

[3] Hallam's *Liter. of Europe*, iv. 306-24. See also Lecky's *Eng. in Eighteenth Cent.*, i. 84. One of the stanzas of his epitaph runs as follows:—

> 'Macte, malæ fraudis domitor, defensor honestæ
> Legum naturæ, justitiæque pugil!
> O quantum debent, quas læserat Hobbius ambas,
> Recta simul ratio, Relligioque tibi!'
>   (Browne Willis, *Cathedrals*, iii. 511.)

almost too old for such an office. Going one morning on a post day into a coffee-house, he took up a gazette, and read to his great surprise that Dr. Cumberland, of Stamford, had been appointed to Peterborough.[1] The well-known saying of its being better to wear out than to rust out originated in an answer of his to some friends who were entreating him to take some relaxation from his unceasing industry.[2] Old age did little to impair his faculties. He did not begin his examination of Wilkins' 'Coptic History' till he was eighty-three years old.[3] He appears to have been in all respects a man most deserving of honour. His descendant, R. Cumberland, after describing him as being 'as truly a Christian as he was perfectly a gentleman,' says of his charity, that every year, after reserving a few pounds for his burial, he gave all the overplus to the poor.[4]

A sort of slur rests, undeservedly, on the memory of Richard Kidder, from his having superseded Ken in the bishopric of Bath and Wells (1691–1703).[5] The revered name of his predecessor seemed to make him an intruder upon ground which belonged of right to one of the saintliest of men. Yet he was by no means deficient in good qualities. The Nonjurors spoke and wrote of him as an 'Erastian and Latitudinarian Traditour,'[6] but could bring no specific charge against him except on some points of doctrine, and that in their opinion he was too lax in admitting Dissenters into the service of the English Church without demanding full acknowledgment of their previous errors.[7] He was a simple-hearted, charitable man, of much learning, especially

---

[1] Macaulay's *Hist.*, ch. xvii. [2] Burnet's *Own Times*, p. 569 (note).
[3] Noble, p. 87.   [4] R. Cumberland's *Memoirs of Himself*, i. 27.
[5] An arrangement was made through the queen and Lord Weymouth, with Kidder's consent, of restoring Ken to Bath and Wells, and translating Kidder to Carlisle; but Ken refused (*Life*, by a Layman, 700).
[6] Ken to Lloyd, *Life of Ken*, by a Layman, p. 713; and note to *id.*, p. 603.
[7] Bowles' *Life of Ken*, p. 247.

in Oriental languages, on which account the Revision Committee of 1689 had entrusted him with the charge of retranslating the Psalms from the original.[1] His ejection in 1661 from the vicarage of Stanground had been a signal example of the unseemly and oppressive haste with which the Bartholomew Act was carried through. He had no objections to episcopacy or to the liturgy, but the new Book of Prayer had not yet reached that part of the country, and he chose rather to be deprived of his living than to make a declaration of faith in ignorance of what it really was.[2] Archbishop Sancroft afterwards offered him promotion, and Robert Nelson specially recommended him to Tillotson. A story is told of him, curiously illustrative of the attempts which were often, and sometimes not unsuccessfully, made to gain out of ecclesiastical appointments influence for the Court. One of William's ministers tried unsuccessfully to gain his vote for a measure desired by the king, and at last arrogantly said, 'Consider whose bread you eat.' 'I eat no man's bread,' said the bishop, 'but poor Dr. Ken's. I had not thought of giving a vote, but now I shall vote contrary to your commands.'[3] Kidder was killed in the great storm of November 26, 1703, when a part of the palace at Wells fell down, and buried him in its ruins.

Of the seven bishops who were committed to the Tower in 1688, five were afterwards Nonjurors, and three of these—Sancroft, Lake, and White—died before the end of the seventeenth century. Turner passed away in 1700. The three survivors were Ken, the deprived Bishop of Bath and Wells, William Lloyd of Worcester, and Sir Jonathan Trelawney of Exeter.

[1] Birch's *Life of Tillotson*, p. 125. Tillotson valued his commentary on the Pentateuch, and sent it as a present to Le Clerc (*id.*, p. 197).
[2] Cassan's *Lives of the Bps. of B. and W.*, quoted in Ken's *Life*, p. 601.
[3] Noble's *Cont. of Grainger*, ii. 106.

William Lloyd, Bishop successively of St. Asaph, Lichfield, and Worcester (1680–1717), must not be confused with his namesake and contemporary, the Nonjuring Bishop of Norwich. Burnet, who was his intimate friend, speaks in the warmest terms of his great worth. He was an excellent scholar, he says, especially in Biblical theology,[1] and a man who would never pass from any subject until he had thoroughly mastered it. Yet his love of learning had not hindered him from administering ' the greatest cure in England,' St. Martin's, with an application and diligence beyond any about him. He was a holy, humble, and patient man, ever ready to do good. He endowed schools, set up a public library, and kept many curates to assist him in his indefatigable labours. And Whitehall lying within that parish, he stood as in the front of the battle all King James's reign, and maintained as well as managed that dangerous post with great courage and much judgment.[2] Burnet further adds that he was very instrumental in delivering the English pulpit from the pedantry with which it had lately been overrun. This is the eulogium of a warm friend. His learning and piety is unquestioned; the excellence of his judgment is more than disputable. It was scarcely possible that a man should keep a clear head for the events of his time, who was so fascinated by the hopeless study of the Apocalyptic visions as to see mysterious import in every movement of Italian, Muscovite, and Turk, and who could be firmly persuaded that the years

---

[1] He left a large folio Bible, interleaved, with the blank leaves filled with remarks which overflowed even over the margins of the chapter. Queen Mary wanted him to publish it (Nichols' *Lit. Anecdotes*, iv. 731). His manuscript papers were prodigious in number, and Dr. Johnson says that they supplied his successor's kitchen at Lichfield with paper for many years (Noble's *Cont. of Grainger*, ii. 83). Burnet's *History of the Reformation* was mainly compiled from materials given to him by Lloyd (*Own Times*, p. 130, note). He was considered the most eminent chronologist of his time (Green's *Hist. of Worcester*, i. 219).

[2] Burnet's *Own Times*. p. 130.

between 1712 and 1716 would certainly inaugurate the millennium.[1]

Lloyd took an important part in the Declaration of 1688. It was he who headed the petition to King James; and one of the most vivid pictures in the story is that of the Bishop of St. Asaph, unable to escape from the multitude, who detained him in the palace yard and kissed his hands and very garments in an enthusiasm of delight, till he was rescued at last by Lord Clarendon, who drove him home in his carriage by a circuitous way.[2]

Lloyd was strongly in favour of King William, and his rather ingenious reasoning is said to have gained over to the new Government a great number of the clergy. A large proportion of them were wishful to transfer a more or less willing allegiance to the new dynasty. But how they could do so with a good conscience was a very perplexing matter to men who had been brought up all their lives in a firm belief in the dogmas of the divine right of kings, and the duty of passive obedience on the part of subjects. There was a means of escape from the difficulty, but it was one which in itself no Englishman would willingly resort to. If William had become king by right of conquest, their principles in no way forbade them to accept this as the divinely ordained answer to the solemn appeal of combat. It was a great national ordeal, in which Heaven was called upon to award victory to the right. Could this be fitly argued in the present case? Could it be shown, without violence to facts, and without wounding their susceptibility as citizens of a

---

[1] Burnet's *Own Times*, pp. 644-45, and note; Calamy's *Life*, ii. 383.

'Then old Mysterio shook his silver hairs,
  Laden with learning, prophecy, and years.'

—Shippen, quoted in Noble's *Cont. of Grainger*, ii. 83. 'I have heard,' said Whiston, 'Bishop Lloyd thank God for being able to read the prophecies as he could read history.'—Whiston's *Memoirs*, p. 33.

[2] Macaulay's *Hist.*, chap. viii.

free country, that William and his successors possessed this right? 'Yes,' answered Lloyd—and in their balanced state of feeling such reasoning brought light and relief— 'with relation to the people of England the Prince was indeed no conqueror, but a preserver and deliverer, well received, and gratefully acknowledged. But with relation to King James there had been, to every intent and purpose, an appeal to arms in a righteous war, and the decision of a higher Power had been given. The Prince's success against the King had given him the right of conquest over him, and by it all his rights were transferred to the victor.'[1] Such an argument was not one that would convince unwilling listeners, but was a welcome solution to Churchmen who had entangled themselves in their own theories, and only wished to be extricated from them.

Early in Queen Anne's reign, Lloyd's zeal for propagating his own political opinions showed itself in a more questionable form, and brought him into some disgrace. A formal complaint was laid before the House of Commons of his having used all his interest in Worcestershire to prevent Sir J. Pakington's election, and of having written a libellous letter on the subject. The new Tory majority took up the question hotly, and carried a resolution that the bishop's action had been 'malicious, unchristian, and arbitrary, in violation of the rights of the Commons,' and moved a request to the queen that he be removed from the post of High Almoner.[2] The letter had been rather intemperately worded, but there can be little doubt that the resolution was conceived almost entirely in the spirit of party.

Lloyd was more rigidly scrupulous than were some of his contemporaries as to whom he admitted into holy orders. A regular form of compact is still extant in which Sancroft, Ken, the two Lloyds, and Turner bound themselves toge-

[1] Burnet's *Own Times*, p. 523.   [2] *Parl. Hist.*, vii. 33.

ther, by solemn mutual consent in ten articles, by which all laxity on this point should be strenuously resisted.[1]

With the exception of Ken, not one of the seven bishops is so readily remembered as Sir Jonathan Trelawney, who was translated from Bristol to Exeter, and thence to Winchester (1685–1721). It is not that he was very memorable in his episcopal character. He was a good man, of competent learning and well versed in affairs, of ardent temper, open-hearted, generous, and charitable.[2] But his memory has been kept alive by his extreme popularity in Cornwall, where he was looked up to and reverenced as the worthy head of a very ancient Cornish family. Hence the vehement agitation of the miners when they heard of his being committed to the Tower. The echoes of the familiar doggrel, 'And shall Trelawney die?' not only sounded at the time from the far south-west to the most distant extremities of the island, but have lingered in remembrance through all the years that have elapsed from then till now. It is a curious instance of the strange vitality which sometimes attaches, without any very apparent reason, to snatches of old ballads, when the circumstances which originated them have long passed out of popular knowledge.

For some time before the crisis of the struggle Trelawney had taken an active part in the contention against Rome. Some words of his, written in days when none knew what extremity of peril for English Churchmen might not be near at hand, are well worthy of being quoted. They occur in a letter to Archbishop Sancroft, of which Ken was the bearer: 'No courage shall be wanting, . . . for my

[1] *Life of Ken*, by a Layman, p. 314. This care is referred to in his epitaph: 'In episcopali munere obeundo quam sollicitus fuerit, et indefessus, testentur quotquot ad ecclesiarum curam ab ipso sunt admissi.'— Browne Willis, *Cathedrals*, ii. 657.

[2] *Athenæ Oxonienses*, quoted in note to Burnet's *Own Times*, p. 816.

resolutions are entirely fixed not to do anything which may reflect on the honour or interest of the Church, in which as I had the blessing of initiation by the baptism of water, I am ready to go out of it with the other of blood.' [1]

Trelawney was sometimes charged with being a Jacobite in disguise, and with a political tergiversation which was entirely alien [2] to his truthful and manly character. At the time, however, of the Revolution he was greatly exercised as to the course he ought to take. His sentiment and decided Tory feeling was all on the side of James; his detestation of Rome, and love of liberty, inclined him more strongly to the other party. Eventually he gave a frank and hearty support to William, welcomed him at Bristol, and joined in drawing up the form of thanksgiving for the deliverance which had been effected.

It may be said of him, lastly, that he merited the gratitude of the Winchester boys by insisting, in his capacity of visitor, 'that there should be bed-makers appointed by the warden for them, and that they should be relieved from the servile office of making their own beds and keeping their chambers clean.' [3] He also required that during the winter half-year they should not be obliged to rise before six in the morning.

John Hough was a bishop for no less than fifty-three years, from 1690 to 1743, first of Oxford, then of Lichfield (1699), and afterwards of Worcester (1717). In 1715 he declined the primacy. Born three years before Cromwell had

---

[1] *Life of Ken*, by a Layman, p. 359. Atterbury spoke very highly of his 'zeal for the true faith of Christ, and for the dignity and honour of the priesthood.'—Williams' *Life of Atterbury*, i. 175.

[2] I see, however (Overton's *E. Ch.*, 1660-1714), that in some of his letters in the *Trelawney Papers* this bishop does not always appear in a very favourable light.

[3] *Life of Ken*, p. 9.

been made Protector, and living on till nearly the middle of the following century, he seemed to be a veritable patriarch of the Church, and held a reputation worthy of the name. Pope and Horace Walpole were about the last men of their day to spend their praise on any prelate; but the one speaks of 'Hough's unsullied mitre,' and the other of 'the good old bishop.'[1] Lord Lyttelton, both in his poems and in his 'Persian Letters,'[2] was enthusiastic in his admiration of 'good Wor'ster':

> He who in youth a tyrant's power defied,
> Firm and intrepid on his country's side,
> Her boldest champion then, and now her mildest guide!
> O generous warmth, O sanctity divine!
> To emulate his worth, my friend, be thine.[3]

In truth, he and another, scarcely younger, and no less venerated than he, Wilson, Bishop of Sodor and Man, must have seemed to Churchmen of the Georgian epoch like the survivors of a nobler age. With those two exceptions, the great names which at the beginning of the century did honour to the English episcopate had all passed away, and little was left to relieve the decent mediocrity which was all that the lethargy of the time allowed. There was, indeed, a vast contrast between the sluggish torpor of those days—Hoadly the most prominent figure in the Church, Walpole in the State—and the ferment and exaltation of feeling half a century before, when Hough and his fellows were expelled for defying James's illegal mandate, and Magdalen was 'stocked with Papists,' and a contest involving weighty consequences to religion and to liberty was seen to be drawing nearly and visibly to its issue.

Hough's character seems to have been a very beautiful

---

[1] H. Walpole's *Letters*, i. 278; quoted from Pope in note to *id*.
[2] Lyttelton's *Persian Letters*, No. 57.
[3] Lyttelton's *Poems*, 'To Dr. Ayscough.'

one, and remained unchanged throughout his long career. Even at the close of his life his conversation and letters had the cheerfulness and spirit of youth;[1] while the same sweet and calm piety which breathes throughout a letter to Lord Digby very shortly before his death was no less conspicuous in his earlier years. In all private relations he knew no distinctions of party: in public life he was so far a Whig and moderate Low Churchman that he did not altogether escape the imputation, so common among the hot-headed partisans of Queen Anne's time, of being 'an enemy to the Church.'[2] He rebutted the foolish charge with dignity and a seemly consciousness of desert.[3] Perhaps the worst that his High Church friends could truthfully say against him was that they were scandalised at 'his having made Friday his great day for treating strangers, &c.'[4] Tolerant measures of every kind always found a firm friend in him.[5] He lamented the bitterness which had lately risen up against Dissenters.[6] In the same spirit he complained of the great hardship of not giving toleration to the Episcopalians of Scotland. It was an unworthy truckling, he said, 'to the Presbyterian high-fliers, for the birds are common to both churches.'[7]

George Hooper was nominated to St. Asaph in 1702, and to Bath and Wells in 1703. Burnet, in that spirit of prejudice against his opponents which is the special blot upon his character, has spoken of him as 'reserved, crafty, and ambitious.'[8] These imputations were notoriously unjust. That he was not ambitious is sufficiently clear from his refusing both the bishopric of London and the

---

[1] Valentine Green's *Hist. of Worcester*, i. 213.
[2] *Parliamentary Hist.*, vi. 197.   [3] *Id.*
[4] *Reliquiæ Hearnianæ*, ii. 30.
[5] *Parl. Hist.*, vi. 163, 497, &c; Nicolson's *Correspondence*, p. 485.
[6] Stoughton's *Queen Anne*, p. 51.   [7] Nicolson, p. 399.
[8] Burnet's *Own Times*, p. 690.

primacies of York and Ireland.[1] But perhaps the gentle suavity of manner which contributed to endear him to his friends, and to the clergy of his diocese, may have seemed like craft to one as impatient of opposition as Burnet was. He was not only as warm a High Churchman[2] as Burnet was the contrary, but was also Prolocutor of the Convocation which condemned that prelate's book upon the Articles as lax and latitudinarian. He was a great friend of Ken, who was delighted[3] when he succeeded to his episcopal seat at Bath and Wells, as he had previously followed him in his rectory at Woodhay. The queen had begged the Nonjuring bishop himself to resume the charge from which he had been ejected, and Hooper had importuned him to consent. But Ken could not overcome the difficulties of the oath, and felt also that the infirmities of age were fast disabling him for active life. He returned, therefore, his grateful acknowledgments of the queen's favour, and besought God's blessing upon her, but added that 'he desired only to see his flock in good hands, and he knew none better to whom he might entrust it than Hooper's.'

Hooper lived a zealous, ascetic life, winning by it the praise even of Whiston, whom he had expelled as a heretic from the Holy Communion. He was a learned and polished man. His distinguished schoolmaster, Dr. Busby, had prophesied of him that he would be 'the best scholar, the finest gentleman, and the completest bishop ever educated at Westminster;' and that though he might be 'the least favoured in feature of any in the school, he would be the

---

[1] Noble's *Cont. of Grainger*, iii. 76.

[2] Though he always voted as a High Churchman in religion, and a Tory in politics, he was not a party man, and in the House of Lords lamented the use of the terms 'High' and 'Low' Church, as introducing invidious and injurious distinctions.—*Parl. Hist.*, vi. 698.

[3] *Life of Ken*, by a Layman, p. 703.

most extraordinary.'[1] Among other attainments he was an accomplished student of Oriental languages, a subject on which he kept up a frequent correspondence with his old master, Dean Pococke. In London, Jewish Rabbins often consulted him on difficult or interesting questions.[2]

Two very distinguished men, whose lives belong almost exclusively to a preceding age, were nevertheless not raised to the episcopate until the eighteenth century had begun. George Bull, born in 1634, spent the last few years of his life (1705-9) as Bishop of St. David's; William Beveridge, born in 1638, was Bishop of St. Asaph from 1704 to his death in 1707.

[3] Both in his lifetime and afterwards, Bull has always been held in deserved repute as one of the most illustrious names in the roll of English bishops. Robert Nelson called him 'a consummate divine,' and by no means stood alone in his opinion. Those who attach a high value to original and comprehensive thought will scarcely consider him entitled to such an epithet. He was a man of great piety, sound judgment, and extensive learning, but not of the grasp and power which signally influences a generation, and leaves a mark in the history of religious progress. He loved the Church of England with that earnestness of affection which in the seventeenth century specially characterised those who remembered its prostration and had shared its depressed fortunes. Dr. Skinner, ejected Bishop of Oxford, had admitted him into orders at the early age of twenty-one. The canon, he said, could not be strictly observed in such times of difficulty and distress. They were not days when the Church could afford to wait for the services of so zealous

---

[1] Mist's *Journal*, Oct. 11, 1723; quoted in Nichols' *Lit. An.*, iv. 570.

[2] *Life of Ken*, p. 78.

[3] The account of Bishops Bull and Beveridge are taken almost *verbatim* from what I had previously written in the chapter on Robert Nelson and his friends, in *The English Church of the Eighteenth Century.* pp. 123-26

and able an advocate. He proved an effective champion against all its real and presumed adversaries, Puritans and Nonconformists, Roman Catholics, Latitudinarians, and Socinians. An acute controversialist, skilled in the critical knowledge of Scripture, thoroughly versed in the annals of primitive antiquity, he was an opponent not lightly to be challenged. A devoted adherent of the English Church, scrupulously observant of all its rites and usages, and convinced as of 'a certain and evident truth that the Church of England is in her doctrine, discipline, and worship most agreeable to the primitive and apostolical institution,'[1] his only idea of improvement and reform in Church matters was to remove distinct abuses, and to restore ancient discipline. Yet he was not so completely the High Churchman as to be unable to appreciate and enter to some extent into the minds of those who within his own Church had adopted opposite views. He used to speak, for example, with the greatest respect of Dr. Conant, a distinguished Churchman of Puritan views, who had been his rector at Exeter College, and whose instructions and advice had made, he said, very deep impression on him.[2] So, on the other hand, although a strenuous opponent of Rome, he did not fail to discriminate and do justice to what was catholic and true in her system. And it tells favourably for his candour, that while he defended Trinitarian doctrine with unequalled force and learning, he should have had to defend himself against a charge of Arian tendencies,[3] solely because he did not withhold authorities which showed that the primitive fathers did

---

[1] Speech before the House of Lords, 1705; Nelson's *Life of Bull*, p. 355.
[2] Nelson's *Life of Bull*, p. 11. Archdeacon Conant stood very high in Tillotson's estimation as a man 'whose learning, piety, and thorough knowledge of the true principles of Christianity would have adorned the highest station.' Birch's *Life of Tillotson*; *Works*, i. ccxii.
[3] Nelson's *Life of Bull*, pp. 243–49; Dorner's *Prot. Theology*, ii. 83.

not always hold very defined views upon the subject. His most notable and unique distinction consisted in the thanks he received, through Bossuet, from the whole Gallican Church[1] for his defence of the Nicene faith; his most practical service to religion was the energetic protest of his 'Harmonia Apostolica,' in favour of a healthy and fruitful faith, in opposition to the Antinomian doctrines of arbitrary grace, which, at the time when he published his Apostolic Harmony, had become most widely prevalent in England.

Bull had been ordained at twenty-one; he was consecrated in 1705 Bishop of St. David's, at the almost equally exceptional age of seventy. He succeeded a bad man, who had been expelled from his see for glaring simony; and it was felt, not without justice, that the cause of religion and the honour of the episcopate would gain more by the elevation of a man of the high repute in which Bull was universally held, than it would lose by the growing infirmities of his old age. He accepted the dignity with hesitation, in hopes that his son, the Archdeacon of Llandaff, who, however, died before him, would be able greatly to assist him in the discharge of his duties. But he was determined that if he could not be as active as he could wish, he would at all events reside strictly in his diocese.

Beveridge, Bull's contemporary at St. Asaph, 1704-7, was a man of much the same stamp. Both were divines of great theological learning; but while Bull's great talents were chiefly conspicuous in his controversial and argumentative works, Beveridge was chiefly eminent as a student and devotional writer.[2] His ' Private Thoughts on Religion and

---

[1] Burnet's *Own Times*, 767. He calls it 'the most learned treatise that this age had produced.'— *Id.*

[2] Of his argumentative writings, Noble (*Cont. of Grainger*, ii. 92) says that they are weak and not always orthodox, and that they should not have

Christian Life,' and his papers on 'Public Prayers' and 'Frequent Communions,' have always maintained a high reputation; and his 'Excellency of the Book of Common Prayer' had, in 1788, already passed the twenty-eighth edition. Like Bull, he was profoundly read in the history of the primitive Church, but possessed an accomplishment which his brother bishop had not, in his understanding of several Oriental languages.[1] Like him, he had been an active and experienced parish clergyman;[2] and, like him, he was attached almost to excess to a strict and rigid observance of the appointed order of the English Church. It was to him that Dean Tillotson addressed the often-quoted words, 'Doctor, Doctor, charity is above rubrics.'[3] Yet it must not be inferred, therefore, that he was stiffly set against all change. In a sermon preached before Convocation, at their very important meeting of 1689, he had remarked of ecclesiastical laws other than those which are fundamental and eternal, 'that they ought not indeed to be altered without grave reasons, but that such reasons were not at that moment wanting. To unite a scattered flock in one fold under one shepherd, to remove stumbling-blocks from the path of the weak, to reconcile hearts long estranged, to restore spiritual discipline to its primitive vigour, to place the best and purest of Christian societies on a base broad enough to stand against all the attacks of earth and hell, these were objects which might well justify

---

been published. Dodsley, also, in his *Art of Preaching* (p. 254), speaks disparagingly of them, and calls him 'jingling Beveridge.'

[1] One of his publications is a Syriac Grammar in three books (Noble, *id.*); another was on 'The Excellence of the Oriental Languages.'

[2] His contemporary, Denis Granville, spoke of 'the piety and indefatigable diligence of the renowned Dr. Beveridge;' and added that 'the devout practice and order of his church doth exceedingly edify the city, and his congregation increases every week.'—Quoted in Overton's *Life in the E. Ch.* (1660-1714), p. 77.

[3] Birch's *Life of Tillotson*, lxxxviii.

some modification, not of catholic institutions, but of national and provincial usages.'[1]

Beveridge was one of the bishops for whom the moderate Nonjurors had much regard. In most respects he was of their school of thought; and although, like Wilson of Sodor and Man, and Hooper of Bath and Wells, he had not scrupled for his own part to take the oath of allegiance to William and Mary, he fully understood the reasonings of those who did. He greatly doubted the legality and right of appointing new bishops to sees not canonically vacant, so that when he was nominated in the place of Ken, he after some deliberation declined the office.[2]

The pathetic earnestness of his sermons is said to have been particularly impressive. An eminent layman, his contemporary, who speaks of him as 'a pattern of true primitive piety,' says of them that 'he had a way of gaining people's hearts and touching their consciences which bore some resemblance to the apostolic age,' and that he could mention many 'who owed the change of their lives, under God, to his instructions.'[3]

In the period that followed upon the Restoration, Beveridge had taken a prominent part with Dr. Horneck and others in the formation of religious societies among young men, and had won many from lax and dissolute ways.[4] In the beginning of the eighteenth century he took great interest in the proceedings of the Christian Knowledge Society, and left to it the greater part of his property. It was his special care that through its means religious publications should be circulated among the Welsh in their own language.[5]

---

[1] 'Concio ad Synodum,' quoted by Macaulay, *H. of E.*, chap. xiv.
[2] *Life of Ken*, by a Layman, pp. 591-97.
[3] Nelson's *Life of Bull*, p. 65.   [4] Curteis on Dissent, p. 348.
[5] Secretan's *Life of Nelson*, pp. 111-12.

No name in the long history of the English episcopate is more honourable than that of Thomas Wilson.[1] For no less than fifty-nine years, from 1696 to 1755, he administered the see of Sodor and Man in a way which excited, as it well might, the amazement and admiration of all Churchmen to whom his fame was known. Nor was his repute confined to England. Cardinal Fleury, shortly before his death in 1743, sent a special messenger to him. He had heard, he said, about him, and he felt the more interest in the account because they were the oldest, and he believed also the two poorest bishops in Europe. He hoped that it might be possible he would accept an invitation from him, and pay him a visit in France. Fleury likewise procured an order that no French privateer—for the war of the Austrian succession was then at its height—should ravage the Isle of Man. Queen Anne and George I. both offered him English bishoprics, and Queen Caroline was specially anxious to keep him in England. 'Nay,' said the bishop, 'I will not leave my wife in my old age, because she is poor.'[2] In his own diocese he was honoured with a reverence which sometimes almost bordered upon superstition. 'The people of the island,' one of his biographers writes, 'were so thoroughly persuaded of his receiving a larger portion of God's blessing, that they seldom began harvest till he did; and if he passed along the field, they would leave their work to ask his blessing, assured that that day would be prosperous. Nor was this opinion confined to the obscure corner of the world where he lived. In Warrington,

---

[1] Cruttwell's *Life of Wilson* has been my principal authority for what is mentioned in this sketch. I was not till afterwards aware of Keble's more elaborate work in two large volumes. Cruttwell was a physician, who was so impressed by the biography of Wilson which he was publishing, that he changed his profession and became a clergyman.—Keble's *Life of Wilson*, pref. xvii.

[2] Cruttwell, p. 228.

even in London, there are those who can remember crowds of persons flocking round him, with the cry of "Bless me too, my lord."'[1]

Two things are particularly worthy of record in Wilson's earlier life, while he was yet a young clergyman. At a time when chaplains in great houses—mess-Johns, as they were sometimes contemptuously called—often occupied a position of which South said that 'he who serves at the altar has generally as much disdain as he who serves in the kitchen,' Wilson, alike to his own honour and to that of the Earl of Derby, was always the revered and trusted friend. At a time when pluralities and non-residence were a growing scandal and reproach to the Church, Wilson made a fixed resolution, which he steadily adhered to, 'never to accept two Church livings, though ever so conveniently seated, nor trust to others what ought to be my own particular care.'

The Church Constitution for the Isle of Man, as framed by the bishop, agreed to by the clergy in Convocation, ratified by the Earl of Derby, and published in the Tinwald Court, 1704, would, under any circumstances, have been a very remarkable one. Compared with the general ecclesiastical surroundings of England in the eighteenth century, it seems almost like a strange anachronism that it should have been through so many years a vigorous working reality. But the isolation of his little island diocese gave full scope to the authority which Wilson commanded through the love and reverence of his people. He was also greatly helped by his constitutional position. In the Isle of Man the early English usage still prevailed which had been universal in the old days of Alfred and Edgar. The bishop, or his deputy, sat in the great court along with the Governor. He withdrew only in capital cases; the question which

[1] Cruttwell, p. 228.

the dempster put to the jury being not 'Guilty or not guilty?' but 'May the man of the Chancel continue to sit?'[1]

The system of Church discipline to which, under Bishop Wilson's guidance, the Manxmen submitted themselves was something like that of a Moravian settlement, or of Paraguay under its missionary fathers, or, in some respects, of Geneva under Calvin's rule. All parents and masters of families were rigorously fined who did not send their children and unconfirmed servants to the regular catechising at evening service. None might be admitted as sponsors or to matrimony who had not been confirmed, and had not received the holy Sacrament. The rubric of unworthy receivers was to be religiously observed, and ministers admitting such were to be severely censured. Commutation for penance and other ecclesiastical penalties was to cease. Penance was to be strictly enforced in its fullest primitive form. 'After censure and penance no person, upon incurring the same censure a second time, shall be admitted to absolution until the Church is satisfied of his sincere repentance; during which time he shall not persevere to come within the church, but shall stand in a decent manner at the church door every Sunday and holiday the whole time of morning and evening service, until, by his penitent behaviour and other instances of sober living, he deserve and procure a certificate from the minister's churchwardens, and some of the soberest men of the parish, to the satisfaction of the ordinary; which if he do not deserve and procure within three months, the Church shall proceed to excommunication. And during these proceedings the Governor shall be applied to not to permit him to leave the island. And this being a matter of very great importance, the ministers and churchwardens shall see it duly performed,

[1] Cruttwell. p. 379.

under penalty of the severest ecclesiastical censures.' On the last Sunday of every month the names were to be set down of those who, without just cause, absented themselves from church, who neglected to send their children and servants to be catechised, or their children to school.'

With these and similar regulations the see of Man was administered throughout Wilson's lengthened episcopate. It is not to be supposed that such a system of Church discipline could be carried out in its integrity without occasional difficulties of a serious kind. On one occasion the wife of the Governor was put to open penance for a gross slander. The archdeacon of the island, who was also the Governor's chaplain, received her to Holy Communion, upon which the Bishop at once suspended him. The Governor then charged the bishop with illegal conduct, and, upon his refusal to pay a fine, committed him to prison; and though the Council, upon appeal, reversed this sentence, Wilson was meanwhile under close confinement for no less than nine weeks. We find, also, laments of the pernicious books and principles introduced, and of the 'evils arising from inroads upon the excellence of our discipline and the willing submission to it.' But except on occasional instances, the ecclesiastical constitution seems to have been willingly submitted to and substantially carried out. Mackay, travelling in the island about twenty years after it had been set on foot, speaks of the 'penances imposed on all offenders without distinction, and generally done patiently.'[1] He adds that when he was there the people did not often reckon time by the hours of the day, but by the 'Tra Sherveish,' or service-times, namely, nine in the morning and three in the evening. A person would say it was an hour or two hours before or after service-time. His biographer tells us, what otherwise we should hardly have expected,

[1] Mackay's *Journey through England*, ii. 241.

that 'he was a great friend of toleration. The Roman Catholics in the island loved and esteemed him, and not unfrequently attended his sermons and his prayers. The Dissenters, too, attended even the communion service, as he had allowed them a liberty to sit or stand, which, however, they did not make use of. A few Quakers who resided in the island held him in great honour.' As for the Moravian brotherhood, Tyerman records that he was so respected by that community as to be chosen 'Antecessor of their General Synod.'[1] It was only against opinions suspected of a rationalising tendency that his wide-hearted charity was closed.

Wilson's 'Sacra Privata' is well known as a valuable devotional work. In the life of that excellent man, General Oglethorpe, there is a letter from him to the bishop, praising warmly a manual which he had written at his request to be translated for the use of the Indians.[2]

Though Francis Atterbury was not raised to the episcopate till he succeeded Spratt at Rochester (1713–23), his name is very prominent throughout the first twenty years of the century. The fame which he had won at Oxford for wit and talent and great command of language followed him to London, where he was appointed lecturer at St. Bride's in 1691, chaplain to William and Mary in 1694, and preacher at the Rolls in 1698. Among the many distinguished preachers who adorned the London pulpits of that period, none held a place superior in general estimation to that of Atterbury. Leading men of every party thronged to the Chapel Royal to listen to his persuasive reasonings and impassioned appeals, adorned with every grace of voice and gesture. The testimony of the Jacobite Duke of Wharton is naturally a favourable one. But in what he

---

[1] Tyerman's *Oxford Methodists*, p. 188.
[2] Wright's *Life of Gen. Oglethorpe*, p. 90.

says of his speech, 'as honey sweet, as soft as heavenly dew,' of his forcible expression, of his 'manly sense in easy language dressed,'[1] he does but repeat the praise with which Steele in the 'Tatler' points his satire on the heavy, lifeless manner of preaching too prevalent among the clergy of his day.[2] Doddridge, dwelling upon the beauty and purity of his language, calls him 'the glory of English orators.'[3]

Atterbury's later Jacobitism sometimes brought upon him the charge of disloyalty to his Church no less than to the established dynasty. 'While we were in the church,' wrote Thoresby in 1723, 'there was a mighty shout in the street, which we were told was upon the Bishop of Rochester passing by, some crying out, "No Popish bishop! no English cardinal!" But the guards restrained them as much as possible. From mobs of all sorts, libera nos, Domine.'[4] There was no real ground for the imputation. He was, indeed, among the highest of High Churchmen; but, like other High Churchmen of that period, he was a firm and thorough Protestant. Towards the close of the seventeenth century he had joined with ardour in the controversy against Rome, and one of his literary works was a warm defence of Luther against the attacks of Roman polemical writers. It is told of him that he made various efforts to gain over to Protestantism Pope, who, like most other eminent literary men of Queen Anne's time, was one of his friends and frequent associates. Even in his later days, when he was living in exile as a banished man in the daily company of Roman Catholics, he asserted that he would rather die at the stake than abandon the principles of the Church of England.

---

[1] Wharton's *Poems*, quoted in F. Williams's *Memoirs, &c., of Atterbury*, i. 314. [2] *Tatler*, No. 66.
[3] Williams, p. 71. [4] Thoresby's *Diary*, ii. 377.

As opposed to the Whig and Latitudinarian Churchmen, who were particularly strong on the Episcopal bench, Atterbury was one of the straitest of his party. His enemies called him 'a fiery and factious bigot.'[1] He was made Prolocutor of Convocation, and none pressed with such vehemence as he for all the utmost rights of the assembly of which he was the chief representative, and of that mass of indignant clerics[2] who complained that they were misrepresented and betrayed by the very men who should be their fathers and guides. It was he who chiefly composed Sacheverell's defence. It was he who drew up the most violent protests of discontented peers in Parliament. Clarke and Whiston, and all leaders of the heterodox, found in him their most uncompromising opponent. He abstained, it is true, so long as Anne was upon the throne, from lending much countenance to that 'Church in danger' cry which proved so effectual in fanning the flames of ecclesiastical and political partisanship. But so soon as the Queen was dead, the new-made prelate was vehement with voice and pen in denouncing the ungodly league of Whig politicians and Whig bishops to subvert the constitution of the Church and confuse its doctrines.

It is not to be wondered at that Atterbury incurred strong hostility on the part of his opponents. Burnet could not bear with a man who, he allowed, had great learning and extraordinary parts, but whom he accused of being 'ambitious and virulent out of measure, with a singular talent in asserting paradoxes with a great air of assurance, and showing no shame when he was detected in

---

[1] *Gentleman's Magazine* for 1750, p. 406.

[2] He was almost idolised by many of the extreme High Church party, and 'in the Tower received more homage than is often paid to the Crown' (Noble's *Cont. of Grainger*, iii. 82).

them.'[1] Hoadly, whose whole tone of mind was entirely opposite to his, pursued him with a dogged pertinacity of opposition, which gave occasion to a witty quotation. It was said of him, in allusion to his lameness,—

> Raro antecedentem scelestum
> Deseruit pede pœna claudo.[2]

Whether it were a sermon, or a pamphlet, or a treatise; whether the subject were passive obedience, or the rights of Convocation, or the power of charity to cover sins, or the temporal rewards of virtue;—no sooner had Atterbury published, than it might be reasonably expected that Hoadly was preparing his 'Exceptions,' or his 'Remarks,' or his more elaborate Confutation of certain arguments used by his eloquent adversary. Such opposition was fair enough; but Hoadly did himself little credit when he joined, with what appeared a personal animosity, in the outcry that attended Atterbury's fall. There was a not unmerited sting in Lord Bathurst's taunt when he turned to the Bench and said that 'he could hardly account for the inveterate hatred and malice some persons bore to the learned and ingenious Bishop of Rochester, unless they were intoxicated with the infatuation of the wild Indians, who fondly believe they inherit not only the spoils but the abilities of every great enemy they kill.'[3]

Atterbury's Jacobitism did not take any very overt form until the accession of George the First. So long as Anne was reigning, it was quite possible to be both a Jacobite and a loyal subject. But he was one of a considerable party with whom allegiance to the daughter of James was not lightly to be transferred to an alien ruler in whom the blood of the royal martyr did not flow. Even among the great body of

[1] Burnet's *Own Times*, p. 671.   [2] Bp. Newton's *Life and Works*, p. 12.
[3] *Parl. Hist.*, viii. 333.

the people the memory of Charles the First was held in affectionate and pitying remembrance. Their attachment to the Protestant succession was by far the stronger feeling. But if the grandson of Charles could have been induced by the urgent persuasions of his English followers to be so untrue to his convictions as to give even a dissembling adherence to Anglican tenets, he would probably have succeeded Anne without a struggle.

Meanwhile, apart from Nonjurors and open Jacobites, there were many men—and some of them high in power—who would have rejoiced, even without conditions, to hail a Stuart for their king. Their number had greatly increased in the latter part of Queen Anne's reign. Atterbury was one of them. The story (though its authenticity is not certain) is well known how, immediately on the Queen's demise, he proposed to Bolingbroke to proclaim James at Charing Cross, and to head the procession in his lawn sleeves, and how, when Bolingbroke shrank from the enterprise as desperate, Atterbury exclaimed, 'There is the best cause in Europe lost for want of spirit!'[1] His Jacobitism was not quite that of the Nonjurors, who felt that a transfer of allegiance was prohibited them by the sacred obligations of religion. Neither was it quite that of the many country gentlemen who could not bear the break in the old succession, and hated the Whig settlement and the German dynasty. If Atterbury could have persuaded himself that the Church would be as safe under George as it had been under Anne, he would have engaged in no Jacobite plots. But it is evident that he was full of alarm at what might happen under the new rule. Not one man in the kingdom would have been so rapturously delighted if the Pretender had renounced his Roman Catholic opinions. But as this was not to be, he became convinced that it was far better for

[1] Mahon's *England from the Peace of Utrecht*, chap. iv.

Church and State that Tory and High Church principles should flourish under a Papist king, than that dogmas which he abominated should triumph under a Protestant succession. When, two or three years before, he had drawn up, at the request of the Lower House of Convocation, a 'Representation of the Present State of Religion,' he had not disguised the gloomy forebodings with which he looked abroad. And now it appeared to him that such forebodings were being indeed realised. The venerable assembly of which he had been the champion was prorogued and silenced; impugners of received doctrines were permitted to vent their blasphemies ('for I cannot,' he said, 'give the tenets of Mr. Whiston, or even of Dr. Clarke, a softer name'[1]) without punishment or rebuke; schismatics were lifting up their heads, and were already clamorous to be released from the restraints which 'the wholesome policy of our good queen' had so lately imposed; the Bishops' Bench would be more than ever replenished with traitors in whose hands the bulwarks of the Church would be yielded to the enemy; the gracious edifice itself, tampered with and betrayed, would lose all its fair distinctiveness, and be handed over to the mercies of Arians and heretics, Presbyterians and Dutch Protestants. Such, with little exaggeration, were the fears which drove Atterbury into Jacobite intrigues.

But plots and intrigues flourish in an air very unfavourable to rectitude and high principle, and Atterbury's virtue was not proof against the temptations which now beset it. He was not disposed to be a martyr to the cause he cherished; and when he saw the unsparing severity practised against men who, by overt act, or even by carefully worded doubts, disputed the legality of George the First's title to the crown, he was only too ready to make use of all

[1] Atterbury to Trelawney, Williams, i. 175.

the dissembling artifices of conspirators. There may still be a faint shadow of question as to the genuineness of Atterbury's letters in the Stuart correspondence. But if, as is almost universally agreed,[1] they are authentic, it is certain that a dark blot of dissimulation and falsehood must rest upon this latter period of his life.[2] Such conduct can be but slightly palliated by a consideration of the extreme difficulty of the position in which the death of Queen Anne had placed him, and by the fact that political virtue was at this time corrupted and undermined, even in the highest quarters, by an utter decay of loyalty. It was a period when it might appear that no professions of sincerity could anywhere be trusted in those who took any part in the intricate politics of the day. Painful as it is to read Atterbury's strong disavowals of complicity in machinations into which his whole energy was thrown, it is some satisfaction to know that, although he sacrificed truth to the fear of death or disgrace, he at all events did not yield to those more sordid temptations under which so many of his contemporaries fell. Had he given way to the solicitations of Walpole and Sunderland, both of whom thoroughly recognised his great abilities, he might not only have avoided banishment and poverty, but could have obtained from them ampler revenues and high promotion.[3]

If we could but forget Atterbury's protestations of injured innocence, or if we could believe, notwithstanding

---

[1] Overton in *The E. Ch. of the Eighteenth Cent.*, i. 101-2. Warburton says that even Pope, Atterbury's devoted admirer, was before his death convinced of his Jacobite intrigues (Note to *Parl. Hist.*, viii. 271).

[2] Secure as Atterbury's fame is for eloquence and wit, posterity is far enough from endorsing what Samuel Wesley declared would be the judgment of posterity —

> 'Thou still shalt live, to deathless fame consigned -
> Live like the best and bravest of mankind.'
> (*Elegy on Atterbury*, Williams, ii. 468.)

[3] Williams, *Memoirs, &c., of Atterbury*, i. 129.

the evidence, that up to the time of his trial he had kept aloof from actual conspiracy, we should feel nothing but pity for this distinguished prelate in his exile. It was a sad conclusion to a life in which high abilities, generous affections, and unwearied energy had been lavishly spent in the cause, as he believed, of his country and his Church. An alien among strangers who looked upon his countrymen as enemies and upon his creed as heresy, he saw month by month his hopes dwindling away, and the cause he had attached himself to wrecking itself by incompetence and neglect. Paltry jealousies were rife in the factitious Court of the Pretender, and before long the unfortunate bishop found himself neglected and cast over by the worthless Prince for whom he had made such unsparing sacrifices. In his declining years he began at last to long for rest.[1] But he was too valuable an ally for such rest to be permitted him, and the air of intrigue in which he had lived so long encompassed him to the end. He became ill; but it was only after humble solicitations and heavy payments that his daughter was at length permitted to visit him. And when he died, although his bones were suffered to rest in the great Abbey which he had so often adorned by his eloquence, the indignity was offered to his remains of careful search, in the fear that traitorous papers might perchance lurk within his coffin.

With Atterbury might be closed the list of the more distinguished names which gave lustre to the English episcopate in the reign of Anne. There are, however, several men of note among those who yet remain to be mentioned.

Thomas Sprat was Atterbury's predecessor at Rochester from 1684 to 1713. An elegant scholar and an accomplished

[1] Pope had urged him to use his exile for some great literary work (Bp. Newton's *Life*, p. 14).

preacher, a writer whose prose composition is notable for the purity and excellence of its style, a friend of scientific inquiry, and Fellow and Historian of the Royal Society, a man, moreover, of polished address and marked conversational power—he maintained with ease a certain prominence of position. But his elevation to the episcopate was a mistake, or rather it was a relic of the careless days which followed upon the Restoration. For he had been made a bishop by Charles the Second, whom he had attended for some time as chaplain.[1] He was a courtier both by nature and habit, of easy and indolent good temper, and far too skilful in trimming and veering to every political gale. In early manhood he had culled every figure of rhetoric to extol in ambitious dithyrambics[2] the unequalled fame of the great Protector. Afterwards he was a zealous Royalist, and in his romancing history of the Rye House Plot was no less effusive in his praises of the King than he had been of Cromwell before. In James the Second's time he was not ashamed to act in that ecclesiastical commission by which the king sought to stifle the freedom of the subject and the liberties of the Church; and though the paper trembled in his hand, and his voice was drowned by angry murmurs

---

[1] He had been, before he was made a bishop, the chaplain and confidential friend of the Duke of Buckingham, who delighted in his wit and readiness. An anecdote is told that the first time he dined as a young man at his patron's table the duke observed a goose near him, and remarked that he wondered why it generally happened that geese were placed near the clergy. 'I cannot tell the reason,' said Sprat, 'but I shall never see a goose again without thinking of your Grace' (Noble's *Cont. of Grainger*, ii. 83).

[2] Thus, for example, to take half a dozen lines almost by chance:—

'Thy only sword did guard the land,
   Like that which, flaming in the angel's hand,
      From men God's garden did defend.
      But yet thy sword did more than this,
   Not only guarded but did make this land a paradise.'

Sprat's *Poems*, 'To the Happy Memory of the Lord Protector,' stanza ix.

and by the noise of people hastening from the choir,[1] he had ventured to read in Westminster Abbey the Declaration which brought the struggle to a crisis. It cannot be reckoned to his discredit that he deserted James when he showed himself bent on pushing matters to extremities. At all events, at the Revolution he took the new oaths without hesitation, joined with Burnet, Lloyd, and Compton in the coronation of William and Mary, and drew up those sentences in the Service for November 5 which express the gratitude of the Church for the second great deliverance wrought on that day.[2] An attempt was made a few years after to involve him in a charge of treasonable designs. But it signally failed, and Sprat yearly celebrated his deliverance by a solemn day of thanksgiving.[3] The latter part of his life was, indeed, more exemplary than the earlier. The worldliness by which his talents and high ecclesiastical position had been so grievously sullied seems to have passed away, nor does there seem any reason to doubt what is said of him, that from the beginning of the century to his death in 1713, his life was spent in the quiet, beneficent, and pious discharge of his pastoral duties.

John Hall, Bishop of Bristol from 1691 to 1710, was to some extent a representative man, as being a decided Puritan. He was the only bishop upon the Bench of a school of thought which once numbered so many distinguished names in the English hierarchy. Perhaps it may even be said that he was the last of his race. Low Church bishops, as the term was understood in that era, abounded to a somewhat disproportionate extent: and later in the century there were some excellent men in the Episcopate who were deeply interested in the Evangelical movement. But in the time of Anne and the Georges, the old Puritan

---

[1] Macaulay, chap. viii. [2] Macaulay, chap. xviii.
[3] Johnson's *Lives of the Poets* (Sprat).

type,[1] though it lingered on, no doubt, among individual Churchmen far more largely than was apparent from any outward indication, was fast becoming obsolete in the public life of the English Church. In John Hall of Bristol it survived, but with none of the energy which had fired the Puritanism of a previous age. He was a good man, and the old-fashioned form which his piety had taken, while it stirred the mirth of some, was honoured and venerated by others.[2] But he lived the life of a scholar only and a recluse. In those days, and for long afterwards, it was unfortunately considered not inconsistent with the functions of a bishop that he should also be the head of a college in one of the universities. It was so with Hall, who was apt to let his episcopal duties at Bristol fall into neglect, while he pursued the quiet tenor of his way at Oxford,[3] uncon-

---

[1] Thus J. Scott, in his excellent work on the Christian Life, published towards the end of the seventeenth century, in a section upon brightness in religion, speaks of the many Christians of his time who held that their faith was 'an enemy to mirth and cheerfulness, and a severe exactor of pensive looks and solemn faces,' people who 'retire themselves from the most innocent pleasure and festivities of conversation' (*Christian Life*, chap. iv.). So De Foe, *id.*, 1701, of men 'rigid and zealous, positive and grave; And every grace but charity they have' ('True-born Englishman,' *Works*, xx. 26). Thoresby was a singular mixture of the Puritan and High Churchman. Thus he speaks of cards as 'a wicked diversion' (*Diary*, i. 183); and on December 31, 1713, 'was disturbed with foolish, or rather sinful, mummers, and was perhaps too zealous to suppress them' (*id.*, ii. 188). Mrs. Oliphant remarks on a similar combination of Puritanism and High Church feeling in the Wesley family (*Sketches of the Reign of George II.*, p. 20). It was, however, very long before the general aversion to Puritanism which had set in with the Restoration began gradually to abate. 'Nearly half a century of licence had not dimmed the hatred with which men thought of a government that had undertaken to repress vice by penal laws' (Wedgwood's *Wesley*, p. 116). By the middle of the century religious men began once more to recognise the nobler elements of Puritanism, and even to vindicate a revived use of the term. Thus James Hervey in 1748: 'Is it Puritanical? Be not ashamed of the name' (*Works*, pp. 6, 24).

[2] Stoughton's *Church of the Rev.*, p. 306.

[3] Burnet's *Own Times*, pp. 5, 9. 'He was a scholar,' says Noble, 'and a pious divine; but known more in than out of Oxford' (*Cont. of Grainger*, i. 102).

scious, as it seemed, that an exemplary private life of study and religion did not compensate for the omission of the duties for which he had been specially appointed to be a ruler in the National Church. It was somewhat ominous of a coming period of inactivity that he should have been contemplated by many as a proper person to succeed [1] Tenison in the Primacy.

John Williams, Bishop of Chichester from 1696–1709, was a great friend of Tillotson, and is highly spoken of in one of the Archbishop's letters, as 'one of the best men I know, and most unwearied in doing good, and his preaching very weighty and judicious.'[2] As Lecturer at St. Mildred's, Poultry, he had held a worthy place among the most eminent of the London clergy. In the controversies of the time he took a considerable part—first against Rome; then, in his Boyle Lectures, against the Deists[3]; lastly, in that friendly discussion with Dissenters entitled a 'Collection of Cases,' in which most of the leading Churchmen of the time took part, and which passed through several editions, and attracted much attention.[4] He wrote also the second part of 'The Whole Duty of Man.'[5]

Offspring Blackhall, Bishop of Exeter[6] from 1707 to 1716, had been, like Williams, a London preacher and Boyle Lecturer.[7] He wrote against Toland upon the authenticity of Scripture, and against Hoadly on the question of Nonresistance.[8] But he was chiefly known by his sermons, which were for some time much read and commended as 'rational, instructive, and familiar.'[9] They were published in two folios by Archbishop Dawes, who prefaced them

[1] Kennet, quoted in Perry, pp. 3, 95. [2] Birch's *Life of Tillotson*, i. 149.
[3] *Id.*, pp. 151–52. [4] Hunt's *Religious Thought in England*, ii. 149–54.
[5] Skeats' *Hist. of the Free Churches*, pp. 225–26.
[6] Dallaway's *History of Sussex*, i. 93. [7] Hunt, iii. 103–5.
[8] Lathbury's *Hist. of the Nonjurors*, p. 231.
[9] Dean Stanhope, in Nichols' *Lit. Anec.*, iv. 168.

with a high panegyric upon the writer. 'I,' he said, 'who had the happiness of a long and intimate friendship with him, do sincerely declare that in my whole conversation I never met with a more perfect pattern of a true Christian life than in him.'[1] Though eventually he gave in his adhesion to King William and became one of his chaplains, he is said to have been a Nonjuror for two years.[2] Like many other Churchmen, he acquiesced in the validity of the new Government, while he looked back with affectionate memory to the period when the Stuarts were yet firm upon the throne. He wrote warmly in defence of the arguments which ascribed to Charles the authorship of the 'Eikon Basiliké,' and did not cease to maintain strongly the essentially divine origin of civil government, and the duty of non-resistance.

Sir William Dawes was Bishop of Chester from 1707 to 1714, and Archbishop of York[3] from 1714 to 1724. He had taken orders at a time when few men of high family did so except from the highest motives, 'putting aside the elegance of dress for the ecclesiastical habit with the greatest pleasure in the world, and looking upon holy orders as the highest honour that could be conferred upon him.'[4] Without being a man of transcendent ability, he was universally spoken of in terms of the highest esteem. Archbishop Sharp,[5] Bishop Wilson of Sodor and Man,[6] Dr. Waterland,[7] and Doctor Johnson of Connecticut,[8] one of the

---

[1] Note in Burnet's *Own Times*, p. 817.

[2] Perry's *Church History*, iii. 199.

[3] Queen Anne nominated both Dawes and Blackhall as High Tories, without consulting her ministers (Alison's *Life of Marlborough*, i. 351, 359).

[4] Noble's *Cont. of Grainger*, i. 78.   [5] *Life of Sharp*, i. 332.

[6] Cruttwell's *Life of Wilson*, p. 101.

[7] Waterland spoke of him as 'that watchful guardian of the Christian faith' (Van Mildert's *Life of Waterland*, 309).

[8] Beardsley's *Life of Johnson*, p. 28; so also *Hardships of the Inferior Clergy*, 1722, p. 18.

most honoured names in the American Episcopal Church, may be mentioned among those of his contemporaries who have recorded their high opinion of his worth. He was one of the celebrated preachers [1] of his time; though it may be that some part of his popularity in the pulpit was owing to 'a majestic personage and a sweet engaging manner.' [2] In politics he was a strong Tory, and fell at one time into some disgrace with the Whig Government for his staunch advocacy of the Divine right of kings. If his vote was usually given on the intolerant side,[3] his private letters make it very clear how high and pure were his motives. The supposed danger of the Church, and the 'wicked spirit' which he believed to be 'rife,' pressed heavily upon his mind, and led him frequently to such aspirations as these: 'God grant that all orders of men amongst us may grow wiser and better, and especially that our order may be most exemplarily wise and good.' 'God make us all, and especially the clergy, prudent and wise in our zeal for the Church, in proportion at least to the lessening of its outward legal securities.' [4]

Charles Trimnell was Bishop of Norwich from 1707 to 1721, and of Winchester from 1721 to 1723. In those days of violent party spirit, it was something to say of a bishop that 'even the Tories valued him, though he preached terrible Whig sermons.' [5] But though ardently attached to the principles of the Revolution [6] he had not the partisan

[1] Some of his sermons and other works, including an *Analysis of Atheism*, were published in 3 vols.   [2] Drake's *History of York*, p. 468.
[3] See especially his speech on the Bill for strengthening the Protestant Interest (*Parl. Hist.*, vii. 570; also vi. 886, vii. 945, viii. 35; Nicolson, 485, &c.). He denied that Quakers were entitled to the name of Christians at all (Wilson's *Merchant Taylors*, p. 968).
[4] Nicolson's *Correspondence*, pp. 481, 489.
[5] Noble's *Cont. of Grainger*, ii. 75.
[6] In the various ecclesiastical questions that came before the House o Lords he always voted, and sometimes spoke, in support of a liberal and tolerant policy.

temper ; and a kind heart, a cultivated mind, and a good knowledge of mankind greatly endeared him to his clergy,[1] who could depend upon him as a wise adviser and a sympathising friend. There was much sound counsel, and suitable to his times, in some of his charges and special sermons. Such, for instance, were his words in a sermon preached for the sons of the clergy in 1707 : ' Let us take care that while we maintain the distinction and dignity of our order, we do not suffer ourselves to be carried into a separate interest from that of those who are not of our order, or from that of the State. For we cannot pretend to be a separate body without making the worst kind of schism, and the nearest to that which is condemned in Scripture.'[2]

Trimnell was charitable and hospitable, and took a special interest in relieving the distress and promoting the welfare of the foreign Protestants from the Palatinate who abounded in Norwich, as their predecessors had done ever since the time of Elizabeth. His piety, genial as it was, seems to have been of a somewhat ascetic kind. We are told of his long and frequent fastings.[3]

The list of the bishops of Queen Anne's reign having thus far been gone through, it may be well to complete it, without leaving out the names of men of lesser mark, or even of the insignificant and the unworthy.

Gilbert Ironside was Bishop of Bristol from 1689 to 1691, and of Hereford from 1691 to 1713. His father Gilbert had been Bishop of Bristol before him. He was of little note as a bishop, but as Vice-Chancellor at Oxford he had acted with much firmness and resolution in the difficult times when James was bent upon imposing his own creatures upon a reluctant university.[4]

[1] Bingham's *Works*, ix. 418.
[2] Cassan's *Bishops of Winchester*, p. 378.
[3] Stephens' *Funeral Sermon on Trimnell*, quoted in Cassan, p. 386.
[4] Birch's *Life, &c., of Tillotson*, i. 153.

William Talbot was Bishop successively of Oxford (1699–1715), Salisbury (1715–21), and Durham (1721–30). A member of a distinguished family, and a zealous Whig, he was in much favour in the Court of William and Mary, to the latter of whom he especially commended himself by his eloquence in the pulpit.[1] Hence his preferment. His promotion was further advanced in later years by the interest of his son, Lord Chancellor Talbot. Atterbury accused him of sycophancy,[2] not without cause, if we may judge from his adulation of the Queen in his speech on the Sacheverell trial. The speech itself, however, was a weighty one, dwelling chiefly on the duties of free subjects, and the true nature of obedience to rulers.[3] Indeed we are told that his speeches could generally command the attention of the House.[4]

He delighted in magnificence, and at Durham, notwithstanding his princely revenues, he fell into difficulties, from which he was only extricated by the dutiful generosity of his son.[5] Altogether he was too much like his predecessor Lord Crewe in loving to appear in the secular array of prince-bishop of his lordly see. There is a curious picture of him in 1722: 'The Bishop of Durham appeared on horseback at a review in the king's train, in a long habit of purple, with jack-boots, and his hat cocked, and black wig tied behind him like a military officer.'[6]

In theological opinion he was not altogether orthodox.[7] He lamented that Samuel Clarke's refusal to sign the Articles prevented him from giving him the best preferment

---

[1] Note to Burnet's *Own-Times*, p. 851.
[2] Williams' *Life of Atterbury*, ii. 239.
[3] *Parl. Hist.*, vi. 844–46.
[4] Campbell's *Lives of the Chancellors*, iv. 640.
[5] *Id.*, iv. 649–51.
[6] *Flying Post* of June 14, 1722, quoted from Malcolm *Anecdotes* in Surtees' *Hist. of Durham*, iv. 11.
[7] Cassan's *Lives of the Bishops of Salisbury*, p. 195.

in his gift. Rundle also, whose supposed Arian opinions gave much scandal[1] when he was afterwards promoted to the see of Derry, was one of his chaplains.[2] It should be said in compensation that another of his chaplains, to whose elevation in the Church he heartily contributed, was that pattern of exact orthodoxy and strictly moderate views, Secker, afterwards Archbishop of Canterbury.

Peter Mews (or Meaux), Bishop of Bath and Wells from 1672 to 1684, and of Winchester from 1684 to 1706, belonged far more to the seventeenth than to the eighteenth century. His life had been a curious medley of ecclesiastical and military service.[3] He had fought as a young man for Charles the First, had been ejected from his fellowship at St. John's, Oxford, during the Commonwealth, and had spent several years in exile.[4] Then he had held in succession or together a multitude of offices in the Church and university. He had been Archdeacon of Huntingdon and of Berks, Canon of Windsor and of St. David's, President of St. John's, and Vice-Chancellor of the University of Oxford, Vicar of St. Mary's, Reading, King's Chaplain, Prebendary of Durham, Dean of Rochester. Then, when he had mounted to the episcopal throne of Winchester, he broke out anew as a soldier, served against Monmouth, directed the artillery at Sedgmoor, narrowly escaped being hanged by the rebels, did kind service in interceding with Faversham for the lives of the conquered, and suffered all the rest of his days from a wound which he had received in the fight.[5] As a friend alike of Oxford and of the king, the dispute at Magdalen College was referred to him, and he confirmed Hough in his office as President. He signed approval to the Declaration of the seven bishops, but did not forfeit the confidence of

---

[1] It was, however, a supposition which rested on very insufficient grounds.
[2] Hunt, iii. 170, 174.   [3] Cassan's *Bishops of Winchester*, p. 1901.
[4] Cassan's *Bishops of Salisbury*, p. 195; Whiston's *Memoirs*, p. 268.
[5] *Life of Ken*, by a Layman, pp. 282, 409.

James, who sent for him in the extremity of his peril as a counsellor whom he could still trust. 'I pressed him,' wrote Mews, 'with all imaginable arguments, to call a Parliament as the most visible way to put a stop to those confusions which threatened.'[1] In William and Mary's time he was on the commission for revision of the Prayer Book, but retired from it, dissatisfied, at an early stage.[2] Of his general character there are opposite accounts. Burnet, who had no eye for the better qualities of an opponent, calls him weak, ignorant, and obsequious.[3] Elsewhere he is spoken of as hospitable, just, and generous, a man of great personal intrepidity, and a frequent preacher.[4]

Of Thomas Smith, Bishop of Carlisle from 1684 to 1702, nothing is told very worthy of note, but what is told is all to his credit. Browne Willis records of him that 'he was a great benefactor to Carlisle, every day bestowing something on the public.'[5] His successor in the see spoke of him as deeply read, but of great modesty. He had lived in great privacy through the Commonwealth, but was remembered and promoted by Charles the Second.[6] We read of him as writing to the seven bishops to express his sympathy and approval,[7] and of taking an active part in the promotion of societies for the reformation of manners.[8]

His successor, William Nicolson (1702–1718), was Queen Anne's first bishop. In 1718 he was translated to Londonderry, and in 1727, a few days before his death, was made Archbishop of Cashel. He had felt great scruples about taking the oaths to King William, but had satisfied himself at last that 'whenever a sovereign *de facto* is universally

---

[1] Letter quoted in *Life of Ken*, p. 476. [2] Birch's *Tillotson*, i. 127.
[3] Burnet's *Own Times*, p. 382.
[4] *Wood*, quoted in Cassan; *Life of Atterbury*, p. 292.
[5] Browne Willis's *Survey of Cathedrals*, i. 301.
[6] Nicolson's *Letters and Memoirs*, p. 626. [7] *Ken's Life*, p. 416.
[8] Nicolson, p. 163.

submitted to and recognised by all the three estates, I must believe that person to be the lawful and rightful monarch, to whom alone I owe an oath of fealty.'[1] His Church opinions, and his position near the Scottish border, brought him into contact with the Scotch Episcopal clergy and their congregations, and he spoke highly of them, adding a very mistaken opinion that before long episcopacy would be restored in Scotland.[2] He was a man of some capacity, and entered eagerly into the controversy with Hoadly, but with a want of temper and a vehemence of personality which were a subject of amused scandal among Dissenters,[3] and did harm to the cause he advocated. In Church politics he took the narrower and more exclusive side. In a conversation, for instance, which George I. had with him soon after his accession, the king urged that the Dissenters had rendered much service to the State, and that the bill against occasional conformity should be repealed. Nicolson held the contrary opinion. Toleration, he said, was a sufficient recompense, and 'the security of that is all that the honest men among them seem to desire now.'[4] He was proficient in various branches of general learning, had studied German in Leipzic, was an historian of some note, and a distinguished antiquary. He left treatises on Runic inscriptions, and wrote also on astronomical and geographical subjects.[5]

Thomas Manningham was Bishop of Chichester from 1709 to 1722. A preacher of some popularity, he had succeeded Burnet in 1684 as Preacher at the Rolls, and was afterwards Lecturer at the Temple. In politics he was a Whig; in character he seems to have been a quiet man who dis-

---

[1] Lathbury's *Nonjurors*, p. 47.   [2] Thoresby's *Correspondence*, i. 381.
[3] Calamy's *Life and Times*, ii. 375–77.
[4] Stoughton's *Queen Anne and the Georges*, p. 106.
[5] Jefferson's *History of Carlisle*, p. 233; and Sir J. Ware's *Irish Bishops*, p. 296.

liked prominence, and chiefly desired 'to collect himself, to be known by few and envied by none.'[1] But, on occasion, he was not wanting in becoming spirit. A story is told of him, that, when the ladies in attendance upon the Queen requested Manningham to read her the service from an adjoining room, he answered that 'he did not choose to whistle the prayers of the Church through the keyhole.'[2] He had been a Fellow of New College, and contributed much to the building of its library.[3]

Nicholas Stratford was Bishop of Chester from 1686 to 1707. To judge, says Dr. Stoughton, from his primary visitation charge, he was an earnest and faithful man.[4] All that we hear of him leads to the same conclusion.[5] He resided constantly in his diocese; he repaired his cathedral; he acquitted himself with zeal and learning in the Roman controversy; he took very great interest in the work of the societies for the reformation of manners, and started many of them in his own diocese. There is no reason to doubt the eulogium in his epitaph that he was 'pietate plane primæva.'

Philip Bisse (St. Davids, 1710-13; Hereford, 1713-21) is spoken of as a worthy man, but owing more to his fine person than to his fine preaching.[6] A more favourable account of him speaks highly of his 'sanctity, judgment, and learning.'[7] Like his relation Thomas Bisse[8] he was more heedful than most of his contemporaries of the decencies and solemnities of worship, and did much to beautify both the cathedral of Hereford and the parish

---

[1] Nichols' *Lit. An.*, i. 207.   [2] *Id.*   [3] Dallaway's *Sussex*, ii. 94.
[4] Stoughton's *Church of the Revol.*, p. 306.
[5] Ormerod's *Hist. of Cheshire*, vol. i.; Browne Willis, *Cathedrals*, i. 437; Nicolson's *Letters*, p. 170.
[6] Noble's *Grainger*, ii. 100.
[7] Nichols' *Lit. An.*, i. 703.
[8] Author of *The Beauty of Holiness, Cathedral Worship*, &c.

churches of that city.¹ His wife was Duchess of Northumberland.

James Gardiner (Lincoln, 1694–1705) seems almost eclipsed in the greater note of his predecessor, Tenison, and his successors Wake and Gibson. He voted with the Whigs and Low Churchmen; and if the epitaph, in Sapphic verse, on his tomb at Lincoln is any authority, he was a good man.²

Humphrey Humphreys, of Bangor and Hereford (1689–1713), and William Beaw and John Tyler of Llandaff (1679–1724), are also, unless diocesan histories should be closely explored, names, and little more. It may be said of Humphreys that he had been on the Committee for the revision of the Prayer Book;³ of Beaw that, in James's time, he had written without delay to express his approval of the action of the Seven Bishops;⁴ of Tyler, that he was one of those who protested, with an earnestness which did them credit, against the intolerant provisions of the Schism Bill.⁵ John Evans, Bangor (1701–15), does not appear, in some mentions of him, in a favourable light. We find him in the anteroom to the Jerusalem Chamber giving the lie to the Prolocutor of the Lower House of Convocation;⁶ in the House of Lords protesting against the French offers of peace;⁷ in Ireland (for he was afterwards Bishop of Meath) angrily remonstrated with by Swift for his behaviour to a poor curate;⁸ and of his

---

¹ Browne Willis, ii. 530. ² Browne Willis, *Cathedrals*, vol. iii.
³ Birch's *Tillotson*, cxix. ⁴ *Life of Ken*, by a Layman, p. 416.
⁵ *Parliam. Hist.*, vi. 1356.
⁶ 'My Lord of Bangor, did you say in the Upper House that I lied?' The bishop replied in some disorder: 'I did not say you lied, but I said, or might have said, that you told me a very great untruth' (Stanley's *Memorials of Westminster Abbey*, p. 524). Stanley tells it of Humphreys; but in June, 1702, Evans must have been several months Bishop of Bangor.
⁷ *Parl. Hist.* vi. 1152. His protest against the Schism Bill did him better honour.
⁸ Swift to Wallis, Hughes' *Letters of Eminent Persons*, ii. 4.

being specially acquainted with preferments, as if he made it his peculiar province.¹ At the same time it must also be said that his contemporary, Sir James Ware, spoke of him as having been in both dioceses a vigilant pastor;² and that he is spoken of by Mant as a generous benefactor to the Church.³

But of the Welsh bishops in general we hear very little. Wales was still far removed by its distance, its mountains, and its language from the general current of English life, and a Welsh bishop, who stayed in his diocese, and was not very conspicuous for good or evil, might be very exemplary or learned on the one hand, and somewhat scandalous on the other, and yet live and die scarcely known beyond his quarter of the Principality. Beveridge, Bull, and Hoadly were, it is true, Welsh bishops, but the two first had gained all their fame as English clergymen before their connection with Wales, and Hoadly, to his great reproach, scarcely set his foot in the country of which he was consecrated to be a spiritual father. One, however, of the purely Welsh bishops deserves a special and very honourable mention. The historians of St. David's single out Adam Ottley (1713-23) as a noble exception in a list of obscure prelates. They speak in the highest terms of his activity and earnestness, and how in a lax age he went far to revive the character of a primitive bishop.⁴

Two Welsh bishops, on the other hand, were in ill repute, and one of them appears to have been a thoroughly bad man. Almost all the benefices in Wales were in the gift of the bishops, and in the case of these two this important patronage appears to have been scandalously abused. Edward Jones (St. Asaph, 1692-1703) was prosecuted for simony;

---

¹ Nicolson's *Letters*, p. 527.
² Sir J. Ware's *Irish Bishops*, p. 163.   ³ Bp. Mant's *Irish Ch.*, ii. 391.
⁴ W. B. Jones and E. A. Freeman's *History of St. David's*, p. 336.

but though the presumption of his guilt was very strong, the charge was not established with absolute certainty.[1] Not so with Thomas Watson (St. David's, 1687–1705). Against him simony and corruption in their basest forms were clearly proved. He was the most worthless of James II.'s bad bishops. Burnet, who was on the Commission which deprived him, speaks of him as having wickedly disgraced his sacred profession; as 'passionate, covetous, and false in the blackest instances; without any one virtue or good quality to support his many bad ones.'[2] It may be well conceived how much detriment such a man must have done to the cause of the Church, and of religion generally in Wales.

The only bishop remaining to be mentioned among those who occupied sees in Queen Anne's time, is the senior prelate on the bench, Nathaniel, Lord Crewe,[3] Bishop of Oxford from 1671 to 1674, and of Durham from 1674 to 1721. It is with great reluctance that, having shared in the benefactions with which he enriched Lincoln College, Oxford, I am compelled to include him among the few bishops who at this period did discredit to their high position in the Church. Had he been a lay baron, his tergiversation and sycophancy, as common vices of his period, might perhaps have been lost sight of in the hospitable generosity of his private life. At Durham he occupied very much the position of a feudal lord, keeping state with his retainers in mediæval style. Thus we read, '1700, August 9, Lord Crewe, Bishop of Durham, and his lady, came from Auckland Palace to Durham, and were met by a large company of gentlemen and tradesmen. The streets and windows were filled with people, and all the

---

[1] Burnet's *Own Times*, p. 658.

[2] Burnet, *id.* It is right, however, to add that there were some who still believed that he was grossly wronged and had been a victim of a conspiracy of non-residents (Browne Willis, quoted by Freeman and Jones, p. 333).

[3] Last of the Barons of Crewe (Noble's *Grainger*, i. 84).

trade banners were displayed.'[1] But in a spiritual peer, his faults were such as could in no way be redeemed, even in the opinion of the careless, by open-handedness in life, and by posthumous generosity. At the Restoration he had been a young man high in favour with Charles II., to whom he commended himself very pleasantly as an agreeable man, of good person and easy manners, a judge of music,[2] and a supple courtier. The ardent royalists of Lincoln College made him their Rector. The king gave him the Deanery of Chichester, and raised him to the see of Oxford. He won the favour of the Duke of York by marrying him to Mary of Este, with no authority except an order under the king's signet, notwithstanding the repeated protests of the Commons and the warning threats of Shaftesbury. With such interest at Court, he was quickly raised to the bishopric of Durham, not, however (so it is said), without a payment from its revenues of five or six thousand pounds, which the pleasure-loving monarch had promised to Nell Gwyn.[3] His own father was so much ashamed at the means by which the preferment had been obtained that he never entered into the House of Lords after his son had obtained it. Four years afterwards when Crewe tried, though happily in vain, to get the primacy, the old man prayed earnestly that he might not succeed.[4] In James's Court he held the office of Privy Councillor and Clerk of the Closet, as he had done in that of Charles, and served his master only too well for his character as a bishop and an Englishman. He acquiesced in if he did not promote the king's most arbitrary designs; he courted the honour of a place in that commission which was

[1] Surtees' *Hist. of Durham*, iv. 11. From a diary of the time.
[2] Some, however, denied him this accomplishment. At Oxford, where he was a member with Ken and others of a musical society, Antony A. Wood says of him that he was 'always out of tune, as having no good ear' (*Life of Ken*, p. 43).
[3] *Quarterly Rev.*, 39, 336.   [4] *Id.*

intended to crush the liberties of the Church and nation; he condescended to drive compliantly in the train of the papal nuncio;[1] he refused to introduce Patrick to the king because of the dean's[2] zeal against popery. After James's abdication Crewe was excepted from the general indemnity, absconded, and, after the lapse of a couple of years, had to bear with the humiliation of being indebted for his pardon to the kindly offices of his strongest political opponent, Bishop Burnet. It need scarcely be added that his influence among the clergy of his diocese was not of the best. 'I hear,' wrote a correspondent to his friend in 1715, 'that Lady Crewe is dead, but could have wished it had been his Lordship: for as long as we have such bishops we cannot expect good clergy.'[3] But age and the deep sorrow he felt at his wife's loss are said to have had a salutary effect upon the worldly old prelate. This at least we may say of him, that in his case the hackneyed quotation may be inverted, and the good he did lives after him, while the evil is interred with his bones. His servility has indeed left dishonour upon his memory; but, not to speak further of his bequests to his university, tens of thousands have been indebted to his princely benefaction at Bamborough Castle for education in youth, for medicine and attendance in sickness, for bountiful relief in time of death, or for ever-ready help in times of wreck or peril amid the boisterous seas which beat upon that rock-bound coast.

The list of the spiritual rulers of the English Church in Queen Anne's reign is thus completed, yet three other English bishops have to be mentioned, all of them highly venerated by a party, two at least of them honoured and beloved by all who knew them, and one of them a saintly

---

[1] Macaulay's *History of Eng.*, iii. 3. [2] Birch's *Tillotson*, i. 99.
[3] J. Johnson to Henry Liddle, Oct. 23, 1715. *Diary of Mary, Countess Cowper* (1714), app. 180.

name which will be treasured in memory so long as the list of English worthies shall last.

Four of the Nonjuring bishops lived into the eighteenth century; but as one of them, Turner of Ely, died in 1700, mention need only be made of the remaining three—Frampton, Lloyd, and Ken.

. Robert Frampton, Bishop of Gloucester from 1681 to his deprivation in 1689, died in 1708. He was a man of considerable ability and deep earnestness, fervently attached to the tenets of the English Church, and impetuous in his denunciations against schism, yet gentle and kind-hearted in temper, and a man who loved goodness greatly wherever he might find it. In earlier life he had been chaplain to the English factory at Aleppo, a worthy successor there of Pocock, Busire, and Huntington. Like them, he formed a large and familiar acquaintance with the patriarchs and bishops of the Eastern Church, especially with the most learned of them, studied the Oriental languages, and made himself familiar with the history and usages of the Eastern Communion.[1] Among his countrymen there, who some few years after were very highly spoken of by Maundrell as a sober, benevolent, and devout society,[2] he was much beloved, and when after sixteen years' absence he returned to England, the testimonials which he brought of his talents and great services raised him speedily to the Deanery of Chichester. He was an eminent preacher. Pepys writes in his diary: ' I go to church, and there beyond expectation find our seat and all the church crammed by twice as many people as used to be: and to my great joy find Mr. Frampton in the pulpit; and I think the best sermon for goodness and oratory, without affectation or study, that ever I heard in my life. The truth is, he preaches the most like an apostle

---

[1] Evan's *Life of Frampton*, p. 44.
[2] Anderson's *Church in the Colonies*, ii. 466.

that ever I heard man; and it was much the best time that ever I spent in my life at church.'[1] Evelyn, in 1673, spoke scarcely less warmly of him. There is extant an interesting letter which he wrote to Bishop Lloyd of Norwich on his promotion, at the age of sixty, to the see of Gloucester. It is full of very genuine humility, and reveals incidentally his profuse charity. He had spent his profits, yearly as they came, freely, and, as he hoped, to God's glory. Half had always been devoted to charitable uses, and much of the rest had gone to his poor relations. He should abhor, he said, running into debt, and he was afraid the expenses of taking the bishopric would expose him in his old age and his relations to beggary.[2] As bishop, he served his Church fearlessly and dutifully. He brought upon himself the displeasure of James by a sermon in Whitehall, in which he earnestly exhorted his hearers to constancy in the Protestant faith.[3] But when the question came of transferring his allegiance, he refused to do so, and on his ejection from Gloucester retired to the village of Standish, where he spent the rest of his life in the quiet duties of religion, entering into controversy with no one, for indeed he was no friend to controversy where it could be avoided. 'I wish,' he said to Kettlewell, 'our men of war—I mean our disputants—would beat their swords and spears, as you do, into ploughs and pruning-hooks, endeavouring to make their readers turn their thoughts to piety rather than controversy; since the former though never so necessary—yea, the *unum necessarium*—is scarcely heard among the din and clashing of pros and cons.'[4] By the permission of the bishop he still assisted in the service, catechising and preaching from the reader's pew, and saying such of the

---

[1] Quoted in *Life of Ken*, by a Layman, p. 753.
[2] *Life of Ken*, p. 757. [3] *Id.*, pp. 323–24.
[4] *Life of Kettlewell*, Ap. 66.

prayers as he could without mentioning the names of the reigning family.[1]

William Lloyd, who died in 1710, had been Bishop, first of Llandaff, then of Peterborough, and lastly of Norwich, from 1675 to his ejection in 1689. He had been an active and efficient prelate, and his loss had been especially lamented at Llandaff when he was translated from that diocese in 1679. The history of his life comes into constant connection with that of Ken,[2] to whom, though his temper was different and his views occasionally divergent, he was a warm and steadfast friend. In their public life we find them united in 1685 in an attempt to bring about a greater vigilance in the admission of candidates to holy orders. In 1688, it was by a mere accident that he was prevented from joining his friend in the protest of the Seven Bishops against James's usurpations. The next year they had both taken part in drawing up the service of thanksgiving that 'a mighty deliverer had been raised up,' whereby 'our holy reformed religion was not overwhelmed with popish superstition and idolatry.' But, like Ken and his Nonjuring brethren, he could not allow that the throne was vacant, and chose to be ejected rather than to conform. From that time, however, his action did not contrast favourably with the quieter and more temperate line adopted by Ken and Frampton. Resistance to the Government of the time excited and somewhat embittered him—feelings which were perhaps increased by a tumult which arose in the city after the ignominious action off Beachy Head in 1690. The rabble, giving credence to a report that the French had been invited over by the Nonjurors, attacked Lloyd's house, and forced him to take sanctuary in the Temple. At a later

---

[1] Evan's *Life of Frampton*, p. 208.

[2] Most of the facts mentioned in this sketch of Lloyd's life are gathered out of the *Life of Ken*, by a Layman.

period it is by no means certain that he did not give real colour to the belief which on this occasion was entirely unfounded. At all events, although he never went the lengths of Turner, the ejected Bishop of Ely, he steadily resisted every compromise and every expedient by which the Nonjuring schism might have been mitigated if not averted. His energetic disposition, his residence near London, and his intimate and confidential relations with Sancroft, had made him distinctly the leader of his party. Ken's moderate counsels might have led him to take a wiser path; but, having once taken the ill-advised step of joining with Turner in the clandestine consecration of Hickes and Wagstaffe, he fell more and more into their views, and diverged more widely from Ken and Frampton, Nelson, Dodwell, and Brokesby, who were all earnestly desirous that their separation from the Established Communion should be neither wide nor perpetual. How thoroughly irreconcilable he had become was strongly shown at the funeral, in 1698, of White, the Nonjuring Bishop of Peterborough. With Turner he followed the hearse to the grave, but would not stay to hear the service, because a Conforming clergyman had been appointed to read it. His death, in 1710, ended the separation so far as the moderate Nonjurors were concerned. Hitherto they had all agreed in asserting the spiritual rights of the deprived bishops. But now Ken only was left, and it was well known that he, for the sake of healing the schism, was willing and even wishful to forego such claims. With his authority therefore, and at his counsel, Dodwell and Nelson, Cherry and Brokesby returned, with no little gladness, to communion with their brethren in the churches from which they had long been absentees. From the year 1710, the Nonjurors can be considered as little more than a Jacobite sect.

Thomas Ken had been Bishop of Bath for little more

than four years, between 1685 and 1689. He might have resumed his old see in 1703, for Queen Anne offered it to him, and all English Churchmen would have been glad to see him once more occupying it. But he declined it, as unwilling 'to return into the business of the world again.' He remained, therefore, in the peaceful retirement which Lord Weymouth provided for him at Longleat, removed as far as might be from worldly solicitudes. 'In the dedication prefixed to his works Ken compares himself, not (he modestly adds) in gifts or graces, but in the circumstances of his later life, to Gregory of Nazianzen. Like him, he had been driven from his episcopal see; like him he delighted to beguile the pains, the austerities, the infirmities of the seclusion in which he spent his declining years with hymns and "songs devout." But there were points of far more than outward resemblance between Ken and Gregory, or between Ken and Chrysostom, Gregory's still more distinguished successor in the bishopric of Constantinople. The ascetic temperament; the spirit, bold and fearless on occasion, but delighting above all in tranquil contemplative reveries; the poetical imagination; the somewhat cramped sacerdotalism and anxious orthodoxy, combined with utter aversion to controversy, and a tendency to view all Christian doctrines with sole reference to their bearing upon sanctity of life—all these features are observable in Ken as in Gregory and Chrysostom.'[1] Ken was but for a very short time a ruler in the English Church, and, with the exception of two imperishable hymns, he has left behind him no works which have made any impression upon his countrymen. But the sanctity, the intrepidity, the pure and simple guilelessness of his life have become rooted in the memory of English Churchmen, as a fair and noble

---

[1] This passage is taken from my essay on the sacred poetry of the time in *The English Church in the Eighteenth Century.*

example, around which their affections cling. And, undoubtedly, the peculiar beauties of his character gained in attractiveness by the strength of contrast with the more secular age which at his death was already beginning to steal upon the Church.

After passing under review the whole catalogue of English bishops from the opening of the eighteenth century to the death of Queen Anne, it is impossible not to feel that it is one which, on the whole, did much honour to the Church of that time. Of some individual names the contrary has to be said, and it is quite inevitable that, in a list of some forty or more dignitaries who were living within the limits of half a generation, some should have passed away without any memories attached to their name which are in any way worthy of record. But setting apart prelates of more secondary note, that was a remarkable muster-roll which included such well-known and representative men as Fleetwood and Burnet, Patrick, Compton, Fowler, Cumberland and Tenison, Wake and Sharp, Bull and Beveridge, Wilson and Hough, Atterbury, and Ken and Frampton. The Whig or Low Church element is, no doubt, predominant; but the other great section of the Church could look with no less pride to their own especial leaders. The bishops of that period will, as a whole, well bear comparison with those of any other age in history in regard either of piety and practical religious activity, or in general ability, or in learning, or in eloquence, or in attainment to the full level of the culture of their time. No doubt there is an element that is wanting, especially if we must exclude Ken and Frampton as no longer official members of the Episcopate. The Revolution had dealt a great blow upon sentiment both in religion and politics, or rather upon both in one.

With it there departed for a lengthened period that old loyalty which, in England, had entered so largely into the composition both of Church and State: and its departure left a gap in the consciousness of all public men which was immediately and very sensibly felt. For a whole century religious and social life in this country had been deeply interested in matters in which questions of loyalty and religion meet. There had been strife and suffering, action and reaction, vehement feeling on either side. At last, after an interval of angry disappointment, the nation as a whole had acquiesced, as a matter of necessity, in a change of rulers and a new dynasty. But the enthusiasm which had invigorated the political and religious life of the seventeenth century was gone. An age of expedience had already set in. Expedience is not altogether to be despised as a principle of action when interpreted into life by high-minded and religious men. But under no circumstances can it fail to be somewhat deficient in the nobler sentiments. These remarks are by no means intended for a full explanation of that peculiar spirit of the time which dates from the latter part of the seventeenth century. Many causes contributed to it which cannot here be entered into. But what has been said is sufficient for the immediate purpose. Apart from all other causes, the Revolution which placed Mary and William of Orange on the throne was one of those events in the history of a State which have not only a political and social action, but also, so to say, an ethical bearing, by their direct influence upon thought, morals, and religion.

The application of this to the subject before us is evident. A majority of the prelates in the period immediately under review were distinctly bishops of the Revolution. They had been appointed by William in the full tide of his success. As Churchmen and citizens, they had been ardent promoters of the Revolution. They were thoroughly imbued with its spirit. They were good and religious men, active and energetic, zealous for the welfare alike of their country and of their Church. But whatever the spirit of that Revolution, whatever its merits and its defects, it was sure to be represented, worthily, no doubt, and favourably, but still to be represented in the lives and work of those bishops. We must not look for feelings which were wholly alien to it. We may find love of goodness, love of reason, love of liberty, love of truth; we may find rectitude of action and diligence in work; but we must not expect to discover in them lofty aspirations, high enthusiasm, or anything of that kindling elevation of sentiment which sheds upon some lives and upon some periods a dignity which is especially its own.

The influence of the Revolution was by no means limited to that part of the Episcopate who owed their elevation to it. Upon those who belonged most definitely to the defeated party it worked unfavourably. The two, in the period before us, who were most decidedly Jacobite in their sympathies were Atterbury among the Conforming bishops, and Lloyd among the Nonjurors. To the characters of both of these men their Jacobitism was detrimental. It was impossible for any one to take any leading part in the whisperings and intrigues, the secret messages, and the concealed plots—the only conditions under which James's interests in England could be promoted—without great risk to truthfulness and uprightness of tone. Speaking generally, without special reference to either Whig or Jacobite, the years that followed after William had been once securely seated upon the throne were calculated to affect the leaders of the Church with a certain relaxation of fibre, the results of which might not be, and were not, seriously felt for some time, but which gradually began to operate. For the great questions which once stirred their minds were now lulled to rest. Some of the eldest of the bishops remembered well the time of the Protectorate, when Bull's contemporaries in those days— Sanderson, and Jeremy Taylor, and Hammond, and many another worthy—celebrated in private houses, with almost a deeper love than ever, the services and hallowed rites which had been banished from the churches to make place for the harangues of Independents and fanatics; many more remembered amid what tumultuous joy their Church had resumed its place at the Restoration. Then, not many years after, had come an excited and anxious time in which their own anointed king had perversely girded himself to the task of overthrowing the Church of which he was the temporal head. They had all known the perplexities and shared in the ferment of that time. Some of them had suffered no little peril in the cause of their Church; all of them had felt that humiliation, and perhaps even persecution, might be in store for them. There was scarcely one of them who had not contributed treatise, or pamphlet, or carefully studied sermon to the array of arguments with which the pretensions of Rome had been assailed. Then had come the new enthusiasm of active and passive resistance, and many a troubled scruple as to how far resistance might be authorised by the laws of religion and by the constitution of the Church. Then, before the fervour of the movement had yet fully abated, there had been a little interval—very short, indeed, and transitory, but of great interest while it lasted—in which Churchmen of every party, warmed by one common interest, and touched by the sympathy which they had received from Nonconformists, began practically to contemplate the possibility of raising up in England, within the bounds of one Church, one strong united body to head the Protestant interest, and to cope on more equal terms with the great organisation of Rome.

But before the seventeenth century finally closed, these dangers and triumphs, these hopes and fears, these times of interest and expectation had passed away, or, so far as they survived at all, were but artificially prolonged to suit the interests of party. The Church of Queen Anne's reign was undoubtedly full of life, and was occupied to the full with many and varied questions. Nor did it enjoy quietude. It was disturbed, on the contrary, by great restlessness, and its members were often ranged one against another in hot strife. But in external circumstances there was nothing any longer to stir the feeling, or to warm the imagination, or to raise men up above themselves. A prosaic century had begun; and the bishops, excellent and distinguished men as many of them were, could not be expected to be more than the age allowed.

Perhaps if there had been more warmth and enthusiasm in them, they would have been less understood, and therefore less valued. As it was, the country had good cause to be well content with its bishops; and on the whole it was thoroughly content. Beyond all question the bishops were, as a body, in the reigns of William and Anne, held in very high respect. Never was there a time when party feeling was more unsparing in its diatribe upon opponents; and at a time when Church politics entered into almost every question of the day, the leading bishops were far too prominent persons to escape invective. It is therefore all the more remarkable that in all their paper warfare so very little should be found which throws the slightest disparagement upon their collective or individual character. In the Georgian period a reader of the literature of the age will constantly meet with some such slur of dislike or reproach, but not so in this earlier time. He will find, on the other hand, frequent and high encomium: 'Never such excellent bishops since Elizabeth's time'[1]; 'We have (as by all must be acknowledged) as wise and learned bishops as are in the world';[2] 'We never had a better sort of bishops';[3] 'I think this nation never enjoyed more learned and pious prelates.'[4]

[1] *Athenian Oracle*, p. 561.
[2] Eachard, p. 150.
[3] *Clergyman's Advocate*, p. 66.
[4] Thoresby, i. 608.

Thus also a writer, in 1707, on 'The Church and State of England,' speaks of the people as being thoroughly satisfied with the activity, the patronage, and the moderation of the existing episcopate.[1] Many Nonconformists, as Du Moulin the Independent, and Calamy the Presbyterian, expressed a no less ungrudging praise. Although, therefore, the assertion did not come quite well from the mouth of Fleetwood, and although his boast that they had not parted with 'one point of doctrine, one point of discipline, one line of the Common Prayer, nor one external ceremony,' must be qualified by the fact that some upon the bench were quite willing to make such concessions, he was fairly justified in boasting that the bishops had 'gained more ground upon the hearts of the Dissenters than had been for a hundred years before by all their predecessors.'[2] It is obvious that many of such eulogies as those that have been quoted refer only or especially to the Low Church bishops. Those who held views of a more High Church character did not come so much before the public eye in a collective character. But the lives of such men as Bull, Beveridge, Wilson, Dawes, Hooper, Sharp, and Trelawney, show very clearly that they were held in no less estimation. Nor were outward manifestations wanting of the great respect in which the episcopate was held. The reception given to Crewe at Durham was connected with the palatine character of the see. But when Trimnell entered, in 1707, upon his see of Norwich, we are told that thirty coaches and a great number of mounted gentlemen and citizens came out to meet him.[3] 'It requireth,' said Robert Nelson,[4] 'great firmness of mind not to be dazzled with the honour which surroundeth the epis-

[1] Papers on *The Growth of Deism*, p. 266.
[2] Charge of 1710; Fleetwood's *Works*, p. 183.
[3] Cassan's *Bishops of Winchester*, p. 201.
[4] Nelson's *Life of Bull*, p. 318.

copal throne.' At Oxford, and perhaps at Cambridge, the office conferred one singular privilege. In 1704, Charles Talbot, afterwards Lord Chancellor, claimed, as son of a bishop, the right of receiving an honorary degree before the ordinary time for his graduating had arrived. His father, on account of his strong Whig principles, was at that time very unpopular at the university, but it was acknowledged that the claim was one that could not be denied.[1]

Queen Anne's reign was a time when it was argued that to be of no party was to be 'in an infamous neutrality.'[2] The country was pretty equally divided between Tories and Whigs, and the virulence of pamphleteers on either side was extreme. However much the bishops might be respected personally, or as a body, it was a matter of course that there was no reticence nor mercy in the vigour with which their opinions were condemned from the one point of view or from the other. To judge from some violent pamphlets on either side, if a bishop was not 'one of our Dissenting bishops,'[3] he was likely to be a Papist; if he was not pledged to bring England under the rule of James and the Jesuits, he would certainly do his best to give up the Church into the hands of Presbyterians. Taunts, however, such as these, and others yet more vehement and unrestrained, were thought very little of. After all, they were but the ordinary ammunition of party war. Meanwhile, neither Whig partisan nor Tory, neither Dissenter nor freethinker, nor yet that too numerous company who joined to dissolute lives a shallow and flippant infidelity, as yet brought against the bishops as a body the faintest charge of inattention or neglect of duty. In two or three indivi-

---

[1] Campbell's *Lives of the Chancellors*, iv. 650.
[2] *The Examiner*, No. 8; quoted in *Quart. Rev.*, 101, 415.
[3] *Reliquiæ Hearnianæ*, 3. But Hearne did not employ anything like such strong language as some of his contemporaries.

dual cases such imputations were deservedly incurred, and did not fail to be brought; but as a whole the episcopate could hold its high place in public opinion unchallenged.

Owing in great measure to the confidence which is conferred by high repute, there is a feature in the general character of the bishops of William's and Queen Anne's reign which stands out in strong contrast with what is observable later in the century. There was, as a rule, a thorough absence in them of all timidity in speech and action. A bishop was not in the least afraid to maintain to the full his own idiosyncrasy. He spoke and acted as he thought best, without overmuch consideration of what public opinion might say to it. They were heard in Parliament much more frequently than afterwards, and that not merely because almost every political question of the day had also its religious or ecclesiastical aspect. In a word, they had a stronger feeling that they were high dignitaries in the nation generally as well as in the Church, and that they were altogether entitled to speak publicly what they thought on any matter, however secular and temporal, which concerned the interests of the people. We have seen Robinson as a plenipotentiary, and Compton and Mews even resuming on certain critical occasions the office and habit of the soldier. Whether it were well to do so is a different question; at a later date it would have been simply impossible.[1] In any case advancing years would almost certainly have tended to limit episcopal work more and more to strictly ecclesiastical matters. But the rapid falling off of their importance as leading men and legislators was also greatly owing to a falling off in general character. Bishops who owed their mitre not so much to merit and ability, but—as was often the case in the days of Walpole and his successors— to the

[1] In England; in Ireland the case was different.

wish to gain a vote to please a man in power, were not likely to win repute either for themselves or their order. In the early part of the century, when a bishop rose in Parliament to speak he was sure of a respectful audience; there were not many who could be equally sure of such deference a generation later.

It cannot be said that relations were for the most part very satisfactory between the bishops and their clergy. All of King William's bishops and some of Queen Anne's were Whigs, and, in the old sense of the word, Low Churchmen. The clergy, on the other hand, except perhaps in London, were almost all High Churchmen and Tories, men who 'against Dissenters would repine, And stand up firm for right divine.' Hence a great want of harmony. In Convocation there was open war. The contest began in 1697 with the 'Letter to a Convocation Man,' in which the author insisted that Convocation should be again summoned as 'the only remedy for the awful diseases of the time.' From that date until the prorogation of 1717 the contest raged almost incessantly between the Upper and the Lower House. A little useful work was done, and some questions debated which were very important to the practical efficiency of the Church; but the greater part of these stormy sittings were occupied with questions in which the two Chambers were thoroughly out of accord. The bishops in the Jerusalem Chamber were most of them, in different degrees, Whigs and so-called 'Latitudinarians;' the proctors of the clergy in Henry VII.'s Chapel were almost all Tories and High Churchmen. The Lower House spent much labour in examining and censuring works considered to be dangerous or heterodox, by Toland and Emlyn, Clarke and Whiston, Burnet, Hare, and Hoadly. They had much to say on concessions to Dissenters, on occasional Conformity, on Presbyterian baptism, on union with Scotland, on the danger of the Church in general. They held strong opinions as to their rights and powers, and upon their independence in relation to the Upper House. On almost all these matters the bishops either differed entirely, or if they held somewhat similar views, differed so greatly in tone, phraseology, and expression, as to make their opponents almost more furious than if they had dissented entirely. Altercations were hot, and even personalities frequent. Out of Convocation the dispute was carried on with no less vehemence. The bishops did not disguise their irritation at the conduct of the clergy, and were assailed by them bitterly in return. 'Burnet complained that "the prelates were charged as enemies of the Church [1] and betrayers of its interests;" and even Hough mentioned in the House of Lords the opprobrious names the clergy gave the bishops, and the calumnies they laid on them.' [2] It was a lamentable dispute, and one that happened at an unfortunate time. For while these controversies were going on a great opportunity was lost. The Church was popular and strong. The bishops, notwithstanding party clamour, were highly respected by the people, a great power in the State, influential even among Nonconformists, and, to some extent, leaders of thought. The clergy, although as a class prejudiced and bigoted, and in many cases ignorant and squalidly poor, held a yet uncontested position in all the country parishes. They guided the opinion of their congregations, and shared the sentiments of the rural squires. The nation as a whole was decidedly inclined to take interest in what the Church might say and do; the Queen was a Churchwoman to the core; the Governments of the day, both Whig and Tory, would have been exceptionally ready to sanction and further any proposals which would plainly conduce to its welfare and usefulness. Under such circum-

[1] *Parliam. Hist.*, vi. 160.   [2] *Id.*, p. 497.

stances, if only the Church had risen to the level of the occasion, it would seem that the road lay open before it to do a great work. The bishops (and in speaking of them in their corporate capacity we mean especially those Whig bishops who formed the strong and compact majority) had their faults, and doubtless some of them, if they had their way, might have consented to changes which the Church would have had good cause for regretting. Neither then, nor at any time, could it afford to lose the love and loyalty of its High Churchmen. But if, without any extreme change in their opinions, the inferior clergy could have had more of the tolerance and breadth of view which might be found in many of the prelates, and if there had been mutual confidence between the two orders, and they had consulted in harmony together only for the spiritual and moral good of the people, surely the subsequent chapter of Church history would have differed widely from what it proved to be. As it was, the nation looked on interested to a far greater degree than might have been expected,[1] but not edified, at the innumerable jealousies and animosities with which the precious time was consumed; and when at last the strife was exhausted, both combatants and lookers on fell back more listlessly than ever into the heavy stillness which was about to oppress the energies of the Church and the spiritual life of all.

[1] Whiston, a tolerably impartial witness on such a matter, says that the Bangorian controversy (which was all intimately connected with the other questions at issue) 'seemed for a great while to engross the attention of the public' (*Memoirs*, i. 245).

CHAPTER III.

THE ENGLISH CHURCH. 1714–1760.

With George I.'s accession, many of the questions which in Queen Anne's reign had occupied attention, both in the Church and in the country generally, began at once to lose interest and to recede from view. The peaceful acknowledgment of the new king, and the battle of Preston in the next year, almost ended the Jacobite hopes. Nonjurors became a persecuted remnant, interesting to the ecclesiastical student, and entering largely into the history of the depressed Episcopalians of Scotland, but lost to thought and view from most Englishmen. Tory High Churchism, which had risen to its flood tide of popularity at the time of the Sacheverell trial, ebbed rapidly and lastingly. A queen devoted from her heart to the interests of the Church was followed by a king who knew nothing of it, and, except in his official position, cared nothing for it. With the fall of the Harley ministry a period of Whig predominance set in. To Churchmen it was not a Whiggism like that of William and Mary's times, full of hope to some, full of alarm to others, but exciting and invigorating to all. As then, so now also, it was friendly to the Church at large, and favourable to Low Churchmen; but was as far from any thought of startling the Church with reforms and reorganisations as it was from renewing the folly of a Sacheverell prosecution. The Church could no longer be pronounced in danger, in any form at least which could stir the susceptibilities of the multitude. A minister was about to rule whose special maxim it would be never to run a risk of any ecclesiastical commotion, never to move what could any way be left at rest. Thus also the strength of party feeling died gradually away. The great war, too, had come to an end with the peace of Utrecht. The fire of Protestant ardour was abated, leaving indeed a settled hatred and mistrust of Rome, but no longer kindling thought into action, no longer so full of sympathy for oppressed churches abroad, nor calling interested attention to the points at issue between England and Rome. Convocation came to an end, its useful discussions no less than its heats and follies. Questions with Nonconformity were greatly lulled. Dissenters were satisfied with the repeal of the Schism and Corporation Acts; their numbers had dwindled; they became occupied with differences among themselves; there was a great increase of tolerant feeling; and thus causes of discussion and dispute were wanting. Amid the growth of this general cessation of exciting questions, it must be added that there was a visible falling off of the practical activities of Churchmen. The zeal of the Reformation societies cooled; church building rested; the educational and the missionary movements were somewhat slackened. The Deistical controversy was alone full of life. Added to this was the varied strife which gathered round the Bangorian dispute. These arguments, whatever might be their ultimate results, brought little immediate profit to the Church. Presently a new life gradually awakened in the Wesleyan movement.

The period included in this chapter completes, to all practical purposes, the history of Jacobitism. Even at the beginning of George III.'s reign it had already become a sentiment, perfectly compatible with thorough loyalty to the reigning dynasty. But at the beginning of George I.'s reign there can be little doubt that quite the majority of country clergymen and country squires were Jacobites at heart. The great opportunity had been lost when the new king had succeeded without resistance. But still they hoped. The excitement at Oxford in May 1715, when 'No usurper!' had been shouted in the streets, and 'every one was toasting to a new restoration,' met with warm sympathy in many a parsonage and many an ancient manor-house.[1] In the December previously it had been felt necessary to circulate directions to the bishops 'that none of the clergy in their sermons and lectures presume to intermeddle in any affairs of State and Government, save only on such special feasts and fasts which are or shall be appointed by public authority, and then no further than the occasion of such days strictly requires.' It was also enjoined that the canonical prayer before sermon should be regularly used, with the royal titles not omitted.[2] Whereupon it was said that a certain Dr. M—— varied the 'Let us pray for King George' by 'We *must* pray for,' &c. It is possible, however, and indeed probable, that all this disaffection in the Church was not a very vigorous feeling. The German dynasty was looked upon by such men with much distaste; the old line was looked back to with regret; they felt that if some guarantee were given for the liberties of the Church, they could put up even with a Papist king,[3] so long as he was of the older and wholly English line; but they were not inclined to be so hearty in his cause as to submit to sacrifice on his behalf. There was not a particle of the intense feeling which their ancestors felt for Charles I. and at the

---

[1] *Reliq. Hearnianæ*, ii. 4.

[2] *The Justice and Necessity of restraining the Clergy in their Teaching*, 1715.

[3] It was a frequent hit against the High Tories that they held the Church of England would always be in danger till it had a Popish king for its defender (Addison, in the *Freeholder*, No. 14, Feb. 6, 1716).

restoration of Charles II. There was almost nothing left of the religious and political convictions which half a generation before had made men Nonjurors. The House of Brunswick could be tolerated if the House of Stuart was no longer to be had. We need not speculate how the Tory clergy would have acted if the insurrection of 1716 had been more successful. It was quickly and severely crushed, and henceforth English Jacobitism took, with rare exceptions, no very overt form. There was immense sympathy with Atterbury in his imprisonment,[1] great readiness to catch up accusations and ill-natured stories against the king,[2] and much affection professed for the Pretender. A weekly periodical entitled 'The Scourge,' first published in 1720, 'in vindication of the Church of England,' bore as its frontispiece medallions of the Stuart sovereigns, with the motto—

> In their time
> Rich industry sat smiling on the plain,
> And peace and plenty told a Stuart's reign.

In the third decade of the century there was not much display of clerical Jacobitism except at Oxford.[3] In the fourth decade the coldness with which the Jacobite invaders were everywhere received showed clearly how well satisfied the country gentry and clergy were to remain in grumbling content under the existing constitution.[4] At the time of the Pretender's inroad into England Archbishop Herring exerted himself with much success in organising the yeomanry against him; and Secker congratulated even the clergy of Oxfordshire on a behaviour which had 'abounded in proofs of loyalty and affection.'[5] Fielding's writings about this time display in various lights the Jacobitism of

---

[1] Notes to *Parliam. Hist.*, viii. 350.
[2] *A Memorial to the Clergy*, &c., 1723.
[3] Lady Sundon's *Memoirs*, ii. 182 (1732).
[4] Tyerman's *Oxford Methodists* (1736).   [5] Secker's *Charges*, p. 87.

the day, and how harmless it generally was. We have his Squire Western in 'Tom Jones'; and in his 'True Patriot' (1745–46) there are some lively and amusing papers on the subject. One is an imaginary journal of an honest tradesman after the Jacobite conquest. Another is a supposed letter from a Nonjuror to his son at Oxford.[1] The insurrection had, however, grave effects upon Episcopalian Churchmen in Scotland. We find some of the bishops using their best efforts in Parliament to plead for a mitigation of the disabilities that were piled upon them.[2] In the fifth decade Horace Walpole speaks of Oxfordshire as still 'a little kingdom of Jacobites.' The university itself was of course the centre of it. Pitt spoke of the violent Jacobitism common there, both among the lads and others. Many of them were 'learned and respectable, and so much the more dangerous.'[3] Perhaps elsewhere an innocuous Jacobite sentiment was more widely diffused than might be expected. Southey, for instance, mentions that at Bristol in the end of George II.'s reign there were many 'who from political scruples of conscience refused to take King William's halfpence; and these persons were so numerous that the magistrates thought it necessary to interfere because of the inconvenience which they occasioned.'[4]

After the accession of George I. the history of the Nonjurors in great measure merges partly into that of the Jacobites, partly into that of Episcopacy in Scotland. Those among them who had been for some years estranged from the English Church because they could admit of no ecclesiastical allegiance, except to the dispossessed bishops, had joyfully returned to her communion when their scruples had

---

[1] Fielding's *Works*, viii. 103, 127–29. [2] *Parliam. Hist.*, xiv. 276, 304.
[3] Walpole's *Memoirs of George II.'s Reign* (1756), pp. 406, 413. There is a warm reproof of Oxford Jacobitism (1748) in Mason's 'Isis'; Mason's *Poems*, p. 179.
[4] Southey's *Life and Correspondence*, i. 17.

been removed by the death of the other Nonjuring bishops, and Ken's absolute surrender of all episcopal rights. If the oath of abjuration were imposed, as often in the queen's reign it was not, their principles would generally have prevented their holding office either in Church or State, but otherwise they were thorough English Churchmen and loyal English citizens. If their Churchmanship, so far as it touched upon politics, was favourable to the Jacobite cause, so, too, was that of the national clergy, and so, too, it might be fairly said, was that of the queen herself.

The Nonjurors, therefore, who continued separate at the end of Queen Anne's reign were either uncompromising adherents of the Pretender, or men whose estrangement from the English Church was gradually hardening into hostility. Hickes was their first leader; who, as far back as 1693, had been, together with Wagstaffe, consecrated by Lloyd, White, and Turner to the nominal office of suffragan bishop, in strictest privacy, and greatly against the wish of the moderate Nonjurors. Wagstaffe died in the midst of the warm controversy which arose upon the return of Robert Nelson, Dodwell, Brokesby, and others to the English communion. Therefore, in 1713, Hickes called to his aid two Scotch Nonjuring bishops, and consecrated to a nominal Episcopacy Jeremy Collier, Hawes, and Spinckes. Thus was perpetuated what appeared to be a gratuitous schism even to many who had cordially sympathised with the original Nonjurors. They themselves, on the other hand, did not scruple to advance the claim that 'the true Church Regent, or College of Bishops, and the true Church of England depending upon it, are in the little and faithful suffering number, and will be in those who regularly succeed them in the royal priesthood unto the end of the world.'[1]

[1] *Constitution of the Cath. Church*, 1716; quoted in *Life of Ken*, by a Layman, p. 773.

The rent became wider still when the Brunswick dynasty succeeded. The Nonjuring ranks had indeed an accession to their number in one distinguished Churchman, whose whole spirit was utterly averse to ecclesiastical divisions and political intrigue. William Law,[1] then Fellow of Emanuel College, Cambridge, was unable to take the oath imposed after the coronation of the new king upon all who held fellowships or benefices. But his position as a Nonjuror was one of isolation. He was too deeply interested in the vital principles of Christianity to care greatly for discussing questions which had no intimate concern with conscience and the spiritual life. Nor did he ever separate himself in word or thought from the English communion. Sunday and week-day, he never, unless by necessity, omitted a service in his parish church.[2] As Nonjuror, no less than in the days when he spoke of Anne as the best of queens, William Law continued one of the most eminent worthies of our Church and one of its ablest writers.

But the Nonjurors generally, after the accession of George I., were mainly occupied by their differences with the polity of England, and by their differences with its Church. In the interval before the Jacobite rising of 1716 they were excited and alert,[3] full of hope that they might soon be, not in pretension, but in happy reality, the veritable Church of these islands. For the same reason they were fast beginning to be looked upon by the nation generally as its declared enemies. 'Papists and Nonjurors'[4] was becoming a combination of words ominous to them of trouble. At Drury Lane, in 1718, they were held up alike to the derision and detestation of the multitude as 'the stiff Nonjuring separation,'—

[1] Overton's *Life of W. Law*, p. 469.   [2] *Id.*, p. 225.
[3] Lathbury's *History of the Nonjurors*, p. 258.
[4] *Reliquiæ Hearnianæ*, i. 188; Hoadly's *Answer to Convoc.*, p. 309.

> Who at our surest, best foundation strike,
> And hate our monarch and our Church alike.

Then, referring to the disabilities which were heaped upon them after the collapse of the Jacobite movement,—

> Each lurking pastor seeks the dark,
> And fears the justice's inquiring clerk.
> In close back rooms his routed flocks he rallies,
> And reigns the patriarch of blind lanes and alleys;
> There, safe, he lets his thundering censures fly,
> Unchristens us, and gives our laws the lie,
> And excommunicates three stories high.[1]

Nor can this feeling of aversion be wondered at. If even a learned and accomplished man like Dr. Hickes could write that 'the English clergy can perform no valid acts of priesthood. Their very prayers are a sin, their sacraments no sacraments; . . . though they should die martyrs in their schism, their martyrdom would not be accepted,' &c.,[2] what violence of language would some others stop short of? It seems like going back to the old days of Donatists and Circumcellions, when little African sects unchristianised the whole Catholic body, and scraped as if from pollution the very altars of the churches which they had invaded. But virtue and learning—for the Nonjurors as a body were not wanting in either—appear to be almost as helpless as barbarism itself against the distorting effects of dwelling too exclusively upon a single set of ideas.[3] These men, who had sacrificed so much for their principles, and who yet could no longer defend the position they had taken except by investing their special opinions with a fictitious importance, lost all sense of proportion when they began to declaim on

---

[1] Prologue to Cibber's 'Nonjuror.'

[2] Quoted from Hickes's *Collection of Papers*, by Kennet, in his *Letter to the Bishop of Carlisle*, p. 39.

[3] *The Freethinker*, No. 32, July 11, 1719.

their favourite subject. The greater their isolation, the more extravagant became their pretensions. The same spirit naturally breeded dissensions among themselves. 'The Nonjuring fanatics,' wrote an essayist of 1719, 'who think themselves the favourites of Heaven, refuse quarter even to their old friends when they happen to boggle at any of their extravagances.'[1]

A little before Hickes's death, in 1715, they were hotly at variance among themselves on the subject of the 'usages,' some adhering to the Anglican practice, others advocating a return to all that had been omitted in the second book of Edward VI.—the mixed cup, the prayer for the dead, the invocation of the Holy Spirit upon the consecrated elements, and the prayer of oblation to express that the eucharist is a proper sacrifice. The question was, of course, not exclusively a Nonjuring one. Many divines in the Established Church had from time to time argued that they were still permissible, and had pleaded for their revival. But among the Nonjurors it became a question that was contended so keenly, that for twelve or fifteen years the two parties absolutely divided, each electing their own bishops. By about 1732 almost all of them had become usagers. But about that time there were already many who separated decidedly from the Anglican Church by publishing a service book of their own, and prohibiting all communion with those who continued the use of the Book of Common Prayer.[2] They all were, throughout, strongly hostile to the Romish Church. Some of them wrote against its corruption, and Charles Leslie, one of their ablest members, not only engaged in the Roman controversy, but braved many painful rebuffs, and much systematic neglect, in vain attempts to convert the Pretender to the Protestant faith. They were, however, very much in earnest in their efforts (1716–

[1] Lathbury's *Nonjurors*, pp. 278–92. [2] Lathbury, p. 390.

23) to establish a relationship of friendship and intercommunion with the Eastern Church. The Eastern patriarchs do not seem to have had a very clear idea who 'the suffering Catholic bishops of the old Constitution of Britain' might be. But they gave the Nonjuring proposals a full and courteous consideration, so far as that can be called consideration where no shadow of concession is granted. In a synodical letter signed by four patriarchs and several archbishops and bishops, they answered that nothing could be added and nothing taken away from the divine doctrines of the orthodox faith, and that all who wish to enter into communion with their Church 'must submit to them with sincerity and obedience, and without any scruple or dispute. And this is a sufficient answer to what you have written.'[1]

The Nonjurors' Jacobite opinions often brought them into sharp collision with the law. About 1720 they were described as very daring and troublesome; and one of their clergy, Laurence Howel, for his aspersions upon George I., was sentenced to be degraded and thrice whipped. The whipping was remitted, but he died in prison.[2] In 1723 Walpole brought forward a Bill for raising 100,000*l.* on the estates of Roman Catholics and Nonjurors.[3] In 1730 Hearne wrote of their prospects in a tone far more sanguine than real facts could have justified. 'I have been told,' he says, 'that at the court at London the Nonjurors are esteemed to be the honestest part of the nation, and that even Queen Caroline says so herself. I am also certainly informed that the Nonjuring Church of England gains ground in London every day.'[4] He speaks also of a difference in opinion among their body as to whether 'going

---

[1] Lathbury's *Nonjurors*, pp. 310-59.   [2] Nichols' *Lit. An.*, i. 31.
[3] Campbell's *Lives of the Chancellors*, iv. 405; Hoadly's Nineteenth 'Britannicus' Letter, *Works*, iii. 57.
[4] *Reliq. Hearnianæ*, iii. 61.

to the sermons at the public churches' could be countenanced, provided they did not attend the prayers.[1]

In the rebellion of 1745 some of their more ardent spirits threw themselves heartily into the Pretender's cause. One of them, by name Deacon, who had taken a prominent part in the later innovations upon the Common Prayer, died upon the scaffold with all the zeal of a martyr, asserting in lofty terms the high claims of the Nonjuring Church.[2] In the debates of 1748 upon the Bill for disarming the Highlands, Secker and Sherlock both pleaded for Scotch Episcopalians, but both drew a broad distinction between Jurors and Nonjurors.[3] Not a voice was raised for toleration of the latter. After the fifth decade of the century such Nonjurors as yet existed in England were quiet enough. In the 'Idler' for June 17, 1758, Jack Sneaker 'cannot believe that the Nonjurors can be quiet for nothing. They must certainly be forming some plot for the establishment of Popery. He does not think the present oaths sufficiently binding, and wishes that some better security could be found for the succession of Hanover.'[4]

The last Convocation of Queen Anne's reign had closed with the session of Parliament of July 9, 1714, not three weeks before the queen's death. In the May of the next year a summons was issued under the king's writ for it to meet and transact business. It seemed as if a course of usefulness were now before it. A list of subjects was submitted to it for discussion, upon which canons might be drawn up for the better regulation of various Church questions. These subjects were excommunications and

---

[1] *Reliq. Hearnianæ*, p. 159. [2] Lathbury, p. 388.
[3] *Parliamentary History*, 14, 276-304.
[4] *The Idler*, No. 10. Notwithstanding suspicions, the Nonjurors were to the last keen opponents of Romanism. It is rather curious that the Gordon phrenzy against Papacy began in Scotland with the letters of Abernethy, a Nonjuring bishop (T. Somerville's *My Own Life and Times*, p. 192).

commutation of penance, terriers of Church property, prevention of clandestine marriages, a form for consecrating churches and chapels, the better investigation of testimonials, &c., for candidates for holy orders, an amendment of the seventy-fifth canon on clerical irregularities, improve regulations for the residence of clergy on their benefices, curates' licences, preparation for Confirmation, and the more orderly performance of that office.[1] Convocation met accordingly, and twelve of the fifty new London churches recently voted by Parliament being now nearly completed, precedence of discussion was given to drawing up a form for the consecration of churches. In this and the ensuing session some progress was also made in some of the other questions upon which they had been requested to consult.

But in the spring of 1717 the Bangorian controversy had started into full life. Hoadly had preached the sermons which so outraged the special form which High Churchmanship had taken, and Convocation, always in that age far too ready to exercise its right of censuring heretical or objectionable publications, had turned zealously to the task. Some remarks will be made in a subsequent chapter upon Hoadly and his writings. As regards the particular charges at this time brought against him, there can be little doubt that, however repugnant the general spirit of his theology might be to most Churchmen, he had propounded no opinion which had not been expressed before him by many eminent divines in the English Church from the Reformation upwards. He had said some things which were very open to misapprehension. But no one can candidly read his 'Answer to the Representation of Convocation,' or even the summary in the concluding pages of it, without either assuming that his original meaning was very different from his explanation,

[1] Wilkins' *Concilia*, quoted in Perry's *Hist. of the Ch. of E.*, iii. 274.

or else granting that he stood upon what must be to Protestants the impregnable ground of Reformation principles. The former assumption, though constantly made, is gratuitous and unfounded. There is little or nothing in his sermons which is not easily and naturally susceptible to his own interpretation of it. He was very much misrepresented or misunderstood even on the point in which he was thought especially to have contravened the Articles of the Church. If, said they, sincerity as such, exclusive of the truth or falsehood of the doctrine or opinion, be alone sufficient for salvation, or to entitle a man to the favour of God—if no one method of religion be in itself preferable to another—the conclusion must be that all methods are alike in respect to salvation or the favour of God. 'But where,' answers Hoadly, 'do they find such a position in any part of my writings? . . . . The subject which gave occasion to what I said related expressly to a man's choice of a church or a communion. What I affirm is that in this choice it is his sincerity in the conduct of himself which will justify him before God. This I maintain to be so far from supposing that no one method of religion is preferable to another, which the learned committee have represented as the very same point, that it relies upon and supposes the very contrary position to this, viz., that one method of religion is preferable to another, and that therefore we ought to the utmost of our powers to choose that one method which is the best; but that, infallibility not being our privilege, Almighty God puts our title to His favour upon our present sincerity and uprightness in this choice.'[1]

The committee appointed by Convocation to draw up their representation were not intentionally unfair, and the wording of their indictment is very moderate; but Hoadly's views on Church authority came at a time when they were

[1] Hoadly's *Answer*, &c., § 21.

particularly offensive to a vast number both of clerical and lay Churchmen. Romanist efforts had been triumphantly defeated; Dissent was in a very depressed condition, and its fortunes apparently in complete wane; the Sacheverell trial had proved, if nothing else, at all events that the Church was very popular with the multitude. Everything flattered and encouraged what is always the innate propensity of human nature, to believe that their own doctrines rested upon peculiar and indefeasible authority and truth. There were doubtless great numbers who believed in their hearts that the English Church had succeeded to the authority which Rome laid claim to, and that its tenets could not be disputed without heresy and sin. The charge, therefore, was drawn up against Hoadly. But before it could be presented to the Upper House of Convocation, Government, alarmed at the movement, intervened. Convocation was prorogued in the first instance for six months, but practically until far into the next century. It never met again under any of the Georges for the regular transaction of business, and heavy as the blow was, and deplorable in some ways as was the injury inflicted by it, it cannot be said with Dean Swift that it was unprovoked.[1] Until its revival in our own days its meetings degenerated into a curt and melancholy form. At the meeting of a new Parliament, Convocation also was convened. The Lower House appointed its prolocutor—Tanner, for instance, afterwards Bishop of St. Asaph, in 1727, Waterland in 1732, and Lisle in 1735. The primate and other dignitaries met the clergy and the civil officials at Westminster Abbey or St. Paul's. The service was read in Latin, and a Concio ad Clerum delivered. They

---

[1] 'During the time that Convocations (which are an original part of our Constitution, ever since Christianity became national among us) are thought fit to be suspended, God knows from what reason or for what provocations'—('Considerations upon Two Bills,' &c., 1731; Swift's *Works*, viii. 342).

then proceeded to the chapter-house, voted an address to the Crown, and adjourned. Occasionally some further symptom of latent life was exhibited. In 1727 the Archdeacon of Lincoln brought forward certain 'gravamina,' which he was requested to put into writing for the next meeting of Convocation.[1] In 1742 an attempt was made by Archdeacon Reynolds to read a paper on Ecclesiastical Courts, but, being of a latitudinarian tendency, it was not acceptable to the House, and was stopped by the Prolocutor.[2] In 1749 the 'Free and Candid Disquisitions' upon the subject of revision of the Liturgy was 'addressed to the governing bodies in Church and State, and more immediately directed to the two Houses of Convocation.'[3] One of the suggestions in this treatise was the need of more occasional prayers, as, among others, for Convocation during their session.[4] In 1755 there was some synodical debate on the occasion of the publication of Lord Bolingbroke's works, and an address to the Crown asking for the suppression of Antichristian writings.[5] Convocation, in fact, maintained an existence just sufficient to keep the memory of it alive, and to make its revival a not unfrequent subject of conversation and argument. There were some Churchmen of the stiff, exclusive type, who liked it best in its worst aspect, and would have rejoiced to see once more the representatives of the people passing Schism Bills, and those of the clergy condemning the Burnets of that time. Thus Jenyns makes his country parson exclaim,—

> Heaven with new plagues will scourge this sinful nation,
> Unless we soon repeal the Toleration,
> And to the Church restore the Convocation.

To whom the squire, a friend of the Church, but not the

[1] Perry, iii. 365.   [2] Stanley's *Memorials of Westminster Abbey*, p. 525.
[3] Nichols' *Lit. An.*, i. 595.
[4] *Gentleman's Magazine* for 1750, vol. xx.   [5] Perry, iii. 366.

least wanting to see the country pedagogued by a narrow-minded synod, makes reply,—

> Plagues we should feel sufficient, on my word,
> Starved by two houses, priest-rid by a third.[1]

There were many others, both on the Whig and Tory side, who had no wish or thought of seeing any diminution of tolerance, but who felt it a gross injustice that the constitutional assembly of the Church should thus be gagged. Dr. Johnson was hot upon this point. '"David Hume told me,"' said Boswell, '"you would stand before a battery of cannon to restore the Convocation to its full powers." Little did I apprehend he had actually said this: but I was soon convinced of my error; for with a determined look he thundered out, "And would I not, sir? Shall the Presbyterian Kirk of Scotland have its General Assembly, and the Church of England be denied its Convocation?" and his eyes flashed with indignation.'[2] Horace Walpole, after his manner, sneered at any suggestion of its revival.[3] Occasionally, and especially a little before the middle of the century, there was some slight movement among the clergy on that subject. Thus, in 1741, the instructions to some of their proctors at a diocesan meeting contained the following: 'It is your lot to have been called to a provincial synod, after a long disuse of synodical conventions; in consequence of which a universal feebleness and debility has seized the whole ecclesiastical system. . . . Since then it is not to be expected that the episcopal government can be uniformly administered without synodical concert and councils, much less that subordinate courts can uphold the exercise of discipline, . . . our instructions to you are to move the synod to represent to his Majesty what advantage true

---

[1] S. Jenyns' *Poems*, 'A Dialogue,' 1719. [2] Boswell's *Johnson*, iv. 397.
[3] H. Walpole, *Mem. of Reign of George III.*, p. 532.

eligion and learning may reap from the councils of the clergy assembled in Convocation, and directed by his Majesty's wisdom, and most humbly to implore his favour to the Church in the revival of this primitive and legal method of discipline.'[1] Many felt that, although desirable on many accounts, its expediency was open to debate. Two long letters passed between Hurd and Warburton relating to it. 'There is no doubt,' wrote Hurd, 'but that the Church has lost much of her dignity and authority by this disuse of her Convocation; and by this means religion itself may have been considerably disserved. But in other respects, I have not light enough at present to determine for myself whether these Church synods would be of all the benefit to religion which Dr. Atterbury supposes. . . . Certainly any abuse or grievance, which it concerned the ecclesiastical state to take notice of, might be represented with more weight and effect to the Legislature. But then have not the bishops authority enough to regulate all material disorders within their dioceses? . . . And as to that part of the Convocation's office which is supposed to consist in watching over the faith and principles of the people, I should question if it would have any good effect. Bad books might be censured; good ones might, too; . . . and had Convocation been as busy twenty years ago as Dr. Atterbury would have it, I should have been in pain for the "Divine Legation."' Even just censures, he added, only increase the circulation of books.[2] 'I know,' answered Warburton, 'you are afraid I might some time or other publicly declare myself with more warmth than was fitting, in favour of so unpopular a thing as Convocation.' He then gave his opinion that, convinced though he was of the rights of Convocation, he also was not certain of the expedience of their frequent

---

[1] *Gentleman's Magazine* for 1741, xi. 481.
[2] Warburton and Hurd's *Correspondence*, H. to W., Aug. 1760, Letter 144.

sitting. His judgment was that it should be empowered by royal licence to examine particular questions, wherever such arose affecting the welfare of the country on Church points, and demanding careful consideration.[1] He has elsewhere said that he thought the laity ought to be represented in Convocation, as they were in Church synods before the Conquest.[2]

Archbishop Secker has left a Latin oration intended for the Convocation of 1761, but which he was unable to deliver on account of ill-health. In it he discussed at some length the suspension of its regular functions. We have met, he said, to consult, if such consultation be committed to us, in the interest of religion and sound morals. But no such question is submitted to us, or at present likely to be; and there are those who ask with ridicule why we continue to meet in solemn but empty form. Our synod, he answered, is a part of the ancient constitution of the realm, no less than the Houses of Lords and Commons; and though its action be suspended, it nowise ceases to exist. It had done good work in the past; and its future services, when opportunity should arise, must not be lightly prejudged. Meanwhile it was a stately meeting of Church representatives, met for prayer and mutual counsel, and testification of loyalty. There were many pious and learned men who earnestly desired a restoration of its power. On the other hand, Deists, and Romanists, and Dissenters, and others cried out against any action of Convocation, and talked of Church tyranny and the like. There were jealousies and suspicions, and he feared that some had not been altogether without ground; at all events, they were not easily to be removed. At the present time there were not many nor difficult subjects for deliberation; but if once Convoca-

[1] *Id.*, Warburton to Hurd, October 1760, Letter 145.
[2] Quoted in Caswall's *American Church*, p. 128.

tion met for business, innovations and differences, offences and attacks, would at once start into life, and Government, without which the king could not act, was particularly anxious that the quiet of the Church should not be disturbed. If Convocation consulted only on small matters, it would be dishonoured and thinly attended. If it dealt with important questions, there would be violent differences of opinion, which might probably be most injurious to the Church, or would at least stir up great hostility from without. Although, therefore, he was well aware that the constitution of the Church was mutilated without its Convocation, he deprecated precipitate action. He would willingly wait till controverted subjects could be debated in a calmer spirit. Meanwhile, if they could not construct canons, they must seek by word and example to instil obedience to the canon of Holy Scripture. If they could not fulminate anathemas against the heterodox, they must endeavour all the more to confute them by their arguments.[1]

At the end of Queen Anne's reign much, and a great deal too much, had been heard of divine right and passive obedience. With the queen's death it all died rapidly away. If any High Churchmen still boasted that 'the Church of England is sincere, loyal, uniform, and generous in her obedience,'[2] either it expressed the thought of one who in heart had no true king on this side the sea, or he spoke of the past rather than of the present. Most of the clergy were fairly loyal, and on occasion expressed their loyalty even with effusion. But Whig Churchmen, who were really attached to the dynasty, had had the old sentiment rooted out of them by the counter-spirit of the Revolution; and Tories, however faithfully they might give their allegiance to the Crown, had no liking whatever for the king. Not

[1] 'Oratio coram Syn. Prov. Cant.,' Secker's *Charges*, pp. 350-75.
[2] *The Scourge*, Feb. 1717, p. 9.

till George III.'s time did the long-ingrained spirit of
loyalty cordially revive. Queen Anne's time seemed so
quickly to recede into the far past that we read with some
surprise that, even in 1726, Sacheverell was, against his
will, followed as much as ever; and that not the Church
only, but the churchyard, was still crowded when he
preached.[1] At Oxford alone, and to some extent in the other
university, the doctrine of 'passive obedience still sat
enthroned,'[2] and gradually transferred itself without an
effort from the Stuart to the Brunswick kings. Of
Oxford and Cambridge, Pope wrote as late as 1762,—

> May you, my Cam and Isis, preach it long,
> The right divine of kings to govern wrong.[3]

In 1772, Dr. Nowell, principal of St. Mary Hall, preached
before the House of Commons a sermon so full of high
Tory sentiment, that although at the time he was as usual
thanked, and his sermon ordered to be printed, the thanks
were afterwards expunged.[4]

The old 'Church in Danger' cry,[5] which had been so great
a force in the latter part of Queen Anne's reign, was also
the occasion of some serious riots after George I.'s accession.
But after the Jacobite rising it was scarcely heard again.
The renewed fear of Popery had overpowered the fear of any
danger from Dissent. Presbyterianism also in England had
suddenly and rapidly declined; and Sir Robert Walpole
was careful to an excess not to give any opening for a
renewal of the old alarm. But it was often spoken of as a
memory of the past; and often, as time went by, the perils
from which the Church was supposed to have escaped gained
in magnitude by tradition. 'It was at a season,' says Parson

---

[1] Lady Sundon's *Memoirs*, p. 314. [2] Wakefield's *Memoirs*, p. 60.
[3] Fourth *Dunciad*, p. 188. [4] Boswell's *Johnson*, iv. 264.
[5] Overton, in pp. 383-86 of *The Eng. Ch. in the Eighteenth Cent.*

Adams, 'when the Church was in danger, and when all good men expected they knew not what would happen to us all.'[1] Thus also the learned Dr. Jortin, in a sermon of 1747: 'Our eyes then viewed her as they pursue the mild and gentle light of the setting sun. We then began to understand her value, because we then feared to lose her.'[2]

A marked feature in the ecclesiastical history of England, for a full generation after the time of the Revolution, had been the prominence of the position ascribed to the English Church as heading the Protestant interest throughout Europe. But when the treaty of Utrecht had ended the war, and when the overthrow of Jacobite hopes early in George I.'s time had made Englishmen feel that Protestantism in their own country was secure, their interest in other churches began rapidly to fade. In the beginning of George I.'s reign, while the recent constitution might at any moment have to confront sudden and formidable danger, the idea of a Protestant confederacy was still one which might very easily be revived. When the new king met his Parliament, he spoke of the need there was that 'all friends of the present happy Establishment should unanimously concur in some proper method for the greater strengthening of the Protestant interest; of which, as the Church of England is unquestionably the main support and bulwark, so will she reap the principal benefit of every advantage accruing by the union and mutual charity of all Protestants.'[3] Both Lords and Commons warmly echoed these sentiments. About the same time, in 1716, there was some practical demonstration of sympathy in the response to a brief read in all churches for the relief of the suffering Protestants in Lithuania.[4] Bennett's book on the Protestant Church of

---

[1] Fielding's *Jos. Andrews*, p. 146.　　[2] Jortin's *Works*, i. 363.
[3] Calamy's *Autobiog.*, ii. 387, &c.
[4] Fleetwood's *Works*, p. 704; Malcolm's *London*, i. 22.

Poland, published the same year, passed at once through a second edition. This was almost the last sign of anything like wide and general interest in the struggle against Romanism on the Continent. High Churchmen had always been more or less inclined to accentuate the differences which separated them from non-episcopal communions abroad, and to offer the hand of fellowship in the cause of mutual defence, or of mere charity, rather than of cordial good-will. Men suspected of Jacobite leanings were constantly accused of minimising all that separates us from Rome, from anxiety to prove to themselves and to others that no great harm would ensue even if the king were personally a Roman Catholic. And though this feeling was not the least shared by Englishmen in general, yet the strong public antipathy to all that was distinctively German in the new king so far extended itself to foreigners in general as to have a visible effect in making opinion more entirely insular. Jealousy of Hanover, of Hanoverian soldiers, and of royal attachment to Hanover, was to be for a long time a far stronger influence than any interest in North German Protestantism. Hoadly, Kennett, Hare, and other Whig Churchmen often dwelt upon the need of uniting for the defence of the common Protestant cause. Wake, Butler, Secker, and other eminent prelates maintained a friendly correspondence with the leaders of other reformed churches in Europe. In 1719, the king, who was then in Germany, made, with universal approval, some strong representations to the ymperor in favour of the suffering Protestants of the empire. The Dissenting deputies, in an address to the king two or three months before his death, hailed him as 'the common father of all Protestants.'[1] In 1732, General Oglethorpe was assisted by Parliament in providing a refuge in Georgia, not only for poor debtors, but also for 'oppressed Protestants of

[1] Calamy, ii. 491.

other countries.'[1] But neither in the country in general, nor in any considerable party, was there any longer much thought of a Protestant confederacy, headed, in its two aspects, by the State and Church of England. In 1751 a renewed attempt was made to effect a general naturalisation of Protestants. Yet it is noticeable that both the promoters of the Bill and its assailants rested not so much upon religious or patriotic as upon economic and commercial arguments.[2] It may be remarked, also, that when the English people were watching with delight the triumphant campaigns of Frederic the Great, there does not appear to have been the slightest admixture of envy that the part of Protestant hero (for it was in this light that Frederic was regarded) should be filled, not by an English, but by a Prussian leader.

It has been seen that in 1710, in a remarkable speech before the House of Lords, Archbishop Wake had recalled to mind the schemes of Church comprehension which had occupied so much attention in the preceding reign, and had lamented their failure. Reference has also been made to his efforts in George I.'s time for promoting closer fellowship both with the Gallican Church and with Protestants abroad. His earnest aspirations after a greater visible unity are no less apparent in his letters to Courayer in 1726.[3] A thoroughly Catholic-hearted man, he was pained and troubled that there should be so much estrangement on this side and on that among those whom he knew to be all true members of the Church of Christ, agreed in essentials, though differing in judgment in certain particulars of

[1] Oglethorpe's *Memoirs*, p. 51.
[2] Mahon's *History*, chap. xxxi.; H. Walpole's *Mem. of George II.*, p. 54; Tucker's *Expediency of a Law for Naturalisation, &c.* Tucker dwells much on the sympathy of distinguished English divines of an earlier age with Protestantism on the Continent.
[3] Several of his letters are given in Lady Sundon's *Memoirs*, i. 81-84.

doctrine. Nine years later we find another good man occupied with somewhat similar thoughts. Bishop Berkeley did not, like the archbishop, cherish designs of comprehension. But as on the one hand he gained, by his never-failing courtesy and consideration, the affectionate esteem of many Roman Catholic ecclesiastics in Ireland, and proposed the admission of their co-religionists into the college at Dublin without any obligation of attending chapel or divinity lectures, so also he wrote to a friend that 'a principal end proposed by me has been to promote a better understanding with the Dissenters, and so by degrees to lessen their dislike to our communion.'[1] In the very opposite spirit to that which had carried the odious Schism Bill, he was of opinion that every encouragement should be given them to improve in all liberal studies. He was also anxious that an order of lay readers should be promoted, so that young men who felt they had a vocation for doing spiritual good might have a ready opening made for them in the English Church.[2]

About this time it would have been felt very unsafe to relax in any way the terms of communion. Deistical writings were more in vogue than at any earlier or later date; Arian and other unorthodox opinions were in favour at court; and there were some, as Potter said, who were ready to embrace 'in the general scheme of comprehension or confusion' all sorts of error.[3]

'Oh, how I do wish,' wrote one of Doddridge's Nonconformist correspondents in 1744, 'for the sake of our common Christianity, for the breaking down of the wall of separation between our brethren of the Church of England and ourselves!'[4] 'Some hints,' writes another in 1745, 'have

---

[1] Berkeley to Johnson, June 1735; Fraser's *Life of Berkeley*, 4, 211.
[2] Id. [3] Quoted in Hunt, iii. 74.
[4] Doddridge's *Correspondence*, iv. 358.

been given towards proposals of comprehension. Pray, good doctor, what are your sentiments? How far is it an object to be wished for, for the honour of our common Christianity and Protestantism? Indeed, where rational piety and solid virtue so visibly languish as in the present age, it matters little what external forms or party names flourish or decay.'[1] Archbishop Herring, as will be seen in the sketch of his life, was as warmly in favour of the project as was compatible with a somewhat careless and indolent temper. Even Archbishop Secker, though very cautious not to commit himself to any scheme of innovation, wrote to Doddridge that 'he agreed with him heartily in wishing that such things as we think indifferent, and you cannot be brought to think lawful, were altered and left free, in such manner that we might all unite. He had no reason to believe that any of the bishops thought otherwise, and he knew some wished it strongly. Nor, perhaps, were the body of the clergy ever so well disposed to it. Still he did not think there was the least prospect of it. There was not enough disposition among men of influence to take any pains about it.'[2] In fact, amid many mutual compliments, and much interchange of kindly wishes, the correspondence ended in nothing. Doddridge wrote also to John Wesley on the subject. It might seem as if through Methodism there were a great hope of promoting Christian harmony. If this great movement could have been retained in close intimacy with the Church of England as a voluntary organisation of all who wished to use it, as helping them to a holier life, it might also, from another point of view, have conduced greatly to the promotion of Christian unity.

In 1768 another very distinguished Nonconformist, Dr. S. Chandler, after speaking of Professor Turretin with approval as engaged in a good work of reconciliation, went

[1] Doddridge's *Correspondence*, iv. 141.   [2] *Id.*, p. 382.

on to express a wish that by a few alterations and concessions the English Church would 'remove some of her enclosures, and open her bosom to receive many now excluded from her communion and ministry.'[1]

The Schism Act of 1714 was happily the last act of legislative intolerance against Protestant Dissenters. Intolerance was indeed far from dead, and much that had been framed in such a spirit remained yet to be repealed, part of it speedily, part of it not for a long lapse of years. The Schism Bill was indeed doomed from its very birth. It came into operation on the very day the queen died. But better counsels in this respect came in with the new reign; and even if the queen had lived, it is very doubtful whether the tide of reactionary extravagance which had set in with the Sacheverell trial, and which alone had sufficed to carry the Bill, would not very quickly have subsided. Its provisions were never enforced, although at least one notable Dissenting academy, that of Henry Grove at Taunton, was for some time closed. A measure for its repeal was brought forward by Earl Stanhope in the December of 1718, and carried, though not by large majorities,[2] early in the ensuing February. Some of the bishops were strongly in favour of the proposal, and some spoke on that side with much earnestness. Others took a different view. Among them, somewhat unexpectedly, was Archbishop Wake, who dishonoured his earlier opinions by the foolish argument that there was no need to repeal a Bill of which no advantage had ever been taken.[3] The Act against Occasional Conformity was removed from the statute-book at the same time, and some clauses of the

---

[1] Chandler's *Case of Subscription*, quoted in Tayler's *Retrospect of Religious Life in England*, p. 261.

[2] In the Lords by 55 to 33; in the Commons by 263 to 202.

[3] *Parliam. Hist.*, vii. 570.

Test and Corporation Acts. Stanhope had obtained permission from the king and Cabinet to move for their entire abrogation,[1] and might perhaps have succeeded if the Nonconformists had not been too easily content with what they had got. But they were afraid of awakening a fresh burst of intolerance, and, in fact, were not quite unanimous in wishing it. There were some very good Whigs who thought the test was a necessary fence against Popish recusants. In 1730, and again in 1734 and 1739, new efforts were made for the abolition of the two Acts. But Sir Robert Walpole would not support the movement. Lord Hervey takes us behind the scenes, and shows us the dilemma in which the minister found himself, and the manœuvres to which he had resort—how he felt he could not directly oppose the measure, but was particularly anxious to avoid the hot contentions to which it would give rise—how he interviewed the queen and gained her to his side—how he schemed, but without much success, to make Hoadly believe that a delay of the measure was necessary even in the interests of toleration—how, finally, he contrived a packed committee to treat with the Nonconformist deputies, and prevail upon them, as they eventually did, that the movement was at present inexpedient.[2] And so the sacramental test remained, fitly described even at that time as 'a scandal to the Reformation, and a handle to libertines and Deists.'[3] It became, no doubt, at last innocuous for actual harm, like a rusty weapon, as Lord Mahon calls it, hung up in an armoury, a mere trophy of past power.[4] But it was not this for some length of time. In 1748 the Corporation of London thought that the conscientious scruples of Dissenters might properly build for the City a Mansion House.

---

[1] Campbell's *Lives of the Ch.*, iv. 395.
[2] Lord Hervey's *Memoirs of the Reign of George II.*, pp. 144–58.
[3] *Gentleman's Mag.* for 1739, ix. 19.   [4] Quoted by Campbell, iv. 494.

Dissenters, therefore, were elected to the office of sheriff, though one was blind and another was bedridden. Six hundred pounds was made by a by-law the fine for declining to serve; and between that time and 1767, when the Lords decided in favour of the Nonconformist objectors, no less than 15,000*l.* had been collected by these fines.[1]

Vehement as the ebullition against Nonconformity had been at the end of Queen Anne's reign, it was soon, to speak generally, succeeded on either side by tolerant and friendly feeling. The mobbing of meeting-houses, the repressive legislation, the threatening of coming measures more coercive still,[2] were followed in a few years by a mutual kindliness which contrasted very remarkably with the spirit which had recently prevailed. Swift, writing in 1732, asked what could be the cause of the change, and why such great tenderness to Dissenters was everywhere prevailing. Was it chiefly owing to the fear of Popery? or did it arise from a worse cause—from such a spread of Deism, scepticism, and indifference that the nature of belief was coming to be thought a small matter?[3] No doubt both these causes had something to do with it. It was clear also that in some directions an intelligent spirit of toleration had been making great strides. Besides this, the fears of danger to the Church had now become quite tranquillised. For nearly a generation the growth of Presbyterianism had been to timid Churchmen a continual cause of an alarm which had sometimes almost risen into panic. In any case these fears would have abated. But Presbyterianism in England began almost of a sudden to suffer under a quick decline. It divided and broke up, some returning to the National Church, others swelling the ranks of Unitarianism or other denominations. 'In less

---

[1] Lord Mansfield's speech, quoted in Rutt's notes to Calamy, ii. 273.
[2] Calamy, ii. 288. [3] Swift's *Works*, viii. 125.

than half a century the doctrines of the great founders of Presbyterianism could scarcely be heard from any Presbyterian pulpit in England. The denomination vanished as suddenly as it had arisen, and, excepting in literature, has left little visible trace of the greatness of its power.'[1] The Quakers increased in numbers, and the Unitarians began to form into a separate body more definitely than hitherto they had done. After a short time the Moravians became numerous and active, though their leaders did not consider that adoption of their views in any way implied separation from the English Church. With these exceptions the decay of Presbyterianism in this country was, to a less extent, shared by Nonconformity generally. While the Church was labouring under the Bangorian controversy, Dissent was being agitated by a still more vehement dispute upon the question of subscription to belief in the doctrine of the Trinity as defined in the first of the Thirty-nine Articles, and in the fifth and sixth answers of the Westminster Catechism. At an important meeting at Salters' Hall, on February 17, 1819, the subscription was rejected by a majority of 79 to 63, on the ground that the imposition of a creed was inconsistent with the principles of Protestant Dissent. This decision increased the ferment; the one party being bent upon vindicating themselves from a Unitarianism which, in many various degrees, was evidently gaining ground; the other protesting against any sort of declaration which was not expressed in the exact words of Scripture. The Presbyterians were chiefly against subscription; the Congregationalists, although much divided on other points, were nearly unanimous on the opposite side; the General Baptists opposed the test; the Particular Baptists were in favour of it. The contest was very hot, first in the west and in London, afterwards throughout the country

[1] Skeats's *Hist. of the Free Churches*, p. 311.

and in Scotland. Nonconformity was much weakened by it, both by the divisions which it caused, and by the secession to the English Church of some of the best and most learned of the ministers, and also by its distracting effect upon quiet religious life. Indeed, there can be little doubt that the friendly and peaceful feeling which, with many exceptions, subsisted through a great part of the century between the National Church and Nonconformity was not one which was altogether to the praise of either party. It arose in great measure out of a sort of lukewarmness and absence of strong religious motive; and when, through the action of the Methodists and Evangelical movements, spiritual life regained greater force, either party began once more to be too much in earnest in behalf of their distinctive tenets to speak of them in the easy and careless manner which had been frequent heretofore. For the long interval the points on which both were most in earnest were very nearly the same. They had a common enemy in Deism; and the many able defenders of Christian truth who came forward from the ranks of the Established Church were admirably supported by such learned Nonconformist writers as Samuel Chandler and George Benson, Grove and Foster. Both were troubled with very analogous difficulties on questions of subscription; both descanted on the great reasonableness of Christianity; both were scared at the very name of enthusiasm; and consequently most leading men on either side viewed with great suspicion the advances of a popular movement which, through the revival of religious warmth, was to do far more in strengthening both the Church and the old Nonconformist denominations than in weakening them by the multitudes which it withdrew from their congregations. Since, therefore, there was so much in common, there can be little wonder that many leading Nonconformists began to feel very doubtful how far scruples which they felt but weakly could justify a continued separation; or that Churchmen, on the other hand, should often speak with indifference of any concession which it might be thought desirable to make. In any case, it is very certain that the life of Dissent seemed for a long time to be definitely ebbing away,[1] and that there was very generally an excellent understanding between leading men on either side. Nonconformists gladly accepted the small annual grant which, under the name of the Regium Donum, was commenced in 1723; they attended in large numbers the sermons of every Church preacher of any eminence; and, reversely, a great many clergymen swelled the congregations of the eloquent Baptist minister, Dr. James Foster.[2] Doddridge maintained a cordial correspondence with half the bishops on the bench. Similar friendly relations were kept up between the principal Churchmen of their time, and Watts, Chandler, and other prominent Dissenters. Towards the middle of the century there was also much greater concord among Nonconformists than there had been heretofore. Watts was carried to his grave in 1748 by two Independent, two Presbyterian, and two Baptist ministers;[3] and this was but a symptom of an association which was becoming general.

It is evident that among the more educated classes the principles of toleration made immense growth in the forty years that elapsed between the close of Queen Anne's reign and the accession of George III. That they were defective as judged in the light of later opinion will of course be readily granted; but still the change was so great as almost to mark an era in the history of religion. When Locke

---

[1] Mosheim's *Eccles. Hist.*, v. 94; Doddridge's *Corresp.*, iv. 72, 358; Hunt's *Rel. Th.*, iii. 246; Skeats's *Hist. of the F. Ch.*, 334.

[2] Stoughton's *Relig. in England under Q. Anne and the Georges*, p. 332.

[3] Tayler's *Retrospect*, &c., 256.

died in 1704, he was on this point far in advance of all but a small minority of thoughtful men. Had he taught the same doctrines in 1754, he would no longer have been perceptibly in advance of his age. To Mosheim, writing about 1755 at Gottingen, it seemed that England was possessed of an 'unbounded liberty' in religious matters; 'and I do not hear,' he adds, 'that a spirit of intolerance characterises the episcopal hierarchy.'[1] 'Freedom from oppression,' said Doddridge, 'is a redeeming feature of the time.'[2] So also Baptista Angeloni, in 1755, wrote that from much observation, and in justice to the Church of England, he must own there was a generosity and a liberality of sentiment in it greater than he feared was at all good for its welfare.[3]

There were, however, many both among clergy and laity to whom this gentler spirit was yet unknown, and it had not penetrated far into the general populace. As mobs, not without applause from many who should have known better, wrecked meeting-houses in 1714, so they tore down Roman Catholic chapels in 1780, and so also, here and there, they rabbled Methodist meetings. In 1753, and the next year, a disgraceful outburst of savage intolerance was elicited by the Bill for the Naturalisation of Jews, and was so far successful that the Bill was repealed. Were it not that very recent instances have proved that in more than one European country the old fanaticism against Jews is still far from extinct, the passions excited by the measure would indeed seem surprising. The bishops, and almost all the better educated of the clergy, defended the cause of tolerance; but the spirit which prevailed among the populace was so violent that there was fear lest it might possibly

---

[1] Mosheim's *Ch. Hist.*, v. 99.
[2] Doddridge's *Sermon on the Lisbon Earthquake*, p. 37.
[3] Angeloni's *Letters on the English Nation*, ii. 65.

result even in massacre. Warburton spoke of it, not without reason, as a perfect wickedness of intolerance.[1] So long as the ferment lasted the clamour seemed to have been more excited and universal than was caused by any other event in the century. '"No Judaism! no Judaism!" is now,' exclaims a pamphleteer, 'the popular cry in town and country. Invectives against the Jews are what Mercury is still carrying from one end of the British Isles to the other.'[2] An essayist in the 'Connoisseur,' writing as much in seriousness as in banter, describes 'the town I have been speaking of as divided into two parties, who are distinguished by the names of Christians and Jews. The Jews, it seems, are in the interest of a nobleman who has given his vote for passing the Jew Bill, and are held in abomination by the Christians. The zeal of the latter is still further inflamed by the vicar, who every Sunday thunders out his anathemas.... In this he is seconded by the clerk, who is careful to enforce the argument from the pulpit by selecting staves proper for the occasion.' He goes on to speak of 'the little crosses at the breast,' which the ladies were wearing to signify their zeal in behalf of their threatened faith.[3] For, indeed, extraordinary as it may seem, the permission for Jews to naturalise without acknowledgment of Christianity created in vast numbers of the untaught, and of the ill-taught, a very panic lest the country should apostatise from its Christian profession. To be suspected of sympathy with the detested Bill was a formidable barrier to success at the elections;[4] and the bishops lost more popularity by their manly stand

---

[1] Warburton's *Corresp.*, p. 156.

[2] *The Crisis; or, An Alarm*, 1754, pt. ii. So also the *World*, No. 50; Walpole's *Memoirs of the Reign of George II.*, pp. 361-64, &c.

[3] The *Connoisseur*, No. 13, April 25, 1754.

[4] On this and other points some interesting details are given in Overton's chapter on 'Church Cries,' in the second volume of *The Eng. Church of the Eighteenth Cent.*

against the outcry than they had forfeited on the part of many of their number by real shortcomings.

The exceedingly severe measures adopted against Popery at the beginning of the century have already been referred to. For some time Jacobitism kept alive the fear that a life and death struggle between Rome and Protestantism in England might be yet impending; and so long as this dread could with any reason be entertained there was no thought of relaxing the stringency of the law. In 1721, about the time of Atterbury's trial, a hundred thousand pounds was raised upon the property of Popish recusants. A few lifted their voice against it as an act of persecution; but, for the most part, even the greatest champions of toleration upheld on political grounds the justice and expediency of the fine.[1] At the same time all Papists were required to depart from the cities of London and Westminster, and from within ten miles of the same, and to keep strictly within their own dwellings.[2] After this there was a lull. But when, towards the middle of the century, Jacobite machinations began to be again formidable, the position of a Roman Catholic, especially of a priest, became precarious. 'He was a priest,' wrote Fielding in 1742, 'but those who understand our laws will not wonder he was not over-ready to own it.'[3] After the rebellion of 1745 popular feeling became yet more exasperated.[4] It was not very long after this that Blackstone interpreted the law in the dreadful sense that 'where a person is reconciled to the see of Rome, or procures others to be reconciled, the offence amounts to high treason.'[5] The statute was not, indeed, ever carried out to this sanguinary extent, but it rendered the priest liable to perpetual imprisonment, and the proselyte to loss of all his property.

---

[1] Especially Hoadly, in his letters signed 'Britannicus.'
[2] Rutt's Note to Calamy, ii. 654.   [3] Fielding's *J. Andrews*, B. III. ch. viii.
[4] Whiston's *Memoirs* (1748), ii. 602.   [5] Gibbon's *Memoirs of his Life*, 38.

The extracts from different journals of the day, in the 'Gentleman's Magazine' during the invasion of 1745,[1] show how the press was then teeming with invectives against Popery; with laments that the zeal against it should have slackened; with highly coloured representations of its superstitions; with warnings against its political tendencies; with propositions for the adoption of yet more stringent measures in opposition to it. One writes to show that the whole system is utter Paganism; another to argue that it may be doubted whether it is not worse than Atheism. The poet Shenstone, about this time, or a little later, after speaking of Rome as 'a hated fiend,' goes on to describe with exultation 'the righteous havoc' which, since the days of James II., had levelled so much that remained of the old monastic buildings, 'covering distant fields with the wrought remnants of the shattered pile.'[2] There were many whose prejudice or timidity so got the better of them, that they were half ready to believe that the last comer into their village might be a concealed Jesuit, and that 'Papists might be busy with French gold among the bishops and judges.'[3] The most ridiculous suspicions and imputations were levelled against distinguished men whose religious or ecclesiastical opinions did not quite fall into the general groove. Bishop Butler had set up a cross in his chapel, and therefore had become a proselyte of the Pope.[4] John Wesley was an 'enthusiast,' and was, therefore, continually charged with Papistical opinions; Doddridge himself, that most worthy Nonconformist, was, because of his Christian charity to Connell, declared to be half a Jesuit.[5]

It is clear, however, that during the generation which

---

[1] *Gent.'s Mag.*, vol. xv.   [2] Shenstone's *Ruined Abbey.*
[3] The *Idler*, No. 10, June 17, 1758.
[4] Bartlett's *Life of Bishop Butler*, 91, 190.
[5] Note to Doddridge's *Life and Correspondence*, iv. 29.

elapsed between the first and second Jacobite insurrections general feeling, and especially that of the more educated classes, had become very much mitigated towards Romanism. This may be attributed to several causes. There was no longer any serious fear of a revolution which would imperil Protestantism and place a descendant of James upon the throne. The National Church was powerful, and Romanism shared in the depression which had befallen Nonconformity in general. But Protestant Dissenters were prosperous and secure; Roman Catholics could only depend upon the indulgence of the law. It was difficult, therefore, to cherish any strong feelings against a people who were of necessity timid and retiring. Meanwhile a kindly feeling of a more definite kind had been gradually arising in many Churchmen who were none the less thoroughly staunch to their own principles. They had been struck with the charity and moderation exhibited on either side in the correspondence between Archbishop Wake and the Gallicans. They were pleased with Courayer's defence of Anglican orders. The strong High Church reaction at the close of Queen Anne's reign, and the cry of danger to the Church from Presbyterianism, had led many to declare that, of two evils, Romanism was better than Dissent. Men whose open or concealed sympathies were with the Jacobites, when at last they despaired of the Pretender becoming a Protestant, began to take a somewhat less hostile view of Romanism, in order to convince themselves or others that the interests alike of Church and State might be safe, even if a Roman Catholic were on the throne. It was of course to the interest of Rome to encourage this belief; and it is quite possible that, in view of the great advantages which would have been secured to the Vatican by a restoration of the Stuarts, large and unwonted concessions might have been granted. Hearne, exaggerating these possibilities, writes in 1725 that letters from Rome stated that it was a common saying there that the Pope was almost turning Protestant; that he was recommending the general reading of the Scriptures in the vernacular; that he declared customs and ceremonies were no matters of faith, and might be laid aside as parts of its drapery by provincial churches; that he thought of calling a general council; and that even the populace of Rome no longer had the same frightful notions of a heretic.[1] It may be added that the attacks of Daillé, Middleton, and others upon the authority of the primitive Fathers shocked not a few good Churchmen, and made them feel more clearly than they had done the common ground which they held in this respect with the great upholders of all ecclesiastical tradition. Lastly, the evident growth of Deism, and the loud assumptions of its teachers that they were the special champions of reason, inclined some minds to look less unfavourably than hitherto they had done upon a church in which doubts, or at least their open expression, were summarily laid to rest by a sterner voice of authority.

When external impediments are removed or slackened, Roman Catholicism will always and inevitably assert its attractiveness to minds of a certain class. Although, therefore, Romanism was comparatively inactive, not only because of the repressive statutes by which its energies were fettered, but also because it shared in the comparative indolence and weakness which seemed to have overtaken for the time almost every form of religious belief, it yet made a somewhat considerable increase in England. A great number of writers speak in every tone of alarm of the growth of Popery;[2] special lectures were in many places

---

[1] *Rel. Hearnianæ*, ii. 217.

[2] *E.g.* the *Freethinker*, Nos. 5 and 6; Doddridge's *Corresp.*, 3, 182; Secker's *Charges*, p. 19; De Foe's *Tour* (1727), iii. 189; Mackay's *J. through England*, i. 280; Chubb's *Works*, 'On Reason,' &c., p. 23; *Gent.'s Mag.*, ix. 31, &c.

given upon the subject; and in **1734**, Gibson, then Bishop of London, issued a circular letter on the necessity of using every means to provide the needful antidotes.[1]

Questions of subscription to the Articles, and of the interpretation which should be given to it, came forward most prominently in the latter part of the century. Yet they were much discussed in George I.'s and George II.'s reigns. Two or three causes rendered this inevitable. The subject has so much to do with the respective rights of authority and private judgment, that it was continually touched upon in the course of the Bangorian controversies. Neither was it possible that a discussion of this nature, when it was distracting every section of Nonconformity, should fail to attract attention in the National Church also. The Arian controversy brought it forward in more direct practical bearings; for a strong effort was being made to establish a right of holding office in the Church, notwithstanding opinions which were of a definitely anti-Nicene character. The question thus became more serious and more complicated than it had been before. So long as the main contention was that an Arminian construction might be legitimately put upon articles which wore a Calvinistic appearance, or while High Churchmen claimed to understand in one sense the words of a formula, and Low Churchmen in another, the difficulty might seem to be contained within manageable bounds. It became a matter of graver consequence when many feared that any increased laxity of interpretation might gradually deluge the Church with Arians or Deists.

The controversy, however, gradually recovered its natural proportions—partly because the revived Arianism was a temporary phenomenon, and soon abated; partly because it was tolerably apparent that nothing which could

[1] *Gent.'s Mag.*, iv. 702.

be said upon the subject would do much either to contract or extend the latitude which had hitherto existed. No honourable or honest man would enter upon a ministry in which every prayer he uttered would accuse him of hypocrisy or insincerity; and if the dishonourable and dishonest were not otherwise deterred from entering, they would not be excluded by the barrier of subscription. Even then there were remedies against heresies in the pulpit. As for minor differences, where men could honestly use the words of the Liturgy, it was certain that such liberty as had hitherto been conceded could not now be drawn in. A man might for his own part be of opinion that an article might bear no other sense than that which had been in the mind of its compiler, but when he was aware how many distinguished divines of every variety of thought had argued without censure for a wider latitude, it was no longer in his power to deny to others the right which he did not claim for himself.

By far the strongest writer in defence of a restricted view of subscription was Dr. Waterland. It may be readily acknowledged, even by many who do not quite agree with his conclusions, that he did a very good service to the Church. His clear and forcible reasonings must have often convinced even those who allowed a far wider interpretation of the Articles than he did, that Arianism had no right to offices of trust in the English Church. Here and there a clergyman might to his own satisfaction conscientiously defend his maintenance of such opinions; and it was quite certain that Anglican divines might with perfect sincerity hold various views as to the mode in which Christ's true divine nature was united with His humanity. But Waterland's writings, published at a time when both orthodox and heterodox divinity had a very large circulation, did much to counteract what was for the time a great danger. Perhaps

Waterland himself would have excluded from the ministry of the Church all who did not hold Trinitarian doctrine in its most definite and formulated sense; but he greatly strengthened the feeling, which in some influential quarters was growing weak, that at all events Antitrinitarians had no place there.

On other less material points the general result of the controversy was to confirm the reasonable liberty which English clergymen had hitherto enjoyed. Hoadly fairly maintained his position that 'the Articles were never so much as confined to any one particular determinate sense; but, on the contrary, were by public authority, as long ago as the time of King Charles I., declared to admit of several senses, which was then found expedient even for the honour and use of the highest and strictest Churchmen themselves.'[1] Thus also Archbishop Wake wrote to Professor Turretin of Geneva, in 1718, that it was very right to guard by subscription against the promulgation by ministers and professors of doctrines contrary to accepted confessions.[2] But, added he, we should be very careful not to multiply subscriptions, nor to inquire into private opinions on difficult points of doctrine nor lay down definitions not clearly revealed. On such matters no one had a right to impose any such burden upon men's consciences.[3]

Towards the middle of the century the question of subscription, which had not ceased to be much discussed,

---

[1] Hoadly's *Ans. to Conv.*, chap. ii., sect. 20, § 5.

[2] In support of subscription to articles which he held to be fundamental Archbishop Wake was ready to go to lengths which did not stop short of odious persecution. In 1721 he supported a Bill, happily thrown out by a large majority, which would have made stubborn Arians liable to perpetual imprisonment. It would have increased the stringency of what was already a severe law of William III. Wake in his latter years was a strange compound of liberality and intolerance.

[3] 'Conscientiis hominum credenda imponere, nisi in rebus claris et perspicuis, et ad salutem omnino necessariis, nec potest magistratus Christianus nec debet.' (Wake to Turretin, July 1718, Mosheim, *Eccl. Hist.*, v. 175.)

came again to the front. It was, as before, discussed partly in direct connection with the Arian heresy, and partly on independent grounds. In the latter aspect it entered into the controversy started by 'The Free and Candid Disquisitions,' published in 1749 by John Jones, vicar of Alconbury. This work, which received, as it deserved, great attention, suggested, among its other propositions in the direction of revision and reform, that 'the Thirty-nine Articles may be liable to just and reasonable exceptions when compared with the genuine sense of the Word of God, as that sense appears (at this day) to learned and inquisitive men. It may not be improper to observe that there are instances in the Christian world of churches which require no tests of this kind, and yet maintain a harmony of belief.'[1] It was about this time that Dr. Jortin wrote an able and well-considered treatise upon the varying senses in which subscription has been understood, and in defence of the wider and more general view.[2] This interpretation was, however, almost immediately afterwards much discredited by the advocacy of Clayton, Bishop of Clogher, whose opinions were almost avowedly Arian; and by that of Archdeacon Blackburne, whose dissatisfaction with the formulas of the English Church was so great as to be hardly compatible with his position as a clergyman of it.

The same year that 'The Free and Candid Disquisitions' were published, subscription was more incidentally considered in two larger publications of importance, David Hartley's 'Observations on Man,' and the 'Considerations on the Theory of Religion,' by Edmund Law, afterwards Bishop of Carlisle. Hartley, as might be expected, was averse to all subscriptions.[3] A man of deep and gentle

---

[1] § xxii. in the analysis of the work in the *Gent.'s Mag.* for 1750, xx. 164–66.
[2] 'Strictures on Subscription,' &c., Jortin's *Tracts*, ii. 417–21.
[3] Hartley's *Observations on Man*, pp. 344–60.

piety, his opinions were, however, of a very indefinite and undogmatic character. He had been prevented by conscientious scruples from taking holy orders, but was greatly interested in religious questions, and much concerned in the well-being of the English Church. Edmund Law's 'Theory of Religion' is a work well deserving careful study. He follows partly in the steps of the 'Essay on Redemption' published two years before (in 1747) by William Worthington. Like him, he was strongly impressed with the progressive character of Christianity. 'I am far,' he said, 'from imagining that Christianity is yet come to its mature state; that it is understood in the whole extent and held in its utmost purity and perfection in any one church.'[1] He considered that the Scriptures were far from being exhausted of their meaning, and in an excellent passage in which he speaks of the respect due to the past, of the advantages of the present, and of the hopes for the future, he says, 'Instead of looking back, and labouring to confine religion to the model of past times, or even to tie it down to its present state and model of improvement, we learn rather, with the great apostle, "to forget those things which are behind, and to reach forward to those things which are before."'[2] It is plain that such words are incompatible with holding that any church has a right to bind any of its members stringently down to one exclusive interpretation of truths which have not been revealed with absolute clearness.

At the beginning of the century there had been, of course, many Churchmen who had warmly advocated the revision of the Liturgy, as proposed to the Commission of 1689, and who greatly regretted the failure of the scheme. No one, however, contemplated the possibility of any re-

[1] Worthington's *Considerations on the Theory of Religion*, p. 208.
[2] *Id.*, p. 291.

newal of the attempt. There was a considerable party who would have resisted, as dangerous innovations, even the reformation of gross abuses, and who stoutly held that 'to alter anything in our Establishment is to bring a plague into the very bowels of it.'[1] The very name of reform had a savour to them of revolution or fanaticism. But in the middle of the century the desirability of it was again widely and vehemently discussed. The author of the 'Free and Candid Disquisitions' suggested, in 1749, a number of additions and alterations which he thought would add to the usefulness of the Liturgy, and increase the efficiency of the Church. His suggestions were many of them reasonable and well considered; and although in some quarters they were denounced with the utmost vehemence, the reception given to them was on the whole decidedly favourable. Several bishops and other eminent Churchmen expressed a cordial approval, so that for some years it was very commonly and generally expected that a revision was immediately impending.[2] Two or three things prevented it. One was the prevalent 'vis inertiæ' in Church matters. There were few who cared to exert themselves much in favour of changes which they thought desirable. Another cause was the absence, now that Convocation had been silenced, of any regular organisation for the discussion of such questions. A third and weighty objection was felt in the ominous activity of some who were notoriously heterodox.

> A liturgy wants mending : are free-thinkers
> The only coppersmiths—the only tinkers?
> Where are the clergy? doth not reformation,
> Purely religious, need a Convocation?[3]

And so the design dropped; and probably it was well it

---

[1] *The Scourge*, Oct. 21, 1717, No. 38.
[2] Jas. Hervey's *Works*, Letter 155 (1756), ix. 230.
[3] *Gent.'s Mag.*, Jan. 1750, vol. xx.

did. Alterations would have been, no doubt, cautious for the most part and sensible. But a liturgy improved to the taste of 1750 calls up too strongly the idea of a church renovated and repewed at that date, to make us feel otherwise than grateful that Secker and Sherlock and Herring, with the help of Doddridge and Chandler, were not more zealous in carrying out their plan.

Deism in England can only be spoken of here in general terms, and some remarks have been already made upon it in a previous chapter. It was there noticed how free-thought, after accomplishing the great work of the Reformation, was for several generations chiefly occupied with the questions which more immediately sprang out of the breach with Rome; how it gradually extended itself to wider fields; and how Locke, by popularising a systematic exercise of reason on theological subjects, set an example which, for good and evil, was diligently followed throughout the greater part of the eighteenth century. It was seen how Toland, in his 'Christianity not Mysterious,' laboured to remove from our faith whatever doctrines transcend the grasp of human reasoning. Reference was made both to the light and jesting scepticism of Shaftesbury, and to that really noble principle of his philosophy which insisted upon a belief in disinterested virtue. It was observed how Pope borrowed from Shaftesbury something of that easy optimism which undermined the barriers of right and wrong; and how Mandeville carried out the principle to its ultimate results, and proclaimed the demoralising theory that in politics, if not in ethics also, vice was but a modified form of virtue. It was noticed, lastly, how the earlier Deists of the century, dissembling their ulterior designs, or not yet fully aware how far their mode of thinking would carry them, professed adherence to what they considered the substance of Christianity, and directed their assaults most especially against the clergy of the Church. They proposed to show—and in this respect their successors followed in their wake—how a mass of corruption had been built up upon the foundations of Christianity by the imposture and self-seeking of its ministry.

But till near the end of Queen Anne's reign the Deism of the century was only in its prefatory stage. The distinctively Deistical period was that which extended through a little more than forty years from about 1713. In that year were published Collins' 'Discourse of Free-thinking,' Shaftesbury's 'Characteristics,' and Mandeville's 'Fable of the Bees.' Toland's 'Nazarenus' and 'Pantheisticon' appeared in 1718 and 1721; Collins' 'Grounds of the Christian Religion,' and his 'Scheme of Literal Prophecy,' in 1724 and 1726; Wollaston's 'Religion of Nature' in 1724; Tindal's 'Christianity as Old as Creation' in 1730; Woolston's 'Discourses on the Miracles' in 1727-30; Chubb's 'Enquiry concerning the Books of the New Testament,' his 'True Gospel,' &c., and other works, at various dates between 1739 and 1749; Morgan's 'Moral Philosopher' in 1738; Annet's 'Free-thinking the Great Duty of Religion' in 1739; Bolingbroke's posthumous works in 1753. In a sort of midway position between the assailants of Christianity and its strictly orthodox defenders may be mentioned the younger Dodwell's 'Christianity not founded on Argument' in 1741, and Middleton's 'Free Inquiry' in 1749. The 'Essay on Spirit' was published by Clayton, Bishop of Clogher, in 1751.

The remarks on this conflict will be only general. No attempt will be made to speak in detail either of the Deistical writers, or of the very numerous defenders of revealed religion by whom their arguments were combated. The struggle was at its height[1] about the time when Tindal

[1] Hunt's *Rel. Th. in E.*, iii. 159; Cairns' *Unbelief in the Eighteenth*

published his 'Christianity as Old as Creation.' Warburton[1] and Doddridge[2] both spoke of that work as an attack upon Christianity more artful and desperate than any subsequent to the time of Porphyry; and the former, exulting in his sense of power, and feeling that it was indeed a contest, as he said, 'pro aris atque focis,' set himself, like another Samson, and, like Samson, with too much of the earthy in him, 'to overturn the pillars of this famous edifice of iniquity.'[3] Few were more competent than he to detect ignorance, to expose false reasoning, and to overwhelm his opponents with a storm of learned and vituperative satire; and if he were not quite the advocate whom a church would do best to choose, his style of argument was perhaps more fitted to combat Deism in the minds of those over whom it had gained most power than the calmer reasoning of Butler, or William Law's appeals to the deeper springs of Christian feeling. Warburton was far indeed from being alone. Not in England only—though English divines took perhaps the foremost place—but in most European countries, Christianity, impressed with the importance of the crisis, but with no less confidence than before, ' undertook anew a like systematic course of self-defence with that which, fifteen centuries before, it had for the first time carried through with so much credit.'[4]

It may fairly be claimed that, upon the whole, the defenders of Christian doctrine remained masters of the

---

Cent., p. 85. The latter calls Tindal's work 'the key of the Deistic position.'   [1] Warburton's *Works*, iv. 714.

[2] Doddridge's *Works*, iii. 404.   [3] Warburton to Hurd, pp. 171 and 267.

[4] M. J. Matter, *Histoire du Christianisme*, iv. 391. The author, enumerating some of the most distinguished apologists, remarks, ' L'Allemagne, dans cette lutte, se montra toujours savante et grave ; l'Angleterre, sérieuse et convenable ; la France, parfois instruite, quelquefois moqueuse, toujours spirituelle. Un écrivain du Danemark fut plus éloquent que tous les autres apologistes, en montrant simplement ce qu'avait fait le Christianisme.' (*Id.*, 392.)

position. By the middle of the century the peculiar type of unbelief which had gone by the name of Deism was almost vanquished. Bolingbroke's works, published in 1753, gave some amount of new life and spirit to it.[1] But, notwithstanding their brilliant and effective style, they fell more flat on public attention than was generally expected. A contemporary attributed this to their being too bulky for the popular taste.[2] In no case would they have made the same stir as if they had been published fifteen years before. Some among the cultivated classes had cast aside their belief too entirely and decidedly to care any longer for what might be said on one or the other side. Many, on the contrary, who greedily read the more covert assaults of the earlier Deists had been alarmed and disgusted by the ribaldry of Woolston, and by the undisguised irreligion of some other writers. Deistical pamphlets had been very widely circulated, but so also had been those of the more eminent Christian writers, as is sufficiently proved by the number of editions called for. The Methodist revival had an indirect influence even upon the classes who were to no perceptible extent carried away by it, and Evangelicalism was already beginning to arise. Apart from all other causes, mere weariness of a long controversy carried some natural effects.

Thus the Deistical period passed away, to be succeeded in part by a gradual but real revival of religion, in part by a more thoroughgoing scepticism. Although the controversy had not been by any means an unmixed evil, it had evidently done much to loosen for the time the foundations of faith; and the evil, most conspicuous in upper-class society, had indirectly permeated even to the most illiterate. Throughout the century complaints of the immorality and infidelity

[1] *Connoisseur* for March 28, 1754, p. 44.
[2] Brown's *Estimate of the Manners of the Times*, i. 56.

of the age continually recur, but they are most frequent and best grounded in the middle of it. We may take a short space of seven or eight years immediately after 1750, and adduce a few testimonies from contemporary literature. 'It is impossible,' writes Bishop Butler in 1751, ' to forbear lamenting with you the general decay of religion in this nation, which is now observed by every one. . . . As different ages have been distinguished by different sorts of particular errors and vices, the deplorable distinction of ours is an avowed scorn of religion in some, and a growing disregard of it in the generality.'[1] Scepticism, said Doddridge in 1755, is general, and Christianity is openly renounced and blasphemed by multitudes of the great and vulgar.[2] Sherlock spoke in 1750 of ' the dissolute wickedness of the age,' and of ' the manifest and almost general contempt, or at least neglect, of the duties of religion.'[3] Secker, in 1758, of ' the dreadful progress which wickedness, profaneness, and avowed infidelity have made in the nation.'[4] Samuel Johnson, of Connecticut, speaking of the state of manners in England in 1756, exclaims, ' But what can be expected of such an age as this? O Deus bone, in quæ tempora reservasti nos!'[5] 'In Holland,' said Brown, in his ' Estimate of Manners,' 1756, ' religion *seems* yet to exist; while in England it is evidently destroyed.'[6] A paper in the ' World,' 1753, speaks of ' Christianity ' as 'entirely reasoned out of these kingdoms.'[7] Warburton in the same year, 1753, wrote impatiently of the way in which people spoke 'of the

[1] Butler's *Primary Durham Charge*, 1751, at beginning.
[2] Doddridge's *Sermon on the Lisbon Earthquake*, 1755, p. 37. Wesley's *Treatise on Original Sin*, Nov. 1756, might be quoted to the same effect (*Works*, vol. ix.), but the extremely dark view he takes in it of mankind in all times and countries deprives it of special value in this connection.
[3] Sherlock's *Works*, iv. 332, 337.   [4] Secker's *Charges*, p. 239.
[5] Johnson to Berkeley, Dec. 10, 1756; Beardsley's *Life of Johnson*, p. 230.
[6] Brown's *Estimate*, &c., 1756, i. 175.
[7] The *World*, May 24, 1753, No. 21.

wretched state of religion with the same phlegm and indifference as they speak of the broken power of the States of Holland.'[1] Horace Walpole, in 1751, records the appointment of a committee to consider on amending the laws against vices which had increased to a degree of robbery and murder beyond example.[2] The 'Connoisseur,' speaking in 1753 of Bolingbroke's writings, tells of infidel clubs, such as the 'Robin Hood' Society, where 'lawyers' clerks, petty tradesmen, and mechanics harangue on Toland, Tindal, Collins, Chubb, Mandeville, and Bolingbroke, and talk about "Paul" and "Peter." . . . Our polite ladies are, I fear, in their lives and conversation little better than free-thinkers. Going to church, since it is no longer the fashion to carry on intrigues there, is almost wholly laid aside.'[3] Fielding also, in 1752, speaks of the clubs, and especially of the 'Robinhoodians,' and of the discussion of its learned members 'whether relidgin was any youse to socyaty.' One great scholar said he 'made no doubt but that this society, by means of their free inquiry after truth, would in the end discover the whole; and that the manner in which a man was made would be no more a mystery to posterity than it is to the present age how they make a pudding.'[4] The 'Adventurer' for 1752 says, 'To dispute on moral and theological topics is become a fashion. . . . In almost every tavern and every alehouse illiterate petulance prates of fitness and virtue, of freedom and fate; and it is common to hear disputes concerning everlasting happiness and misery, the mysteries of religion and the attributes of God, intermingled with lewdness and blasphemy, or at least treated with wanton negligence and absurd merri-

[1] Warburton to Hurd, June 1753, *Correspondence*, p. 139.
[2] H. Walpole's *Memoirs of the Reign of George II.*, p. 41.
[3] The *Connoisseur*, March 28, 1754, No. 9.
[4] Fielding, in the *Covent G. Journal*, Jan. 18, 1752; *Works*, x. 13.

ment. . . . The effect as well as the manner of these fashionable disputes is always ill; they tend to establish what is called natural religion upon the ruins of Christianity; and a man has no sooner styled himself a moral philosopher than he finds that his duty both to God and man is contracted into a very small compass, and may be practised with the greatest facility.'[1]

The beginning of the last-quoted passage implies that amidst an abundance of flippant unbelief there was also a real and widespread interest in theological and moral subjects, which in itself was a more promising sign than mere dead indifference. Religion had been shaken and unsettled, rather than, as some thought, banished and destroyed. The minds of numbers were disturbed, prone to extremes, feverishly anxious to find a panacea for their perplexity, either in yet unexplored powers of reason, or in that which they had so long looked upon with horror— emotion and enthusiasm. This is vividly expressed in a letter written in February 1757 by Warburton to Hurd: 'There is an epidemic madness amongst us: to-day we burn with the feverish heat of superstition; to-morrow we stand fixed and frozen in Atheism. Expect to hear that the churches are all crowded next Friday, and that on Saturday we all buy up Hume's new Essays.'[2] Morbid as it often was, there was yet a movement in the soul of the nation, out of which improvement was likely to arise. The tens of thousands who flocked to the preaching of Wesley and of Whitefield bore ample testimony that a desire of better things, that a sense of sin, and even a thirst for holiness, might be quickened into life even in classes of men who had been considered vicious almost beyond precedent. In much the same way other large sections of society, upon

---

[1] The *Adventurer*, Dec. 9, 1752, No. 13.
[2] Warburton and Hurd's *Letters*, p. 239.

whom that wonderful movement had little or no effect, were, to a considerable extent, not unprepared to welcome back again a gospel which they had too hastily and inconsiderately abandoned.

The wave, so to say, of irreligion which appears to have passed through the country towards the middle of the century is by no means to be ascribed entirely to the Deistical movement, but it was certainly connected with it both in cause and effect. The Deists were in some cases men of high character, sincerely desirous of clearing away corruptions and following the truth. There were some of them who called themselves—and deserved to be called—Christian Deists, religious-minded men who were actuated by a pure desire of freeing Christianity from what they considered mere concretions that had encrusted upon it. And though this can hardly be said of Collins—for his hold on distinctively Christian doctrine must have been very slight—his upright principle and religious feeling caused it to be said of him that if he made shipwreck of his faith, he would certainly get to heaven on a plank.

Other leading Deists may have been men of very different character. At any rate, there can be no question that the opinions advanced by some of them, especially by Mandeville and Bolingbroke, were such as might easily be construed into encouragements to laxity of life. Speaking generally of them, their immediate and direct influence was in some most important respects altogether bad. Even if it be granted that their objects were good, that some of their objections were well worthy of very serious consideration, and that the free-thought which they were never weary of extolling was a principle which only requires qualification, and which, with such qualification, no one who really loves truth can assail without taking the standpoint of Rome, it is none the less plain that their religion or philosophy exactly suited worldly men and women, who wished—without breaking altogether with religion—to have a creed which would interfere as little as possible with their passions and their ease. Its teaching was essentially negative in its character, and, as Dorner says, exhausted itself in self-praise, and in attacks on the Christian religion as the work of priestcraft.[1] Although some of the Deists would have indignantly repudiated the charge—so far, at least, as their own intentions were concerned—Bentley did not overstate what appeared to ordinary observers the general result of their arguments, 'That the soul is material, Christianity a cheat, Scripture a falsehood, hell a fable, heaven a dream, our life without providence, and our death without hope—such are the items of the glorious gospel of these evangelists.'[2] It was a professed religion which was singularly deficient in all the essential elements of a religion. Some of its preachers imagined that by establishing what they called a reasonable religion of nature they were combating scepticism and infidelity. But 'there never has been any real religion consisting exclusively of the simple tenets which nature teaches.'[3] Deism scarcely endeavoured to search out in earnest even what nature by itself can tell of God. Nature does reveal God in part, although it reveals Him in power, greatness, beauty, order, and infinity, and scarcely at all in His moral attributes of goodness, justice, and mercy. But the Deists, preserving Christianity in form, looked for no other base for human action, and did not even explore what nature could teach them. On the other hand, looking at Christianity almost entirely as a 'republication of the law of nature,' they missed almost all its depths of meaning as a spiritual revelation. They had little sense of anything that really moves the soul, little

---

[1] Dorner's *Hist. of Prot. Theology*, ii. 83.   [2] Bentley, quoted in *id.*
[3] Max Müller's *Introd. to the Science of Religion*, 116.

sympathy with the inmost wants of humanity, little consciousness of sin, little craving for redemption, little aspiration after a better holiness, little perception of the great need of a divine Spirit comforting and strengthening the weak or labouring spirits of mankind.

Thus Deism could not but fail, even if regarded at its best, although it was not in its best, but in its worst aspect that it was commonly taken up in fashionable society, and made to encourage indifference and vice. Nevertheless it had some genuine elements of strength; nor were its influences altogether detrimental to the cause of religious progress.

Its main strength is unquestionably to be found in its firm insistence upon liberty of thought. Free-thinker was the popular synonym for Deist. The Deists gloried in the title, and made exorbitant use of it in arrogating to themselves an almost exclusive claim to be the sole champions of man's free right of reason. Or, on the other hand, by a slight inversion of argument, they could make it a title to honour in a somewhat different sense. Like Collins, in his 'Discourse on Free-thinking,' they could ask how any one could do otherwise than commend free-thinkers when they were but the successors of men who held the most honoured names. Milton, Cudworth, Henry More, Locke, Tillotson—were they not all free-thinkers? where would the Reformation, where would Christianity itself have been? where would be the right to send missions among the heathen, if free-thought were not alike the privilege and the duty of man? It was easy for his opponents to answer that these were but commonplaces, which they did not deny, and that they also exercised their free right of reason in exposing his blunders and false reasonings. But it was none the less true that free-thought did, in general, lie under a stigma much more decided and universal than in our day, and that, nevertheless, it was an innate right which could not easily be impugned. Many Churchmen, especially of the Whig or Low Church party, saw this clearly, and did their best to bring the name of free-thinking into better repute, and to deprive the Deists of the vantage which they got from the name. They did not succeed in this well-meant attempt; and though the Deists outrageously abused the word, clothing under the cover of free-thought every invective which they chose to hurl against Christianity, the Church, or the clergy, they partly gained their point in making it appear to the popular mind that Christian doctrine and free-thinking were incompatible terms. Indeed, there seems to have been a real danger of religious opinion becoming petrified within a set range of regularly recognised variations. Reason was to be duly exercised on matters of faith. Everybody felt bound to speak in the highest terms of reason. But though the state of the case might properly be disguised, reason was not to be free. Reformation had taken place once, and, so long as people kept fast to its formulas, would never be needed again, unless (as one party excepted) to bridge over in some minor respects the differences between Church and Dissent. If, therefore, this danger existed, as almost certainly it did, Deism was not unserviceable in asserting the liberty to think, even if liberty should sometimes lead to heresy or unbelief. Although the individual may suffer, the wider interests of Christianity have never yet been the worse, and, we may trust, are not likely to be, for any research of friend or enemy.

It was a result of the Deistic controversy, which went far to make up for many evils in it, that in the end it widened and enlarged Christian thought. Much that the Deists advanced was far from being, in itself, adverse to the progress of Christianity. Certainly, in their use of it, it generally wore an Antichristian aspect, and often had this intention. Their arguments were generally aimed at the establishment of a 'natural religion,' coloured, more or less superficially, by whatever could be retained of acknowledged Christian morality. But when their system had collapsed, Christianity, by the power it has ever possessed of gradually assimilating whatever is most sound in the reasonings of its opponents, began to admit, at all events as permissible opinions, various positions which the Deists had endeavoured to establish. It may be granted that the generality of good Christian people adhered rigorously to the exact ground which their fathers had taken, and that modifications of it were but slowly admitted in the gradual lapse of time through more than one generation. Here and there, however, theologians of high character in the Church became sensible that some conclusions which had been directed against the Christian faith might prove, if true, not hindrances, but confirmations and developments of it.

Thus, in the earlier part of the century, a man would have been thought hopelessly sceptical, and almost a confessed Deist, if he ventured to doubt the absolute accuracy of all Old Testament history. No view of inspiration could be allowed as orthodox but one that made Christianity dependent upon the literal exactness of every statement in Genesis or the Kings. Many of the evidence writers reasoned as if the least concession would imperil the very foundations of religion. It is still quite admissible to hold this view, and to argue that nothing which sacred historians have told has ever yet been fairly disproved. But, at all events, no well-educated man thinks the worse of any divine who refuses to be bound by this acceptation of what inspiration means, and who maintains that Scripture is indeed the record of a revelation from God, but not the actual message, precluding all human error in the instrument of it. When an eighteenth-century Deist thought he had detected an error in the sacred record, he handled it with triumph, as if he thought its establishment would explode out of the world the whole Christian Church, and those who argued against him were filled with a corresponding fear. The controversy hastened the time when sober and zealous Christians might calmly believe that such triumph and such fears were alike unfounded, that Scripture itself never laid claim to any such infallibility, and that the supposition of it did but place a stumblingblock in the way of belief.

The Deists often wrote about the atonement, and in no subject which they took in hand were their worst characteristics more prominent. Their cold, rationalistic, unspiritual view of that which lies so nearly at the heart of all Christian faith revealed to the utmost the poverty and wholly unsatisfying nature of what they proposed as the new creed. It was, therefore, one of the happiest results of the struggle, that the alarm which Deistic theories inspired tended, as Warburton said, 'to bring back the slighted doctrine of redemption, and to reinstate it in its ancient credit.'[1] It was satisfactory that this same prelate, whose influence upon the thought of the age was so considerable, but who was so entirely out of sympathy with the Evangelical and Wesleyan movements, should yet assert in the same passage that 'the doctrine of redemption is the *primum mobile* of the gospel system.'[2] Nevertheless it was not only by reaction, as some at least will hold, that Deistical writings on this subject were productive of ultimate good. The authors of them attacked with no little vigour certain popular opinions on the subject, and, after shaking thereby the faith of many, passed on their way amid the applause of the unbelieving and profane. But there was at least one man of profound thought and eminent piety who took up their negative conclusions, and built up around them a theology

[1] Warburton's 'Doctrine of Grace,' *Works*, iv. 716.   [2] *Id.*, 717.

full of deep feeling and spiritual faith. William Law, in one of the most valuable of his works, quotes from a Deistical tract of 1746 a passage in which the author remarks, 'That a perfectly innocent Being of the highest order among intelligent creatures should personate the offender and suffer in his stead, in order to take down the wrath and resentment of the Deity against the criminal, and dispose God to show mercy to him, the Deist conceives to be both unnatural and improper, and therefore not to be ascribed to God without blasphemy.'[1] On these words, as upon a text, Law goes on to set forth his own thoughts upon the great mystery of redemption. Some may cordially assent to them; others may disapprove; but none can doubt the intense Christian earnestness of the writer.

Some of the strongest arguments brought forward by the Deists against the truth of Christianity were derived from generally accepted teaching on the subject of future punishment. This doctrine, they said, of endless torments destined for a large portion of the human race is absolutely incompatible with goodness and justice in God. As, therefore, it is a part of the Christian faith, Christianity stands condemned. Chubb perpetually recurs to this; so also does Collins; and so do other of the Deists. There can be no doubt whatever that by so doing they greatly promoted their cause, and that multitudes were staggered by such reasonings, who yet believed that the tenet was vital to Christianity, and that the rejection of it was almost equivalent to accepting Deism. This assumption was greatly strengthened among the mass of the people by the very prominent and emphatic place given to the doctrine in question by the most popular teachers in the great religious revival which took place in the middle of the century.

It was a matter which needed diligent and thoughtful

[1] W. Law's 'Spirit of Love,' *Works*, viii. 73.

investigation more than any other in the whole range of theology. Yet it was almost left to the Deists, or rather to them and to others who were indeed far from being Deists, but who were yet either unorthodox, or considered by ordinary English Protestants to be not quite trustworthy as religious guides. The tenet still accepted in full force in popular religion was openly disputed for the most part either by Deists, or by Arians, or by Mystics, or by some who were called by the suspected name of Latitudinarians. Among the Arians who held these opinions the most prominent was Whiston. He had, he said, 'for many years thought that the common opinion in this matter, if it were for certain a real part of Christianity, would be a more insuperable objection against it than any or all of the present objections of unbelievers put together.'[1] Dr. Clarke, he added, and Sir Isaac Newton thought as he did on this point. He published a treatise on the subject, for which we find Bishop Berkeley inquiring.[2] Le Clerc, about 1705, wrote to the same effect. In the course of what he says, this author mentions the name of a man of some note who was on the point of giving up the Christian faith until he found that the doctrine of eternal punishment could be otherwise understood.[3] Among English Mystics who held a very different opinion from that popularly received as to the teaching of Holy Scripture on this most solemn question is William Law.[4] It is exceedingly likely that on this as on other points he had been influenced by Deist reasonings; but the contrast is indeed great between the flippant scepticism of some of the Deists and the intense and loving faith of this saintly Churchman. Another Mystic, also a Non-

---

[1] Whiston's *Memoirs of S. Clarke*, p. 75.
[2] Berkeley's *Life and Works*, iv. 301.
[3] Le Clerc's *Bibliothèque Choisie*, vii. 325.
[4] Law's *Spirit of Love*, &c.

juror, a man of very holy life, Francis Lee,[1] thought in this as Law did. So also did Francis Okely, a very learned and good man, a Mystic and Moravian, but none the less an English Churchman;[2] and so, some years later, did Henry Brooke, the pious and accomplished writer of 'The Fool of Quality.' Two of the most thoughtful and eloquent of the Cambridge Platonists in the end of the preceding century—Henry More[3] and Cudworth[4]—may be classed with them. But even these two men, lofty and spiritual as their Christian philosophy is, were often regarded with some doubt as rationalist and latitudinarian and somewhat mystical. Tillotson raised against himself a storm of indignation, and was said by his opponents to be almost a Deist, for insinuating, in guarded language, some qualifications of the prevailing opinion. Among Liberal Churchmen of the eighteenth century, Blackburne,[5] Jortin,[6] Edmund Law,[7] Worthington,[8] and Watson[9] have all made it more or less evident that they did not consider Christianity pledged to the terrible doctrine which was commonly maintained. But, as a rule, throughout the century, Churchmen and most religious people of all denominations held tenaciously to the received opinion; or if they did doubt, thought it best to hold their peace. With the exception of the Mystics, who were not widely known, the Deists stood almost alone

[1] In his 'Exposition of Esdras's Vision,' Whiston's *Mem. of Clarke*, p. 286.
[2] Nichols' *Lit. An.*, iii. 93.
[3] H. More on the *Immort. of the Soul*, B. IV. ch. xix. § 8.
[4] Cudworth's *Works*, iv. 319.
[5] Blackburne, *On the Intermediate State*, p. 161.
[6] Jortin, *Works*, i. 439; *Discourses on the Christian Religion*, pp. 263, 273.
[7] E. Law's ed. of Abp. King's *Origin of Evil*, p. 85, note.
[8] Worthington, *On Redemption*, p. 3.
[9] Watson's *Autobiog.*, ii. 409. Reference may also be made to Bishop Newton's last sermon in his third volume, quoted in Maty's *Review*, i. 384; A. Barbauld's *Works*, xlviii.; Southey's 'Vision of the Maid of Orleans,' *Works*, x. 81. It is well known how Dr. Johnson would have gladly welcomed a doctrine of purgatory in a Roman or any other form if no other resource were left.

in questioning it. They nearly succeeded in identifying such doubts on these matters with Deistical opinions. When, on one occasion, Collins appealed to H. More and Tillotson, Swift spoke of it as a shuffling attempt to screen Deistical notions by great names.[1] It was a pity that Churchmen should have left Deists in almost undisturbed possession of their vantage-ground, and that they should not, as William Law did, have turned their opponents' best weapon to the support of the Christian faith. Yet it was perhaps better that Deists should moot the question than that it should have been passed over in silence. In nothing has Christianity more gained in our own day than that, owing to a deeper study of Biblical eschatology, opinions such as those supported by William Law should be acknowledged as at all events so far well founded as to be deserving of great respect; and that those who cannot accept that teaching may at all events conceive of the unutterable pain of loss in a sense less utterly opposed to our highest instincts than any which was commonly open to English Christians in the century before.

The objections raised by the Deists, and especially by Woolston, to the miracles as recorded in the New Testament were often as frivolous and unreasonable as they were coarse and offensive. It is, however, very probable that good eventually arose out of the discussion. Assaults made upon them did not permanently invalidate their authority. These instances of divine power are so inwoven into the whole texture of the gospel narrative, that to resign belief in them is much the same as to give up the credibility of the whole. It is also obvious that if a single miracle, as that of the resurrection of our Lord, is considered to be established, the difficulty of believing in others at once disappears. Woolston's attack made no lasting impression upon the English mind. But when attention was once turned to the

[1] Swift's *Works*, viii. 180.

miracles, a good deal of fresh light was gradually thrown upon their whole scope and purpose. It was felt, not so much by the eighteenth century evidence writers as by those who came after them, that to look upon the miracles mainly as proofs and evidences of the Christian message is to misjudge their nature, and that in these later days the gospel does more to prove them than they the gospel. They follow by natural sequence upon a revelation of the world's Saviour. They reveal the God of holiness and love as one with Him who rules the universe with His power. It was not so much to prove the incarnation as because of it, and as a natural accompaniment of it, that He, whose purpose was to redeem the whole being of man, should be seen able to control the corruptions and infirmities of the body, no less than those which ruin the welfare of the soul. If life and immortality were brought to light by the gospel, it was but fit that some glimpse should be manifested of a world where not only sin is vanquished, but also pain and death. We can scarcely imagine that Christ, being what He was, should have come uninvested with some such majesty of miraculous power. And all this seems the more probable when it can be so readily imagined that such signs of present Godhead need involve no infraction, nor even any suspension of fixed laws. If even human faculties, cramped as they are by innumerable limitations, rise to new and hitherto unknown powers, as they ascend to the knowledge of higher laws, and can so modify and so guide into fresh channels the ordinary action of physical agencies as would convey to the mind of a savage an overwhelming impression of the supernatural and miraculous, it may well be supposed that to carry out any purpose of the divine will, infinite power has no need to undo aught that it has done, or to infringe for a moment's space upon the solemn unerring movement of an eternal law.

If Woolston's attacks on the miracles gave rise to a fuller examination on the subject, and by degrees to a better understanding of their design and nature, a similar remark may be made of Collins's scheme of prophecy. Unlike Woolston, who had mingled coarse insults upon Christianity with strange visionary utterances which made his sanity doubtful, Collins's work did but express the difficulties of a mind which was indeed thoroughly sceptical, but yet far from irreligious. In this respect he was a worthy opponent. But there seems to have been a great want of grasp of the subject both in him and in some of those who answered him. It was a question which, like many others of great theological importance, had received little consideration since the liberation of thought in the sixteenth century, and it was quite time that it should receive the closer study of learned and judicious minds. Objectors took this or that saying of the prophets, and seemed to expect from it that, if it were to be received as prophetical at all, it must contain a simple, clearly defined prediction. Many, on the other hand, who undertook to answer objections took a somewhat similar view, as if the evidential value of prophecy were staked upon the clearness with which it could be proved that certain detached words of Scripture, looked upon by themselves alone, foretold of things to come. Both seemed apt to imagine that, to constitute a prophecy, the mind of the speaker must be wholly projected into the future. Allusions in such passages to current events were spoken of by the objector as if they blocked all further meaning; and, on the other side, were either passed over, or minimised to the utmost, as if they were difficulties that needed to be explained away.

Collins would not allow that there was among the Jews an early and general expectation of a coming Messiah. This opinion, which none, it has been observed,[1] have more

---

[1] Cairns' *Unbelief in the Eighteenth Cent.*, p. 78.

thoroughly confuted than Strauss himself, brought this advantage, that it led Bishop Chandler and others to dwell more fully and forcibly than otherwise they might have done upon the Messianic spirit which pervades the Old Testament. It was shown what immense additional weight this gives to the testimony of prophecy. The evidence rests on no mere single words, however forcible in themselves. Separate texts gain cumulative strength when they are reinforced by a multitude of others, all bearing on the same common expectation. Even those prophecies which seem clearest and most indubitable, if they were regarded as detached instances, single and unsupported, might with no great difficulty be explained as chance coincidences, or references to other events. But when, striking as they are in themselves, they are also parts of a great system of Messianic hope, links in a protracted series of self-consistent prophecy, their weight is indefinitely increased. That confident hope of a Deliverer to come, which appears and reappears in men of the most different types, in one generation after another through the whole history of a race, expressed at one time in written words, at another in oral tradition, at another in type and ceremony, is in itself a kind of prophecy strongly impressed with the marks of a providential ordering. With this hope before them, growing in vividness as time went on, nothing was more natural than that the Hebrew prophets, the spiritual teachers of their age, should often begin with some present lesser deliverance of their own day, and rapidly and almost unconsciously pass on to the larger hope; and that it should be quickly seen, by the swelling grandeur of their language, that their thoughts were no longer limited to the smaller hopes and fears which for the moment were occupying the minds of their people. It would be contrary to all analogy in the moral and spiritual world for prophecy to give that wholly unmistakable and demonstrative testimony, which in all religious matters we are ever craving for in vain. But, short of this, prophecy presents a very imposing mass of evidence in its connected and collective character, as each revolving age gradually gave new touches and fresh definition to the image of Him for whom saint and seer were hoping, the looked-for Messiah, the Prophet, Priest, and King. If a Saviour of the world were indeed foreordained before the beginning of man's history, surely that wonderful hope, and that development of intimation, was quite what we might most anticipate. It was full enough to invigorate the faith and spiritualise the religion of those to whom it was given; but it was not too full and clear to be out of harmony with a time not yet ripe for the more perfect dispensation. The prophecies are indeed great witnesses to Christ, but they are far from being mere evidences to satisfy a later age. Their first purpose was to strengthen faith and hope, courage and patience, in the ancient Jewish people. But such and similar considerations were taken too little into account by many who, in the last century, discussed the subject of prophecy. The writers on the Christian side were as bent on searching out and defending the external evidences as the Deists were on disparaging them. They discussed, therefore, the prophecies much in the same manner as they did the miracles. Both were apt to be looked upon almost entirely in the light of detached wonders, which could be separated, so to say, from their context, to be regarded, according to the mind of the inquirer, as satisfying or insufficient proofs. There were, however, in the course of the controversy some valuable contributions to the theology of the subject.

Tindal's 'Christianity as Old as Creation' was in some respects the climax of Deism. The most characteristic feature of English Deism is the main thesis of his argument. Christianity is with him simply the religion of nature. All taht si vital and essential in it is 'what mankind at all times were capable of knowing.'[1] The name of Christianity may be of later date, but the thing itself is as old and extensive as human nature.[2]

It was a doctrine that readily lent itself to all that was worst in the Deistical system, and to the subversion or weakening of whatever is most precious in Christianity. But it also contained much which is wholly reconcilable with the Christian scheme, and not to be rejected without distinct injury to it. To show that his thesis was not necessarily antagonistic to Christianity, Tindal quoted on his title-page various passages from well-known theological writers, as from Eusebius, St. Augustine, Grotius, Clarke, and Sherlock.[3] He might have multiplied his authorities. The mystical writers, in particular, have taken pleasure in pointing out that, although not yet revealed in any outward form, the spirit of Christ and the true vital life of Christianity have never in any age been denied to earnest and religious-minded inquirers, and that He who is the light that lighteth every man that cometh into the world has been the Giver of grace and salvation to multitudes who never heard His name. ' There be members, therefore, of this Catholic Church, both among heathens, Turks, and Jews, and all the several sorts of Christians, men and women of integrity and simplicity of heart, who, though blinded in some things of their understanding, and perhaps burdened with the superstitions and formalities of the several sects in which they are engrossed, yet being upright in their hearts before the Lord, chiefly aiming and labouring to be delivered from iniquity, and loving to follow righteousness, are, by the several touches of the holy light in their

---

[1] Quoted by Overton on ' Deism,' in *The Ch. of Engl. in the Eighteenth Cent.*, i. 198.   [2] Hunt, *Rel. Th. in Eighteenth Cent.*, ii. 635.

[3] That from St. Augustine is especially apposite : ' Res ipsa, quæ nunc religio Christiana nuncupatur, erat apud antiquos, nec defuit ab initio humani generis ; quousque Christus venerit in carnem, unde vera religio, quæ jam erat, cœpit appellari Christiana ' (Aug., *Retract.*, i. 13).

souls, enlivened and quickened, thereby secretly united to God, and therethrough become true members of the Catholic Church.'[1] Much in the same manner, that favourite and kindred saying of the Deists that Christianity is a republication of the law of nature, although miserably inadequate as a complete account of Christianity, contains nevertheless a very important truth; for a religion which was not fundamentally based on the essential nature of things would soon stand convicted of unreality.[2] William Law, in his 'Spirit of Love,' published in 1754, has expressed this in words no less deserving of quotation than those of Barclay. 'You are to know, Eusebius, that the Christian worship is no arbitrary system of divine worship, but is the one true, real, and only religion of nature; that is to say, it is wholly founded on the nature of things, has nothing in it contrary to the power and demands of nature, but all that it does is only in, and by, and according to the workings and possibilities of nature.... Nor can any fallen creature be raised out of its fallen state, even by the omnipotence of God, but according to the nature of things, or the unchangeable powers of nature: for nature is the opening and manifestation of the divine omnipotence; it is God's power-world, and therefore all that God does is and must be done in and by the powers of nature.... Now right and wrong, good and evil, true and false, happiness and misery, are as unchangeable in nature as in time and space.... Divine revelation is not to appoint an arbitrary system of religious homage to God, but solely to point out and provide for man, blinded by his fallen state, that one only religion that, according to the nature of things, can possibly restore to him his lost perfection.... A

[1] Barclay's *Apology*, p. 259. There are several other somewhat similar passages in the same work.

[2] Thus Sherlock: 'Natural religion is the foundation upon which revelation stands; and therefore revelation can never supersede natural religion without destroying itself' (*Disc.*, liv.; *Works*, iii. 26).

religion is, then, the one true religion of nature when it has everything in it that our natural state stands in need of, everything that can help us out of our present evil, and raise us and exalt us to all our nature is capable of having.'[1]

Tindal's book had been considered so strongly opposed to revealed religion, that many people were much displeased that orthodox prelates like Sherlock, divines of liberal opinions like Jortin,[2] and men whose piety took a mystic turn, like W. Law, Brooke,[3] and J. Byrom, should thus far make common cause, as they said, with Deistical writers.[4] John Wesley charged William Law with holding doctrine on this point which was 'the very essence of Deism; no serious infidel could contend for more.'[5] Warburton, generally opposed to Wesley, on this subject cordially agreed with him. Christianity, he said, had indeed come to a pass when eminent divines could talk of it being a republication of the law of nature, and could quote without condemnation the paradox of its being old as creation itself. That such objections should be felt was natural and reasonable enough. At a time when in general society there was only too strong an inclination to attenuate Christianity into little more than a lofty system of morals, a writer might do great harm who conceded, or even seemed to concede, to the Deists anything more than was just. The fear, however, was scarcely well founded. A few, like Middleton, might give some colour to it. But a saintly and contemplative ascetic like William Law, and a practical and thoughtful prelate like Sherlock,[6] were both of them

[1] W. Law's 'Spirit of Love,' *Works*, viii. 136–39.
[2] Jortin's *Discourses on the Christian Religion*, p. 73.
[3] H. Brooke's *Fool of Quality*, ii. 251.
[4] Letter to Mr. Law, Wesley's *Works*, ix. 193.
[5] *Doctrine of Grace*, p. 3, chap. iii.; Warburton's *Works*, iv. 712.
[6] Sherlock's remarks occur in his sermon before the S.P.G.: 'The religion of the gospel is the true original religion of reason and nature. It is so in part; it is all that and more.' And, two or three pages after—'The

very unlikely men to do any such injury to the cause of faith. They were far more likely to benefit religion by sifting out the truth in a Deist argument, and supplementing its great deficiencies.¹ In a question of practical religion, Wesley, above all other men of his time, had a right to speak with authority. But the relations of natural to revealed religion constituted the very point on which it may be said that his theology was weak. It is true that Wesley declared that 'the religion we preach is evidently founded in, and in every way agreeable to, natural reason, to the essential nature of things, and to the nature of God.' But such words do not in practice lessen what has been called by a modern writer 'the dreary antithesis of God and mere nature characteristic of Wesley and his followers.'² For after defending, against the mystics, the use of reason in religious matter, Wesley goes on to say that on such subjects natural reason profits nothing until the new birth has supplied it with true judgments upon which to ground it. 'It is necessary that you have a new class of senses opened in your soul, . . . not depending on organs of flesh and blood. . . . And till you have these internal senses you can have no apprehension of divine things, no idea of them at all.'³ It is clear that to men, by whom 'unredeemed nature,' in its connexion with the spiritual life of man, was thus handed over, as it were, to the

consequence is manifestly this, that the gospel was a republication of the law of nature, and its precepts declarative of that original religion which was as old as the creation' (Sherlock's *Works*, iii. 312-314).

¹ Chubb, who quoted Sherlock's saying with great approval, speaks as if these deficiencies were very unimportant. The promises, he says, of life and immortality and spiritual help 'are not in their own nature constituent parts of religion, but only means and helps to it' ('Enquiry into the Grounds,' &c., p. 98; Chubb's *Works*, vol. iv.). It would be difficult to conceive what could be more important in religion than these 'non-constituent parts,' of which the Deists spoke so slightingly.

² Wedgwood's *John Wesley*, p. 78.

³ Wesley's *Earnest Appeal*, quoted in *id.*, 259.

dominion of ignorance and sin, there was something wholly abhorrent in the attempt to show the close intimacy between Christianity and the common inborn nature of mankind. To most Wesleyans, and perhaps also to their chief founder,[1] even outward nature seemed to lie under a cloud; as if it had no divine voice except to the 'converted,' while to them it was but a passing show of little worth, compared with other things upon which alone their thoughts were to be fixed. This sort of estrangement between religion and ordinary nature, though it did not interfere with the success of the great revivalist movement, and possibly even added strength to it among those who were most affected by it, was yet a grave defect. In that age especially, when natural science, in all its branches, was beginning an advance which in all former ages had been unparalleled, it was more than ever desirable that theology should not narrow the field upon which are manifested on the human heart the operations of divine grace. Consciously, therefore, or unconsciously, the Deists did in this respect a real service to Christianity, if their reasonings led to a greater consideration of those natural foundations which religion, if it is to command the thought and reasoning of mankind, can never afford to neglect.

There was one very important respect in which the Deistical controversy, in its effect upon religious minds, was directly subsidiary to the impression made on thoughtful men by the Methodist and Evangelical movements. It led such men to think that external evidences, however firmly they may be established, are far from being the only or even the chief supports upon which Christianity depends. Faith rests also upon other ground, which is impregnable against such assaults—upon feeling and conviction, and

[1] There is a fine passage in one of Wesley's later works ('Estimate of the Manners,' &c., *Works*, xi. 159-62) on the beauties of the universe, but it is mixed with much melancholy reflection on 'a total ignorance of God, almost universal among us.'

adaptation to the wants and necessities of the soul. This was expressed in a very exaggerated form in a work which attracted much attention, and of which it was never certainly known whether it was intended for a defence of the Christian faith or for a covert attack upon it.[1] This was the 'Christianity not founded on Argument,' published in 1743, by Henry Dodwell, son of the learned Nonjuror of the same name. Just in the same way as the father had been accustomed to push an argument to its extremest possible consequences, utterly regardless of extravagance in the conclusions it might lead him to, so did the son. He maintained that 'the judging at all of religious matters is not the proper office of Reason, or indeed an office in which she has any concern.'[2] He quoted the admonition of the Preacher, 'My son, trust thou in the Lord with all thy heart, and lean not on thine own understanding.' A divine spirit was given 'not to teach the rudiments of logic, but to irradiate the soul with a thorough conviction, and perform more by a secret whisper than a thousand clamorous harangues from the schools.'[3] Whether that still voice were called intuition or any other name, at all events there was an absolute impossibility of apprehending spiritual objects in any other way. 'Be satisfied henceforth there is a kind of evidence of power beyond what reason can ever pretend to furnish, such as brings with it that cordial peace and assurance to which all conviction by human means is an utter stranger.'[4] Dodwell's treatise might be regarded in two ways. In one aspect it led to pure scepticism.[5] It was said of it that it

[1] The uncertainty of Dodwell's contemporaries as to its drift is also felt by the German historian of English Deism: 'Ist der ultra-orthodoxe Supernaturalismus, den er aufstellt, seine eigentliche Meinung? Oder nimmt er die Maske eines Schwärmers an, um die Bibel lächerlich zu machen?' (Lechler's *Geschichte des Englisch. Deismus*, p. 421).

[2] Dodwell's *Christianity not founded*, &c., p. 7.

[3] *Id.*, p. 56.   [4] *Id.*, p. 115.

[5] 'Wir nehmen sie als den Anfang einer neuen Periode des Deismus, nämlich, seiner Auflösung in Skepticismus' (Lechler, 412).

made Scripture superfluous, and 'that other candle of the Lord, human reason, a false light and dangerous.'[1] Still this tendency is owing only to his exaggerations. There is abundant room for the full exercise of reason on religious subjects, while accepting almost all that he had said of the illumination of divine grace. In this latter aspect Dodwell's words fell gratefully on the ears of many who were wearied with ceaseless appeals to the supremacy of reason, and long controversies on evidences which seemed to make faith, if it depended upon them, the prerogative of the learned.[2] Some of those who had felt the power of the new revival hailed the book as a valuable contribution to the cause of true religion. 'Our good Methodists,' wrote one of Doddridge's correspondents, 'do not much approve of your "Answer to Christianity not founded," &c.; Seagrave was but this day in the coffee-house vindicating the book you wrote against.'[3] In fact, the interest which the treatise aroused was a sign of the times. Unbelief and belief had alike begun to pass through a certain change in outward form. The Deists were getting less attention paid to them, and so were the evidence writers. They had said most that at the present time had to be said. And, after all, it was clear that the future of Christianity was not staked upon the contest, as to many it had once seemed to be. Whatever else might be thought of the Wesleys and of Whitefield, they had made it unmistakably evident that the faith of Christians is at all events not always founded upon argument. When Christianity had proved itself to a man's heart by its reasonableness, its fitness, its beauty—or when it had been brought home to the heart by what would seem a more direct action

---

[1] Bp. E. Law's *Considerations on the Theory of Religion*, p. 27, and note by his son and editor, the Bishop of Chester.

[2] Dorner has some remarks on Dodwell's book as thus regarded (*Protestant Theology*, ii. 87).

[3] Doddridge's *Correspondence*, iv. 170.

of divine grace—might it not then be time enough to return again to the evidences, not so much to gain faith as to inform and strengthen it?

The way in which Deism often acted beneficially upon the Church by direct reaction is too obvious to need many words. It led men to think that in its recoil from Puritan fanaticism, religion in England had grown over-timid and distrustful of whatever was not wholly clear to reason. An over-rational theology might perchance land the inquirer on cold and barren shores of Deism. Aversion to mystery might undermine faith's foundations. We are told by Warburton [1] what we might naturally expect would be the case, that the writings of Collins and Tindal had led the clergy generally to dwell more frequently and emphatically than for some time they had been wont to do upon redemption and atonement, and whatever other doctrine belongs most specially to the gospel message.

It may be added that the feeling of common danger had a distinct influence in lessening the estrangement between Churchmen and Dissenters.[2] When Chandler, Leland, Doddridge, and other learned Nonconformists were contending side by side with eminent Church divines in defence of the common cause, their mutual differences were sure to appear smaller by comparison.

The transition from Deism to Methodism is less abrupt than might appear at the first glance. Strong as the contrast was between the cold scepticism of the one movement, and the intense earnestness of faith by which the other was pervaded; great as the dissimilarity was between the controversialist divines who were defending the external evidences of Christianity with arms of learned criticism, and

[1] Warburton's 'Doctrine of Grace,' *Works*, iv. 716.

[2] 'The Deistic period had resulted in an extension of the right hand of fellowship over many a wall of separation, both within and without the Church' (Dorner's *Protest. Theol.*, ii. 487).

those fervid preachers, on the other hand, whose appeal lay to the faith, the conscience, and the emotion of the multitude; there is yet a very marked connection between the two. The foremost apostle of that great revival—to apply to him a hallowed title which few indeed have equally deserved—was himself well aware that there were no more powerful weapons against Deism than those which he was wielding; and that however forcible might be the other evidences upon which Christianity was based, none were more reliable or convincing than those which he was daily preaching. No apology, therefore, is needed for quoting somewhat at length a remarkable passage from Wesley's own writings. 'You have no senses,' he writes, 'suitable to eternal and invisible objects. . . . A thinking man wants an opening, of whatever kind, to let in light from eternity. He is pained to be thus feeling after God so darkly, so uncertainly, to know so little of God, and indeed of any but material objects. He is concerned that he must see even that little, not directly, but in the dim, sullied glass of sense, and consequently so imperfectly and obscurely that it is all a mere enigma still. Now these very desiderata faith supplies. It gives a more extensive knowledge of things invisible, showing what eye hath not seen. . . . For it resolves a thousand enigmas of the highest concern by giving faculties suited to things invisible. Oh, who would not wish for such a faith, were it only on these accounts! How much more if by this I may receive the promise, I may attain all that holiness and happiness! So Christianity tells me, and so, I find it, may every Christian say. I now am assured that these things are so; I experience them in my own breast. . . . And this I conceive to be the strongest evidence of the truth of Christianity. I do not undervalue traditional evidence. Let it have its place and its due honour. It is highly serviceable in its kind and in its degree, and yet I cannot set it on a level with this. It is generally supposed that traditional evidence is weakened by length of time, as it must necessarily pass through so many hands in a continued succession of ages. But no length of time can possibly affect the strength of this internal evidence. . . . It passes at once, as it has done from the beginning, into the believing soul. Traditional evidence is of an extremely complicated nature. . . . On the contrary, how plain and simple is this, and how level to the lowest capacity! . . . The traditional evidence of Christianity stands, as it were, a great way off; . . . whereas the inward evidence is intimately present to all persons, at all times, and in all places. It is nigh thee, in thy mouth and in thy heart, if thou believest in the Lord Jesus Christ. If, then, it were possible (which I conceive it is not) to shake the traditional evidence of Christianity, still, he that has this internal evidence (and every true believer hath the evidence or witness in himself) would stand firm and unshaken. . . . . I have sometimes been almost inclined to believe that the wisdom of God has, in most later ages, permitted the external evidence of Christianity to be more or less clogged and encumbered for this very end, that men (of reflection especially) might not altogether rest there, but be constrained to look into themselves also, and attend to the light shining in their hearts. Nay, it seems (if it may be allowed to us to pry so far into the reasons of the divine dispensations) that, particularly in this age, God suffers all kinds of objections to be raised against the traditional evidence of Christianity, that men of understanding, though unwilling to give it up, yet, at the same time they defend this evidence, may not rest the whole strength of their cause thereon, but may seek a deeper and a firmer support for it. Without this I cannot but doubt whether they will long maintain their cause; whether if they do not obey the loud call of God, and lay far more stress than they have hitherto done on this internal evidence of Christianity, they will not, one after another, give up the external, and (in heart at least) go over to those whom they are now contending with, so that in a century or two the people of England will be fairly divided into real Deists and real Christians. And I apprehend this would be no loss at all, but rather an advantage to the Christian cause. Nay, perhaps it would be the speediest, yea, the only effectual way of bringing all reasonable Deists to be Christians. . . . [Then to the Deists,] Go on, gentlemen, and prosper. Shame these nominal Christians out of that poor superstition which they call Christianity. Reason, rally, laugh them out of their dead empty forms, void of spirit, of faith, and love. . . . Press on, push your victories, till you have conquered all that know not God. And then He, whom neither they nor you know now, shall rise and gird Himself with strength, and go forth in His almighty love, and sweetly conquer you altogether.'[1]

There can be no expectation of saying anything new of the Wesleys and their fellow-workers. For my own part (to speak in my own person), it is with hesitation, and almost with reluctance, that I enter upon a subject which, not in my judgment only, has been so admirably treated by my late colleague.[2] But though the Methodist movement has occupied many able writers, it does not appear to me, after a careful study of John Wesley's writings, that the subject is by any means exhausted. In any case it is obviously impossible, in the most general review of the religious thought and movement of the eighteenth century, to pass over that which is undoubtedly the most conspicuous feature in it. I shall, however, feel at liberty to assume

[1] Wesley's Letter to Dr. Middleton, 1749; *Works*, x. 74–77.
[2] Canon Overton's chapter on the Methodist and Evangelical movements, in the second volume of *The English Church in the Eighteenth Century*.

much as known to every tolerably informed reader, and shall confine most of my observations to certain special features of this most remarkable revival.

The greatness of the movement need not here be dwelt upon. It speaks for itself, clearly enough in England, far more so still in America. Its indirect results, or rather those which are less material and visible to the eye, cannot so easily be estimated. Certainly they were very great. We cannot define how far it affected the whole spiritual life of the nation, how far it stemmed the tide which had once seemed setting towards general irreligion and immorality; how far it restamped upon entire sections of the population a soberness and sedateness of thought which had been the inheritance, in great part lost, of the old Puritanism; how far it influenced the Evangelical movement, and so worked upon classes which it did not directly reach; how far it stimulated the relaxed energies of the whole Christian Church in England; how far it saved this country from the fierce passions by which, in the revolution period, Continental feeling was upheaved. Whatever may be the estimate of different judgments on these and such like questions, no one can at all events doubt that the impression made by the preaching of these zealous men was very wide and deep.

Whatever these results were, they certainly did not exceed, rather they fell far short of Wesley's expectation. Devoted to his work, and wrapped in it, keenly alive to the great realities of it, certain, through lengthened and intimate experience, that he beheld no transitory thing which could pass away with his own life, it is very noticeable with what a hushed feeling of solemn awe he sometimes speaks of what was being done through his hands and those of his fellow-labourers. Whitefield had hoped that 'the whole world would be set in flame'[1] with it. To Wesley, although

[1] Whitefield's *Letters*, June 13, 1741, p. 274.

so much calmer and less impassioned, it was much more than a hope. The fire had begun to burn, the earthquake was felt already, a great and strong wind was already rending the mountains, and breaking in pieces the rocks before the Lord.[1] God was spreading holiness over the land.[2] It was the dawn of the latter day glory.[3] Glorious times were even at the door. What unprejudiced man, he asked, could fail to see the signs of the times? 'Those who were blind from their birth, unable to see their own deplorable state, and much more to see God, . . . now see themselves, yea, and the light of the glory of God. . . . Those that were before utterly deaf to all the outward and inward calls of God, now hear not only His providential calls, but also the whispers of His grace. Those that never before arose from the earth, or moved one step towards heaven, are now walking in all the ways of God, yea, running the race that is set before them. The leprosy of sin is now clean departed from them. . . . At this day the gospel leaven, faith working by love, outward and inward holiness, righteousness and peace and joy, have so spread in various parts of Europe, particularly in England, Scotland, Ireland, in the islands, in the north and south, from Georgia to New England and Newfoundland, that sinners have been truly converted to God, thoroughly changed both in heart and life, not by tens only, or by hundreds only, but by thousands, yea, by myriads. The fact cannot be denied.'[4] 'Behold, the day of the Lord is come. He is rolling away our reproach. Already His standard is set up. His Spirit is poured forth on the outcasts of men, and His love shed abroad in their hearts. Love of all mankind, meekness, gentleness, humbleness of mind, holy and heavenly affections, do take place of hate, anger, pride, revenge, and vile or vain

[1] 'Further Appeals,' Wesley's *Works*, viii. 239.
[2] Letter 248, Sept. 16, 1774; *Works*, xii. 280.
[3] Sermon 63, *Works*, vi. 283.   [4] Serm. 66, vi. 307-8.

affections. Hence wherever the power of the Lord spreads, springs outward religion in all its forms. The houses of God are filled; the table of the Lord is thronged on every side. And those who thus show their love of God show they love their neighbour also, by being careful to maintain good works, by doing all manner of good, as they have time, to all men. They are likewise careful to abstain from all evil. Cursing, Sabbath-breaking, drunkenness, with all other (however fashionable) works of the devil, are not once named among them. All this is plain demonstrable fact. For this also is not done in a corner.'[1] 'A few years ago, if we heard of one notorious sinner truly converted to God, it was matter of solemn joy to all who loved or feared Him. And now that multitudes of every kind and degree are daily turned from the power of darkness to God, we pass it over as a common thing.'[2]

Such experiences might well justify his most sanguine expectations. There was something overwhelming in the very spectacle of those great multitudes who often gathered to hear. 'I judged the congregation, closely wedged together, to extend forty yards one way, and about a hundred the other. Now, suppose five to stand in a yard square, they would amount to twenty thousand people. The same evening I began preaching, at Leeds, to just such another congregation.'[3] Sometimes, especially under Whitefield's preaching, the whole vast audience would be visibly thrilled with religious emotion as by a magnetic shock. Of one such gathering of more than twenty thousand, Whitefield writes to a friend, 'Such a universal stir as I never saw before. The motion fled as swift as lightning from one end of the auditory to the other. You might see thousands bathed in tears.'[4] Or if there were no such strong excite-

---

[1] *Earnest Appeal*, viii. 41.   [2] *Journal*, May 16, 1749, ii. 135.
[3] *Journal*, Aug. 10, 1766, iii. 261.
[4] Whitefield's *Letters*, July 20, 1742, p. 413.

ment, the deep and earnest attention with which the preachers were often listened to was scarcely less impressive. Thus, of a great congregation in Northumberland, 'It was a delightful evening, and a delightful place, under the shade of tall trees; and every man hung upon the word; none stirred his head or hand, or looked to the right or left.'[1] 'I preached at Biddick to a multitude of colliers, though it rained hard all the time. They seemed all to be melted down as wax before the fire.'[2] Or again, 'The wind was high and very sharp, but the people little regarded it.'[3] 'Although it was a cold and stormy day, the people flocked from all quarters.'[4] On another occasion, 'In the midst of the sermon a large cat, frighted out of a chamber, leaped down upon a woman's head, and ran over the heads and shoulders of many more; but none of them moved or cried out, any more than if it had been a butterfly.'[5]

It is a question of great interest to inquire into the causes of the wide and deep impression which Methodism made upon great masses of the people. It is no less interesting and important to ask how it was that other great sections of society remained untouched by it, or rather untouched by other than its indirect influences. In either case, Methodism, so far as it was a great organised movement, and not merely a temporary revival, may practically be identified with the life and thought and teaching of John Wesley himself, and it will be almost entirely from his writings that these remarks will be illustrated.

An apostle's work requires an apostle for the worker; and if pure Christian motive and unwearied diligence in carrying that purpose out can give a title to that name, few have deserved it better than he. It may be granted that he started upon his apostolic career with the lower aim of

[1] Wesley's *Journal*, July 18, 1748, ii. 104.
[2] *Id.*, May 20, 1752, ii. 262.   [3] *Id.*, April 15, 1774, iv. 11.
[4] *Id.*, April 22, 1774.   [5] *Id.*, June 24, 1761, iii. 64.

'saving his own soul.'[1] But the self-interested purpose was quickly lost in a nobler longing, in which self had little part. 'We see (and who does not?) the numberless follies and miseries of our fellow-creatures. We see, on every side, either men of no religion at all, or men of a lifeless, formal religion. We are grieved at the sight, and should greatly rejoice if by any means we might convince some that there is a better religion to be attained, a religion worthy of God that gave it. And this we conceive to be no other than love; the love of God and of all mankind; the loving God with all our heart and soul and strength, as having first loved us, as the fountain of all the good we have received, and of all we ever hope to enjoy; and the loving every soul which God hath made, every man on earth, as our own soul. This love we believe to be the medicine of life, the never-failing remedy for all the evils of a disordered world, for all the vices and miseries of men.'[2] The history of his life is the record of the single-hearted devotedness with which he carried out this evangelistic purpose. Many will strongly feel that there were some grave defects in his theology and general views of human nature; but no one who knew anything of the man could doubt the simple integrity of heart, the earnest zeal, the unflinching self-denying courage, the pure love of God and goodness, which inspired his whole life. Whitefield, on the day that he was ordained, wrote, 'I call heaven and earth to witness that when the bishop laid his hands upon me, I gave myself up to be a martyr for Him who hung upon the cross for me.'[3] Wesley would have expressed himself with greater calmness and self-restraint; but he, no less, throughout his long career, counted life, and all that earthly life can give, as nothing

---

[1] 'My chief motive, to which all the rest is subordinate, is the hope of saving my own soul. I hope to learn the true sense of the gospel of Christ by preaching it to the heathen' (Wesley's *Letters*, Oct. 10, 1735, xii. 37).

[2] *Earnest Appeal*, viii. 3.   [3] Whitefield's *Letters*, June 20, 1736, p. 15

in comparison with what he believed to be his Master's will. As for money, not even a St. Francis or a St. Dominic could have held it more utterly as dross in respect of all it could supply beyond his personal and immediate necessities.[1] Having on all points an exalted, and even stern view of what the gospel law demands or recommends, with unreserved and unaffected simplicity he made it his rule of life. Thus his character as a man not only gave great weight to his words as a preacher, but caused him to be looked up to by his followers with unbounded respect. 'Next to God and my Saviour,' writes one of the early Methodists, 'I reverence Mr. Wesley.'[2] And something of this feeling was undoubtedly shared by great numbers of those who came most directly under his benevolent but autocratic sway.

Wesley's prolonged life of zealous work was made far longer still by his indefatigable industry and methodical use of time. Rising regularly for at least fifty years at four in the morning, his day of nearly eighteen hours was so carefully stewarded, that but very few fragments of it were lost. He generally preached eighteen or nineteen times every week,[3] beginning very commonly at five in the morning. Every two or three months, whatever might be the weather, he travelled seven or eight hundred miles,[4] and never less than four thousand five hundred miles in the year.[5] But the hours spent in travelling were almost always occupied. It was the time he chiefly reserved for reading, whereby, in addition to his theological reading, he was able to keep himself well informed in most general literature.[6] Whether

---

[1] On this point, however, he resembled the great founders of the mendicant order more in the spirit than in the letter. He was scrupulously neat and correct in his own dress, and used to insist upon it in others. 'Let no one,' he said, 'ever see a ragged Methodist.' His rule for money was, 'Gain all you can, honestly and wisely; save all you can, and then give all you have to God' (Sermon 50, vi. 133).

[2] Rowe's *Diary of an Early Methodist*, p. 251.

[3] *Id.*, viii. 38.   [4] *Id.*   [5] *Id.*, iv. 21.

[6] John Wesley's general reading was thus very considerable. Opening

driving or riding, with the reins on his horse's neck, to town or village, along the miserable roads of that age, his mind was for the most part as busily at work as if he were in the quiet of his study. 'History, poetry, and philosophy I commonly read on horseback, having other employment at other times; and I aver that in riding above a hundred thousand miles I scarce ever remember any horse (except two, that would fall head over heels any way) to fall or make a considerable stumble while I rode with a slack rein.'[1] Preaching, reading, writing, advising, administrating, reflecting—he did indeed fill his years with active work. It was no ordinary constitution that could have borne such unceasing demand upon his energies. For some years he frequently suffered with severe feverish attacks, to which he fully expected he should shortly succumb. But even then, at the first respite from pain or sickness, he was preaching and travelling as before. After a time he quite outlived these bodily infirmities. On his birthday, June 28, 1784, he wrote in his journal, 'I am as strong at eighty-one as I was at twenty-two, but abundantly more healthy, being a stranger to the headache, toothache, and other bodily disorders which attended me in my youth.'[2]

If Wesley had been asked what outward means most contributed to the extension of the Methodist movement, he would certainly have answered, 'Field preaching.' No great

his journal almost at random, we find, for instance, during the years 1768–73, that he had read during that time, among other works, Leland's *History of Ireland*, Bonavicini's *History of the War in Italy*, Wodrow *on the Persecution in Scotland*, Dalrymple's *Memoirs of the Revolution*, Walpole's *Critical Notes on the Times of Richard III.*, much of Mosheim's *Ecclesiastical History*, Hooke's *Roman History*, *Belisarius*, *Life of Pope Sixtus V.*, *An Account of the European Settlements in America*, a great part of Homer's *Odyssey*, Thomson's *Poems*, Dr. Byrom's *Poems*, Blackburne *on the Penal Laws*, *Medical Essays*, Priestley *on Electricity*, the pleadings in the Douglas Case, several of Swedenborg's writings, &c. On most of these he makes in his diary a few short and sometimes pithy remarks.

[1] *Journal*, March 1, 1770, iii. 393. [2] *Works*, iv. 282.

good, he used to say, could be done in any place without it.¹ He was always glad when a church was open to him, and was well aware there were many who would not listen to him except in a church.² But he knew also that 'the novelty of our manner of preaching has induced thousands and tens of thousands to hear us who would otherwise never have heard us at all, nor perhaps any other preacher.'³ Though one in the pulpit had 'preached like an angel, it had profited them nothing; for they heard him not. But when one came and said, "Yonder is a man preaching on the top of the mountain," they ran in droves to hear what he would say, and God spoke to their hearts.'⁴ It was under open heaven, and there only, that he could reach to any wide extent 'the tinners in Cornwall, the keelmen at Newcastle, the colliers in Kingswood or Staffordshire;' there only that he could touch 'the drunkards, swearers, Sabbath-breakers of Moorfields, or the harlots of Drury Lane.'⁵ The good which he had seen arise out of this out-of-door preaching led him, no doubt, now and then to over-estimate its value; as where he said 'he was well assured that he did far more good at Epworth by preaching three days on his father's tomb than he had done by preaching three years in his pulpit.'⁶ The two things are different. The regular order of religious worship scarcely admits of comparison with the special missionary efforts, which in some important points resemble it neither in character nor in aim. Yet surely Wesley's example has been, ever since the Reformation, too much neglected in the English Church. An order of well-instructed and approved itinerants might add greatly to what the Church can do.

Wesley was far too wise as a leader of men to permit his associations, when once formed, to fall through for want of

---

¹ Letter 530, *Works*, xii. 438. ² *Works*, ii. 53. ³ *Id.*, xii. 90.
⁴ *Id.*, viii. 230. ⁵ *Id.*, xii. 79. ⁶ *Id.*, 88.

being organised. It is not within the design of these remarks to tell in detail of the bands, the classes, the leaders, the stewards, the visitors, the weekly meetings, the quarterly visitations, the yearly conferences, the tickets of membership, the mutual confessions, the periodical inquiries. To many, however much they might be in general accord with the principles of the society, such semi-monastic discipline, such absence of spiritual self-reserve, such inquisition into the inner life, would be wholly intolerable. There is, however, no evidence that these regulations were otherwise than quite congenial to the great bulk of members; and where thus willingly submitted to, their value in strengthening and binding together the societies can scarcely be over-estimated.

Over the whole Wesley exercised a personal supervision with a strength of memory and power of will which was in every way worthy of himself. He would not delegate an iota of his own supreme authority. 'As long as I live,' he wrote in the last year of his life, 'the people shall have no share in choosing either stewards or leaders among the Methodists; we are no republicans, and never intend to be.'[1] He would advise with his preachers, but they should not control him. 'So long as I remain with them the fundamental rule of Methodism remains inviolate. As long as any preacher joins with me he is to be directed by me in his work.'[2] He knew his own powers. Impossible as it might have seemed to be, he not only made a quarterly visitation to all his principal societies, but 'generally knew two-thirds of the congregation in every place, even on Sunday evening, and nine in ten of those who attended at most other times.'[3] He knew 'not only the names, but the outward and inward states, the difficulties and dangers of twenty thousand persons.'[4] At his centres of Bristol, London,

---

[1] Letter 612, Jan. 13, 1790, xii. 439. [2] Letter 822, Jan. 1780, xiii. 115.
[3] *Further Appeal*, viii. 116. [4] *Id.*, 226.

Newcastle, and Kingswood, he 'determined, at least once in three months, to inquire at their own mouths, as well as of their leaders and neighbours, whether they grew in grace;'[1] and to those only of whom he found no cause to doubt would he grant each time the valued ticket which declared in his own handwriting that he believed the bearer to be one who feared God and worked righteousness.[2] Nor would he grant his certificate to any who would not comply with rules. 'I told the London society, "Our rule is to meet a class once a week, not once in two or three. I now give you warning, I will give tickets to none in February but those that have done this." I have stood to my word.'[3] His reproofs were sometimes of the bluntest description, perfectly unqualified by any phrase. 'I met the society (in Norfolk) at seven, and told them in plain terms that they were the most ignorant, self-conceited, self-willed, fickle, untractable, disorderly, disjointed society that I knew in the three kingdoms. And God applied it to their hearts, so that many were profited, but I do not find that one was offended.'[4]

But noble motive, devoted zeal, indefatigable industry, new modes of preaching, able organisation, excellent discipline—all these were but the instruments and favouring circumstances of a great work. Whatever might be the qualifications of the messenger, the message itself was the main and essential matter. Had it a stamp and character of its own, which gave it among large classes of the population a peculiar success? The question is not so wide a one as might at first appear, for it is certain that both the successes and the failures of the Methodist preaching had very little to do with those accessories of faith in which differences of opinion are chiefly to be found, but in the presentation of that central doctrine of deliverance from sin which

[1] *Further Appeal*, p. 256. [2] *Id.*
[3] Letter 453, Feb. 22, 1776, xii. 407. [4] *Journal*, Sept. 9, 1759, ii. 512.

is the vital principle of universal Christianity. It is well known that although Wesley himself was strictly orthodox and strongly attached to the tenets of the English Church, he thought very little of any controverted point which did not bear plainly and immediately on practical religion. That sort of latitudinarianism which is indifference to all opinions he abhorred, and called 'the spawn of hell.' 'Hold you fast that which you believe is most acceptable to God, and I will do the same. We must both act as each is fully persuaded in his own mind. . . . However, let all these smaller points stand aside. If thou lovest God and all mankind, I ask no more: give me thy hand.'[1] In this spirit he often spoke with warmly expressed reprobation of the manner in which, at the period of the Reformation, good men on either side, High Churchmen and Puritans, spent so much energy on questions which seemed to him utterly unimportant. He did not scruple to declare, and even strongly to insist, 'that orthodoxy, or right opinions, is at best but a very slender part of religion, if it can be allowed to be any part of it at all.'[2] All that was important was repentance towards God and faith in our Lord Christ.

In the main, and with some important qualifications, Wesley's great success as an evangeliser was quite what his words imply. It was in the main a triumph of Christianity at large, independent of any such differences as divide church from church. It was a great advantage to him that he was an English Churchman; but if he had been a Presbyterian or a Lutheran, an Independent or a Baptist, his preaching would not have greatly differed in its character, nor, except for the greater difficulties he would have had to encounter, in its results. If he had been a preaching friar in a Roman Catholic country, the difference would of course have been considerably greater, but even then it

[1] Serm. 39, *Works*, v. 499-502.   [2] *Plain Account*, &c., viii. 249.

would not have widely differed, and the work he did might perhaps have been as great. It would still have been the same good news of deliverance from sin through a Redeemer's love, preached through a long life with that conjunction of power and perfect devotedness which is so rare, but which, when it does appear, has always been so fruitful in great achievements. Wesley's theology might have been in one direction or another widely different from what it was, and yet have remained the same in its most essential character.

If what has been said of Wesley in the preceding pages were in any respect an adequate account of John Wesley's preaching—if it were enough to speak of him as a saintly man gifted by nature and training with no ordinary powers of influencing extensive classes—a great preacher of repentance, faith, and love, at whose earnest words even the most neglected and godless and profligate were constantly stirred to their innermost hearts, and awakened to new perceptions, hitherto dead or wholly dormant in them, of the evil and misery of sin, and of the unspeakable blessedness of a future from that very moment opened to them, a future in which the past was forgiven and wiped away, and faith and love and goodness theirs, to grow in them for all coming time—then indeed it would have been inexcusable, beyond all attempt at palliation, if such an evangeliser had not been everywhere welcomed by all good men as the glory of the Church he loved.

Such indeed was Wesley, and such was his preaching and its results. But there was also a great deal in it which no doubt added all the greater force to it in the mind of multitudes of his hearers, but which others, especially among the more thoughtful and intelligent classes, might, without blame, very strongly disapprove. If in the middle of the eighteenth century the English Church had been as full of energetic life as it was, unhappily, wanting in it, it might still be very open to question whether without detriment to itself it could have taken any measure which, in the eyes of the nation at large, would seem to identify it with the Methodist movement. In such a matter gain is not to be measured by any consideration of temporary utility, in however high a sense that word be used. Even if the result had been permanently to strengthen the Church with the millions whom Methodism had won, even if it had quickened its energies in every direction, and kindled in it a noble revival of spiritual life, even such advantages, enormous as they would be, might be dearly bought if they implied opinions which would in any way lower the type of religion, and tend to estrange from it cultivated thought. Wesley himself accounted for the utter failure of Methodism in his time among the more educated classes by assuming that all worldly advantages were, in the great majority of those who possessed them, too great a snare to the souls of men to allow of their accepting the pure and simple gospel. Perhaps there was a grave flaw in his teaching, to which they were more sensitive than the general multitude, and which made them dull to understand even that which was most excellent in it. Perhaps there was some important feature in his view of Christianity which was essentially repugnant to the ideas of most thoughtful men. If it were so, it would plainly not be right or reasonable to impute the practical rejection of Methodism by the English Church merely to a torpid circulation of religious life and a culpable want of flexibility in the Church system. Churchmen of our own day, well aware of Wesley's thorough loyalty to their Church, and thinking of him chiefly as a holy man, who was at once a most powerful missionary and an admirable organiser, are apt to feel convinced that if he lived in our day, when the Church is everywhere seeking new outlets for its energy, room would certainly be found within its borders for Wesley and all the machinery of Methodism. If, however, Wesley were living now, exactly what he was, it is exceedingly doubtful whether, with the best intentions, and the sincerest longings for unity and co-operation, it would be possible to carry this out. It does seem perfectly possible that, with a cordial wish for it on either side, modern Methodism might enter into a close and beneficial association with Anglicanism. But Wesley, liberal and tolerant as he was in some respects, was much more rigid and exclusive than modern Methodism. He was patient of almost any divergence of opinion on many points of doctrine, but there were some tenets, far from universally received, upon which his 'quicunque vult' was very stern and uncompromising. We shall see how very dark was his view of the world in general, how few and scanty he considered to be the slender gleanings of Christianity. It may be doubted whether this one opinion alone, entertained by him as it was with the utmost conviction, and entering essentially into his whole system of practical as well as speculative theology, would not be sufficient even in our own day to prevent any wide co-operation with him.

On this point, therefore, it seems necessary to enter more in detail upon Wesley's views, and to quote his own words as used at different times and in different writings.[1]

The fall of man was, according to Wesley, utter and complete. 'From that moment Adam died, his soul died, was separated from God; separate from whom the soul has no more life than the body separate from the soul. . . . Dead in spirit, dead to God, dead in sin, he hastened on to death everlasting, to the destruction both of body and soul in the fire never to be quenched. . . . Thus, " through the

[1] His first fifty-three sermons, though preached in some cases in the earlier part of his public life, received his special imprimatur at their publication in 1771, and are specially referred to in the trust deeds of Methodist chapels.

offence of one," all are dead, dead to God, dead in sin, dwelling in a corruptible, mortal body, shortly to be dissolved, and under the sentence of death eternal.'[1] The heart of man, therefore, in itself is 'altogether corrupt and abominable.'[2] 'With all his good breeding and accomplishments, he has no pre-eminence over the beast; nay, it is much to be doubted whether the beast has not the pre-eminence over him.'[3] For in ourselves 'we bear the image of the devil, and tread in his steps.'[4] 'Evil spirits roam to and fro in a miserable disordered world'[5]—a world in which there is 'an entire depravation of the whole human nature of every man born into the world.'[6] Wheresoever he looked, every nation, age, and time presented to his eye the same uniform picture of general gloom and desolation. The Jews were 'stupidly, brutishly ignorant, and desperately wicked.' If so, 'what can we expect from the heathen world? . . . Are they not one and all without God in the world, having either no knowledge of Him at all, . . . or such conceptions as are far worse than none?' The Mahomedans, 'destroyers of human kind, . . . have no knowledge or fear of God.' Nor was so-called Christendom much better. The Greek Church, steeped in 'gross, barbarous ignorance, deep and stupid superstition,' was 'scarce worthy of the Christian name.' As for Romanists, 'wherein do they excel the Greek Church, except in Italianism, received by tradition from their heathen fathers, and diffused through every city and village? . . . They excel it, too, in Deism.' His picture of the Protestant nations is all but as dark,[7] and his account of his own countrymen is darkest of all. 'Ungodliness is at present the peculiar glory of England, wherein it is not equalled by any nation under heaven. We therefore speak

[1] Sermon 5, v. 55. [2] Serm. 1, v. 7. [3] Serm. 44, vi. 61.
[4] *Id.*, 60. [5] Serm. 41, vi. 31. [6] Serm. 41, vi. 63.
[7] The last quotations are all from his 'Treatise on Original Sin,' 1756, *Works*, ix. 210 21.

an unquestionable truth when we say there is not on the face of the earth another nation (at least that we ever heard of) so perfectly dissipated and ungodly; not only so totally without God in the world, but so openly setting Him at defiance. There never was an age that we read of in history since Julius Cæsar, since Noah, since Adam, wherein ungodliness did so generally prevail, both among rich and poor.'[1] The Irish were 'a little better than the Hottentots, and not much.' 'The generality of English peasants, grossly ignorant of all the arts of life, were eminently so with regard to religion.'[2] Yet there was more hope for them than for the higher classes. In fact, 'a total ignorance of God is almost universal among us. The exceptions are exceeding few, whether among the learned or the unlearned. High and low, cobblers, tinkers, hackney coachmen, men and maid servants, soldiers, sailors, tradesmen of all ranks, lawyers, physicians, gentlemen, lords, are as ignorant of the Creator of the world as Mahometans or Pagans.'[3] England was no Christian country.[4]

In 1738, Wesley returned from America, with a despondent feeling that he himself was as yet no Christian. He had laboured abundantly, he said. He had given up his substance and his labour. He had thrown up friends, reputation, ease, country. He had put his life into his hands, wandering into strange lands. 'In all outward righteousness he was blameless.' And after all, 'this have I learned in the ends of the earth, that my whole heart is altogether corrupt and abominable. . . . Alienated as I am from the life of God, I am a child of wrath, an heir of hell.'[5] In his later foot-notes he modifies these assertions; but there is no such later qualification of what he says in the October of the same year, after his conversion, or, as he would have

[1] Serm. 79, vi. 448.   [2] Id., ix. 225.
[3] 'An Estimate of Manners,' 1782. Works, xi. 159-62.   [4] Id., ix. 164.
[5] Journal, Feb. 1728, i. 76.

preferred to call it, his 'justification' and new birth. He there makes it a part of the conscious proof of his being a new creature that he judges of himself ' to have no good thing abiding in him; but all that is corrupt and abominable; in a word, to be wholly earthy, sensual, and devilish— a motley mixture of beast and devil.'[1] Notwithstanding the earnest wish he even then had to do the divine will, he believed that before his eyes were thus opened he had but lived, according to the straitest sect of his religion, a Pharisee.[2] Thus, in 1753, when he thought his death was near, he wrote a few lines for his epitaph, in which he simply described himself as 'a brand plucked out of the burning.'[3] His mother had always lived what others would call the purest of Christian lives. But she was strongly impressed by the spiritual experiences of her sons, John and Charles, and in September 1739 believed that she also, while receiving the Holy Communion, had suddenly received the forgiveness of her sins.[4] As John Wesley considered this to be the true birthday of her soul's life, he felt bound to consider that her previous Christianity had been at best a mere legal service. When, less than three years afterwards, she died, her son's verses on her grave recorded how,—

> True daughter of affliction, she,
> Inured to pain and misery,
> Mourned a long night of griefs and fears,
> A legal night of seventy years.[5]

If the sudden change by which, as he thought, her night ended had not taken place, there can be no doubt that at this period, at all events, of his life (for there may have been a slight modification of his views afterwards) he could only have considered her as a Christian by treating it as one of

---

[1] *Journ.*, Oct. 1738, i. 161.
[2] *Journ.*, Jan. 1743, i. 409.
[3] *Journ.*, Nov. 1753, ii. 309.
[4] *Journ.*, Sept. 1739, i. 222.
[5] *Journ.*, Aug. 1742, i. 384.

those 'exempt cases' about which there was a difficulty to which he could not close his eyes.[1]

There is something painfully touching in the sad tone of pity with which Wesley, in the same spirit with which he viewed the world in general, regarded the sports of children. 'Pretty little creatures, with the wrath of God abiding on them.'[2] The sense of a mistake in his religion falls yet more jarringly on the ear when he listens with great satisfaction to the account of a teacher telling how his voice could not be heard amidst the cries and groans 'of children flying from the wrath to come;'[3] and to another teacher telling of a child 'eight years and a half old, but as serious as a woman of fifty;' and of another boy of eleven 'wise and staid as a man.'[4] In his school at Kingswood, 'as we have no play days (the school being taught every day in the year but Sunday), so neither do we allow any time for play on any day. He that plays when he is a child will play when he is a man.'[5] It is impossible not to feel a perverse pleasure in Wesley's vexation that though 'they ought never to play, yet they do every day; yea, in the school.'[6] But even Wesley's most devoted admirers were ready to grant that he was 'disposed to be too stern towards children.'[7]

How frightful beyond all imagining was the condition of human nature according to Wesley's conception of it cannot be fully realised without taking into thought what was his belief as to the punishments which awaited the ungodly. In his teaching no ray of hope or mitigation alleviated the horrors of that state. Fire 'unquestionably material,' torments as much greater than those of the Inquisition as the skill and malice of superhuman can be greater

---

[1] *Conversations*, Aug. 1745, viii. 282.   [2] *Journal*, June 1762, iii. 96.
[3] *Id.*, Sept. 1770, iii. 415.   [4] *Id.*, Sept. 1772, iii. 471.
[5] *Short Account of Kingswood School*, 1768, xiii. 251.
[6] *Remarks on the State of Kingswood School*, 1783 xiii. 268.
[7] *Diary of an Early Methodist*, p. 159.

than those of human agents; senses exquisitely quickened, 'agonising at every pore,' without rest or intermission, through periods in which millions of ages count as nothing; sufferings of soul no less than of body; wickedness unrestrained;[1]—such was the representation of suffering inexpressible which may be found in his seventy-third sermon, and which is not tempered by anything else that can be found in his writings. It has been said that he believed in varieties and degrees of punishment. To some extent he did. Suffering would be 'perhaps more intense to some than others;' and since each would receive his own reward, there might be infinite variety in punishment, but still it would be 'essentially the same for all.'[2] And 'there is not,' he has elsewhere said, 'and cannot be, any medium between everlasting joy and everlasting pain.' The soul is 'unspeakably happy or unspeakably miserable.'[3] In one single passage of his early journals he has used words which might seem to imply a belief that the unquenchable fire might have the salutary office of purging away the dross.[4] But at no later period does there appear to be the slightest intimation of such a possibility. On the contrary, he warmly contended against any such idea of purgation as Popish, mystic, and unscriptural.[5] In his controversy with William Law there was nothing in all the writings of that saintly-minded divine which so stirred Wesley's indignation[6] as the earnestly expressed conviction[7] that the fire of God's wrath was an operation of His love, inflicted for no other purpose than only to correct and purify.

Into that abyss of misery Wesley believed, without

---

[1] Serm. 73, vi. 381–89. [2] *Id.*, 385. [3] Serm. 54, vi. 195.
[4] *Journal*, Feb. 1738, i. 76. 'If the oracles of God are true, though when ennobled by faith in Christ they (the deeds of the law) are holy and just and good, yet without it they are dung and dross, meet only to be purged away "by the fire that never shall be quenched."'
[5] Letter, Sept. 1753, xii. 198–99. [6] Letter to W. Law, 1756, ix. 481, &c.
[7] W. Law's 'Spirit of Love' and 'Spirit of Prayer,' Law's *Works*, vol. vii.

apparently a shadow of doubt or misgiving, that the great mass of mankind was sinking. 'The gate of hell,' he said, 'is wide as the whole earth, broad as the great deep.'¹ 'If many go with you, as sure as God is true, both they and you are going to hell. . . . Here is a short, a plain, an infallible rule. In whatever profession you are engaged, you must be singular or be damned.'² There was no question with him as to the justice of all this. So far from questioning it himself, he did not even see how it could be questioned. Speaking of one whose conscience has suddenly been awakened, he says, 'His guilt is now also before his face. He knows the punishment he has deserved, were it only on account of his carnal mind, the entire universal corruption of his nature; how much more on account of all his evil desires and thoughts, of all his sinful words and actions! He cannot doubt for a moment but the least of these deserves the damnation of hell.'³ Thus also he speaks of 'a sinner of any kind or degree' coming to 'a sense of his total ungodliness, and his absolute meetness for hell fire.'⁴

It has seemed impossible to avoid entering somewhat at length into this subject. A man of Wesley's depth and sincerity of religious feeling could not hold such views without being most profoundly impressed by them. They did not affect his happiness; nothing has power to throw any permanent shade of gloom over the mind of a man who spends a healthy and active life in ways of goodness and beneficence. 'I feel and grieve,' said Wesley, 'but I fret at nothing.'⁵ Much in the same way as a successful and experienced surgeon loses to a great extent the sense of pain at what he sees, though that of active pity may be strengthened, so it was with Wesley. His thought of the awful ruin into which he judged that the millions of man-

¹ *Further Appeal*, viii. 109.   ² Serm. 31, v. 412.
³ Serm. 21, v. 251.   ⁴ Serm. 5, v. 62.
⁵ *Journal*, June 1776, iv. 79.

kind were rushing did not make him unhappy, but it made religious thought and religious life inexpressibly grave and serious to him. It made a very deep impress upon the whole of his theology; and while it added tenfold to the effect of his preaching to the multitude, it tended greatly to alienate others from it.

We can understand the detestation in which Wesley held the Calvinistic doctrine of reprobation. By fixing his mind on goodness and happiness open to every soul of man who would not reject such priceless benefits, he was able to hold with calmness a dogma which might well drive those who held it into madness, and to believe it consistent with infinite justice and mercy. But there was a limit which he could not pass. 'I would sooner,' he said, 'be a Turk, a Deist, yea, an Atheist, than I could believe a doctrine of reprobation. It is less absurd to deny the very being of God than to make Him an almighty tyrant.'[1] He thought it 'a horrible decree, and inconsistent with the great principle that the Lord is loving to every man, and His mercy is over all His works.'[2] 'All the devices of Satan,' he said, 'for these fifty years have done far less toward stopping this work of God than that one single doctrine.'[3] 'O God,' he exclaims in another place, 'how long shall this doctrine stand?'[4] His temporary break with Whitefield on the ground of his Calvinism is sometimes spoken of as something of a discredit to him. It is rather to his honour that a difference upon which he felt so very strongly should have done so little to interrupt the affection and esteem which he felt for his warm-hearted fellow-labourer.

If Wesley's preaching had been only a loud and earnest call to fly from the wrath to come, he would never have

---

[1] *Treatise on Justification*, 1764, x. 334.
[2] *Letters*, 1755, xii. 491.   [3] *Conversations*, viii. 336.
[4] *Thoughts upon Necessity*, 1774, x. 480.

been the great evangelist that he was. We come to what was indeed a noble and soul-inspiring gospel. It was blended indeed with much that was very open to question, and it began with those assumptions of an utter and universal depravity which neither reason nor Scripture justifies; but otherwise it was doctrine worthy of a great Christian messenger, and such as might well thrill through the hearts of those to whom it was addressed. Truth seems to gain sometimes, partially at least and for the time, by an alloy of error. Certainly in this case the black and dismal background threw into the strongest contrast the light and glory which illumined those who issued forth from it. Suddenness and violence of transition were no objections to the minds of those to whom he chiefly preached, but served rather to engross their attention, excite their imagination, and stir their feelings more than any calmer presentation of truth could do.

When the preacher had not merely awakened the conscience of a listener, but had convinced him that whether he had been a notorious and profligate sinner, or a respectable 'almost Christian,' had been unimpeachable in outward conduct, and attentive to the forms of religion, he was in either case utterly and hopelessly corrupt, and rushing on to an end of everlasting misery, then straightway salvation was set before his eyes, free, full, and without stint. If he stood on the verge of everlasting burnings, he was no less near to that of everlasting glory.[1] Would he take now and at once the momentous step which separated the one from the other? Past sin was no hindrance. Nay, but the message is to none other than to sinners. 'It is the free gift of God, which He bestows not on those who are worthy of His favour, . . . but on the ungodly and unholy; on those who till that hour were fit only for everlasting de-

[1] Serm. 25, v. 327.

struction; those in whom was no good thing. . . . His pardoning mercy supposes nothing but a sense of mere sin and misery.'[1] It was on this that Wesley was wont especially to insist. He knew his special strength. He knew among whom his preaching was with power, as he knew also with whom it was ineffectual. He could do almost nothing, he was wont to say, with 'the rich, the learned, the reputable, the moral.'[2] None seemed to him so hopeless as they.[3] At all events, he would fain leave them to others. 'Only let us alone with the poor, the vulgar, the base, the outcasts of men. . . . Suffer us to call sinners to repentance; even the most vile, the most ignorant, the most abandoned, the most fierce and savage of whom we can hear.'[4] It was they, after all, who might most be led to 'groan under the wrath of God,'[5] and so to seek deliverance. Because they were nearest to the lowest, it might be that they were nearest also to the highest. To all, but to these most of all, he preached tidings of great joy. With the sense of sin would come, by the free grace of God, the gift of faith, which was the eye, the ear, the palate, the feeling of the soul.[6] And with it would come 'a vast and mighty change,'[7] which might well be called the new birth. For 'it is the great change which God works in the soul when He brings it into life; when He raises it from the death of sin to the life of righteousness; . . . when the whole spirit is created anew; . . . when the love of the world is changed into the love of God, pride into humility, passion into meekness; hatred, envy, malice, into a sincere, tender, disinterested love for all mankind. In a word, it is that change whereby the earthly, sensual, devilish mind is turned into the mind

---

[1] *Earnest Appeal*, viii. 6.   [2] Serm. 1, v. 15.
[3] *Id.*; and Serm. 31, v. 410; Serm. 61, vi. 264; *Letters*, xiii. 54; *Journal*, ii. 348; *Earnest Appeal*, viii. 19, &c.
[4] *Further Appeal*, viii. 239.   [5] Serm. 5, v. 39.
[6] *Earnest Appeal*, viii. 6.   [7] Serm. 10, v. 119.

which was in Christ Jesus. This is the nature of the new birth.'[1] He who was thus reborn was, as it were, in a new world. The old had passed away; all had become new. Whatever the past had been, now it was all cancelled. 'Wilt thou be troubled or afraid of what was done before thou wert born?'[2] In Wesley's theology there were very few half-lights and shadows. 'Look through all the world, and all the men therein are either believers or unbelievers.'[3] The one had been born anew, converted, justified, received into God's love; the other lay in darkness, sin, and death. He did not deny that the night of an unconverted state might not be faintly illumined by some 'drawings of the Father.'[4] The change might in some cases be gradual. It was even conceivable that there might be cases in which the new-born man might not be conscious that the change had happened in him. New birth, as its name implied, was but the beginning of progressive life; it might relapse, and pass again into death. Thus much Wesley allowed. As a rule he judged the process of salvation to be as follows. A man asleep in darkness and in the shadow of death is touched by God through some awful providence, or by some powerful word. 'He is terribly shaken out of his sleep, and awakens into a consciousness of his danger. . . . Horrible light breaks in upon his soul; such light as may be conceived to gleam from the bottomless pit. . . . He sees God as a consuming fire. . . . His heart is bare, and he sees it is all sin. . . . He feels sorrow of heart, remorse, fear. . . . He struggles with sin, yet for a time sin is mightier than he. . . . At last his miserable bondage ends. . . . His eyes are opened in quite another manner than before, even to see a loving, gracious God. . . . He hath a divine evidence of things not seen by sense, even of the deep things of

[1] Serm. 45, vi. 71.
[2] Serm. 8, v. 94.
[3] Serm. 20, v. 237.
[4] Serm. 17, vi. 99.

God, more particularly of the love of God, of His pardoning love to him that believes in Jesus. . . . Here end both the guilt and power of sin. . . . Here ends also that bondage unto fear. . . . He is dead unto sin, and alive unto God ; . . . and having power over all sin, over every evil desire and temper and word and work, he is a living witness of the glorious liberty of the sons of God.'[1] He believed that in the great majority of cases the gift of faith and joy was as instantaneous as when at the beginning God said, ' Let there be light, and there was light.'[2] He could scarcely imagine otherwise of it. ' But we are concerned for the substance of the work, not the circumstance. Let it be wrought at all, and we will not contend whether it be wrought gradually or instantaneously.'[3] He held that not unfrequently this saving faith was given ' in dreams and visions of the night.'[4]

The vastness of this change, as Wesley conceived of it, may be well judged from this, that he insisted upon the strictest and most literal interpretation of those words of St. John, that ' he who is born of God sinneth not.' Some, he writes, speak as if this meant ' He sinneth not wilfully, or he doth not commit sin habitually, or not as other men do, or not as he did before.' But he insisted that the saying was in no such way qualified by St. John. The best men under the older dispensation did, no doubt, sin. But it was said of John the Baptist that the least in the kingdom of heaven was greater than he. The great salvation from sin belonged entirely to the Christian dispensation. Then, after arguments which few will consider satisfactory, intended to show that no passage in the New Testament speaks of sin still remaining in such a one, he returns to his conclusion that ' a Christian is so far perfect as not to

---

[1] Serm. 9, v. 101-7.
[2] *Further Appeal*, viii. 61 ; *Answer to Lavington*, x. 8; *Journal*, iii. 156 ; Serm. v. 39, &c.
[3] Letter to Potter, ix. 104.   [4] *Conversations*, viii. 284.

commit sin. This is the glorious privilege of every Christian; yea, though he be but a babe in Christ.'[1] There was 'at the very least ... a ceasing from any outward act of sin, from any outward transgression of the law.'[2]

He was careful to add that there are many stages in Christian life, 'some of the children of God being new-born babes, others having attained to more maturity.'[3] The new birth began a work of sanctification, which might sometimes not bring forth its full fruits of perfection until death. Entire freedom from evil thoughts and evil temper was only the blessing of the mature Christian. But that such perfection was attainable by all was a point upon which he was accustomed to insist very strongly. 'This doctrine,' he wrote shortly before his death, 'is the grand *depositum* which God has lodged with the people called Methodists; and for the sake of this chiefly He appears to have raised us up.'[4] So again, 'I see that wherever the doctrine of Christian perfection is not clearly and strongly enforced, the believers grow dead and cold. Nor can this be prevented but by keeping up in them an hourly expectation of being perfected in love. I say an hourly expectation, for to expect it at death or some time hence is much the same as not expecting it at all.'[5] Some of the finest of John and Charles Wesley's poems are those which express the fervent aspiration after such perfectness.

> O grant that nothing in my soul
>   May dwell but Thy pure love alone!
> O may Thy love possess me whole,
>   My joy, my pleasure, and my crown!
> Strange fires far from my heart remove,
> My every act, word, thought, be love.[6]

[1] Serm. 40, vi. 16. [2] *Id.*, vi. 7. [3] *Id.*, vi. 16.
[4] *Letters*, Sept. 1790, xiii. 9. Wesley spoke more than once of Pelagius having taught the doctrine of going on to perfection, and thought his teaching had been grossly misrepresented (vi. 328; xii. 224).
[5] *Journal*, Sept. 1762, iii. 113. [6] By John Wesley in 1738 (xi. 369).

The perfection attainable by men was perfect love.[1] It did not exempt from ignorance, mistake, and temptation, nor dispense from any of the ordinances; but it did imply complete immunity not only from any outward act of sin, but from every sinful thought and temper. He granted that there were not many to whom it was given. Yet 'several persons have enjoyed this blessing without any interruption for many years. Several enjoy it at this day; and not a few have enjoyed it even unto their death.'[2]

It is very easy to understand how intensely the Methodist preaching must have affected those who thoroughly accepted it and fully realised it. The violent bodily agitation by which the hearers of these sermons were very frequently affected—the groans, the cries, the convulsions, the swoons—were attributed by Wesley himself to various causes. Often they might be 'designed of God for the further manifestation of His work, to cause His power to be known, or to awaken the attention of a drowsy world.' On other occasions he has 'no doubt it was Satan tearing' the sufferers, 'when they were coming to Christ.' But the natural causes to which he also attributed them were quite sufficient in themselves. 'If the mind be affected to an exceeding degree, the body must likewise be affected, by the laws of the vital union.'[3] It was not, he remarked, unheard of in Scripture that, under the impulse of strong religious emotion, men should 'exceeding tremble and quake,' or 'cry with a loud and bitter cry,' or 'roar for very disquietness of heart.'[4] Fear of God's wrath, fear of death, fear of the devil, 'may sometimes even border upon distraction, suspending the exercise of the memory, of the understanding, and of all the natural faculties.'[5] 'Some could give no account at all, only that of a sudden they dropped

---

[1] *Journal*, 1738, i. 151.   [2] *Journal*, 1743, i. 415.
[3] Letter to the Bishop of Gloucester, 1762, ix. 142.
[4] *Further Appeal*, 1745, viii. 62.   [5] Serm. 9, v. 103.

down, they knew not how. Others could just remember they were in fear. Several said they were afraid of the devil, and this was all they knew. But a few gave a more intelligible account of the piercing sense they then had of their sins, both inward and outward, which were set in array against them round about; of the dread they were in of the wrath of God, and the punishment they had deserved, into which they seemed to be just falling without any way of escape. One of them told me, "I was as if I was just falling from the highest place I had ever seen. I thought the devil was pushing me off, and that God had forsaken me." Another said, "I felt the very fire of hell already kindled in my breast, and all my body was in as much pain as if I had been in a burning fiery furnace."[1]

There were multitudes to whom such pains were truly throes of spiritual birth, and who lived for the future an infinitely purer and higher life than ever they had lived before. Whatever may be thought of Methodism in some respects, it is certain that much of the religious motive which was brought to bear upon the convert's mind was of the noblest kind. Love was to be the ruling principle, perfection the end and aim. With fear in any other sense than of reverence and awe he was henceforth to have nothing to do. Neither was there to be any more wilful sin. For 'the immediate fruits of justifying faith were peace, joy, love, power over all outward sin, and power to keep down inward sin.'[2] No form of Christianity has ever laid down more universally, confidently, and unswervingly so high a standard of Christian living. However far the Methodist practice might commonly be from the Methodist ideal, it was at least an incalculable gain to have raised up so many thousands of men and women from the lowest to the highest aims. The perfection which Wesley taught may

[1] *Journal*, 1742, i. 407. [2] *Conversations*, viii. 296.

perhaps be unattainable on earth. He was himself ready to acknowledge that it was very rare. The striving after it might often involve spiritual pride and gross self-deceit. Yet there is something animating and encouraging in the very thought of perfection becoming a practical object of living among a great body of people. To implant the very idea of moral perfection, not among the philosophical, refined, and thoughtful, but among classes like the Kingwood colliers, was indeed a triumph of Methodist Christianity.

It seems lamentable that a form of Christianity which had so much that was noble in it, and which could show such splendid results, should also have been widely disapproved and discountenanced even by good men. Yet it could not be otherwise. How few there are at the present day, not of English Churchmen only, but among religious people of any school, not excepting perhaps even the great majority of Methodists, who would agree in Wesley's opinions without large qualifications! Yet it would have been almost impossible for any one to work with him who did not in the main agree with him. Wesley was indeed tolerant in the extreme of opinions which he did not consider vital. High Churchman though he was in personal opinion, he soon came to think of the differences which separated Churchman from Churchman, and Churchman from Dissenter, as very unimportant. He would hardly so much as ask whether any fellow-worker with him were High Churchman or Puritan, Baptist or Presbyterian. Although he loved the English Church with a deep affection which nothing could ever greatly shake, and though he always maintained that his was the true doctrine of the English Church, and that others departed from it, not he, yet he soon learnt to be almost equally at home in a Scotch kirk or a Nonconformist chapel. Yet, notwithstanding this perfect tolerance on many subjects in which such tolerance was then very rare, he could hold no intimate fellowship with any who disagreed with him on what he considered matters of very great, if not of vital importance. His great esteem for Whitefield, and their general agreement on other points, induced him barely to tolerate a doctrine of predestination from which he personally recoiled with horror. But to his mind salvation seemed to imply essentially that new birth out of a state of utter corruption which was the key-note of the whole Methodist system. 'Take away that,' he wrote to Dr. Taylor, 'or, which amounts to the same, explain as you do, suitably to your doctrine of original sin; and what is Christianity better than heathenism?'[1] Unfortunately, on the very point in which he felt more strongly than any other, a point in which he considered consequences to be involved more momentous than can be imagined, he found a grave and deep difference of opinion, not merely among the more indifferent and careless of the English clergy, but among a great majority of the most earnest and religious of them. When in 1738 he began to preach these doctrines, pulpit after pulpit which before had been open to him was now refused him. On one occasion he reflects at length upon the cause of it. 'I have seen,' he said, 'more than ever I could have imagined, how intolerable the doctrine of faith[2] is to the mind of man, and how peculiarly intolerable to *religious*[3] men. One may say the most unchristian things, even down to Deism; the most enthusiastic things, so they proceed but upon mental raptures, lights, and unions; the most severe things, even the whole rigour of ascetic mortification.' But, he continues, if faith is preached as discovering to wretched man recovery from thorough

---

[1] *Journal*, July 1759, ii. 492.

[2] This must of course be understood of faith as explained by Wesley in the work of conversion. No religious Churchman ever denied the fundamental importance of faith.

[3] 'Religious' is italicised by Wesley.

pollution, and wresting from him all his honour, all hearts are alienated. 'But this is not to be wondered at. For all *religious* people have such a quantity of righteousness acquired by much painful exercise, and formed at last into carnal habits; which is their wealth both for this world and the next. Now other schemes of religion are . . . only a little rough, but friendly in the main, by telling them their riches are not yet sufficient, but by such acts of self-denial and mental refinement they may enlarge the stock. But the doctrine of faith is a downright robber. It takes away all this wealth, and only tells us it is deposited for us with somebody else, upon whose bounty we must live like mere beggars. Indeed, they that are truly beggars, vile and filthy sinners till very lately, may stoop to live in this dependent condition, it suits them well enough. But those who have long distinguished themselves from the herd of vicious wretches, or have even gone beyond moral men—for them to be told that they are either not so well off, or but the same needy, impotent, insignificant vessels of mercy with the others, this is more shocking to reason than transubstantiation.'[1]

It is inconceivable that any number of sober English Churchmen could ever have become Methodists. Yet the case stood thus, that if they did not agree in the main with Methodism—not necessarily in its discipline, but in its doctrines—Wesley, with all his tolerance, all his Churchmanship, could barely find room for them in the Christian system. And therefore a wide gap inevitably rose up between them, and would in all likelihood have done so even if the Church had been as faultless in its dealings with him as too often it was the contrary. So long as Wesley's opinions on certain religious questions of great importance remained as fixed and uncompromising as they were, there might no

[1] *Journal*, May 1738, i. 95–96.

doubt be sympathy and co-operation, but it is hardly possible that there could be real union. The English clergy have in our time been often blamed far too severely for their attitude towards Wesley and his fellow-workers. When we consider the saintly life of the great leader of the movement, his warm and steady Churchmanship, and the immense results which he accomplished, nothing seems more natural or more reasonable than to censure the blindness and folly of the English Church for not finding room and field within its borders for such magnificent Christian energies. Surely, we impatiently exclaim, it was not necessary that there should be perfect agreement: a Methodist order might have been established without in any way binding the regular clergy to consent to all that it might say and do. This had long been my own feeling. After a more careful study of Wesley's writings I no longer think so. My admiration of the man is higher than ever. But my conclusion now is—and I venture to think that it will be shared by many who may read the preceding pages—that the English Church, as a whole, could not in the last century honestly combine with Methodism; neither could Wesley, thinking as he did, have honestly accepted its organised support. There was no reason whatever why individual Churchmen, clerical or lay, should not become Methodists. Wesley held no doctrine which could in the slightest degree involve separation for himself or any of his supporters. But the spirit of his theology was, in some very cardinal particulars, not that of the Church in general, or of any considerable party in it. There might be less practical difference between a Roman Catholic and a Puritan than between an English Churchman and a Methodist, supposing all four to be equally good men. The first two would think differently on almost every point, yet each could readily allow the Christianity of the other. The latter two might think alike on almost all points which had ordinarily been questions of dispute; but if the Methodist considered the Churchman 'unconverted,' he would be bound by a thousand passages in Wesley's writings to consider that person, however highly he might respect him, either no Christian, with the most awful doom impending upon him, or, at best, a Christian in some miserable 'legal' sense of the word. In such individual cases a closer intercourse between two good men would doubtless be too strong for theory, and the Methodist would be satisfied either that his friend had been new-born, but had not yet gained the clear knowledge of it, or else that it was an 'exempt' case, or else would modify his own views as to the universal necessity of the change. But as between two communities the strain would be too great to admit of any cordial union. The most fundamental differences between the English Church and Methodism were not of a kind to create much controversy, but as causes of alienation were more formidable than many controversies.

Wesley's opponents did not do themselves justice. In reading Warburton, or Douglas, or the elaborate work in which Bishop Lavington 'compared the enthusiasm of Methodists and Papists,' it will often seem that they are condemning their own Church more severely than their antagonist. There often appears to be a striking absence of insight into the deeper spiritual feelings. They appear to imagine that no further argument is needed if they can convict Whitefield, or Wesley, or Seagrave of that which was the theological bugbear of the age—enthusiasm, and if they can point to the selfsame heat, and perhaps extravagance of religious feeling, as earlier ages had seen in a St. Francis or a Loyola. It was easy for them to show that Wesley was credulous, superstitious, always ready to accept the supernatural and miraculous. This was partly owing to an infirmity of natural temperament, but far more to his conviction that earth and air were peopled with unseen spiritual existences, and that every event of life was subject to a special overruling of divine providence. They spoke of the cries and groans of the conscience-stricken as mere signs of fanaticism. They made much of the differences between Wesley and Whitefield, little knowing by what depth of generous feeling and noble self-restraint those differences were for the most part underlaid. They gave the Wesleys little credit for their steadfast loyalty to the Church, and thought of them rather as its open or covert enemies. They dilated upon the Antinomianism which here and there appeared in some of the Methodist societies,[1] but said nothing of the impetuous earnestness with which Wesley denounced it, and how unceasingly he insisted upon faith bringing forth its fruits of pure and righteous dealing. In a word, the impression which would be most naturally formed from a perusal of these writings would be that their objections to Methodism were simply those minor failings and extravagances by which intense religious zeal can scarcely fail to be accompanied. The more serious theological defects of Methodism are almost lost in the long array of charges, which are many of them only evidences how greatly Methodism was needed.

Some elements in the Methodist movement were indeed so greatly needed in the English Church, that I am unwilling to leave the subject with the seeming conclusion that Methodism could not have been amalgamated into the constitution of the Church. Practically, and as a matter of

---

[1] Thus at Bristol: 'I began examining the Society, and not before it was wanted. For the plague was begun. I found many crying out "Faith, faith!" "Believe, believe!" and making little account of the fruits of faith, either in holiness or good works' (*Journal*, Feb. 1716, i. 149). So at Wednesbury, Fetter Lane, &c.

fact, I do not think it could have been possible, even if such union had been earnestly desired on either side. The essential obstacles to it were too deeply rooted in Wesley's theology for it to be conceivable that for the sake of any gain, either to the Church or to his own societies, he could have mitigated their sharp-cut severity. But if it had been possible for the Methodism of that age to be consistent with a different view of the divine nature and a no less modified view in regard of the corruption of human nature, it might then have been invited to work with the Church as a voluntary order, with little further modification of its spirit and discipline. At all events, an attempt to bring this about would have done honour to the English Church. But whether the blemishes of the Methodist system were too fundamentally a part of its early missionary energies to admit of any serious modification, and whether Methodism would have done more or less for the Christianity of the world if it had worked side by side with Anglicanism in England and the colonies—these are questions not easily answered, and certainly not within the scope of this work to enter into.

There is strong contrast between the indefatigable movement of Wesley's life and the hermit-like seclusion of William Law: the one visiting the furthest corners of the British Islands almost as often and as regularly as if they were but the remoter hamlets of his parish; the other wearing two places in the floor[1] where he sat day after day in long and thoughtful study. Yet both were leaders of religious thought, both were in marked opposition to many tendencies of their age, both were men of great saintliness of life, both were earnestly attached to the English Church, both were High Churchmen, yet in both the stream of Christian thought flowed too full and deep to be contained

[1] Overton's *Life of Law,* p 242.

in any party channel; both regarded money in no other ligh
than that of means for doing good; both were honoured
above measure by those who enjoyed their intimacy. Even
in opinion, wide as the difference was, it would be easy to
show how constantly the minds of the two men were occupied on the same special subjects, and how often, even on
points in which their opposition was complete, there is in
certain particulars a close analogy of treatment.

Law's life and writings have been so thoroughly and
thoughtfully discussed in a recent publication,[1] that what is
here said of him may be compressed in much shorter compass than the theological importance of his writings would
otherwise require. To pass his works over in silence would be
impossible. There is certainly no author in the eighteenth
century whose writings on divinity I have found so suggestive of thought, so interesting, and so instructive.

My remarks will be confined to those later treatises which
give him his most distinctive place in eighteenth-century
theology. It is not, however, by these that his name is
popularly best known, but by his 'Serious Call to a Holy
and Devout Life.' That must be a book of no small weight
and value which could so deeply touch the heart and mould
the life of Wesley and of Whitefield, of Dr. Johnson, of
Bishop Horne, of Venn and Scott,[2] without speaking of multitudes in every class who have found in its pages incentives
to a new and higher life.[3]

As a controversialist, Law always commands high respect both for himself and for his reasonings. In particular,
his answer to the depressing, if not immoral, utilitarianism

---

[1] *William Law, Nonjuror and Mystic*, by J. H. Overton (Longmans), 1881.

[2] *Id.*, chap. vii.

[3] Wesley makes the publication by Law of his *Christian Perfection*, in 1725, and of his *Serious Call*, in 1726, the first beginning of a real reformation in manners throughout England (*Works*, vi. 330

of Mandeville has deservedly won in our times the warm commendation of Sterling and Frederick Maurice.[1]

The immense influence upon the cultivated English student of the rugged, uncouth writings of Jacob Behmen, the Gorlitz shoemaker, 'the Teutonic Theosopher,' is at first appearance a curious phenomenon. But in Germany the case is abundantly paralleled. Arndt and Andreas, Spener and Francke, Zinzendorf, Novalis, Kahlman, and Schlegel were all more or less indebted to him.[2] Nor can it be wondered at. For amid all his unintelligible verbiage, amid extraordinary fancies, which sometimes seem like the uncontrolled ramblings of insanity, are scattered passages of great beauty and remarkable spiritual insight. And truly there is a golden thread running through it all. For William Law his writings had a surpassing fascination. He mastered the language in order to read them in the original Dutch, translated and published them in folio, and filled his mind with the thoughts which had inspired them. Although the turbid stream was not altogether infiltrated by its passage through Law's clear and logical intellect, yet he sifted out much of the dregs, while he remained in firm possession of the treasure. To many of his contemporaries it seemed as though he had ruined himself as a divine. They turned with aversion from the too frequent remains of Behmen's strange jargon. But as soon as it has escaped from this the stream is clear and pure. In the opinion, not indeed of all, but of many competent judges,[3] Law gains far more than he loses by his studies, both of

---

[1] F. D. Maurice's Introd. to Law's *Answer to Mandeville*, v, xix, &c.

[2] J. M. Matter, *Histoire du Christianisme*, iv. 314 ; J. A. Dorner, *Protestant Theology*, ii. 184.

[3] Those who wish to form any judgment for themselves of Law's later writings, if they do not find it convenient to refer to Law's works, should at all events read the reprint from the 'Dialogue on the Spirit of Love, published by Bishop Ewing in the *Present Day Papers*.

the mystical theology in general, and in particular of Behmen.

The key-note of all Law's theology, which in his later writings he never loses sight of even for a single page,[1] is an assured belief in the firm, unchangeable will of the Deity to be a good and blessing to every creature. All Christian life, all Christian doctrine, must bend to the truth of all truths, that God is 'a boundless abyss of goodness,' an 'infinite, fathomless depth of never-ceasing love.'

Much which seems to an ordinary reader far-fetched and fantastical in Law's writings was to Law's own mind intensely real and full of meaning, as being the working out of his one central conception. It entered essentially into his explanation of the great and world-old problem, how the existence of evil was consistent with the sovereignty of perfect love. For a full sketch of Law's reasonings on this and kindred points I must refer to a chapter in the work already alluded to.[2] He looked upon the whole work of God in this world as ever one of redemption. He believed, with Behmen, that ages before the days of creation this world had been the kingdom of fallen angels. They had misused the divine power of will, and had severed themselves from the light and spirit and love of God. Their whole outward kingdom fell with them into grossness, wrath, and disorder, and 'darkness was upon the face of the deep.' Then the world as it now is was created, in some partial resemblance to its former perfect state; and man, possessed with angelic freedom of will, was to be the restoring angel

[1] Most of the passages quoted below, or referred to, are in the sixth and seventh volumes of Law's *Works*, especially in the 'Spirit of Love' and 'Spirit of Prayer.'

[2] *William Law*, &c., chap. xiv. Although I have carefully and with great interest read many of Law's writings, I had by no means realised the full scope and connection of his arguments until I had read this lucid and instructive chapter.

of the new creation, until at last it should recover its first heavenly lightness. But Adam fell, not (as Law regarded it) by any single act, but by a gradual process. The forbidden tree was no trial imposed upon him by his Maker. It was a power which the world's mixed nature had gained over him through a first declension in Adam towards the earthly, and against which, when it had grown, God's compassion warned him. The eating was but the climax of a lust towards the world. And when he had fallen from the angelic state, it was impossible that he could generate offspring of a nature essentially superior to his own.

The main point to be here noticed is, that while Law fully accepted the Scriptural record of the fall, and made it the basis of his theology, he was dissatisfied with some important particulars in the popular conception of it. Neither in this nor in any other point of belief could he ever bear with any interpretation which could in any way obscure the trust in perfect goodness, willing only man's redemption from evil.

In Law's mind the whole past history of mankind and all the future of the race teems, amid all its sin and misery, with ineffable hope and promise. The greatness of the fall is a measure of the greatness of the restoration. Trust in the promise that as in Adam all die, so in Christ shall all be made alive; confidence in the answer of divine goodness to the groaning and travailing of a world whose supreme need is regeneration—this, above all else, was the message which the gospel brought. Not that the work of recovery waited for gospel times. Law maintained as a cardinal point of true belief that there never was an interval in which the new birth, the new creation, had not yet begun. The same Word of God, who in the fulness of time became visibly incarnate for man's salvation, had been from the first a Second Adam, and a light to every one that is born in the world. That divine nature had been at once reblended with the human—a seed of heavenly life which in the end would crush the serpent's head. 'This is that Christianity which began with the fall,' and which awakened in every true heart faith, and hope, and desire of the new birth, until it broadened out into the full revelation of salvation in Christ the Saviour. He, 'in whose mysterious person humanity was united,' carrying our nature victoriously through the grave, 'recovered by death for man the first glorious immortal body.' He lived and died, and rose from the dead to be a quickening power in us, 'to quicken and revive that life from above which we had lost in Adam;' 'to atone—to quench and overcome that death, and wrath, and hell, under the power of which man has fallen.' Atonement was not, as some strangely and unworthily imagined, satisfaction rendered to an angry God, but regeneration alone, and re-creation unto righteousness. This ariseth out of faith in Christ. 'True faith is a coming to Him to be saved and delivered from a sinful nature, as the Canaanitish woman came to Him, and would not be denied. It is a faith of love, a faith of hunger, a faith of thirst, a faith of certainty and firm assurance. . . . It is the faith that breaks off all the bars of death and hell in the soul. It is to this faith that Christ always says, "Thy sins are forgiven thee; go in peace."' And 'what is God's forgiving sinful men? It is nothing else in its whole nature but God making him righteous again. There is no other forgiveness of sins but being made free from sin.'

'As for the purification of all human nature, either in this world or some after ages, I fully,' said Law, ' believe it.' 'We may be sure enough that the boundless goodness of God will set no bounds to itself, but will remove every misery from every creature that is capable of it.' Never theless that love may work both in time and eternity in very terrible ways. He was sure that 'every act of what is called divine vengeance ought, with greater strictness of truth, to be called an act of the divine love.' But his feeling of the wretchedness in the world was very dark, scarcely less so than that of Wesley himself. He knew not how deeply ingrained sin might often be in a human soul. He found no difficulty in the terrors which Scripture denounces against sin in a world to come. On the contrary, the whole analogy of temporal punishment on earth bore witness to them. Of this only he was well assured, that suffering, however long, however severe, can only be sent in mercy. Whatever God doth, whether it be creating or sanctifying, whether it be threatening or punishing, all 'is but one and the same essential, immutable, never-ceasing working of the divine nature.'

William Law was born in 1686, was Fellow of Emmanuel College, Cambridge, in 1705, declined the oaths in 1716, and soon after became tutor to Edmund Gibbon at Putney. All the latter part of his life was spent, amid devotions, study, and charitable works, in his native village of Kingscliffe, Northamptonshire. He died in 1761. The 'Serious Call' was published in 1726. His more mystical writings were all written during the last twenty years of his life.

John Byrom, another enthusiastic member of the same mystical school, would have claimed more than a passing mention if he had not been so nearly the echo of William Law, to whom he clung as to an honoured and beloved father. Perhaps he thought he should popularise Law's thoughts by stringing them into doggrel verse; perhaps it was the exercise by which he could best appropriate them to his own mind. In any case, the good prose he borrowed from Law could not have been more hardly used. Yet, in his wilderness of rhyme, it is truly wonderful what gems of epigrammatic expression and real poetical thought occasionally occur.

But Jacob Behmen had another student in these islands, whose life and writings have great interest. Henry Brooke was born in 1708, and died in 1783. A pure and noble-minded Christian gentleman, he lived in the world but not of it. Surrounded by its attractions, versed in its accomplishments, his heart was ever most faithful to his divine Master. It is almost hard to realise, knowing what court and city manners were in the reigns of the first two Georges, that he could have preserved his life so untainted and true. Charles Kingsley's words about him are remarkable: 'The pupil of Swift and Pope; the friend of Lyttelton and Chatham; the darling of the Prince of Wales; beau, swordsman, wit, poet, courtier, the minion once of Fortune, yet unspoilt by all her caresses, he had long been known to Irishmen only as the saintly recluse of Longfield.'[1] His writings were sometimes called Methodistical. They were far from being this; but John Wesley, who speaks of him familiarly as 'Harry Brooke,'[2] admired, adapted, and largely circulated his 'Earl of Moreland.'[3] Of whom else could it have been said, of all whom Wesley favoured and esteemed, that he uniformly supported the stage?[4] He was the writer of a tragedy, 'Gustavus Vasa,' in 1739; and though the Government of the time took offence at the spirit of liberty which breathed in it, and closed the theatres against it, this increased rather than diminished his reputation. Among his tenantry and poorer neighbours, to whom he was not only a friend and generous helper, but also a zealous teacher and director in spiritual matters,[5] he was greatly beloved

---

[1] Kingsley, preface to *The Fool of Quality*, or *Life of Henry, Earl of Moreland*, iv.   [2] Wesley's *Works*, xii. 299.

[3] *Id.*, xiii. 137, and Kingsley's preface, xxx.   [4] Kingsley, *id.*

[5] Preface to his *Plays and Poems*, 1789, xviii. On one occasion, the clergyman, being prevented from coming to church till near the end

and honoured, and their grief was universal when he died.

His 'Earl of Moreland,' or 'Fool of Quality,' in five volumes, is over-long and over-exuberant, not in length only, but in fancy and expression. But it is full of noble thoughts —for which the education of an ideal nobleman gives ample scope—in morals, politics, and theology. Kingsley praises 'its deep and grand ethics, its broad and genial humanity,' and adds that 'there will be some to affirm that they have learned from this book more that is pure, sacred, and eternal than from any that has been published since Spenser's "Fairy Queen."'[1] John Wesley, after praising its beauty, its frequent sublimity, its admirable sense, its important truths, continues, 'But the greatest excellence of all is that it continually strikes at the heart. It perpetually aims at inspiring and increasing every right affection; at the instilling gratitude to God and benevolence to man. And it does this not by dull, dry, tedious precepts, but by the liveliest examples that can be imagined; by setting before your eyes one of the most beautiful pictures that ever was drawn in the world. The strokes of this are so delicately fine, the touches so easy, natural, and affecting, that I know not who can survey it with tearless eyes, unless he has a heart of stone. I recommend it, therefore, to all those who are already, or desire to be, lovers of God and man.'[2]

Wesley's edition of this book was a very abbreviated one, and he expurgated with special care all that savoured of Jacob Behmen and mystical divinity. To do this he must have cut away many of the finest passages, and those in which Brooke poured out his soul most fervently. For he

of service-time, found when he came in that Henry Brooke had, by the request of the people, read the prayers, and was then preaching to a deeply moved congregaton (*id.*).

[1] Kingsley's pref. to *The Fool of Quality*, liv.
[2] Wesley's preface to 'History of E. of Moreland,' *Works*,

had been scarcely less fascinated than William Law by Behmen's writings. There are whole chapters of the work in which every page, and almost every line, prove the hold which this theology had gained over him. A great deal of it, however, is not so much Behmen directly, as the clearer and more thoughtful mysticism of William Law. The nature of the fall and its universality, the corresponding greatness of redemption, the deep and measureless love of God, the inward birth in man of Christ the Redeemer and Purifier of all nations, light brought out of darkness and life out of death, reclamation to the utmost bound of possibility, the beneficent work of suffering, all nature groaning for its final restitution—these are the special topics upon which Henry Brooke, no less than William Law, dwelt upon with eagerness and enthusiasm. It seems strange that this author should have been read with delight by Wesley, whose views of the general doom of the bulk of humanity were very dark and terrible. Possibly in his later years there may have been some unconfessed modification in his thought.

For about thirty years towards the middle of the century the Moravian community occupied a place of considerable interest in the records of the English Church, and was certainly more nearly associated with it than any other external communion had ever been. For some time there had been among English Churchmen a special regard for what Zinzendorf justly called 'the most ancient of all the Protestant churches.'[1] In the year of Charles II.'s restoration Comenius had drawn up an account of its history, and sent it to the king, with an affectionate address to the Church of England. The address had been received with much favour, and recommended by Archbishop Sancroft, and Compton, Bishop of London, to the attention of Christian

---

[1] Wedgwood's *Wesley*, p. 93.

people.[1] At the opening of the eighteenth century, when the foundation of the great Church societies had turned much attention to missionary enterprise, the zeal and success of the Moravian missions had evoked cordial admiration. The English Church societies were quite disposed to help them, and in Georgia and South Carolina were almost prepared to hand over to the brethren the care of Anglican congregations.[2] In 1717, Archbishop Wake expressed his sympathy with them, and his satisfaction at what he heard of their episcopal orders.[3] In 1728 one of their societies was invited into England, and received a kindly welcome from the court of Queen Caroline. Under their eminent leader, Count Zinzendorf (born 1700), the society made further advances in this country. In 1737, Archbishop Potter wrote to him in terms of high respect and warm friendliness.[4] When the question was referred to him whether their orders were to be acknowledged by the English Church in the colonies, he answered that although it was not within his power, without the royal consent, to make a formal acknowledgment, he personally was convinced the Church of the Brethren was a true apostolic and episcopal church, and that he heartily advocated their cause.[5]

In 1749 an Act of Parliament was passed to enable them to settle with greater advantage in British dominions,[6] and formally recognising the body as a Protestant episcopal church. In the debate which arose upon the subject Bishop Madox spoke with earnestness of the benefit conferred on

---

[1] Anderson's *Colonial Church*, ii. 685.

[2] Stoughton's *Q. Anne and the Georges*, p. 337.   [3] *Id.*, 356.

[4] He speaks of the 'sancta, vereque illustris Moraviensis cathedra;' and soon after 'vos autem præ cæteris amem atque amplectar, qui nec periculis territi, nec aliis quibusvis Satanæ πειρασμοῖς seducti, una cum purâ primævâque fide primævam etiam ecclesiæ disciplinam constanter adhuc, ut accepimus, tuentes arctiore nobiscum vinculo conjuncti estis' (Doddridge's *Correspondence*, iii. 264).

[5] Hutton's *Memoirs*, quoted in Stoughton, p. 357.   [6] Doddridge, p. 356.

evangelical Christianity throughout the world by every favour that could be shown to 'this ancient confessor church.' Sherlock also spoke to the same effect.[1] During the same year the venerable Bishop Wilson, then eighty-seven years old, accepted the office of chief ' antecessor ' over the Moravian societies in communion with the Church of England.[2] Zinzendorf was particularly desirous of founding in different churches, and especially in that of England, societies of ' United Brethren,' who should use the Moravian organisation for the advancement of their spiritual life, without in any way breaking off allegiance to their own communion.

But it was through John Wesley and his brother that Moravianism came chiefly into contact with Church history in England. The Brethren who were on board ship with him when he went to Georgia in 1735 made a very deep impression upon him. Full of piety and faith, 'always employed, always cheerful themselves and in good humour with one another, they had put away all anger, malice, and uncharitableness. They walked worthy of their vocation.' As he watched their worship and their daily life, it seemed to him as if time had rolled back seventeen hundred years, and that he saw before him the first primitive Christians,[3] and his own heart was filled with grave and sad misgivings lest after all his zeal, all his self-denial, he had yet to learn from these holy, simple-minded men almost the first principles of the Christian faith. Such at least was the feeling with which he returned to England; and thinking not only of his own spiritual welfare, but of that of his Church, he expressed his gratitude that ' God had been pleased by him to open the intercourse between the English and the Moravian Church.'[4] He held about this time much and frequent

---

[1] Stoughton, p. 362.   [2] Tyerman's *Oxford Methodists*, p. 288.
[3] Wesley's *Works*, i. 26, &c.   [4] *Id.*, i. 80.

intercourse with Peter Böhler. He was full of self-dissatisfaction and disquietude, listening with deep attention to what Böhler and other of the Brethren said to him of resting simply and implicitly in Christ, apart from all works and all reasonings, and yet unable at first to break from what he had thought before, and not assured that what they said to him was not foolishness.[1] Then came what Wesley always considered his conversion; after which one of his first purposes was to go to Germany ' to converse with these holy men.'[2] He went to Herrnhut, joined in their prayers, their hymns, their conferences, their love-feasts, kept ' in gladness and singleness of heart, in praise and thanksgiving.'[3] He conversed with them one by one, listened to their experiences, and wrote them down for his own guidance. 'I am with a Church,' Wesley wrote to his brother, ' whose conversation is in heaven, in whom is the mind that was in Christ, and who so walk as He walked.'[4] Whatever might be his later differences from them, it is evident that the impression Moravianism made upon him, at a time when his whole nature was almost morbidly open to new spiritual influences, was deep and ineffaceable.

But even at Herrnhut differences began to arise between Wesley and his German friends. The deep ferment of his soul at this period was not very congenial with the glad and quiet tenor of their artless lives. He was, they said, a ' homo perturbatus.' His active and logical mind was displeasing to men who abhorred what they called human reasoning. ' His head,' they said, ' had gained ascendency over his heart.' Lastly, they were somewhat wearied with his opinions as a zealous English Churchman, and thought he might be left without interference to do good in the

[1] Wesley's *Works*, i. 98. [2] *Id.*, 106. [3] *Id.*, 116.
[4] Quoted in Wedgwood's *J. Wesley*, p. 169.

ministry of his own Church.¹ Wesley, on his side, thought they were not careful enough to practise self-denial, that they were too apt to wear gay and costly apparel, that they often talked of trivial and unprofitable subjects, that they were not zealous in good works to other than their own brethren, and that among some of their leaders there was some lack of straightforwardness and truthfulness.² Though he exceedingly admired 'their mutual love, their excellence of doctrine and of life,'³ yet he thought there were faults among them which needed amendment, and did not fail to tell them what they were.

After Wesley's return to England differences between him and the Moravians in feeling and opinion gradually ripened into complete estrangement. Even if he had continued to see Moravianism at its best, his growing aversion to every form of mysticism would gradually have alienated his sympathies. But in England he met with members of the Brotherhood who held opinions as perilous to sound morality as to pure religion. He saw developing among many of them three of the most dangerous affections under which religion can suffer. One was a disparagement of all the outward rites and ordinances of religion. Christ was the only means of grace, all else was unprofitable.⁴ Nought else need be done but simply and quietly to rest in Him. The second was an aggravated form of the same error. It was the Antinomianism which made the very

---

¹ Tyerman's *Oxford Methodists*, p. 89. They were also quite indisposed to admit the supernatural character of those physical agitations by which Wesley and other Methodists were so much impressed (Wedgwood, p. 207).

² *Id.*, ii. 30, &c. Although Wesley always held that 'orthodoxy was but a very small part of religion,' he thought the views of Zinzendorf and other Moravian leaders were far too accommodating. But it was a community of which it has been said that it was 'Calviniste-ci, Luthérienne-là, Catholique partout, avant tout Chrétienne' (Matter, *Hist. du Christianisme*, p. 348).

³ *Id.*, i. 246, 248, 307, &c.   ⁴ Wesley's *Works*, i. 248, &c.

name of 'good works' an abomination. 'They would have nothing to do with the law. They would preach Christ, as they called it, but without one word either of holiness or good works.'[1] There was no error in religion which gave Wesley so much trouble and anxiety as this. Himself a most earnest preacher of righteousness, he was yet well aware that his cardinal doctrine of justification by faith only was liable to a terrible perversion. He has in one place acknowledged that true religion as he understood it did indeed lie on the very verge alike of Antinomianism and Predestinarianism,[2] the two things which he considered to be most fatal to true religion. He was, therefore, all the more strenuous in his opposition to the Antinomians, of whom he judged the Moravians to be 'the most plausible, and therefore the most dangerous.'[3] The third error was one which did more harm to the good repute of Moravianism in England than anything besides. This was a sort of grossness and voluptuousness of expression which repelled with something like loathing many who had before been greatly interested in the Brotherhood. There were often expressions in the Moravian hymns which no manly Christianity could possibly tolerate. It seems to be entirely owing to this that Moravianism in England fell with some suddenness, about the middle of the century, into disrepute and disgrace, out of which it gradually rose again through the various accounts which came in of the wonderful zeal and love of their missionaries.[4] Nor had there been any falling off in

---

[1] *Id.*, viii. 350.

[2] 'Q. Does not the truth of the Gospel lie very near both to Calvinism and Antinomianism? A. Indeed it does; as it were within a hair-breadth. So that it is altogether foolish and sinful, because we do not quite agree with one or the other, to run from them as far as ever we can' (Conversations, 1745; Wesley's *Works*, viii. 284). [3] Wesley's *Works*, x. 231.

[4] Mosheim's *Eccl. Hist.*, v. 86; Hughes' *Letters*, ii. 204; *Gentleman's Mag.* for 1750, p. 503; Doddridge's *Works*, iii. 271. Wilberforce's *Practical View*, p. 79; where he speaks both of the grave suspicions under which they

the life of the Herrnhut community. This is strikingly borne witness to at the end of the century by Schleiermacher, who, during his residence among them, was no less alive to the beauty and simplicity of their religion than he was to its intellectual defects. What an enviable place of abode it might be, he exclaimed, if only, remaining in all essentials what it is, it could yet be modified to the needs of this later age![1]

A few very excellent English Churchmen permanently joined the Moravians. Benjamin Ingham had gone with the Wesleys to Georgia, and was no less impressed than they with the 'good, devout, peaceable, and heavenly-minded people'[2] who were their fellow-travellers. He did not share in Wesley's revulsion of dislike, and his steady adhesion both to William Law and to the Moravians gradually caused a separation between him and his old companion. We see the worst side of quietism in his advice not to expect much from any ordinances of religion, nor to think of finding Christ in them.[3] On the other hand, it was perhaps not unseasonable advice to Wesley that his newer converts should, in the earlier stages of their new life, be kept still and quiet, and urged to search more deeply into their hearts.[4] Ingham established many societies in different parts of England, and these ultimately seceded from the English Church.[5]

Moravianism gained a very good man in John Gambold. He was among the first of the Oxford Methodists, and for nine or ten years vicar of Stanton Harcourt. The writings of the early Christian fathers, especially those of a mystical

---

had laboured, and of the 'ardent, active, and patient zeal,' in which 'they have, perhaps, excelled all mankind.'

[1] Rowan's *Life of Schleiermacher*, p. 267.
[2] Ingham's *Diary*, quoted by Tyerman, *Oxford Methodists*, p. 68.
[3] Wesley's *Works*, iii. 375.   [4] Tyerman, p. 92.
[5] Wesley's *Works*, xiii. 230.

turn, were his special delight, and it is said of him that his whole mind was steeped in the thought and feeling of the primitive days of Christianity. A visitor at his secluded Oxfordshire living would find 'a very agreeable strangeness in hearing a man of the eighteenth century converse like one of those of the second or third of the Christian era.'[1] In 1737 he fell in with Peter Böhler, and a little later with Zinzendorf, and determined to join their community, 'to partake of their happiness, and to live amongst them in love to Christ and to one another, and to unite with them in promoting the glory of God and the good of mankind.'[2] In 1742, in spite of the earnest solicitations of Secker, he gave up his living. He did not, he said, separate from the Church of England; and even as late as 1765 he wrote a 'Summary of Christian Doctrine,' chiefly 'in the sound and venerable words of the Prayer Book of the English Church.'[3] But 'he longed for intimate fellowship with a little flock whose great concern was to build up one another in faith.'[4] He went to Herrnhut in hopes of finding there the community he craved for. He was made one of their bishops in 1754, and died in 1771. John Wesley kept up his old friendship with him, visited him from time to time, and deplored almost pathetically the difference of thought which kept them so much apart. 'Spent some time with my old friend John Gambold. Who but Count Zinzendorf could have separated such friends as we were?' So also a little later, after another visit, 'How gladly could I join heart and hand again! But, alas! thy heart is not as my heart.'[5] Gambold's verses contrast in tone with the usual poetry of this age. His tragedy, for instance, on the martyrdom of Ignatius abounds in interesting passages. A few lines may be quoted:—

A glorious day, O Philo,
When persecution lowers! I call it sunshine,
Which quickens the dull bosom of the Church
To bold productions, and a bloom of virtues.
Yes, such a worthy juncture I much long for,
When Christian zeal, benumbed and dead through ease,
Glows with young life, feels the more copious blow
Of ghostly aids; and as the danger rises,
Heightens its pulse, and fills up all its greatness.
Then is the time of crowns, of grants profuse,
Complete remission, open paradise,
With power to intercede for common souls,
For generous motives of intenser duty,
Which, while the sufferer sees, serene and glad,
He thanks the impious hand that helped him forward.[1]

A third who should be mentioned was Francis Okely, also one of Wesley's contemporaries at Oxford. After serving for some time as deacon among the Moravians, he offered himself for priest's orders in the English Church. Finding, however, that the bishop could not recognise his past diaconate, he withdrew, and continued to officiate only in the Brethren's congregations. He was a great admirer of Behmen and William Law. Those who knew him spoke of him in the warmest terms as among the best of men, and very valuable as a Christian guide and friend.[2]

About the middle of the century a set of opinions came into some notice which, from the name of their founder, gave to the party the name of Hutchinsonians. These views were held by some Churchmen of considerable mark, as by Horne, President of Magdalen, Oxford, afterwards Bishop of Norwich, and by Jones of Nayland, a clergyman of great learning and piety, whose name is still familiar to many.[3]

[1] 'Ignatius,' act i. sc. 1. Tyerman quotes some fine lines from him upon Christian perfection (*Oxford Methodists*, p. 151).

[2] Nichols' *Lit. An.*, iii. 93.

[3] Bp. Horsley speaks in great praise of that 'faithful servant of God. He

Others were Wetherell, master of University College, Oxford; Berkeley, son of a much more distinguished father;[1] and Samuel Johnson of Connecticut, one of the principal leaders of the English Church in America.[2]

The opinions of John Hutchinson—he was born in 1674, and died in 1737—do not appear to have been in themselves very deserving of record, and have their chief significance as reactionary to certain tendencies of his age. His admirers called him 'the famous Mosaic philosopher,'[3] and were never quite satisfied that he had not quite refuted the 'speculations' of Sir Isaac Newton. He had been an energetic opponent of the Newtonian system. It might be more correct to say that he did not so much deny his facts, or in general under-estimate his skill in the discovery and calculation of natural forces, as dispute the inferences which he feared were being drawn from them. He believed that Newton and Dr. Clarke were working with Collins, Toland, Tindal, and others to undermine the theology of Scripture, and to introduce some heathen 'anima mundi' into the place of the true God. Materialism, atheism, and general heathenism were the opponents rising up anew with fresh and formidable weapons, whom Christian reasoners had to encounter with all their might.[4] Strongly possessed with this idea, and always ready to push his arguments to their

was a man of great penetration, of extensive learning, and the soundest piety; and he had, beyond any other man I ever knew, the talent of writing upon the deepest subjects to the plainest understanding' (Horsley's *Charges*, p. 123).

[1] Bishop Berkeley looked askance upon Hutchinson, as upon that bugbear of the age, an enthusiast. 'I am not,' he said to a correspondent, 'acquainted with his writings, only I have observed that he is mentioned as an enthusiast, which gave me no prepossession in his favour' (Fraser's *Life of Berkeley*, iv. 326).

[2] Beardsley's *Life of S. Johnson*, pp. 234, 305.

[3] Jones's *Life of Horne*, p. 9.

[4] See account of Horne's 'Impartial State of the Case between Sir I. Newton and Mr. Hutchinson,' in *id.*, p. 20-22.

ultimate consequences, he did not hesitate to assert that many of the most illustrious writers on the Christian side in the Deist controversy were only less inimical to religion than their opponents. For they also allowed that there was 'a religion of nature,' and he on his part insisted that if it was to be called a religion at all, it was only that of Satan or of Antichrist. Religion was derived from no other source than from Scripture and tradition. Some of the most celebrated divines had done, he said, infinite mischief in extolling the dignity of human nature, and it was a grievous mistake to suppose that anything but harm could come out of the study of ethics or metaphysics. From Scripture was derived the sum-total of all knowledge that was of any value to man's supreme interests, however much some other branches of learning might be subsidiary to it. He considered that Scripture was a mine of knowledge which had been hitherto but very superficially worked; that Hebrew was a perfect language; that its etymologies were full of divine meanings, which had been neglected chiefly because they had been studied in the light of Jewish, and not of Christian learning; and that where natural objects were referred to in the sacred writings they generally, if not invariably, had a spiritual inward meaning.

Hutchinson's admirers did not by any means feel bound to follow him in all his fantastic imaginations about Hebrew roots, or in all that he objected against the Newtonian philosophy. They honoured him, they said, not so much for any minor opinions which he held, but because he had so strongly insisted that religion was a thing far remote from man's philosophy, and that direct revelation was the one paramount and unique authority upon which all spiritual knowledge rested.[1] Warburton, in his usual language, vented upon them unmeasured scorn. Hutchin-

[1] Jones's *Life of Horne*, p. 92.

son, he said, was a mere 'cabalist,' and his opinions were 'a disgrace to human reason.'[1] But they were men highly deserving of respect. Their lives were most estimable. They zealously laboured in the cause of religion; and if their views were in some respects erroneous and retrogressive, they did service in dwelling upon aspects of Christianity which many of their contemporaries were apt to neglect. It may be added that they opened a fertile and suggestive field of thought in their reflection upon the analogies between the worlds of nature and of grace.

The 'evangelical' movement in the Church had fully begun before George III.'s accession; but its general history belongs so much to the latter part of the century, and its earlier records are so much intermingled with those of Methodism, that whatever is said about it in this work may properly be postponed to a later chapter.

It cannot be said that in any part of the century the clergy, as a body, stood very high in general estimation. No doubt passages may be quoted in which the whole order is spoken of with respect and honour. Thus in the 'Athenian Oracle' for 1716 we read, 'None, we think, but those who are extremely prejudiced will deny that the clergy of England are at this time as considerable a body, both for piety and learning, good preaching and good living, as any in the world, or perhaps as any that have lived in any age of the Church since the apostles.'[2] A somewhat similar passage may be found in Hughes' prefatory essays to S. Chrysostom's 'Treatise on the Priesthood,' 1710.[3] 'We never,' writes a layman in 1711, 'had a more regular

---

[1] Warburton to Doddridge, May 1738, Doddridge's *Correspondence*, iii. 327.　　　　[2] *Athenian Oracle*, iii. 382.

[3] ' Sive enim ingenium, sive doctrinam, sive morum probitatem integritatemque consideremus, vel inimicissimi concedant necesse est, nihil Ecclesiâ Anglicanâ superius unquam exstitisse' (quoted by Babington in his *Answer to Macaulay*, p. 12).

and learned clergy than at this time.'[1] It will be observed that all these passages occur in or about the second decade of the century, a period when the Church, as a national institution, was at the height of its popularity. Such general encomiums of the clergy would not easily be found at a later date.[2] Lord Lyttelton's commendation of them, about 1730, is pitched in a lower key. He praises them as 'moderate, quiet, useful members of the commonwealth, better friends to liberty, better subjects, better Englishmen, than at any previous period.'[3] Towards the end of the century the frequent notices that may be found of reviving activity[4] of the clergy in general, are in themselves significant of an unsatisfactory condition in previous years.

There was of course no period in which there were not a great number of clergymen who were in every way worthy of respect. If Fielding has his Parson Trulliber and his Parson Barnabas, he has also good Parson Adams, and another excellent clergyman, 'well worthy of the cloth he wore; and that,' says he, 'is, I think, the highest character a man can obtain.'[5] There were not a few who corresponded fairly well to the picture of the country pastor in Goldsmith's 'Deserted Village;' or to the clergyman in the 'Spectator's Club,' 'a man of general learning, great sanctity of life, and the most exact good breeding;'[6] or to 'the choice and

---

[1] *The Clergyman's Advocate*, by a Layman, 1711, p. 66. The *Tatler*, in 1709, speaks of the clergy as, 'I believe, the most learned body in the world' (No. 66).

[2] There is no great value in the testimony of a university preacher in 1715, that, amid many examples to the contrary, the clergy as a body did 'honour both to their nation and to their religion, and were the defence of both' (W. Gardner's Univ. S. on 'the Faithful Pastor,' p. 26).

[3] Lyttelton's *Persian Letters*, No. 60.

[4] It may be added that Chateaubriand, writing of England in 1792–1800, speaks with praise of its clergy, as 'savant, hospitalier, et genereux' (*Essai sur la Lit. Anglais*, ii. 285).

[5] Fielding's *Amelia*, B. VII., ch. ii.

[6] *Spectator*, No. 2.

excellent spirits among our divines'[1] of whom the 'Tatler' speaks; or to the rector of South Green, in one of the later essayists, who was 'almost worshipped by his parishioners, their clergyman, doctor, lawyer, steward, friend, and cheerful companion.'[2] There were many who, as the poet Thomson said of his father, were 'with no titles blest, But that best title, a good parish priest;'[3] or of whom their people could say, as the poet Somervile of his friend, 'He taught them how to live and how to die. Nor did his actions give his words the lie.'[4] Those who were severest on the lives of many of the clergy were quite ready, if they were candid men, to make large exceptions; as when David Hartley adds, 'But there are some of quite a different character, men eminent for piety, for learning, and the faithful discharge of their duty. . . . The clergy in general are also far more free from open and gross vices than any other denomination of men among us.'[5] Wesley spoke, reticently for the most part, but sadly and earnestly, of what he considered the great shortcomings of the clergy, but not unfrequently records the good works and teaching which he sometimes found.

It is very evident that, throughout the century, the clergy were, as a body, a good deal open to censure. To come to this conclusion it is not necessary to take greatly into account the bitter and systematic assaults made against them by the Deists, nor yet the reflections of men fired with the zeal of the Methodistic movement, who might perhaps condemn as cold and formal anything that fell

---

[1] *Tatler*, No. 206. [2] The *World* for May 21, 1753, No. 21.
[3] Thomson, 'On my Father.'
[4] Somervile, 'In Memory of Rev. Mr. Moore.'
[5] Hartley's *Considerations on Man*, p. 451. So also in 1737, a writer, who draws a severe indictment against the prevalent negligence in the Church, speaks very highly of many of the clergy as 'men of knowledge, courage, piety, and patience' (*Complaint of the Ch. of Eng. against Pluralities, &c.*, p. 31).

clearly short of their own impassioned ardour. But almost all the literature of the century tells the same story. Poets, essayists, novelists, moralists, writers on social subjects, politicians, pamphleteers, writers on theology, bishops in their charges, the friends of the Church no less than its enemies, all agree that the ranks of the clergy were filled to a serious extent with men who did very little to advance the cause of religion; that there were many grave abuses, and that scandals were not unfrequent. These complaints rarely, if ever, go beyond a certain point. The reader of them never gets the impression that anything like corruption or moral badness is imputed to the order; on the contrary, it is often acknowledged that the general level of clerical living was higher than that of any other section of the community. This, however, does not by any means indicate anything very exemplary, or inconsistent with highly censurable faults. No reader of eighteenth-century literature can fail to be struck by the uniform despondency with which the morals and manners of the age are regarded. Many pages might be filled with quotations from authors of every sort, all of them deploring a prevalent wickedness and godlessness which they seem to consider almost portentous and phenomenal. Such passages lead to a twofold conclusion. It is impossible not to feel that there must have been some solid ground for so general a verdict. It is also impossible not to feel that there was something of a fashion in this style of speaking; that this depth of depreciation was not fully justified; that the case was not so bad as was described; and that, at a period when England was teeming with the germs of political and material progress, it was far from being so unsound at the core as these laments and denunciations might be thought to imply. It may, however, be considered as established that in most classes of society the common standard of principle and duty was abnormally low. In this depression the clergy proportionately shared. Abuses which had been enumerated and deplored by Kettlewell[1] and others in the latter years of the preceding century had gained ground rather than become less with the lapse of time. All serious-minded Churchmen felt that the offices of the Church were often very unworthily filled. 'What honest-hearted man,' exclaims a writer of 1737, 'finds not a sad despondency, with a holy impatience arising in his soul, while he sees so many weak shoulders, such unwashed hands, such unprepared feet, such rash heads, such empty souls, as are now suffered publicly to intrude themselves upon holy duties?'[2] Indolence and lazy self-indulgence, absenteeism and neglect, factiousness and bigotry, servility and preferment-seeking, were the offences, by one or another of which it was commonly said that a considerable proportion of the clergy were affected. Here and there, but not very often, there were greater scandals. The offences enumerated, if they were indeed common, as evidently they were, needed no further aggravation to account for the sarcasms and reproaches in which the writings of the time abounded. The clergy were not disliked; a zealous man who, whether connected or not with Wesley and his party, had incurred the name of 'Methodist' was apt, until he had won for himself esteem and perhaps love, to be a much more unpopular man than his easy-going clerical neighbours who farmed and sported in the adjoining parishes. Meanwhile, amid the jests of the careless, the laments of the true friends of the Church, and the taunts of its enemies, the same causes of offence which had prevailed in one generation of clergymen were still perpetuated in the next. Dilapidated churches and slovenly services were too often the external symbols of a secular and negligent way

[1] *Life of Kettlewell*, iii. §§ 11-12, pp. 90-91.
[2] *Complaint of the Ch. of Eng.*, p. 31.

in which religious duties were regarded, scarcely less by the priest than by his congregation. There may be no reason for supposing that the rectors and vicars whom our great-grandfathers knew were worse men than their successors now. We may think of them as we do of the statesmen of that and of the present day. The general standard of sufficiency has happily become raised to a higher level. A fairly conscientious politician would not dream of dishonouring himself by jobbery to which his ancestors a hundred years back would have consented with scarce a scruple. In a similar manner, the incumbent of his parish could not let things pass as they did then without being conscience-stricken at a dereliction of duty, of which, when clerical opinion was lower, he might perhaps have been almost unaware.

Absenteeism and pluralities were the great blots in the Church system, out of which many of the evils above mentioned rose. 'When I look,' said Bishop Buckner in 1798, 'for the chief and fundamental cause of all the ministerial negligence which I trace, whence such an evident decline of religion among the people, such great inattention to the ordinances of the Church, such rudeness of manner, such disorderly conduct, such profaneness and debauchery proceed, I feel myself constrained to believe it is in no inconsiderable degree attributable to the non-residence of the clergy.'[1] 'Nothing,' said Bishop Horsley about the same time, 'has so much lessened the general influence of the clergy; nothing so much threatens the stability of the national Church.'[2] Throughout the century the bishops were constantly in their charges[3] adverting to this crying

---

[1] Buckner's *Primary Charge*, quoted in *Gentleman's Magazine*, Nov. 1799, p. 962. [2] Horsley's *Charge* of 1796, p. 58.

[3] As, for instance, Secker's *Charges*, pp. 207, 217; Sherlock's *Works*, iv. 127; Bishop Newton's *Life*, pp. 127, 219; Watson's *Memoirs*, i. 415; Porteus's, *Life*, i. 107, &c.

evil, although unfortunately they did not always set a corresponding example in their own practice. The neighbourhood of Cheddar, which, at the time when Hannah More began her good work there, presented the disgraceful spectacle of six large parishes without a single resident clergyman,[1] was undoubtedly a very exceptional instance. But throughout the period the number of non-residents was probably as great as in 1737, when a catalogue, which was then drawn up, showed that about 2,700 out of 12,000 incumbents were not living on their cures.[2] Bishop Porteus twice endeavoured to carry through a Bill by which the pernicious custom should be materially checked, but was both times unsuccessful.[3] Burnet also, in the earlier part of the century, had been disappointed in his attempt[4] to restrain what Archbishop Sharp properly called the 'odious' system of pluralities. But 'the Lords,' says Prideaux, 'were too fond of their privilege of qualifying their chaplains for pluralities to allow the Bill to be even once read.'[5] It must be acknowledged that in some cases there was also a better ground than this for permitting the evil practice to remain, though it ought to have been curbed within very definite limits. 'An answer,' said J. Johnson in 1709, 'to many arguments rises from the great law of necessity. For one quarter, I had almost said one half, of the churches in England are not of themselves sufficient to maintain their proper curate or minister; and such churches must be served by halves or not at all.'[6] In Ireland, as will afterwards be seen, the case was yet worse. It appears, also, that very frequently there was a great want of houses for the

---

[1] *Memoirs of H. More*, i. 452, 459.
[2] *Complaint of the Church of England*, &c., p. 11.
[3] The 'Curates Act' of 1794 was a valuable measure so far as it went (Horsley's *Charges*, pp. 61–80).
[4] *Life of Sharp*, i. 261.   [5] Prideaux's *Life and Letters*, p. 82.
[6] Johnson's *Account of the Present Church of England*, &c., i. 88.

clergy to reside in.¹ In fact, although there were numbers of comfortable benefices where non-residence was utterly inexcusable, a large number afforded only a miserable pittance, sufficient only to meet the absolute necessities of an unmarried or a peasant clergy. There are many clergymen, says one writer, who just sustain themselves 'by God's mercy and man's charity,'² and sometimes by menial duties or coarse manual labour. Trulliber in labourer's smock, feeding his pigs,³ may be matched by Churchill, in his Welsh cure, eking out his scanty maintenance by the management of a little cider-shop.⁴ When Mackay, about 1722, made his tour through Britain he found that in Wales 'the alehouse is generally kept by the parson, for their livings are very small.'⁵ Often, on account of the difficulty of getting tithes which were paid in kind, a living was worth much less than its nominal value. It is clear that this deficiency was great, although estimates differed widely as to its amount. In 1782, in a sermon for the Sons of the Clergy, it is spoken of as frequently a third of the income.'⁶ Cave, in his 'Inquiry into the Policy of a Commutation,' published in 1800, goes so far as to say that tithe-holders received little more than a fourth part of their real value.⁷ Independently of the non-residence and pluralism which it caused, the great poverty of many livings was in many respects an evil. Lofty aims, or even a thoroughly cultured mind, may triumph over the most unfavourable outward circumstances ; but to minds less than the highest, the depressing struggle with poverty has an effect quite the con-

---

¹ Apthorp's Sermon at the Consecration of Bishop Halifax, p. 20.
² *Complaint of the Ch. of Eng.*, &c., p. 16.
³ Fielding's *Joseph Andrews*, chap. xiv.
⁴ *Life of Churchill*, prefixed to his poems.
⁵ Mackay's *Tour through England*, ii. 136.
⁶ W. Jones, *Sermon for the Sons of the Clergy*, p. 18.
⁷ Polwhele's Introduction to Lavington, cclxxix.

trary of salutary. Some of the indigent clergy of the last century won for themselves the highest respect; but very often great poverty was joined, if not, as was sometimes the case, with sordid habits, at all events with ignorance and narrow-mindedness. One who travelled much has remarked that he scarce 'ever met with a polite clergyman among the clergy but who was for the laws and liberties of the country, nor a clown among them but was all for arbitrary power.'[1] In the latter part of the century the interval between the higher and lower social positions of the clergy became far less marked than it had been. The ranks of the clerical body were recruited more frequently by men of standing, means, and education, and much less often from the lower grades.

Some mention was made in a previous chapter of the condition of the universities in the time of Queen Anne. Their condition did not improve as the century advanced. The inefficiency which prevailed there materially tended to a corresponding inefficiency too often found in the Church. For from them came all the clergy. It was very rarely that any bishop would confer orders on any one who was not a graduate of Oxford or Cambridge; and Church questions, in a very narrow acceptation of the term, were almost the only subject outside university routine which, after the decline of Jacobitism, stirred in them anything like real interest. Even this interest was for the most part a lazy and a languid one, chiefly showing itself in a jealous fear of any infringement of the existing order. When the 'Church in danger' cry faded away, there was nothing greatly to disturb the tranquil air of the Common Rooms until the mooting of the 'subscription' question in 1771. It is true that Methodism was originally an Oxford movement. So also was that far less important one, though

[1] Mackay, Preface, xvi.

real and earnest in its kind, which took its name from its founder, Hutchinson. Even when things were at their worst, the universities could not help being to a certain extent centres where both intellectual and religious thought would be originated and represented. But movement of any sort was repressed rather than encouraged. There were many individual scholars, diligent and zealous, but no intellectual stir.[1] There were many men of earnest practical piety, but they had very little effect upon university life. Methodism went forth from Oxford, but never retained a hold either there or at Cambridge. It was flouted and rejected, and treated almost as if it were a disgrace or a crime. When the author of the 'Weekly Miscellany' had reflected upon the University of Oxford for 'letting the Methodists alone, and permitting them to take their degrees, which was giving them encouragement,' Warburton, instead (as Lowth said) of 'turning to its praise this absurd reproach,' resented it hotly as 'an iniquitous and scurrilous reflection on so illustrious a body. . . . The magistrates of the place did use all lawful means to suppress them. . . . The worthy Vice-Chancellor went and reprimanded Mr. Whitefield before a large congregation which he had gathered about him, and obliged him to leave the town, where he has not been heard of since.'[2] Perhaps no fault need be

---

[1] Frequent complaints may be found about the middle of the century of a general distaste for learning. Thus Markland speaks of the great decay of ancient learning, especially of Greek (Nichols, iv. 311). Warburton declared in a letter to Hurd that learning was shamefully neglected by Church grandees (Warburton and Hurd's *Corresp.*, p. 378). *Cf.* also Secker: 'Olim tractatibus omnium generum, doctrinâ, judicio, acumine conspicuis, inclaruimus: nunc non exaruit quidem, sed arescit uberrimus ille laudium fons' (*Concio ad Convoc.*). So also Churchill:—

> 'What now should tempt us, by false hopes misled,
> Learning's unfashionable paths to tread?'
> (Churchill's *The Author*.)

[2] Warburton's pref. to second edition of *The Divine Legation*; quoted by Lowth in his *Letter to Warburton*, pp. 67-8.

found with this prohibition of Whitefield's preaching in Oxford, particularly if it were likely to be a systematic course. It might have been fairly argued that his passionate declamations, and the scenes of excitement which attended them, were not quite the form of religion most adapted to the edification of undergraduates. But the expulsion, in 1768, of the six students from St. Edmund's Hall [1] was a flagrant act of intolerance. 'This occurrence,' said Wesley, ' and the still more remarkable one of Mr. Seagrave refused the liberty of entering it (by what rule of prudence I cannot tell any more than of law and equity), have forced us to see that neither I nor any of my friends can expect either favour or justice there.' [2] The whole passage breathes a mingled note of love for his old university and regret that it should be doing so little. 'I had,' he says, 'so strong a prejudice in favour of our own universities, that of Oxford in particular, that I could hardly think of any one finishing his education without spending some time there. I therefore encouraged all I had any influence over to enter at Oxford or Cambridge, both of which I preferred in many respects to any university I had seen abroad. . . . I love the very sight of Oxford; I love the manner of life; I love and esteem many of its institutions. But my prejudice in its favour is considerably abated. I do not admire it as once I did. And whether I did or not, I am now constrained to make a virtue of necessity.' Then, after the passage already quoted relating to the expulsion of some Methodist students, he goes on to speak of the small advance com-

---

[1] Full accounts of this proceeding may be gathered from Sir R. Hill's defence of these students in his *Pietas Oxoniensis*, and in T. Nowell's *Answer to Hill*. Cambridge partly followed the example in 1772, when the master of St. John's refused testimonials to a son of Rowland Hill for preaching in Cambridge and the neighbouring villages in connection with Mr. Berridge of Clare, a coadjutor of Wesley (Nichols' *Lit. An.*, i. 574).

[2] Wesley's *Works*, xiii. 263.

monly made there in any branch of academical learning. He continues, 'As to the professors, how learned soever they be (and some of them I verily believe yield to none in Europe), what benefit do nine in ten of the young gentlemen gain from their learning? ... For about fourteen years, except while I served my father's cure, I resided in the university. During much of this time I heard many of these lectures with all the attention I was master of. And I would ask any person of understanding, considering the manner in which most of these lectures are read, and the manner in which they are attended, what would be the loss if they were not read at all? I had almost said what would be the loss if there were no professorships in the university? ... Some of the tutors are worthy of all honour. They are some of the most useful persons in the nation. They are not only men of eminent learning, but of piety and diligence. But are there not many of another sort, who are utterly unqualified for the work they have undertaken? ... The public exercises I never found any other than useless interruptions of my studies.'[1]

The general impression conveyed by the notices we find of the state of the two universities in the eighteenth century is one that very much corresponds with Wesley's account. The opportunities for learning and cultivated thought were always present; and those who ardently set themselves to make the best of their time there might find nearly all they wanted, and might leave with no other feeling than generous love for a university where residence had been full to them alike of happiness and improvement. Lowth's eloquent eulogy is too well known to be transcribed in full. It is clear that one who could extract the good and refuse the evil might yet find in Oxford, to use Bishop Lowth's words, 'a well-regulated course of useful discipline and

[1] *Id.*, 362-64.

studies,' an 'agreeable and improving commerce of gentlemen and scholars,' 'a society where emulation without envy, ambition without jealousy, contention without animosity, incited industry and awakened genius; where a liberal pursuit of knowledge and a generous freedom of thought was raised, encouraged, and pushed forward, by example, by commendation, and by authority.'[1] Dr. Parr has spoken to a not dissimilar effect of Cambridge as he found it in 1765. He could not, he said, speak for what Gibbon might have found at Oxford, but he did know that at Cambridge he would have seen many elegant scholars and many deep mathematicians among the tutors; he would have seen the most generous emulation and the most indefatigable diligence in the younger members of the university; he would have seen plans of study recommended for their use—exercises prescribed for the display of their ingenuity—rewards proposed for their merits in mathematics, in poetry, in prose, in Greek composition, in Latin, and in English.[2] So also Bishop Watson declared of Cambridge, in 1759, that 'there is no seminary of learning in Europe in which youth are more zealous to excel during the first years of their education than in the University of Cambridge.' But he adds that this was true only of those who were obliged to take their B.A. degree, and at the usual time; others were much neglected, and nothing done to stimulate their exertions. He speaks very highly of the scholastic disputations there, which he says stood out in very honourable contrast to those at Oxford. Dinner was at twelve; and at two, students flocked in to the disputations in philosophy and theology. They were supported with much seriousness and solemnity, and he had seen the divinity schools filled with auditors from top to bottom. He feared, however, that the growing custom of

[1] Lowth's *Letter to Warburton*, p. 64. It is better known as quoted in Gibbon's *Autobiography*. [2] Parr's *Works*, i. 45-47.

dining late¹ would soon reduce these exercises to as miserable a state as they were at the sister university.²

Evidently, both on the Isis and on the Cam, intellectual life was far from dead. At the same time there is copious evidence that such energies were somewhat exceptional, and that the prevalent spirit was a torpid indolence which could not but act prejudicially both upon the clergy and upon the educated classes in general. The lazy life of Fellows of colleges was throughout the century a constant butt of satirists, essay writers, and others. One jest was, that at all events some branches of physical science were studied, for 'the doctrine of the screw is practically explained most evenings in the private rooms, together with the motion of fluids.'³ As Southey expressed it much later in the century, 'the waters of Helicon were far too much polluted with the wine of Bacchus.'⁴ Newman thinks that about 1770 was, in this respect at least, the worst time in the university. There was 'a head of Oriel then who was continually obliged to be assisted to bed by his butler.'⁵ Dr. Taylor, in 1730, spoke of Cambridge as pervaded by solemn slumbers, interrupted mainly by whist and politics.⁶ Lloyd,

---

¹ Gilbert Wakefield also bemoaned, about 1790, the evil consequences of the later hour for dining at Cambridge, as tending to idleness and intemperance (*Memoirs*, pp. 149-50). In 1723, on a Shrove-Tuesday, Hearne writes that up to that day, so long as he had been at Oxford, they had dined that day at ten. Whereas that year 'they went to dinner at twelve and to supper at six; nor were there any fritters for dinner, as there used always to be. When laudable old customs alter, 'tis a sign learning dwindles.' (*Hearniana*, ii. 156.)

² Watson's *Anecdotes of his Life*, i. 28-37.
³ Warton's note to Pope's *Works*, vii. 39.
⁴ Southey's *Life and Corresp.*, i. 278, March 1793.
⁵ Pattison's *Memoirs*, p. 203.
⁶ 'Though politics engross the sons of Clare,
. . . .
Though Bene't mould in indolence and ease,
And whist prolong the balmy rest of Kays,
And one continued solemn slumber reigns
From untuned Sydney to protesting Queen's.'
(Quoted in Nichols' *Lit. Anecd.*, i. 581.)

about 1760, speaks of 'Fellows who've soaked away their knowledge By sleepy residence at college,' men whose attachment to the graver pursuits of eating and drinking leave little time 'for the impertinence of thinking.'[1] The 'Idler,' in 1758, amuses its readers with the imaginary diary of a Fellow at one of the universities. He adds, however, that it is not intended to imply that such magnificent idleness is universal. Greatly as Oxford and Cambridge had degenerated, the number of learned persons in them was still considerable.[2] Cowper, in 'The Task,' after deploring how discipline had perished in the universities, and how—not without noble exceptions—study, emulation, and virtue had languished and fled, asks indignantly what the results must be. His words may be quoted, though the metaphor he employs does not add much force to them:

> See then the quiver, broken and decayed,
> In which are kept our arrows! rusting there
> In wild disorder, and unfit for use,
> What wonder if, discharged into the world,
> They shame their shooters with a random flight,
> Their points obtuse, and feathers drunk with wine!
> Well may the Church wage unsuccessful war
> With such artillery armed. Vice parries wide
> Th' undreaded volley with a sword of straw,
> And stands an impudent and fearless mark.[3]

Gibbon's picture of Oxford as it appeared to him in 1751 is known to most readers.[4] Doubtless he did not see it to advantage. No class of so-called students were so notoriously idle as the Fellow commoners, who came to 'while away a couple of lazy years, their golden tuft a badge of honour and of ignorance.'[5] Gibbon, then a boy

---

[1] Lloyd's *Poetry Professor*. [2] The *Idler*, No. 33.
[3] Cowper's *Task*, book ii. [4] Gibbon's *Autobiography*, pp. 21-24.
[5] The *Connoisseur*, No. 41, 1754. There appears, however, to have been a healthy feeling that where the golden tassel chiefly represented ignorance,

of fifteen, coming up as member of this privileged order, was probably expected to be idle as a matter of course. But though he did not see anything of the better side of university life, his account, much as it was controverted, was certainly in the main correct. A few opinions similar to his may be referred to. In 1737, Dr. J. Hoadly, in a conversation with John Byrom, condemned the education at the universities with much severity. If it were not necessary for preferment, he would never, he said, send a son there.[1] Dr. Hartley, however, who was present, did not quite agree with him. About 1750, Brown, in his 'Estimate of the Times,' lamented the abuses which had crept into the universities and greatly impaired their use and credit. The professorships, in particular, had become mere gainful sinecures. 'The great lines of knowledge are broken, and the fragments retailed at all adventures by every member of a college who chooseth to erect himself into a professor of every science.' He said also that the few young men of fashion yet found there were scarce under any moral and literary discipline.[2] Dr. Johnson praised Oxford, but his praise is tantamount to blame, for, however admirable the theory might be, he was obliged to allow that the practice was very faulty. 'That the rules are sometimes ill observed may be true, but is nothing against the system. The members of a university may, for a season, be unmindful of their duty. I am arguing for the excellence of the institution.'[3] Adam Smith said of the seven years he spent at Balliol (1740–47), that the discipline in general seemed contrived merely for the ease of the teachers. Vicesimus Knox, though anxious to uphold the credit of the

the rank of its owner could give it no honour. We read in Mrs. Delany's *Diary* for Feb. 2, 1760, that it is an 'error, now much encouraged in Oxford, that peers are not worth being acquainted with' (iii. 583).

[1] Byrom's *Remains*, iii. 167.
[2] Brown's *Estimate*, &c., i. 33.   [3] Boswell's *Johnson*, ii. 61.

English universities, confessed his shame at the immorality, 'the habitual drunkenness, the idleness, the ignorance, which he used to see openly and boastfully intruding itself on the public view, and triumphing without control over the timidity of modest merit.' Wilberforce spoke of the dissoluteness at Cambridge about 1770. The Fellows, he said, seemed only to wish to keep him idle.[1] T. F. Dibdin speaks of the distressing somnolency in the university about 1790. 'There seemed to be no spur to emulation and excellence. Whatever was done was to be done only by private energy. Several members of different colleges wished to meet privately as a society for scientific and literary discussion, in which all religious and political subjects were carefully to be avoided. But the Vice-Chancellor, after a week's consideration, interdicted the meetings. It was impossible, he judged, to predict what might be the tendency, especially in disturbed times, of innovations of this sort.'[2] Wakefield, it should be further added, said that when he was at Cambridge the chapel services were seldom attended by the Fellows at all, and that the doors were open for any until the psalms began.[3] In 1757, Gray, writing to his friend Mason from Cambridge, mentions that he had been to the university sermon on the preceding Sunday, but that, except the heads, no one but his companion and himself was present.[4]

If the universities, generally speaking, were in a very unsatisfactory state, so also were the public schools. Doubtless there were some very learned men at the head of some of the great foundations. Eton especially stood high for the scholarship that could be acquired there. 'That school,' says Gilbert Wakefield, speaking of a period extending from

---

[1] Quoted by Stoughton, *England under the Georges*, ii. 115.
[2] Dibdin's *Reminiscences*, i. 96.   [3] Wakefield's *Memoirs*, pp. 147-8.
[4] Gray and Mason's *Correspondence*, p. 79.

about 1770 to 1790, 'sends out, as far as my experience can form a judgment, much the best scholars in the kingdom. . . . The produce of all our other great schools were to a man inferior.' But though Eton might take the lead at one time, as Winchester or Westminster at another, there were from time to time very able masters in all of them. There was much severity. 'Those "plagosi Orbilii," those pedagogical Jehus, those furious school-drivers,' whom South was wont to denounce, were always common enough. It was a boy's own fault if, taught by some of the most learned men of the day, and aided by the incentives of emulation and the rod, he did not at any one of the great endowed schools get a fairly good intellectual training. But the discipline and tone of character seems to have been sadly defective, and this almost without exception. A passage in Fielding's 'Joseph Andrews' does but express what was evidently a very common opinion. 'Public schools, said Adams, are the nurseries of all vice and immorality. All the wicked fellows I remember at the university were bred at them. . . . It is written, "What shall a man take in exchange for his soul?" But the masters of great schools trouble themselves about no such thing. . . . Discipline, indeed! said Adams; because one man scourges twenty or thirty boys more in a morning than another, is he therefore a better disciplinarian?'[1] Lord Chesterfield, writing to his son in 1750, remarks casually that 'Westminster School is undoubtedly the seat of illiberal manners and brutal behaviour.'[2] Winchester is spoken of by Sydney Smith as being, about 1780, a deplorable place for boys. 'My father suffered here many years of misery and positive starvation. There never was enough provided, even of the coarsest food, for the whole school, and the little boys were of course left to fare as they could.

[1] *Joseph Andrews*, B. III. chap. v. [2] Chesterfield's *Letters*, i. 105.

Even in old age my father used to shudder at the recollections of Winchester, and I have heard him speak with horror of the wretchedness of the years he spent there: the whole system was then, he used to say, one of abuse, neglect, and vice.'[1] At Shrewsbury, one of the most eminent of its eminent masters is said to have replied to a parent who complained of the deterioration of his son's character, 'My business is to teach him Greek, not morality.'[2] Lord Lyttelton spoke of the morality of public schools in his time as very low.[3] So did Southey.[4] Cowper is a more exceptionable witness. His delicate and timid nature ill qualified him for the rough life of Westminster School, and it can be no matter of surprise that he always spoke of public schools as if their faults and vices were redeemed by no merits.[5] Gibbon's bodily infirmities as a boy were as great as those of Cowper, and the time he spent at Westminster was to him also one of little happiness. But he shared, he said, in the common opinion that, with all their faults, the great schools were suited to the genius and constitution of the English people. The teaching, though too limited, was sound so far as it went; and boys learnt truth, fortitude, and prudence, and to value one another for personal merit rather than for birth or riches.[6] If, even at their worst, the public schools could thus far fulfil their office, there was clearly so much that was sound in them, that their shortcomings, however grave, might well seem to be of the times and of individuals rather than of the system in general. Improvement and reform might come at any time.

Some of the larger and best endowed grammar schools

---

[1] Sydney Smith's *Memoirs*, p. 4.
[2] Roberts's *Social History of the S. Counties*, p. 406.
[3] Lyttelton's *Persian Letters*, xcvi.
[4] Southey's *Life and Correspondence*, p. 178.
[5] Cowper's *Tirocinium*.   [6] Gibbon, *Life and Works*, i. 22.

were, in many particulars, like public schools on a smaller scale; probably much more so in the middle of the last century, when locomotion was difficult, than at a later date. But many grammar schools, though they kept up a feeble shadow of classical education, were mere elementary schools.

If the son of a squire or clergyman was sent to one of the little academies which swarmed throughout the country, he might well fare much worse. Grose, in his 'Olio,' written near the end of the century, speaks of the extreme negligence which parents, even of the upper and upper middle classes, showed in choosing schools for their children: 'Nine-tenths of the masters and governesses have scarcely one qualification requisite for their profession.' A little further he continues, in words which must be taken with some allowance, to describe more in detail what they often are: 'The master, who is perhaps a broken exciseman, rarely professes more than to teach writing and arithmetic, though, not to be idle, he hears the lesser boys repeat Lilly's grammar rules by heart. French is taught by a Swiss, an Irish Papist, a deserter from the brigades, and the learned languages by an undergraduated Welsh curate. Dancing is taught by a German valet de chambre, and music by a quondam fiddler to a puppet show. Their bodily food is not more exquisite than that prepared for their minds. . . . Their playrooms are miserable. . . . The qualifications of a governess of young ladies are still lower.[1] . . . Such are in general the instructors of the rising generation. What

[1] R. Southey, speaking of the bad state of female education about the middle of the century, says, 'Two sisters who had been mistresses of the most fashionable school in Herefordshire, fifty years ago, used to say when they spoke of a former pupil, "Her went to school to we!" And the mistress of the best school near Bristol spoke, to my infant recollection, much the same style of English.' (Southey's *Life and Correspond.*, i. 20.) Hannah More's *Strictures on Female Education,*' published in 1799, did good service.

can be expected of such an education?' Things, he adds, were worse in this respect than they used to be. Earlier in the century 'no one could keep a school without a licence from the bishop of the diocese, who, it must be presumed, would not grant one without a previous scrutiny into the moral character and literary abilities of the candidate for such licence. This regulation was made to prevent the growth of Popery and fanaticism; but as neither is at present feared, and religion being pretty much out of fashion, the law, though still in force, is grown into disuse.'[1] Much in the same way Gilbert Wakefield lamented 'that inundation of dreadful evils which are let in upon society by the tribe of profligate and ineffective schoolmasters.' Boys, he said, went up to the universities from that teaching, scarcely knowing even the first rudiments of the languages. 'Can Imagination represent to herself a more melancholy case than that of an ingenious, enterprising youth wasting his time and blasting his hopes in a seminary of one of those ignorant, heedless, insipid schoolmasters with which this kingdom is overrun? . . . Men should learn the knowledge of themselves; nor should he aspire to adorn the mind who is fit only to trim a periwig.'[2] In comparison with many of these 'academies' there was really much to say for some of the homely dame schools, which were by no means confined to the elementary education of cottagers. Thus the poet Wordsworth speaks of the old dame at Penrith, under whom both he and his father had practised reading and spelling: 'A remarkable personage, who had taught three generations of the upper classes, chiefly in the town of Penrith and its neighbourhood.'[3]

Elementary education, in the utter absence of any

[1] Grose's *Olio*, Essay xiii.   [2] Wakefield's *Memoirs*, pp. 31–35.
[3] *Memoirs of W. Wordsworth*, by Chr. Wordsworth, p. 17.

regular system, differed very greatly according to the locality. The educational movement which in Queen Anne's reign had made a considerable start, and promised extensive results, dwindled into much smaller proportions than had seemed probable, but still did not die away. Englishmen were, without much reason, rather proud of the position which their country held as a comparatively educated population. 'All foreigners remark,' says a periodical of 1758, 'that the knowledge of the common people of England is greater than that of any other vulgar. This superiority we undoubtedly owe to the rivulets of intelligence which are continually trickling among us, which every one may catch, and of which every one partakes.'[1] The writer goes on to speak of certain inconveniences in 'this universal diffusion of instruction.' It might seem to a reader of our own times that, to say the least, there was something rather premature in such reflections. But it is very evident that throughout the century a great many worthy people were not a little disturbed at the progress which popular education was making. It was a complaint quite frequently heard that the charity schools were ruining servants, and that the results of a general knowledge of reading and writing might be very serious.[2] Idleness, disloyalty, and pride were among the disastrous effects which such persons expected to see.[3] And, apart from such special anticipations, there were probably not a few who would have said there was a great deal of sound sense in the dictum of the poet-painter Blake: 'There is no use in education. I hold it wrong. It is the great sin. It is eating of the tree of the knowledge of good and evil.'[4]

The advocates of popular education had much prejudice to contend against; and at the end of the century these

[1] The *Idler*, No. 7. [2] *Id.*, Nos. 26, 29, &c.
[3] Secker's *Charge* of 1738, p. 27. [4] Gilchrist's *Life of Blake*, p. 339.

prejudices gained new life through the alarms excited by the French Revolution. Wrong and faithless as it was, there was then a very common feeling that ignorance was safest. Before that time the opposition raised to schemes of education was chiefly one of sluggishness and indifference, and this was getting less than it had been. Thus a clergyman, writing to Dr. Parr about the Bewdley Charity Schools, instituted in 1784, speaks of the doubts and questionings which had been first raised, and how in time they had been silenced or overcome, until the inhabitants of the neighbourhood of all political opinions were gradually giving their support.[1] Throughout the century there had been more or less interest in the subject. The charity-school movement, though it did not recover the activity which it had begun to show in Queen Anne's time, continued to extend. In Wales, about 1730, a system of circulating schools, founded on a definitely religious basis, did much good. Sir J. Thorold, writing to Doddridge in 1740, spoke of 'the extraordinary' work of these 'blessed seminaries.'[2] In 1747, Bishop Wilson writes, 'We have a most surprising account of what has been done in Wales within these six years in this glorious work. No less than 36,800 persons, young and old, have been taught to read.'[3] The good bishop was himself setting an admirable example of educational activity, having established, as early as 1724, schools and libraries in all the parishes of his diocese.[4] In many parts of Ireland industrial schools had been before the middle of the century founded, in which two hours every day were devoted to elementary learning, and the rest of the working time to manual labours.[5] The Christian Knowledge Society never ceased to supply a continuous stream of

---

[1] Parr's *Works*, viii. 203.   [2] Doddridge's *Works*, iii. 470.
[3] Cruttwell's *Life of Wilson*, p. 213.   [4] *Id.*, p. 144.
[5] Sermon by Bishop Wilcox of Rochester on the Irish Working Schools, 1739.

cheap, simple, sound-principled literature. In 1748, S. Johnson of Connecticut, who was then in England, spoke of the number of schemes of education which were being projected.[1] And though most of such schemes came to nothing, and though the work was left far too much to the scattered and desultory energies of individuals, more was done for popular education in the last century than is perhaps generally supposed.

Some mention has been already made of the better sort of dame schools. Similar ones of a yet humbler kind were to be found, as Shenstone said, 'in every village marked with little spire.' The teaching given in them was often very inadequate, even to the unambitious wants of those for whom they were provided. Often, on the other hand, so far as it went (for it was unpretentious in the extreme), it was sound and good. Shenstone gives a lively and pretty sketch, marred only by a slight tone of affectation, of these 'little tenements of learning.' We have the picture of the schoolmistress, 'goody, good woman, gossip, n'aunt, forsooth, or dame.'

> A russet stole was o'er her shoulders thrown,
> A russet kirtle fenced the nipping air;
> 'Twas simple russet, but it was her own;
> 'Twas her own country bred the flock so fair,
> 'Twas her own labour did the fleece prepare.
>
> . . . . .
>
> Her cap, far whiter than the driven snow,
> Emblem right meet of decency does yield.
> Her apron died in grain, as blue, I trow,
> As is the harebell that adorns the field;
> And in her hand, for sceptre, she doth wield
> Tway birchen sprays.

We have her homely garden, with its herbs for use and physic, and the one ancient hen,—

[1] *Works* of S. Johnson of Connecticut, v. 211.

Which ever and anon, impelled by need,
Into her school, begirt with chickens, came.

Then we see her at her daily task,—

Where sits the dame, disguised in look profound
And eyes her fairy throng, and turns the wheel around.

. . . . . .

Right well she knew each temper to descry;
To thwart the proud, and the submiss to raise;
Some with vile copper prize exalt on high,
And some entice with pittance small of praise;
And other some with baleful sprig she 'frays.
E'en absent, she the reins of power doth hold,
While with quaint arts the giddy crowd she sways;
Forewarned, if little bird their pranks behold,
'Twill whisper in her ear, and all the scene unfold.

Lo! now with state she utters the command,
Eftsoons the urchins to their tasks repair:
Their books of stature small they take in hand,
Which with pellucid horn securèd are,
To save from fingers wet the letters fair.

And lastly we have the story of her simple piety:—

Here oft the dame, on Sabbath's decent eve,
Hymnèd such psalms as Sternhold forth did mete,
If winter 'twere, she to her hearth did cleave,
But in her garden found a summer seat;
Sweet melody to hear her then repeat
How Israel's sons, beneath a foreign king,
While taunting foemen did a song entreat,
All for the nonce untuning every string,
Uphung their useless lyres—small heart had they to sing.

For she was just, and friend to virtuous lore,
And passed much time in truly virtuous deed;
And, in those elfins' ears, would oft deplore
The times when truth by Popish rage did bleed.

And tortious death was true devotion's meed,
And simple faith in iron chains did mourn,
That nould [would not] on wooden image place her creed,
And lawny saints in smouldering flames did burn :
Ah, dearest Lord, forefend thilk days should e'er return ! [1]

The foundation of Sunday schools belongs too exclusively to the latter part of the century to be further referred to in this chapter.

The general religious and moral condition of the country was often, as we have seen, spoken of in a tone of somewhat exaggerated despondency and alarm. But none denied that there was at least one great redeeming feature, the favour and encouragement given to works of Christian philanthropy. The rapidly increasing wealth of the country naturally made these efforts more considerable than they had been before. If they had not proportionately decreased, they could not but become more prominent. Yet, apart from this, it was felt, and often remarked in a spirit of not unworthy complacency, that notwithstanding all that could be said against their age, it nevertheless held a high place, as compared with most that had preceded it, in at least two important virtues. One, already alluded to, was the growth of toleration ; the other was the advance of philanthropy.

Already in the end of the seventeenth century Archbishop Tillotson had spoken of this. He had said that amid the strange overflowings of vice and wickedness in our land, and the prodigious increase and impudence of infidelity, the greatest comfort he had had under many sad apprehensions of God's displeasure had been this, that though bad men were perhaps never worse in any age, yet the good, who he hoped were not a few, were never more truly and substantially good. 'I do verily believe there never were at any time greater and more real effects of charity ; not from a blind

[1] Shenstone's *Poems*, 'The Schoolmistress.'

superstition and ignorant zeal, and a mercenary and arrogant principle of merit, but from a sound knowledge and a sincere love and obedience to God.'[1]

Remarks more or less to the same effect often occur in the literature of the eighteenth century. Even in its dullest period there were never wanting good men conspicuous for works of beneficence. 'It must be confessed,' said Steele, in the 'Guardian' of 1713, 'that if one turns one's eyes round the cities of London and Westminster, one cannot overlook the exemplary instances of heroic charity in providing restraints for the wicked, instructions for the young, food and raiment for the aged, with regard also to all other circumstances and relations of human life.'[2] 'Let the charities of this age,' said Defoe in 1724, 'be cast (money bestowed on mere acts of charity to the poor, not reckoning gifts to the Church), it will appear they are greater by far than can be found in England in any the like number of years, take the time when we will.'[3] 'There is indeed,' said Doddridge, 'as has been often and justly observed, one token for God amongst many symptoms of danger; I mean a variety of charitable foundations and institutions amongst you, so far as I know unequalled throughout the whole world, as well as a great freedom from those detestable evils, persecution and oppression.'[4] 'Charity,' said Fielding, in a charge to the Westminster grand jury in 1749, 'is the very characteristic virtue of the nation at this time. I believe we may challenge the whole world to parallel the examples which we have of late given of this sensible, this noble, this Christian virtue.'[5] 'I may be allowed to advance,' said Edmund Law about 1745, 'that we have certain virtues of the first magnitude now in greater perfection—particu-

---

[1] Tillotson's *Works*, Sermon xx. [2] The *Guardian*, June 11, 1713.
[3] De Foe's *Tour through Great Britain*, ii. 133.
[4] Doddridge's *Sermon on the Earthquake*, 1750.
[5] Fielding's *Works*, x. 78.

larly more of true, well-regulated extensive charity—than ever appeared since the time of primitive Christianity;' and he urged that therefore at least 'some partial fondness for the present times may be pardonable amid so much evident partiality against them.'[1] So also a writer in the 'Idler' of 1758, while he grants that the age 'is not likely to shine hereafter,' yet adds that its examples of charity are very worthy of imitation. 'No sooner is a new species of misery brought to view, and a design of relieving it professed, than every hand is open to contribute something, every tongue is busy in solicitation, and every art of pleasure is employed for a time in the interests of virtue.' He considered that in charity 'almost all the goodness of the present age consists.'[2] Brown also, in his rather gloomy 'Estimate of the Manners of the Times,' saw something at least to acknowledge and applaud in 'the many noble foundations for the relief of the miserable and the friendless, the large annual supplies from voluntary charities to these foundations, and the frequent and generous assistance given to the unfortunate who cannot be admitted into them.'[3] 'It is certainly true,' said Hannah More, 'that it is to a great extent an age of benevolence.'[4] We find it, however, more than once remarked that these benefactions rarely came from the wealthiest classes; they were almost exclusively the gifts of 'the middle kind of people.'[5]

Of all these charitable foundations, no doubt the charity schools already spoken of stood first, established, as Malcolm well expresses it, 'by a divine impulse' in all parts not only of the metropolis, but of the country in general. Then came

[1] Bishop E. Law's *Considerations on the Theory of Religion*, p. 281.
[2] The *Idler*, May 6, 1758.   [3] Brown's *Estimates*, &c., i. § 3.
[4] H. More's 'Religion of the Fashionable World,' *Works*, xi. 88.
[5] *Guardian*, No. 79. So also in Harte's *Eulogius* :—

'The charitable few are chiefly they
Whom fortune places in the middle way.'

the hospitals; Guy's, for instance, was founded in 1720, and many others about the same time. It was estimated that already by the middle of the century 20,000 persons every year were cured in them.[1] Next comes—

> The generous band
> Who, touched with human woe, redressive searched
> Into the horrors of the gloomy jail,
> Unpitied and unheard, where misery moans,
> Where sickness pines, where thirst and hunger burn,
> And poor misfortune feels the lash of vice.[2]

These lines of Thomson, written on occasion of the Gaol Committee being formed in 1729, were well within the truth. Dr. Bray's efforts, in the last years of his noble life, and those of Oglethorpe and others, disclosed in many of the prisons abuses and horrors passing description. Kettlewell in the previous century had spoken with pity of the 'very lamentable case, both in body and soul,'[3] of poor prisoners confined both for crime and debt. But hitherto things had improved but little, or perhaps not at all. The brutality and extortion of the keepers of prisons was a very proverb, and to 'rot' in gaol an expression as true as it is horrible. Physically and morally, it might be too often said that all was in keeping with the loathsome atmosphere which decimated their inmates. But from the time of Dr. Bray the conscience of the country gradually awoke to the iniquity of the system, and many good men expended much care in lightening it. 'Parson Hale's' ventilators so greatly reduced the mortality from gaol fever, that after their introduction into the Savoy Prison in 1749, the loss of life was at once reduced from between fifty and one hundred

---

[1] Malcolm's *Manners and Customs of London*, i. 34. This work gives much interesting information about the London charities.
[2] Thomson's *Seasons* (Winter).   [3] Nelson's *Life of Kettlewell*, p. 158.

in the year to four in two years.[1] General Oglethorpe, who died in 1786, at the patriarchal age of one hundred and three, had the satisfaction of seeing the benevolent labours which he had begun in early years splendidly worked out, not in England only, but abroad, by the indefatigable zeal of John Howard.

To enter into detail on the various works of charity instituted in the eighteenth century would far transcend the scope and limits of this work. As a sample of their varied character, mere reference may be made to the 100,000*l.* sent to Lisbon after the earthquake, to the clothing and other kind attentions extensively given to the French prisoners, to the large contributions made on two or three occasions for distressed Germans, to the ransom of persons from slavery at Morocco, to Crewe's noble charity for mariners, to Fielding's plans for reformatories, county workhouses, public laundries, &c., to John Campbell's labours for forlorn girls, and to those of Jonas Hanway for young chimney-sweepers, whose hard lives were often miserably ended by cancer and distortions. Nor should reference be omitted to the pathetic interest bestowed by Dean Swift on idiots. 'I hear,' wrote Pope to him, 'with approbation and pleasure that your present care is to relieve the most helpless in the world, those objects which most want our compassion.'[2] Some mention must be made later of the great movement in the end of the century for putting down the slave trade. It may be sufficient to add that although in many, and perhaps the great majority of cases, munificent works of charity were chiefly the results of strong and definite Christian feeling, it was by no means always so. Many, whose faith had been sorely shaken by the distraction of the Deist and other controversies, were glad to take refuge in that of which Pope had said that—

[1] Jortin's *Tracts,* ii. 247. [2] Swift's *Works,* pp. 18, 368.

> In faith and hope the world will disagree,
> But all mankind concur in charity.¹

And doubtless it might well happen that charity would restore to them hope and faith.

The Societies for the Reformation of Manners, of which much had been heard from about the time of the Revolution to the middle of George I.'s reign, languished soon after into insignificance. It needed no little genuine earnestness to bear up against the storm of invective, the lampoons, the taunts and angry ridicule, with which they were assailed; so that when their early zeal abated, they lost their power and dwindled away.² After 1750 there was a considerable revival of them, partly, but not altogether, in connection with the Methodist societies. John Wesley, in a sermon which he preached before some of them in 1763, after speaking of the 'incredible good done by the older societies for nearly forty years,' and how they had then grown faint and ceased, gives some interesting statistics of their late partial renewal. There were then about twenty in connexion with Whitefield, about fifty under Wesley's superintendence, about twenty managed by Churchmen not connected either with Wesley or Whitefield, and a good many among the Dissenting bodies. Between 1757 and 1763 there had been 10,588 prosecutions for profanation of the Sunday, and for various forms of immorality and vice. Wesley strongly insisted upon the great need of special care in the selection of members. The old societies, he said, became less and less useful, until they finally died away, because there had been great want of discrimination in the choice of those whom they admitted into them; it was very essential that this error should not be repeated.³

These later societies subsisted for several years, and

---

¹ *Essay on Man*, iii. 308. ² *Gent.'s Mag.* for 1737, p. 749.
³ *Wesley's Works*, vol. vi. serm. 52.

were often very active, and sometimes perhaps indiscreet. They came to a rather sudden and violent ending, by a verdict against them with damages on some appeal to the King's Bench. Twenty years later, in 1786, a new association was formed with similar objects, but on a different footing. The strength alike and weakness of the previous Societies for Reformation of Manners were chiefly to be found in their personal and local character. They received no doubt some general instructions from a central authority, but their general nature was that of clubs of earnest-minded men who were bent on checking the growth of vice in their own neighbourhood. The organisation of 1786 was simply a central society 'for enforcing the king's proclamation against immorality and profaneness.' There was, however, great activity and zeal on the part of its promoters, the most conspicuous of whom were Bishop Porteus and Mr. Wilberforce.[1] A great public effort, they urged, was needed, to check if possible the increasing profligacy of the times; for which great purpose persons of distinguished name and character should combine together to enforce the execution of the laws, and to support the magistrates in the conviction of offenders. The design was carried out with much perseverance and through many obstacles. Wilberforce was especially devoted in the cause. 'God has set before me,' he said, 'the reformation of my country's manners;' and in this society he saw one primary means of working out this great purpose of his life. He gained for the scheme the warm approval of the Archbishop of Canterbury. He visited in succession the Bishops of Worcester, Hereford, Norwich, Lincoln, York, and Lichfield. The Duke of Montagu was its first president; the second was Lord Chancellor Bathurst, and after him Bishop Porteus.[2] It

---

[1] Porteus' *Life and Works*, i. 100-1; *Life of W. Wilberforce*, by his Son, p. 49.   [2] *Id.*, p. 50.

did much good, greatly checked the spread of blasphemous and indecent publications, and some valuable Acts of Parliament were obtained by its influence. But at best it was a society working with more or less efficiency through the familar machinery of such organisations; and a society, as contrasted with a number of small religious associations, needs clear and specific objects to be in any high degree successful. The society in question was excellently adapted for drawing the attention of the Legislature, and of the public in general, to some desirable reforms, and for removing some glaring evils. It could do little in battling against more ordinary forms of immorality. Some, like Bishop Watson, withdrew from it sooner than they need have done, from a conviction of its inefficiency for carrying out its large designs.[1] Even those whose heart and soul were in the work became before long convinced that the bounds within which such a society could do much good were very limited. After a few years it was dissolved, and its promoters turned their energies into other directions. In 1794 we find a new 'Association for discountenancing Vice, and promoting the knowledge and practice of the Christian Religion.' It was inaugurated with a sermon of remarkable eloquence by Dean Graves.[2] This body continued its labours for half a century or more, but seems chiefly to have confined itself to the dissemination of religious literature of a strictly evangelical type.

The religious societies of a more purely devotional character, which had once flourished under the direction of men like Horneck, Beveridge, and others, showed, in the middle of the eighteenth century, few signs of continued life, except in the maintenance of certain services and lectures in London churches. About 1737, Whitefield speaks once

---

[1] Watson's *Anecdotes of his Own Life*, ii. 66.
[2] *Life and Works of Dean Graves*, i. 37.

or twice of preaching, as at Bow Church, before 'the religious societies.'[1] He makes mention also of one that had been formed, apparently upon a similar type, among some of the garrisons at Gibraltar.[2] In many cases these societies seem to have merged into those which the Methodist leaders were founding.

The Society for the Promotion of Christian Knowledge continued uninterruptedly, even through the dullest years of the century, its valuable labours. In 1745, Bishop Butler justly spoke of it as 'a society for carrying on almost every good work.'[3] For indeed there were very few labours of Christian benevolence in which it did not to some extent co-operate. Perhaps there was some flagging in its activity after the death of Bray and Nelson, and those other noble-hearted Churchmen, lay and clerical, whose lives form so bright a page in the religious history of the earlier portion of the century. Certainly, after the death of Queen Anne its work no longer so continually recurs, nor with the same marked prominence in the Church annals of the time. This may in great measure arise from its being no longer a new society. Its routine of action was for the most part marked out, and good Churchmen no longer watched it with the same enthusiastic interest as in its earlier days. Nevertheless, apart from such considerations, the feeble support which it received, and the consequent slowness of its development, marked only too clearly the decline of spiritual energy which had set in. In the year 1749, its fiftieth anniversary, the annual subscriptions which it received amounted only to 470*l*. 9*s*. 6*d*., and even at its centenary in 1799 only to 1,734*l*. 7*s*.[4]—the former especially a very small sum with which to carry out the

---

[1] Whitefield's *Letters*, Sept. 28, 1737.   [2] *Id.*, Feb. 25, 1738.
[3] W. H. Sewell's *Account of the S.P.C.K.*, p. 4.
[4] T. B. Murray's *Jubilee Tract of the S.P.C.K.*, 1850.

great and varied work which it had undertaken, and a very small growth as compared to the fourteen or fifteen thousand pounds to which the subscriptions to it have since attained. In 1728 it received its first legacy, a most welcome gift of 6,000*l.*, at a time when its work was sorely hampered by the deficiency of its funds. But its finances were far from being the measure of its work. In education especially it did very much to promote and encourage a beneficent activity which was not carried out under its direct auspices. Most of the ward schools in London were founded at its suggestion, and a vast number of the charity schools in general were more or less indebted to its help. On one occasion a donation is entered on its minutes of fourteen guineas from an unknown donor, with an inscription on the paper in which it was enclosed ' that he could neither read nor write, and that his want of learning induced him, as God had enabled him, to encourage it in others.'[1] Industrial schools, circulating schools, and school inspection were all subjects which came under the consideration of its council; and it was only prevented by the narrowness of its funds from establishing training schools for teachers. In 1741 it organised, especially in Wales, a successful system of evening schools.

Its annual report of the publications issued by it did not begin till 1733, but from the first its press had always been very busily employed in the issue both of Bibles and Prayer Books, and of innumerable publications which it sought studiously to adapt to the religious needs of all sorts and conditions of men. The well-known saying of George III., that he wished every child in his dominion should have a Bible and be able to read it, though far indeed from reaching its fulfilment, was at all events furthered by this society to the best of its power. Already by 1714 it

---

[1] Sewell, p. 37.

had begun to publish, not only in Welsh and Gaelic, but in Greek, at the request of Arsenius, for the distressed Greek Christians, in Tamil for its missions in Hindostan, and was considering the question of issuing the Bible and Psalter in Arabic for the use of Christians in Palestine and elsewhere. Besides giving and selling its publications, it also continued loyally to carry out Dr. Bray's original project of lending libraries. In addition to those which were founded in the British Islands, and for the army and navy, more than fifty libraries were sent out during the century to different colonies and plantations in India, the Cape, and America.

The relations between the Christian Knowledge Society and Lutheran Churchmen in Denmark had been so close and continuous, that although it had passed over to the younger society the spiritual care of the colonies in general, it retained throughout the century the care of missionary work in South India.[1] In 1715, Ziegenbalg, who had come to Europe to consult both with the University of Halle, and with his friends in England, about the now completed Malabar dictionary, was received at a general meeting of the society, and afterwards presented to the king. Archbishop Tenison died that year; but Wake was no less interested than his predecessor had been in the Indian missions. He felt the most cordial admiration for the devoted men who were labouring there, and did all he could to encourage and extend their work. Some interesting letters of his are extant which he wrote to missionaries in South India in 1718, as well as others in 1721-23, to Francke at Halle, earnestly imploring him to urge more

---

[1] Information as to these missions is taken from Anderson's *Colonial Churches*, vol. iii. chap. xxi.; T. Smith's *History of Missionary Societies*, xii.–xiii., and Professor Watkins's speech at the opening of the new S.P.C.K. buildings in 1879, in pages 56–60 of the Society's account.

students to devote themselves to the work. His letters were read before the university, and in response to his appeal three more missionaries came to London, were welcomed by the society, had an interview with the king, and were sent on to India. In 1728 the society established a mission at Madras under Schulz, where, in conjunction with Sartorius and Geisler, he soon gained a thousand converts, as he had previously won over about seven thousand at Tranquebar. He returned to Halle through ill-health in 1742, and there found out and invited to the work a man whose missionary labours were even more successful, as they were also far more prolonged, than had been his own. This was Christian Frederic Schwartz, who came to England on his way to India in 1749, and arrived next year at Tranquebar. He remained there twelve years, and then visited Trichinopoly, where he took the spiritual charge of the English garrison, and laboured indefatigably among the natives, travelling almost every day with his catechist into one or another of the circumjacent villages. There and at Tanjore and Tinnevelly, and at many points along the south-east of the peninsula, he and his fellow-labourers in the English and Anglo-Danish missions left good proof what earnest labours can sometimes do. Schwartz died in 1798. The young prince of Tanjore shed tears when he heard of his death, and wrote to England for a monument to his memory.

Meanwhile the Society for the Propagation of the Gospel was industriously carrying out in America and the adjacent islands its threefold work among colonists, negroes, and Indians. In 1725 it supported 36 missionary clergy; in 1750, 70; and before the proclamation of American independence, 101.[1] In 1743 it was maintaining 67 clergy in America, at the annual cost of 3,165*l.*; and each mis-

[1] Caswall's *American Church,* p. 68.

sionary when he went out was further allowed 10*l.* for books, and 5*l.* for tracts for distribution.¹ In 1741, Secker speaks of its labours as greatly impeded by narrowness of income, and by a heavy debt. The next year, in accordance with the powers of its charter, and by a recommendatory letter from the king, there was to be a general collection for it, which there had not been for more than twenty years past.² It received in 1753 from the poet Young, author of the 'Night Thoughts,' a generous gift of a thousand pounds, the proceeds of some of his works.³

The chief interest of the English Church in America during the reigns of the first two Georges centres round the work of Bishop Berkeley in Bermuda and Rhode Island, of General Oglethorpe in Georgia, in the labours of the Wesleys and Whitefield, in the Church movement in Connecticut, and in the futile efforts to establish in the colonies a branch of the episcopate.

Of Bishop Berkeley's scheme (1725-32) for a central missionary college at Bermuda further mention must be postponed. It is a most interesting incident in the life of a noble-hearted man, and will best be told in the sketch that is given of his life.

The Parliamentary grant which had been voted, but never paid, to Berkeley's College, was devoted, in 1732, to founding a colony in Georgia. Its leader, General Oglethorpe,⁴ was a man of much mark both as a soldier and philanthropist. After gaining high military reputation under Prince Eugene, he had returned to England, succeeded to his family estate near Godalming, and become Member of Parliament for Haslemere. Though an ardent

---

¹ *Report of S.P.G.*, appended to Bishop Gilbert's sermon of Feb. 17, 1743-44.
² Secker's *Charge* of 1741, p. 80.
³ Johnson's *Lives of the Poets*, iii. 340.
⁴ R. Wright's *Life of Oglethorpe*, pp. 30-63.

advocate of the Protestant succession, he was a strong Tory, and his first speech in Parliament had been one in defence of Atterbury. He was well adapted to be a leading man in any undertaking into which he had thrown his energies. Those who had once met him would not easily forget the commanding appearance given by his tall and dignified stature and his handsome features, nor the favourable impression created by his generous and kindly temperament. Into all he did he brought an earnest and enterprising spirit, warm religious feeling, great attachment to the Church, and an ardent desire to benefit his fellow-men. On the other hand, he was over-impetuous, rather choleric, and sometimes imprudent in judgment. Such was the man who led the colony into Georgia. He had lately thrown himself with characteristic zeal into a movement for the amelioration of the state of prisons. The colony might be described as a part of the same reform, its special object being to find a provision for poor debtors, and others whose misfortune rather than their fault had brought them into peril of suffering the miseries of the Marshalsea and other gaols. His benevolent scheme included also the persecuted Protestants of Germany, numbers of whom were flocking to the English shores for refuge. Utterly free from all ignoble and interested motives, Oglethorpe, and those who acted with him, fully carried out the motto of their charter, 'Non sibi sed aliis.'[1] By their own request they were expressly restrained from receiving any grant of land, or any emolument whatever, for their services. They were to be proprietaries of the new province, solely, to use the words of the deed, 'in trust for the poor.'[2] It was an honourable distinction of the new colony that there was to be no

---

[1] The seal which carried this motto represented a group of silkworms at work, in reference to an expected produce of the colony.

[2] Mahon's *History of England from the Peace of Utrecht*, chap. xliii.

slavery. This was prohibited, not only from the fear lest it might discourage the poor emigrants who were to be the strength of the colony, but also on deeper grounds of principle. 'Slavery,' said Oglethorpe, 'is against the gospel, as well as against the fundamental law of England. We refused, as trustees, to make a law permitting such a horrid crime.'[1] He was also very much bent on establishing Christian and civilising relations with the native Indians. Oglethorpe sailed with 120 emigrants, and founded Savannah in 1733, consecrating the day with services of solemn thanksgiving. In a letter written soon after, he said an alliance had been made with the Indians. Their king came constantly to church, was desirous of being instructed in the Christian religion, and had given him his nephew and heir to educate.[2] The next year he returned to England, taking with him a company of Indians under their chief, who were received with much interest and kindliness by the king, the Archbishop of Canterbury, and other leading Englishmen. In 1735 he returned to Georgia, accompanied by 300 emigrants, among whom were a number of Salzburg Moravians with their pastors, and John and Charles Wesley with other clergymen of the new Methodist school. 'I send these lines,' wrote Burton to an American correspondent, 'by my friends who accompany Mr. Oglethorpe to Georgia. They go purely out of religious motive—a circumstance not so common among our American missionaries. They are all members of the University of Oxford, men of piety, learning, and zeal. . . . We promise to ourselves much good from their pious endeavours, under the assistance and influence of Mr. Oglethorpe, both with regard to the Indians and to the colonists.'[3] The Wesleys went out under the auspices of the Society for the Propa-

---

[1] Mahon's *History of England from the Peace of Utrecht,* and Wright's *Oglethorpe,* p. 54.
[2] Wright, p. 63. [3] Beardsley's *Life of Johnson* (of Connecticut), p. 90.

gation of the Gospel, and were also the bearers of a parochial library sent to Savannah by the associates of Dr. Bray.[1] It is evident that in England many good men looked upon the colony with much hope and interest, as being also a true missionary expedition. Old Samuel Wesley said that if he had been ten years younger he would gladly have devoted to it the rest of his life.[2]

There is some satisfaction in seeing that in this last of the American colonies there was still, at a time when it would scarcely have been expected, something of the same religious spirit as had been so conspicuous in many of the early colonists.[3] There was, however, much that was disappointing in the progress of the colony. Oglethorpe soon found that many of the colonists he had brought with him, if saved from misery at home, were only too likely to fall into misery of other kinds abroad.[4] 'The settlement of Georgia,' Franklin wrote, 'had been lately begun, but instead of being made with hardy, industrious husbandmen, accustomed to labour, the only people fit for such an enterprise, it was with families of broken shopkeepers, and other insolvent debtors, many of indolent and idle habits, taken out of the jails, who, being set down in the woods, unqualified for clearing land, and unable to endure the hardships of a new settlement, perished in great numbers, leaving many helpless children unprovided for.'[5] It is suggestive of much suffering and disappointment that one of the earliest institutions established there by Christian benevolence was

---

[1] Wesley's *Works*, i. 45.   [2] Tyerman's *Oxford Methodists*, p. 378.

[3] The following sounds quite like a note from the records of some of the founders of the New England colonies : 'Feb. 6, 1736.—Landed. Mr. Oglethorpe led us to a rising ground, where we all kneeled down to give thanks.' (J. Wesley's Journal, *Works*, i. 23.)

[4] Oglethorpe attempted to remedy this by introducing in 1736 a number of Highlanders with their families. The Salzburgers were very industrious, and very good material for a young colony.

[5] Franklin's *Autobiography*, chap. viii.

the orphanage which occupied so much of Whitefield's care. The young colony was indeed overburdened with troubles, which included war with Spain, and a want of supplies so serious as at last to result in mutiny. Oglethorpe, hampered by subordinates whom he could not trust, contended courageously with his difficulties. But it had become a struggle for life, to which the high-minded and philanthropic hopes which had inspired the beginning of the expedition became gradually subordinate. The Indian missions failed; and soon after Oglethorpe's return to England, in 1743, slavery was introduced, the Moravians agreeing with Whitefield that slaves 'might be employed in a Christian spirit.'[1]

John Wesley's visit to America, although fruitful in consequences both to his own religious life and to that of the Transatlantic colonies, was not in itself a success. He soon relinquished the thought of doing much good among the Indians, whom he spoke of with an unmixed horror, which gave little promise of success in working among them. 'They are all,' he wrote, 'except perhaps the Choctaws, gluttons, drunkards, thieves, dissemblers, liars; they are implacable, unmerciful,' and so forth.[2] Among the colonists his intolerant discipline and sermon personalities made him for the most part very unpopular. Oglethorpe charged Charles Wesley, his secretary, with sedition, as well as with laying excessive stress on forms in religion. To John Wesley he behaved with asperity and even harshly. For though he admired the earnest zeal of the brothers, his hasty and impetuous temper was often provoked beyond measure by what he considered their extravagances. When Bishop Wilson sent him a little book which he had written for the use of missionaries, the general, speaking of it with much praise, said how favourably it contrasted with 'the

[1] Caswall's *American Church*, p. 15.   [2] J. Wesley's *Journal*, i. 66.

lofty imaginations of our Methodists.'[1] Yet, notwithstanding frequent irritation and collision, the two men honoured one another. Wesley, while referring to some misunderstandings, said nevertheless in a letter to him, 'I bless God that ever you was born;'[2] and on his return to England, Oglethorpe, without much perception of Wesley's great vocation, but anxious to promote his interests, exerted himself to procure for John Wesley his father's living of Epworth.

To Wesley himself the voyage to Georgia was an eventful epoch in his life. The devoted faith of his Moravian companions had touched him to the heart, and their doctrine of instantaneous conversion had disquieted him with sore fears as to his own religious state. He was unremitting in his labours, constant in his prayers, so strenuous in austerities of self-discipline that for some time he lived upon nothing but bread and water.[3] Yet he feared that all was vain, and that this only had he learned 'in the ends of the earth,' that all he had done and borne was but 'dross, meet only to be purged away.'[4] His journal about this period reveals unreservedly the commotion of his soul, and makes it easy to understand not only the fiery struggle through which he passed into his intense and lifelong convictions, but also the restless excitement which hindered his success in Georgia.

In the 'Gentleman's Magazine'[5] for September 1737 is a letter from Wesley entreating further help. He could only, he said, offer food and raiment, but the need was great. The letter breathes throughout the true spirit of earnest self-devotion, and stirred much sympathy among religious people in England. This was especially the case among his fellow-workers at Oxford; and Whitefield, after interviews

---

[1] *Life of Oglethorpe*, p. 185. [2] *Id.*, p. 179.
[3] Wesley's *Works*, i. 29. [4] *Id.*, p. 76.
[5] *Gent.'s Mag.*, vol. vii. p. 575.

with the Archbishop of Canterbury, and with the Bishops of London and of Gloucester, at once set out for the colony. While his ship was yet in the Downs he was met by one with Wesley on board, who, baffled and out of heart, had become persuaded that his work lay in England, and that after all, if Whitefield went, he too would lose his labour.

Whitefield none the less continued on his way, and on his arrival in Georgia found much to stimulate and encourage him in the work of his predecessors. 'Surely,' he wrote, 'I must labour most heartily, since I came after such men. The good Mr. John Wesley has done in America is inexpressible.' He did not, however, in this his first visit stay more than four months, and then returned to England to take priest's orders, and to collect money for the orphanage. This interval of three quarters of a year in England thoroughly established his wonderful powers as a preacher. Already the congregation which swarmed round his field pulpit frequently numbered as many as twenty thousand; and the tears which streamed in white gutters down the black cheeks of the Kingswood colliers bore witness to the strong impression made by his burning words. In the early autumn of 1739 he sailed again for America. The trustees of Georgia had given him the living of Savannah, though he declined to accept the emoluments of it. They also gave him five hundred acres of land for the orphanage. When, however, after an evangelistic tour in the more northerly colonies, he arrived at his destination, he found few there except the soldiers, and such as were connected with the charitable institutions he was interested in. The colony had not prospered, and great numbers of the settlers had left it. Henceforth, although the parsonage at Savannah continued to be his home in America, at all events until the orphanage was in full working order, Whitefield's work, in his frequent visits to America, was scarcely more in Georgia than in the other colonies.

For a short time the churches were everywhere opened to him, and were crowded with hearers of all denominations. But he soon very much estranged Churchmen, in America as well as in England, and that without much fault on their part. Like Wesley, he held views of mankind in general which were dark and dismal in the extreme. His terms of condemnation were unsparing, and invectives which were tolerable so long as they were general could be ill brooked when they were directed against individuals or against a class. The clergy would have been superior to human nature, or rather they might have seemed to acquiesce in the justice of the imputations, if they had not resented the mode in which, about this time, he was wont to speak even of those among them whom they held most in honour. That Tillotson knew no more of Christianity than Mahomet or an infidel, that his works and 'The Whole Duty of Man' had sent thousands of souls to hell—such sayings, and many others somewhat similar to them, made many a worthy clergyman think of Whitefield as nothing better than a reckless and dangerous enthusiast, and in America rendered the breach between him and the clergy of his own Church far more speedy and universal than in England. The Methodism of the Wesleys, however uncongenial it might be to large numbers of the clergy and educated laity, was still unmistakably a movement of thorough Churchmen. Across the Atlantic, Methodism, except at its first introduction into Georgia, was almost entirely the result of Whitefield's preaching; and he, although in English orders, and warmly attached to the English liturgy, was yet by his temperament, by his theology, and by circumstances, far less likely to give a Church character to his influence. In the northern colonies, where the Episcopal Church was in many places barely tolerated, the comparative absence of this element doubtless contributed to the success.

Franklin, who, although personally unaffected by Whitefield's preaching, was throughout his sincere friend, is an excellent and important witness to the great impression which he made. 'The multitudes of all sects and denominations that attended his sermons were enormous, and it was a matter of speculation to me, who was one of the number, to observe the extraordinary influence of his oratory on his hearers, and how much they admired and respected him, notwithstanding his common abuse of them by assuring them they were naturally half beasts and half devils. It was wonderful to see the change soon made in the manners of our inhabitants. From being thoughtless or indifferent about religion, it seemed as if all the world were growing religious, so that one could not walk through the town in an evening without hearing psalms sung in different families of every street.'[1] He speaks also of the admirable accent, emphasis, and modulation of his voice, with an articulation so loud and clear, that upon calculation he found that he could well be heard by more than thirty thousand people.

In a review by John Wesley of the progress of Methodism in America,[2] he said that although Whitefield, every time he visited America, had more and more reason to be thankful for what had been done there, yet that he found in his last journey thither that a vast majority had turned back. Organisation, which John Wesley was very careful to establish on a secure footing whithersoever he went, had been greatly wanting in America. There had been no discipline, no regular societies; and it appears that it was not until near the beginning of the war that Methodism began to take the strong and rooted position which it thenceforth held.

---

[1] Franklin's *Autobiography*, chap. viii.
[2] Serm. 131, pub. 1778; *Works*, vii. 410-19.

Apart from the new life given to almost every religious body in America as well as in England by the impulse of the Methodist preaching, the English Church in the northern colonies gained by the distaste, felt by large numbers, especially among the more educated classes, for what they called the 'enthusiasm and confusion' of the new preaching.[1] It was on this account, says Johnson of Connecticut, that 'many sober and thoughtful persons have lately joined us.'[2]

But nowhere could the state of the English Church in America, while yet the colonies were all under the English Crown, be looked upon with satisfaction. An episcopal church without bishops was a monstrous anomaly, self-condemned by its very nature. In its more important and spiritual aspect the result was worst in the southern provinces. It is easy to suppose what would be likely to be the state of a church established during a careless age, in a general and disorganised manner, but without superintendence and without discipline, among a people often reckless in habits and indifferent to religion, who were scattered thinly over a vast and remote territory. There were some good earnest men among the clergy. John Wesley has, for instance, the following entry in his diary for April 22, 1737: 'It being their visitation, I had the pleasure of meeting with the clergy of South Carolina, among whom in the afternoon there was such a conversation for several hours on "Christian righteousness" as I had not heard at any visitation in England, or hardly on any other occasion.'[3] But it is painfully clear that the English Church in the southern colonies was constantly under the charge of very unworthy ministers. Men who in England were ruined in character or in purse, or whose mean abilities or wretched

[1] Beardsley's *Life of Johnson*, p. 120.   [2] *Id.*, p. 114.
[3] Wesley's *Works*, i. 49.

education gave them no hope of a tolerable livelihood at home, sought and obtained a safe refuge in plantations where they would be safe from oversight, from jurisdiction, and from any burdensome pressure of public opinion. A satirist, in the middle of the century, spoke of pastors making their way thither who were sometimes 'missionary felons,' and sometimes utter ignoramuses; 'some who can't write, and others who can't read.'[1] A remonstrance addressed to the Bishop of London, in 1722, makes mention of the 'poor starved striplings' who became officers of the Church abroad, and of 'fugitive, insolent wretches' who make 'their missions, so called, to foreign parts a safe escape and protection from a jail.'[2] What, again, can be more significant than an incidental remark in one of Bishop Rundle's letters?—'The only discipline that I have yet executed has been to discard three out of my diocese, who, though refused certificates by me and by my clergy, have obtained good livings in America, and found room for repentance.'[3] In Maryland, where the Church had received, not without great opposition, 'all the rights and privileges of the Church in England,' its state in 1767 appears to have been on this account deplorable indeed. 'Of about forty-five clergymen, five or six are men whose names should be mentioned with honour, but to hear the character of the rest from the inhabitants would make the ears of any sober heathen to tingle.'[4] Naturally enough, these men were too well content with the prevailing laxity to desire a change which would be certain to introduce reform. We are told that the southern provinces scarcely joined in the appeal for bishops.[5] In Virginia some of the clergy even joined in a protest

---

[1] Churchill's *Gotham*, Book I. [2] *Hardships of the Clergy*, 1722, p. 80.
[3] Hughes' *Coll. of Letters*, ii. 91.
[4] Chandler to Johnson of Connecticut, Beardsley, p. 311.
[5] Beardsley, p. 325.

against an American episcopate.[1] It is true that their action in so doing was based on political grounds; but the political reasons, if they existed at all, must have been urgent indeed to overrule with any propriety the pressing need which all earnest Churchmen must have felt.

In the northern colonies the state of the Church, depressed though it was at first in outward circumstances, was more satisfactory, and its growth decided, and in some places even rapid. Samuel Johnson, 'missionary of the Church of England in Connecticut, and first President of King's College, New York,' gives a very interesting account[2] of its progress in that State, where until about 1720 it had scarcely obtained a foothold. He tells how he graduated at Harvard College in 1714, and how the young men were cautioned against the philosophy of Locke and Newton, lest it should corrupt the pure religion of the country; how he took Congregational orders in 1720; how deeply impressed he and six of his companions were by a copy of the Book of Common Prayer which they had found;[3] how they met together to talk over difficulties, to consult about modes of worship, and to join in prayer for guidance; and how, upon the arrival in 1722 of a clergyman sent into the State by the Society for the Propagation of the Gospel, three of them—Johnson, Cutler, and Brown—determined to sail for England to obtain episcopal orders. He tells us that they received deacon's and priest's orders in March 1723; and that very soon after Cutler and Brown were seized with small-pox, of which the latter died. He describes their interest and enthusiasm in Church matters, their frequent conversations on such questions at the clerical coffee-houses, the coming to England with the same wish to receive

---

[1] Caswall's *America and the American Church*, p. 133.
[2] E. Beardsley's *Life and Correspondence of S. Johnson*, &c.
[3] *Id.*, p. 12.

episcopal ordination of another of their companions. He
tells how, on his return to Connecticut, he was engaged in
organising there the worship of the Church of England,
which up to that time had not existed there, and how he
pressed upon the English bishops to use every effort to
obtain an episcopate for America. He speaks of the friendship he formed with Berkeley, and of the great interest with
which he read his philosophy; how Yale College, then
strongly non-episcopal, received from England a library of
about a thousand volumes, the finest collection of books
which had hitherto reached America, and how there was
some fear about its reception, lest the minds of readers
should be unsettled. He tells us with what hope he
received intelligence of the arrival of Wesley and his companions,[1] his regret that he was too far away from Georgia
to be of much use to them. Two or three years after, his
tone as regards the Methodist preachers has changed. He
is offended at their 'enthusiasm,' and at Whitefield's
tirades against their Church; he hopes religion and learning
will not suffer from the movement, and sees with pleasure
many accessions to his Church from others who, like him,
looked with suspicion at the prevailing excitement. About
this time he had much friendly intercourse with Benjamin
Franklin, who tried to persuade him to come and preside
over an institution which he had founded in Philadelphia.[2]
Meanwhile the English Church in the north was steadily
gaining ground, and about the middle of the century he
was using his best exertions in favour of the new college
which was being set on foot by episcopal Churchmen at
New York. It was a great hardship, he said, that 'those
churches which are branches of the national Establishment
are deprived not only of the benefit of a regular church
government, but their children are debarred the privilege of

[1] Beardsley's *Life and Correspondence of S. Johnson*, p. 90.   [2] *Id.*, p. 172.

a liberal education, unless they will accept of it on such conditions as dissenters from it require, which in Yale College is to submit to a fine as often as they attend public worship in the Church of England, communicants only excepted, and that only on Christmas and other sacrament days.'[1] Johnson was first president of the New York College. There he lived a religious and intellectual life, much respected both by those of his own communion and by his Congregational neighbours, reading daily in his chapel the morning and evening service, procuring for his college library every new and important book on any subject, teaching his pupils—for whom, he says, he found great difficulty in getting good tutors—and taking deep interest in any theological and church questions which arose. In 1759 he received a grant of 500*l.* in support of the college from the Society for the Propagation of the Gospel.

Johnson never ceased to use every effort in his power to get bishops for America. In 1756 his argument was strengthened by bitter personal experience. In that year his son, who had gone over to England to obtain orders, fell a victim to small-pox—that terrible scourge of the century, to which those who came fresh into England seem to have been specially liable. 'I confess,' he wrote, 'I should scarce have thought my dear son's life ill bestowed (nor, I believe, would he) if it could have been a means of awakening this stupid age to a sense of the necessity of sending bishops. But, alas! what can be expected of such an age as this?'[2] The loss was of a kind that had often happened before. Out of fifty-one who went over to the mother country for ordination during the forty years before 1766, ten died during the journey by sickness or the sea. Many young men of promise who wished to take English

---

[1] Beardsley's *Life and Correspondence of S. Johnson*, p. 212.
[2] Johnson to Bishop Berkeley's son, Dec. 10, 1756; Beardsley. p. 230.

orders were dissuaded by their friends from undertaking what was then a dangerous as well as a tedious and expensive journey, and so turned their thoughts to service in other denominations. Remonstrance was not wanting on either side of the Atlantic. Johnson and others who thought with him were incessant in their urgency; and at home the desired measure, pressed by such Churchmen as saw the need upon the ears of unwilling ministries, seemed more than once upon the very point of fulfilment. At the end of Queen Anne's reign it had, as we have seen, been fully arranged that four bishops should be at once sent. After her death reasons were always found for postponement. Sherlock was so bent upon the need being supplied, that he would not take a patent from the Crown for ecclesiastical jurisdiction in America, and would only consent to ordain candidates, and to supervise affairs in the interim, until a better provision could be made.[1] 'I think myself,' he wrote in 1752, 'at present in a very bad situation. Bishop of a vast country, without power or influence, or any means of promoting true religion, sequestered from the people over whom I have the care and must never hope to see, I should be tempted to throw off all this care quite, were it not for the sake of preserving even the appearance of an episcopal church in the plantations.'[2] Bishop Berkeley exerted himself in the cause; Dr. Johnson was warmly in favour of it. Bishop Butler in 1750 formulated the proposal for submission to the Crown in four articles carefully worded to allay anti-Episcopalian jealousy.[3] Bishop Benson made a bequest to the Society for the Propagation of the Gospel in aid of the fund for settling bishops in the colonies, 'hoping that a design so necessary and unexceptionable cannot but at last

---

[1] Beardsley, p. 117.   [2] Stoughton's *Religion in England*, &c., p. 325.
[3] Bartlett's *Memoirs of Bp. Butler*, p. 123; and Rutt's note to Calamy's *Life*, ii. 335.

be put into execution.'[1] Bishop Johnson, of Gloucester, in 1751 assured an American correspondent that ' the united interest of the bishops here is not powerful enough to effect so reasonable and right a thing.'[2] Archbishop Secker wrote to Johnson of Connecticut, in 1764, that Lord Halifax was favourable to the scheme, and so was the Duke of Bedford, President of the Council.[3] 'Earnest and continued efforts,' he assured him in another letter, ' had been made with successive ministers. The king also was in favour of bishops, and had said they might at least send one to Quebec, where there was already a Roman Catholic bishop.' A chief secret, however, of the opposition in America may be detected in the subsequent words: ' The king is thoroughly sensible that the Episcopalians are his best friends.'[4] Throughout the century, long before there were any definite thoughts of independence, there was in America a very great jealousy of interference. Congregationalists were before long far too strong to have any fear of an attempt to force episcopacy on them; nor, after once the Georges had become firmly seated on the throne, was there the slightest apprehension of anything like headstrong zeal of proselytism on the part of the English Church. But there was a real, and unfortunately not an unwarrantable fear, that if bishops were sent to America, Walpole and his successors would do their very best to make them in great measure political agents. There had been some notable examples of this in Ireland. What guarantee was there that an English minister of State would not be still more anxious to manipulate his patronage in like manner in America? There was all the more fear of this in that a Churchman might well consider that he was acting no unworthy part, but an

[1] Bartlett, p. 135.   [2] Beardsley, p. 93.
[3] Id., pp. 276, 282.   [4] Id., p. 302.

honourable and patriotic one, in doing all that lay in his power to support what was called in Ireland 'the English interest.' It is evident that this fear was widely felt in the American colonies, and that Mayhew represented the feelings of a large party of American Congregationalists when he insisted that the proposed appointment of bishops was an aggressive measure,[1] which on political grounds his countrymen were bound to resist. As American disaffection silently but gradually increased, there was all the greater disinclination to an act that would notoriously strengthen the English Church. For English Churchmen were almost universally thoroughly loyalist in all their sympathies. The Government, therefore, were afraid of complying with what they acknowledged to be a just and reasonable demand on the part of the Church. Already in July 1771 we find Johnson and his fellow-Episcopalians all but giving up their last lingering hopes, and thinking whether they had not better apply at once for bishops to some other Episcopalian Church.[2]

Meanwhile in the northern States the English Church was rapidly and largely increasing. In 1761 in all New England the population was estimated at 435,000, of whom English Churchmen—lately an insignificant fragment—already numbered about 40,000. In the province of New York they claimed to be 25,000, or a quarter of the whole.[3] Some of the Congregationalists charged them as a body with a comparative want of seriousness. Their defenders answered that there was indeed a freedom and outspokenness of manner among them which contrasted with the more formal customs which were generally prevalent, but denied that this was any token of irreligion. Yet it might

---

[1] Nichols' *Lit. An.*, iii. 138 ; Caswall's *Am. Church*, p. 133.
[2] Beardsley's *Life of Johnson*, p. 317.   [3] Caswall, p. 57.

be well, said Apthorp, if each, instead of blaming the other, would meet halfway, and would abate something, the one of a stiffness which bordered on affectation, the other of an unconstraint which might risk the charge of levity.[1]

[1] Apthorp's Rev. of Mayhew, Nichols, iii. 138.

CHAPTER IV.

THE ENGLISH EPISCOPATE. 1714-1800.

THE Episcopate in the reign of Queen Anne had been as distinguished a body of men as had ever at one time adorned the English Church. A new and very different record begins almost simultaneously with the rule of the new dynasty. Of course no such change could happen at once. The causes of deterioration must have been already in working, nor could they suddenly produce their ripened results. Yet it is singular to observe how quickly, and how apparently to all, the bench of bishops did about this time lose its lustre and sink in general esteem. Many prominent names had already disappeared out of the list. The two archbishops Tenison and Sharpe had passed away; so had Bull and Beveridge; so had Burnet and Patrick and Compton; and so had Ken and Frampton; and so had some others, no less notable but scarcely less worthy. Before the close of George I.'s reign Dawes had died, and Hooper and Trelawney, Fleetwood and Trimnell and Blackhall. Nor was the Church any longer adorned with the brilliant eloquence of Atterbury, the thoughtful erudition of Cumberland, or the retired saintliness of Ottley. Wake was still Archbishop of Canterbury, but fast sinking into infirmities which compelled him to retire from active life. Hough only and Wilson remained for many years survivors of the older generation, and preserved to an honoured old age the best memories of a nobler past.

If the very best men had been promoted to the vacant places, it is yet likely they would have taken a less eminent position than their immediate predecessors. During the last three reigns the Church had been conspicuously before the eyes of the people. The perils which had gathered the country round the Church in the days of James II., the Protestant enthusiasm which found a leader in William, the burst of High Church ardour in the reign of Anne, all tended to awaken the energies and develop the resources of those who were called to be the fathers and chief officers of the Church. When ecclesiastical interests ceased to be in the front, and a period of tranquil monotony had set in, which seemed to leave no room for anything approaching to enthusiasm, it was inevitable that the words and doings of the bishops should come less prominently forward.

But the interests of religion do not need external excitement. The English Church, in its position of vantage, and secure from danger, should have pursued the even tenor of its way with all the more diligence and success for being no longer disturbed with the semi-political controversies which had of late been distracting it. If indifference, impiety, and crime were showing signs of increase, if attacks upon the doctrines of Christianity were becoming bolder and more frequent, there was all the more reason why the Church should press on her sacred work with increased zeal and more thoughtful earnestness. I do not propose to dwell here upon the causes which contributed to a state of things the very opposite of this. There is always something obscure in the agencies which bring about such intermittent periods of inactivity. Some of them, however, are not difficult to trace, and were by no means peculiar to any one religious body. But in the Church of England the insidious advance of indolence would no doubt have been greatly counteracted if its chief rulers had been carefully selected for the qualifications which best beseem a bishop. It cannot be said that this was generally the case. There were a great many very worthy men among them. There were some conspicuous for their learning. Respectability and decorum reigned supreme among them. There were very few against whom the austerest critic could authoritatively bring home any grave delinquency. Their faults were in a great measure such as were common to the age. A writer, not himself a member of the English Church, has truly remarked how favourably they contrast with the French dignitaries of the same century.[1] But when all this has been said in justice to them, the truth still remains that, as a body, they were not the men best adapted to raise the religion of their times, so far as their exertions could do so, to a higher level. More than this, the censures and reflections which, by friends as well as by opponents, were often passed upon them were, in far too many instances, not at all undeserved.

The revolution which placed William and Mary on the throne had raised some very able and excellent men to the vacated sees. At the same time it somewhat lowered and secularised the type.[2] The bishop lost something of his older position as a successor of the apostles and a centre of Christian unity,[3] and became rather a chief officer of the Church as by law established. He retained much of the former respect, but it was not quite of the kind it had been

---

[1] Stoughton's *Religion in England under Q. Anne and the Georges*, p. 292.

[2] 'The Revolution of 1688 greatly weakened in the Anglican Church the hold of episcopacy as a divine institution. It lingered for a while in the narrowing body of the Nonjurors, and with them the higher and more spiritual perceptions of the Episcopate passed away.' (Abp. Manning's *Essays, &c.*, p. 4.)

[3] A position which Wilson in the Isle of Man still strongly maintained (Cruttwell's *Life of Wilson*, p. 108).

when the belief in episcopacy as a divinely appointed constitution remained comparatively unimpaired.[1] Lord Thurlow, towards the end of the last century, could scarcely believe that there were bishops in Scotland apart from all prelatical dignity and state;[2] just in the same way as to Mrs. Barbauld there seemed something wholly ludicrous in the one American bishop, 'without title, without fixed diocese, and without lawn sleeves.'[3] In the stirring Whig bishops of King William's and Queen Anne's time there was a great deal which, in the opinion of many, would more than compensate for some deficiency in the more hallowed associations which were wont to gather round a 'father in God.' There was a fuller sympathy with the secular side of life, a closer combination of the Churchman and the citizen, a greater readiness for liberal and tolerant measures. The Church of England might have fared worse than to have had throughout the whole of the century a large infusion of bishops such as those of the Revolution.

Unfortunately, when they died their vigorous individuality perished with them, while the tone of thought which characterised them survived in an inferior form. Tillotson was very worthy of admiration; not so a second-rate copy of him. Burnet, with all his faults, will always hold an honourable place in the roll of English worthies. His was a character not likely to be repeated. But a bishop who should be something like him, and yet not be quickened by Burnet's unwearied sense of duty, would be an unattractive character. And besides, it was not altogether on the Whig and Low Church mould that the bishops of the last three quarters of the eighteenth century were chiefly fashioned. The secular spirit which the Revolution had

---

[1] 'In my younger days,' said Jortin, 'to deny the divine succession of bishops was rank atheism' (Jortin's *Tracts*, ii. 436).
[2] Bp. Horne's *Works*, p. 154.   [3] Mrs. Barbauld's *Works*, ii. 151.

introduced remained and flourished, but with it there was very generally blended a sort of High Church stiffness and formality, which altered but did not improve the type.

There was one very direct and obvious cause why a change for the worse in the government of the Church should set in with the beginning of George I.'s reign. Sir Robert Walpole came into power in 1715. If his government in political affairs was singularly deficient in loftiness of principle, still more was this the case in his management of Church patronage. A friend of the Church in his own way, and bent especially upon maintaining it in a tranquil security in which there should be no excitement nor heat of feeling, he yet did as much as any one man well could do to demoralise it by sacrificing its best interests to his own political uses. In one of the chapters of 'The English Church in the Eighteenth Century' Mr. Overton has abundantly illustrated the disgraceful manner in which both by Walpole and his successors the dispensing of Church patronage was made subservient to the commonest interests of party. The instances which he quotes are striking and might be largely multiplied. It will be enough for our present purpose to repeat from his pages the single remark that 'even Dr. Johnson, that stout defender of the English Church, and of everything connected with the administration of its affairs, was obliged to own that "no man can now be made a bishop for his learning and piety; his only chance of promotion is his being connected with some one who has Parliamentary interest."'[1] Nor is there need of accumulating further examples than he has given of the mischief which such a corrupting influence could not fail to cause. He has shown how common preferment-hunting and court subservience became; how political partisanship was fostered and encouraged in men who were

[1] Abbey and Overton's *E. Ch. of the Eighteenth Cent.*, ii. 22.

bound by the very nature of their high calling to enter upon political questions only in a higher spirit of Christian statesmanship; how even one of themselves could say that he 'saw the generality of bishops bartering their independence and the dignity of their order for the chance of a translation.'[1] He has made it clear that the infection had spread so widely, that even men who were estimable in life and religious in feeling did not hesitate to avow such self-seeking motives with an outspoken frankness which satisfies the reader that they could not have thought them a thing to be ashamed of. It was the fault of the same system that some bishoprics became almost appanages of noble families, and that others were filled by respectable mediocrities, whose chief claim to promotion had been that a brother or an uncle had been serviceable to the minister of the day.

We have seen that through the early years of the century the bishops were frequently spoken of as a body of men who did honour to their Church and country. How different is the tone in later years! We may constantly find high praise bestowed upon one or another bishop, but encomiums on the bench in general have altogether ceased. On one occasion, it is true, in 1775, in answer to an invective of more than usual vehemence, three peers, Lord Lyttelton, the Duke of Manchester, and Earl Gower, rose up to defend the bishops, and to assert in warm language their reverence and esteem for them.[2] But it would be difficult to find any other exception to the more or less slighting tone with which as a body they were alluded to. In some notable cases very considerable allowance must be made for the animus of the speaker. The best of the bishops were scarcely safe from the sneers of Horace Walpole, who never let slip any opportunity of aiming a passing shaft at a

[1] Watson's *Life*, p. 116, quoted in *Engl. Ch. of the Eighteenth Cent.*, p. 25.
[2] *Parliamentary History*, xviii. 641.

bishop in his somewhat ill-natured gossip. The satires of Churchill and Whitehead are too much tinged with venom. The Deists were as unfair to Churchmen as Churchmen often were to them. Whiston, self-conscious of the integrity with which, through poverty and reproach, he had followed out the bent of his own erratic opinions, could scarcely allow that merit should ever attend orthodoxy, promotion, and success. Lord Hervey 'had a peculiar antipathy to the Church.'[1] But there is no need to depend entirely upon such authorities as these, nor yet upon the vehement assaults which, in those days of Parliamentary diatribe, were sometimes levelled against them in the House of Lords. There is something more expressive in the frequent occurrence of chance observations such as these: 'It is very certain you judge right in thinking the bench to be under a great degree of contempt.'[2] 'Our bishop is a better sort of man than most of the mitred order.'[3] 'A man of candour and generosity rarely to be met with in men of his Grace's station.'[4] 'E'en in a bishop I can spy desert.'[5] 'I am sadly grieved for the melancholy condition you give me of some of the chief dignitaries, and the condition of the Church there' (in England).[6]

It is certain, therefore, that through a great part of the century the bishops, as a body, were not in favour, or rather that they were in much disfavour. Yet there was very little that was flagrantly wrong. In one case only was laxity

---

[1] Croker's note to Hervey's *Memoirs*, i. xxv, quoted by Overton, as above, p. 20.
[2] Morice to Atterbury, May 19, 1728; *Life*, ii. 276.
[3] Clarke to Bowyer, Nov. 1749; Nichols, iv. 159.
[4] Nichols, iii. 16.   [5] Pope's *Poems*.
[6] Johnson (of Connecticut) to Bp. Berkeley's son, Dec. 1756; Beardsley's *Life of S. Johnson*, p. 230. So also Cowper's *Poems*, 'The Task;' Bolingbroke, quoted in Schlosser's *Eighteenth Cent.*, i. 79; Delany's *Correspondence*, ii. 389; Hartley's *Observations on Man*, p. 451; Lloyd's *Poems*, 'B. Poets,' x. 623; Lyttelton's *Persian Letters*, lvii.

of life suspected. If report was true, there was one prelate whose qualifications for the primacy of York were certainly of a very extraordinary nature. Horace Walpole declared of Lancelot Blackbourne, 'the jolly old archbishop,' that 'though he had been a buccaneer, he had all the manners of a man of quality, and retained nothing of his old profession except his seraglio.'[1] Such authority would not of itself carry any great weight. But there was almost certainly truth in the story. The principal biographer of the eighteenth century does indeed declare that the stories reported of him were the merest calumny.[2] He denies, too, the story that his promotion from Exeter to York was his reward for marrying George I. to the Duchess of Munster. As for the buccaneer legend, how, he not very pertinently asks, could that be, when he was so well versed in the Greek tragedians? But Drake, who wrote during Blackbourne's lifetime his elaborate history of York, scarcely disguises under a thin veil of reticence his acceptance of the tales that were current there.[3] The account given of him by Polwhele, the historian of Devonshire, is that he was a man of strong passions, and a warm and affectionate friend. In earlier life he had been a chaplain in one of the buccaneering expeditions against the Spaniards, and retained throughout life the bluff and hearty manners of a sailor. At Exeter, where he was first dean and afterwards bishop, he was very useful to Walpole by keeping a strict eye upon such gentlemen around as were thought to be disaffected towards Government. He would have liked to keep in Exeter, holding the deanery of St. Paul's 'in commendam.' This did not suit Walpole, and he was sent north.[4] His genial manners would have made him loved, if people could but

---

[1] Walpole's *Memoirs of the Reign of George II.*, p. 87.
[2] Noble's *Grainger*, iii. 68.   [3] Drake's *Hist. of York*, p. 416.
[4] Polwhele's *Devonshire*, p. 514.

forget that he was a bishop and not an admiral. But he won, as Noble says, more hearts than souls. How easy-going were his ways is amusingly exemplified by an anecdote that in a church at Nottingham, tired with the labours of a Confirmation, he ordered pipes and tobacco into the vestry.[1] There is a characteristic letter of his to Bishop Nicolson, and the tone of it does him credit. The subject is the danger of the Church. Like an old sailor, he talks of winds and storms ahead, rocks and tempests. If he cannot do the good he would, he can hinder some harm, and it does not do to think too much of rumour, for stories die away.[2] After Blackbourne, no one ever dreamed of making charges against any English prelate such as were brought against him. Their offences, whatever they were, were of a wholly different order. Simony would have been a sin more in keeping with the briberies and corruption of the age. But, with the exception of a vague and wholly unsubstantiated suspicion once thrown out by Whiston,[3] the bench throughout the period of the Georges was perfectly clear from any such imputation. Whitehead, in one of his Satires,[4] charged Bishop Sherlock with selling his vote. The ministers of that date were quite capable of making the attempt. We are told that Bishop Atterbury, when leader of the Opposition in the Upper House, was offered by Walpole 5,000*l.* a year if he would fall in with his policy.[5] But that Sherlock should have been guilty of such an act is utterly and almost absurdly improbable. He was perhaps too fond of politics, but no Churchman of his day held a more conspicuous or honourable position. It appears to have been a mere

[1] Noble, i. 270. The vicar, more particular than many clergymen of his century, met the servant and insisted that the smoking be adjourned.
[2] Nicolson's *Letters*, p. 563.
[3] Whiston's *Life* p. 517.
[4] Whitehead's *Works*, 'B. Poets,' x. 846.
[5] Williams s *Life of Atterbury*, i. 377.

unscrupulous aspersion which neither friend nor opponent thought worthy of any notice.

The shortcomings of the bishops were those which in men of lower position were, in the Church and society of the age, looked upon only too indulgently. No one can read the fulsome dedications of the time, or the lavish flattery of its congratulatory verses, without feeling that adulation was an art which few educated men disdained to use. In the Church pluralities were looked upon as a matter of course. Non-residence, though often complained of, was easily condoned in those who were otherwise in good repute. Patronage, whether secular or ecclesiastical, had become so universally a matter of interest and favour, that even gross nepotism was scarcely condemned. Finally, throughout the Church the standard of duty had become distinctly lower. The active were less active than they would have been in a better age; the indolent gave to their indolence a free rein. Although such abuses—so far as they existed in the Church—had awakened not much active hostility, and no zealous determination to remove them, yet they had brought the clergy into somewhat ill repute. Their presence among bishops roused a stronger feeling. *Noblesse oblige.* 'Why,' wrote Warburton, 'are we distinguished from the rest of our brethren with superior title and riches, but that we may also outdo them in the service of the public?'[1] But this was just what even a careless and indifferent age could see to be greatly wanting. There were always a certain number among them distinguished for piety, activity, and learning. But the average impression was one that too often conveyed the notion of a rather worldly-minded mediocrity. When bishops held, in addition to their episcopal charge, deaneries, and headships of colleges, and distant rectories; when it was manifest they

[1] Warburton and Hurd's *Correspondence*, p. 356.

had a keen eye to translations into wealthier or more influential sees; when they were seen to remain absent from their dioceses and cathedral cities for many months at a time, or sometimes, with short intermittent visits, even for years, neglecting their duties both to the clergy and to the laymen under their care, 'huddling over visitations by their archdeacons,'[1] and giving the great proportion of their time—in London or in Bath, or elsewhere—to politics, or to theological or literary or classical studies, or perhaps to mere indolent repose; when men were seen promoted to the highest ecclesiastical stations for nothing in the world but political connection or noble birth; when bishops were seen to follow the precedent of their own promotion, and heap the richest benefices in their gift only upon their own relatives and friends; when reports came down from London that there were prelates than whom no courtiers were more skilled in the nicer arts of sycophancy; and when squibs were handed round in jeering coffee-houses—

> Hither, brethren, incense bring
> To the mitre-giving king;
> Praise him for his first donations,
> Praise him for the best translations,
> Benefices, dispensations;[2]

when, again, they heard of one bishop indulging in displays of unseemly pomp, of another being reproved by the king for the extravagance of his entertainments, of others attending the levées and praising the orthodoxy of a man notorious for licentious living; when they read in the scanty Parliamentary reports of bishops in the House of Lords receiving grave and merited censure, sometimes for illiberal or intolerant sentiments, and sometimes for the un-

---

[1] *Hardships of the Inferior Clergy*, in a letter to the Bishop of London, 1722, p. 234.

[2] *Asylum for Fugitive Pieces*, 2nd ed., 1785, p. 241.

seemly vehemence with which certain of them pressed for operations against the revolted colonies; when one bishop was a dunce, and another able indeed and learned to a remarkable degree, but no less remarkable for the indiscriminating and scurrilous invective with which he overwhelmed even the gentlest of his opponents: when one or another of these varied counts was year after year brought up against this bishop or against that, it was not likely that public feeling should confine its criticism to individuals, that it should select and discriminate, and point to the tranquil virtues of many of their number against whom none of such accusations could ever be whispered. Still less would it be taken into consideration that many who fell signally short of what might have been expected of them were, in a more private capacity, amiable and estimable men, perhaps hospitable and charitable, and beloved by a large circle of acquaintances. The great majority of eighteenth century bishops in England were, without a doubt, worthy persons, whose faults as ministers of religion and chief pastors of the Church were greatly owing to the circumstances and surroundings of the time. But these faults were none the less odious in themselves. It was only through the slackness of the age that many of them could be tolerated at all. There was more than enough to justify the dissatisfaction that was felt. The wonder rather is that dissatisfaction did not express itself in other forms than words.

Throughout George II.'s time there was a ceaseless contest between Queen Caroline and the king's ministers, especially with Walpole, whether she or they were to have the chief voice in dispensing Church patronage. So far as she could gain her point, there was no fear whatever of any political jobbery interfering with the appointment of the best man. Perhaps she had no greater pleasure than in using her powerful influence for the promotion of the learned and the good. Nor were there many who were better qualified to judge of merit. Under her, 'for a brief period, liberality and elevation of mind were passports to promotion in the Church.'[1] Almost all the most eminent bishops of the middle of the eighteenth century—Butler, and Secker, and Sherlock, and Smalridge, and Hare, and Potter—were selected and recommended by her. So, too, was Berkeley, who, 'in the comparative darkness of the Irish Church, shone like a star.'[2] She would greatly have liked to bring Wilson from the seclusion of the Isle of Man, and to have given him the wider influence of an English see. In all these appointments her judgment was excellent. On the other hand, there was no security that the Queen's bishops would be orthodox. Clayton, whom, on her strong recommendation, Lord Carteret, Governor of Ireland, made Bishop of Clogher, was indeed an able writer, and a kind and generous-tempered man; but his opinions, which he never shrank from avowing, and which were of a sceptical if not an heretical cast, made the ears of his fellow-Churchmen to tingle, and he died under the excitement of a prosecution. It was partly, no doubt, through her influence, though chiefly through that of Lord Chancellor Talbot, that Rundle was about the same time raised to Derry. His supposed inclination to a Deistical latitude had created a stir which prevented his promotion to Gloucester; it seemed to matter less in an Irish bishop. But he was a man whose personal qualities won the affectionate and even enthusiastic admiration of most who came in contact with him; and if his theology had not been suspected, the appointment would have been an excellent one. A third instance is Samuel Clarke. All acknowledged his piety, his learning, his massive intellect, and the good

---

[1] Pattison, in *Essays and Reviews*, p. 319.
[2] Fraser's *Life of Berkeley*, p. 209.

service he had done against irreligion and unbelief. He became, however, a leader in that singular revival of Arianism which was a feature in the ecclesiastical history of the period, and few well-wishers of the Church could have been content to see him elevated to a bishop's see.[1] But his heterodoxy was no objection whatever in Queen Caroline's eyes. She inspired Walpole with something of her own eagerness to effect his promotion; and the minister, we are told, 'argued with him to persuade him till the candles burnt out.' He reasoned in vain. Clarke had no wish to resign his living; but he would not, under any conditions, either subscribe a second time to the articles or accept a bishopric.

It could not easily be said what the queen's own theological opinions were. Horace Walpole said of her that she 'had no aversion to a medley of religion, which she always compounded into a scheme of heresy of her own.'[2] Lord Chesterfield, in much the same vein, pronounced that 'after puzzling herself in all the whimsies and fantastical speculations of different sects, she fixed ultimately in Deism, believing a future state.'[3] Doubtless neither Walpole nor Chesterfield was altogether wrong, though both of them were thoroughly men of the world, who looked at such a matter from an amused rather than from a serious point of view. The queen was thoroughly in earnest, devout in all observances of worship, and deeply concerned in the welfare of religion in England.[4] She felt, and not without good reason, that she had proved her sincere attachment to the Protestant cause, for she had refused the hand of the Emperor Charles. 'She scorned an

---

[1] Horace Walpole's *Journal of the Reign of George III.*, i. 12.
[2] Walpole's *Memoirs of the Reign of George II.*, p. 85.
[3] Chesterfield's *Characters of Eminent Personages*, p. 14.
[4] *Diary of Mary, Countess Cowper*, p. 11.

empire, for religion's sake.'[1] To the Church of England she gave a warm and never-failing support. 'The queen's death,' wrote Benson, one of the best of the bishops of his time, in a letter to Berkeley, 'is a severe blow. Those who would not be persuaded, while she lived, how sincere a friend she was to our Church and constitution, have since her death been fully persuaded of it.'[2] She was very fond of all literary reading and discussion, but most of all of theology and philosophy. She told Sale, the Orientalist, that she read Butler's 'Analogy' every morning at breakfast;[3] and mentioned, in talking to Whiston, that she had read three times over Wollaston's 'Religion of Nature.'[4] Perhaps it was mainly her admiration of Wollaston which gave her the reputation of holding Deistical views. Round what she called her Hermitage at Richmond were four busts, representing respectively Sir Isaac Newton, Locke, Samuel Clarke, and Wollaston.[5] It did not, however, follow that because she read and admired Wollaston, or because she protected Voltaire when he visited England, and got subscriptions for him, she therefore identified herself with their views. Within certain wide limits she thoroughly loved liberty of thought and free ventilation of opinion. The orthodoxy of the day was somewhat stiff and timid; and finding what she craved for among the more religious of the Deists, she probably came to sympathise with many of their opinions. Theological argument was a delight to her. In early life she had greatly interested herself in the debate between Collins, Clarke, and Leibnitz on deep questions of liberty and necessity. When she was queen she had no happier evenings than when a select

---

[1] Gay's *Poems*, Epistle I., 'To a Lady.'
[2] Fraser's *Life and Works of Berkeley*, iv. 256.
[3] Seward's *Anecdotes*, ii. 335.   [4] Whiston's *Memoirs*, p. 231.
[5] Noble's *Grainger*, i. 271; *Gentleman's Magazine*, Oct. 1732.

company of learned divines met together in her rooms. When Bishop Butler was in town she would often request his attendance every day from seven to nine for conversation on philosophical and theological subjects.[1] Berkeley would be there, 'not very willingly, but hoping to see some means of advancing his favourite project of a missionary college at Bermuda.'[2] It was no pleasure to him, however great might be the queen's gratification, to enter into a long and fruitless argument with Hoadly and Clarke, supported on his own side by Sherlock and Secker. When the debate had closed, and the graver combatants had departed, there was still no lack of ecclesiastical chit-chat among the queen and ladies of her court. We have a glimpse in Lady Cowper's diary of the gossip as to what this bishop had written, and what that had preached, and what a third had said about the Athanasian Creed, and how one was praised for his saintliness of life, and another suspected of heterodox opinions.[3] It should be added, however, that her love of theological controversy did not in any way divert her from the practical works of religion. The self-denying labours of the Moravian Brethren led to their first mission in England, in 1728, at the special request of a lady in her retinue;[4] and her charities, which George II. continued after her death, were no less than 13,000*l.* per annum.[5] Had she lived a little longer she would certainly have taken great interest in the Methodist movement. She died in 1737, only a few months before the most memorable eras in Wesley's life, his return from America, his 'conversion,' and the commencement of field preaching. With some of the Methodist leaders her cultivated and intellectual mind could have had little sympathy. Perhaps she would not greatly

---

[1] Bartlett's *Life of Butler*, p. 40.   [2] Fraser's *Life of Berkeley*, iv. 109.
[3] Lady M. Cowper's *Diary*, p. 18.
[4] M. Davies' *Unorthodox London*, p. 290.   [5] Bartlett's *Butler*, p. 42.

have appreciated Whitefield, although his wonderful successes would have attracted the thoughtful attention of a temperament which was at once religious and unprejudiced. John Wesley would have greatly impressed her. She would have shared in the feeling, nearly universal at that time among the cultivated classes, against 'enthusiasm,' but the conjunction of intense religious earnestness with a trained and well-instructed intellect would probably have had a charm for the queen which would not have been restrained by a cautiousness like that of ministers and bishops. She would have conferred with Wesley, and such conferences might have borne results of great importance to the Church. George II. always maintained that ministers should have listened to his advice and made Whitefield a bishop.[1] If the queen, whose influence in such matters was nearly as great over ministers as it was over the king himself, had supported such advice in the case of Wesley, there can be little doubt that a bishopric would have been pressed upon him. Would he have accepted it? Certainly not, if he had thought it would interfere with his appointed work. Yet when we remember how warmly he was attached to the Church of England, and how greatly he desired an extension of its usefulness, it is quite possible he might have thought that if the episcopate would in some ways restrict his power, it would in other respects give it greater scope. He believed in himself, as every great reformer must do, and in the divine commission he had received. He knew his capacity for organisation, and the influence he could exercise over all whom he came into personal contact with. If the episcopate had been offered him, it is by no means impossible, though it may be very improbable, that he would have accepted it as a providential opening.

At this point it seems not unfit to give some account of

[1] Pattison, in *Ess. and Rev.*, p. 323.

the attitude of the English Episcopate towards Wesley and the other Methodist preachers. Not that Wesley greatly troubled himself as to what their relations might be; but on such a matter the clergy and other Churchmen naturally looked to their leaders for example and advice. If the bishops had taken a decided and tolerably unanimous line in dealing with the subject, there can be little doubt that either the separation would have been greatly precipitated, or some real effort would have been made to find room for the new evangelisers within the Church system.

There was, however, no such unanimity, or anything approaching to it; nor, in the absence of all power of synodical action, does the least effort ever seem to have been made among the bishops to confer with one another as to what action the Church should take. It is true there was no one of the number who cordially and completely approved of the movement. So far all were agreed. But short of this there were many grades of variation between comparative friendliness and strong hostility. Of four among the most eminent of them Wesley spoke, not only with great respect, but as if, on the whole, they had been his friends. 'No one,' he wrote near the close of his life, 'ever thought or called Methodism leaving the Church. It was never esteemed so by Archbishop Potter, with whom I had the happiness of conversing freely; nor by Archbishop Secker, who was thoroughly acquainted with every step we took; as was likewise Dr. Gibson, then Bishop of London; and that great man, Bishop Lowth. Nor did any of these venerable men ever blame me for it in all the conversations I had with them. Only Archbishop Potter once said, "Those gentlemen are irregular; but they have done good, and I pray God to bless them."'[1]

As may be judged from these last words, Archbishop

[1] Wesley's *Works*, Letter to the *Dublin Chron.*, 1789, xiii. 236.

Potter was very much inclined to give the preachers his favourable support. While Wesley was yet at Oxford, in 1729, Potter had not only given his full consent to Wesley's labours among the prisoners at Oxford, but 'was greatly pleased with the undertaking.'[1] He was quick to see his special powers, and strongly advised him not to seclude himself in a rural parish, nor to spend his time in controversy, but to throw all his strength in 'attacking the strongholds of vice, and in promoting practical holiness.'[2] Whitefield also makes mention in his diary for 1738 of a favourable reception he had received from the archbishop.[3] Moravianism was at this time closely akin to Methodism,[4] and Potter took great interest in it. In 1737, he wrote a most cordial letter to Count Zinzendorf, the principal leader of the Moravians.[5] He also helped and encouraged their missionaries.[6]

Bishop Benson was a good friend to the early Methodists. Whitefield records gratefully, in 1736, that 'our good Bishop Benson has been pleased to give me another present of five guineas.'[7]

Bishop Gibson had once said, 'Why do not these gentlemen leave the Church?' 'But this,' adds Wesley, 'was before I had ever seen him.'[8] His interviews with the Wesleys and Whitefield entirely removed any feeling that their position in the Church was untenable; and though he

---

[1] Wesley's *Works*, i. 8.
[2] Curteis's *Dissent in Relation to the Ch. of E.*, p. 355.
[3] Whitefield's *Diary*, Dec. 9, 1738. A little later, however, it would seem as if one of Whitefield's occasional violent sayings had somewhat changed this feeling. Byrom writes, in 1739, that he thinks the archbishop has forbidden Mr. Piers to let Mr. Whitefield preach again in his pulpit (John Byrom's *Remains*, iii. 249).
[4] We see this not only in J. Wesley's own history, but in the remarks of contemporaries. 'I find Zinzendorf,' wrote Warburton in 1740 to Doddridge, 'a perfect Methodist' (Doddridge's *Correspond.*, iv. 480).
[5] Doddridge's *Correspond.*, iv. 264.
[6] Anderson's *Church in the Colonies*, i. 685.
[7] Whitefield's *Letters*, p. 18. [8] Wesley's *Works*, xiii. 237.

opposed them on some points, it was with friendliness and respect.[1] In 1740 we find him conversing with Wesley on one of the most distinctive features of his doctrinal system. He asked him what he meant by Christian perfection. Wesley explained; and the bishop answered earnestly, 'Why, Mr. Wesley, if this is what you mean by perfection, who can be against it?'[2] Of the extravagances which the Methodist revival soon began to show Gibson wrote in a spirit of not unkindly regret. He pointed out to his clergy how completely it is a necessary part of the Christian faith to believe in the direct influence of the Spirit of God, and warned them against the chilling effect produced by neglect of this truth. But while he urged them to follow the example of the Methodists in shunning lukewarmness, he also, quoting largely from Methodist writings, dwelt upon the serious dangers to quiet and sober religion from a fanatical belief in extraordinary interpositions of Heaven.[3] Gibson appears to have had several interviews with the Wesleys. Their object on one occasion was the rather remarkable one of pressing the bishop to be more scrupulous than they had understood him to be in the matter of lay-baptism, meaning baptism of Dissenters. Silent permission, they urged, was taken for authority.[4] Another time Charles Wesley said of him, 'He showed us great affection, and cautioned us to give no more umbrage than was necessary for our own defence, to forbear exceptional phrases, and to keep to the doctrines of the Church.'[5] When the churchwardens of one of the London churches wrote to him to complain of their rector very frequently asking Wesley to preach there, Gibson at once refused to

[1] Wesley's *Works*, xiii. 236; Whitefield's *Diary*, Dec. 1738.
[2] Wesley's *Works, Letters*, 1770, vi. 234.
[3] Gibson's Pastoral Letter against Lukewarmness and Enthusiasm, 1739, pp. 30-40.
[4] Stoughton's *Religion under Q. Anne and the Georges*, p. 392. [5] *Id.*

interpose. 'Mr. Wesley is a clergyman, regularly ordained, and under no ecclesiastical censure.'[1]

Of Bishop Lowth, Wesley spoke with great esteem. He writes in his journal that he had spent the afternoon with him. 'His whole behaviour was worthy of a Christian bishop; easy, affable, courteous; and yet all his conversation spoke the dignity which was suitable to his character.'[2] An anecdote is told of Lowth refusing to sit above Wesley at table; and of his saying at the same time, 'May I be found at your feet in another world.'[3]

Of some bishop, whose name is not given, Wesley writes, 'I have heard a complaint had been made to the bishop that I drove fifteen mad the first sermon. The worthy prelate wished, as I am informed, that the madness might not be forgotten before next Sunday.'[4] Of another bishop, Wesley tells a yet better answer. 'My lord,' some gentlemen asked, 'what must we do to stop these new preachers?' He answered, 'If they preach contrary to the Scriptures, confute them by Scripture; if contrary to reason, confute them by reason. But beware you use no other weapons than these, either in opposing error or in defending the truth.'[5]

An anecdote, slight in itself, but worth recording, of the hospitality shown to John Wesley by Ross, Bishop of Exeter, will be found later in the account given of that bishop.

Wesley speaks on two or three occasions of 'the good old Bishop of Londonderry,' and of the interesting and useful conversations he had with him.[6]

Bishop Horne was frequently brought into contact with Wesley, partly in friendly correspondence, partly in scarcely

[1] A very similar reply of Bishop Horne is quoted on the next page.
[2] Wesley's *Works, Journal,* Nov. 1777, iv. 112.
[3] Note to Mason's edition of Wesley's *Works,* xii. 150.
[4] Stoughton, p. 388. [5] Wesley's *Works,* ix. 87.
[6] Wesley's *Journal,* iii. 267, 271; iv. 16.

less friendly controversy, in which Wesley did not fail to express the great esteem he felt for his opponent.[1] The bishop was himself sometimes called a Methodist, as was the case with many other men whose piety was above the level of their times. He was always anxious to think of Wesley as a Churchman, who might properly be invited to preach. 'In 1790, Bishop Horne was staying with a gentleman of Norfolk. Wesley came on a circuit to a market town near, and sent to ask the minister for the use of the parish church. The clergyman consulted the bishop, who answered, 'Mr. Wesley is a regularly ordained clergyman of the Church of England, and if the minister makes no objection I shall make none.'[2]

Archbishop Secker does not appear to have had any personal communications with the Methodist leaders; but in his charges he constantly refers to them in a tone which betrays little sympathy, and in some respects strong disapproval, but also a good deal of admiration. He speaks somewhat disparagingly of 'a new sect, pretending to the strictest piety,' and condemned their extravagances, and more particularly the exclusiveness by which they seemed to proclaim that they only pointed out the way of salvation. He charged them with advancing unjustifiable notions as necessary truths—as giving good people groundless fears, and bad ones groundless hopes—of disturbing the understandings of many—of prejudicing multitudes against their proper ministers, and preventing their edification by them — of producing first disorders in the churches and then separation. 'Where these irregularities will end, God only knows.' At the same time he begged the clergy not harshly to condemn, not to speak with anger and exaggeration, nor yet to be so imprudent as to disclaim them as not belonging to us, and

---

[1] Wesley's *Works*, ix. 117.
[2] *Works of G. Horne, with Life*, by Jones of Nayland, p. 160.

so to drive them into a sect. He warmly commended their correct piety and zeal, and earnestly entreated his hearers to correct by their example those deficiencies which had too often chilled the services and sermons of the Church.[1]

Many of the bishops, and among them one or two of the best, considered the irregularities of the Methodist system an invincible bar to any close communion. Thus Hildesley, the worthy successor of Wilson of Sodor and Man, shortly before his promotion, refused Whitefield his pulpit, and defended his prohibition in a sermon.[2] So also Porteus, leader of the Evangelical party, forbade the use of the pulpit even to episcopally ordained Methodists.[3] He could not, he said, consent to any clergyman in his diocese 'vibrating between two modes of worship. Let him not be a Methodist in the morning and a Church of England man in the afternoon.'[4]

Archbishop Herring, in one of his letters to Duncombe in 1756, writes of Wesley and Methodism in the spirit of one who criticises with good-natured censure a passing extravagance. 'The other author (J. Wesley), in my opinion, with good parts and learning is a most dark and saturnine creature. His pictures may frighten weak people who at the same time are wicked, but I fear he will make few converts except for a day. . . . For myself, I have no con-

---

[1] Secker's *Works*, 1st Canterbury Charge, p. 233, 2nd Charge, pp. 279-82, &c.; also his *Oratio coram Synodo*. 'Cavendum, ne, si illi sermones ad vulgi captum nimis accommodant ac demittunt, nos hoc nimis dedignemur; ne, si illi sunt justo vehementiores, nos frigidi videamur et affectuum piorum expertes; ne, si illi efficaciam fidei immoderate cum maximo fidelium periculo extollunt, nos non minus ingrate eam deprimamus et extenuemus; ne, si illi inania visa et phantasmata pro certis pignoribus remissionis peccatorum habent, nos in genuinum S. Spiritus testimonium simus imprudenter contumeliosi' (*Works*, p. 371).

[2] Rivington's *Life of Hildesley*.

[3] Porteus's *Life and Works*, ii. 270.

[4] Richmond, Bishop of Sodor and Man in 1776, even forbade the admission of Methodist preachers to the Lord's table (Wesley's *Works*, iv. 100).

stitution for these frights and fervours; and if I can but live up to the regular practice of a Christian life, I shall be in no pain for futurity, nor do I think it an essential part of religion to be pointed at for any foolish singularities. The subjects you mention of the Methodist preaching are excellent in the hands of wise men (not of enthusiasts). Religion for the practice of the world must be plain and intelligible to the lowest understanding. This is self-evident; and the gospel itself assures us that the love of God is keeping His commandments, and what need we further evidence? As to the notion that men are by nature devils, I can call it by no other name than wicked and blasphemous, and the highest reproach that one can cast upon his wise and good Creator.'[1]

There is an account of an interview which Bishop Butler had with John Wesley, who, in the conversation, pronounced that the sole ground of justification was faith. The bishop answered, 'Our faith itself is a good work, it is a virtuous temper of mind.' 'My lord,' said Wesley, 'whatever our faith is, our Church asserts that we are justified by faith only. But how it can be called a good work I see not. It is the gift of God, and a gift that presupposes nothing in us but sin and misery.' This seemed to Butler to lead to pure Calvinism, and he asked Wesley what he meant by faith. The answer was, that 'justifying faith was a conviction, wrought in a man by the Holy Ghost, that Christ hath loved him, and given Himself for him, and that through Christ his sins are forgiven.' Butler said some good men might have that sort of faith, but not all Christians. In the end, the interview closed with the bishop saying, 'Mr. Wesley, I will deal plainly with you: I once thought you and Mr. Whitefield well-meaning men, but I cannot think so now, for I have heard more of you — matters of fact, sir. And Mr.

[1] Herring's *Letters to Duncombe* Jan. 25, 1756, p. 174.

Whitefield says in his journal, "There are promises still to be fulfilled in me." Sir, the pretending to extraordinary revelation and gifts of the Holy Ghost is a horrid thing, a very horrid thing.'[1]

Bishop Hurd's opinion of the movement may be said to have a special interest, because in many respects he was above all others the typical bishop of his age. He will be spoken of later in this work: it is enough to remark here that in his religion, as in his disposition generally, there was a certain stiffness and propriety, and a deficiency of warmth and energy, which expressed and almost exaggerated what was chiefly wanting in the Church of his time. We scarcely need his words to know how he would have expressed himself in regard to the Methodist movement. But there exists a very characteristic sermon of his 'on the mischiefs of enthusiasm and bigotry.' We seem to hear his very accents, as he descants on 'the exorbitancies of ungoverned piety,' and on 'this turbulence of zeal, this rash infringement of the regular institutions which have been provided for the maintenance of religion and the preservation of public tranquillity.' Yet he is too judicial to be altogether one-sided in his verdict. He has strong condemnation for those who, in their opposition to the new preaching, 'become zealots in their turn.' Nor does he fail to admit that 'one cannot but admire such earnest, at the same time that one pities and condemns such groundless and ill-directed zeal. What true service to religion might not a breast so warmed be able to do, if under the guidance of well-interpreted Scripture and sober piety! What increase of Christian righteousness might not be expected, if every man within his own station and within his proper province would appear thus heartily in the cause of it!'[2]

[1] Conv. with the Bishop of Bristol, Wesley's *Works*, xiii. 464-66.
[2] Hurd's *Assize Sermon on the Mischiefs*, &c., 1752.

It may be added that although Hurd's temperament was utterly unsympathetic with the general tone of Methodism, he was not too prejudiced to understand how beneficially it might affect many. A labourer whom he was accustomed to see constantly in church, listening attentively to his sermons, was no longer to be seen in his usual place. The man hesitated a moment, and then said, 'I will tell you the truth, my lord. I went the other day to hear the Methodists, and I understand their plain words so much better, that I have gone there ever since.' The bishop gave him a present, and said, 'God bless you! go where you receive the greatest profit to your soul.'[1]

In Bishop Newton's autobiography there is a casual but very contemptuous mention of Methodism. He had been speaking of his success in preventing 'a public mass-house' at Bristol. 'The building,' he says, 'was converted into a dwelling-house, and nothing of the kind has been attempted ever since, only a bastard kind of Popery, Methodism, has troubled Bristol since that time.'[2]

Bishop Smallbrook gave his countenance to the not uncommon idea that Methodism was nearly akin to Romanism. In his charge of 1746 he declares that 'if the false doctrines of the Methodists prevail, they must unavoidably create a general disorder in our constitution, and often favour the return of Popery itself.'[3]

The most able, though not, perhaps, the most effective of the opponents of Methodism was Bishop Warburton. There was too little common between the two for the attack to have much force. 'The Methodists,' Jones of Nayland remarked, 'despised Warburton for a part of his character, as much as he despised them for a part of theirs;' and he

---

[1] *Life of Lady Huntingdon*, i. 18; quoted in Kilvert's *Life of Hurd*, 201.
[2] Bishop Newton's *Account of his Life*, p. 117.
[3] Quoted by Overton in *The Church of the Eighteenth Cent.*, ii. 138.

added, with much epigrammatic truth, 'his learning is almost as much unlike to Christianity as their Christianity is unlike to learning.'[1] Warburton looked upon the whole movement as fanaticism, which, 'pretending to be of the Church, disdains to shelter itself under the peaceable shade of a legal toleration.'[2] His treatise upon 'The Doctrine of Grace' is directed chiefly against Methodism, but also against William Law, whom he describes as its original parent, and Zinzendorf, its early nurse. All forms of modern enthusiasm were to his mind a viperous brood, which a champion of sober reason should feel bound at once to crush. He granted that since the middle of the preceding century a reaction which rested religion too entirely on bare reason, had thrown into the background some of the most distinctive doctrines of Christianity. But he was afraid the new 'enthusiasts' would only increase the evil. Alarm had been taken, he said, and efforts made to bring back the slighted doctrine of redemption, and to reinstate it in its ancient credit, 'till the old Puritan fanaticism revived under the name of Methodism, and, as it spread, carried once more, as far as differences of times would allow, those gospel principles to their old abusive extremes.' It seemed to him only a natural consequence that it should result in a widespread disposition to revert to the old latitudinarian excesses.[3] He quoted largely both from William Law and Wesley; but neither in mystics nor in Methodists could he see anything but harm. It is, however, remarkable that Warburton fully grants that a work far transcending what mere reason could do was effected in the first conversions to Christianity by the direct operation of the Holy Spirit. 'When, therefore,' he concludes, 'we see the deepest im-

---

[1] Horne and Jones' *Correspondence*, p. 31.
[2] Warburton's *Doctrine of Grace*, chap. xii.; *Works*, iv. 686.
[3] *Doctrine of Grace*, p. 716.

pressions of evil custom, and the darkest stains of corrupted nature thus suddenly wiped out and effaced, to what must we ascribe such a total reform but to the all-powerful operation of grace?'[1] No wonder that Wesley, fresh from his experience of changes no less striking and complete, should exclaim that 'never were reflections more just than these,' and ask why any one should think it impossible that similar conversions should be happening even now around him.[2]

Lavington, Bishop of Exeter, published in 1747 an elaborate work against the Methodists, entitled 'The Enthusiasm of Methodists and Papists compared.' It was, beyond question, a very effective attack. The leaders of the movement are said to have felt and feared its power, and to have taken great pains in buying up and suppressing the copies.[3] Lavington had not a difficult task before him. Palpably to every observer, and carefully chronicled in the journals of the preachers, were to be found innumerable instances of extravagance and superstition, of ignorance, credulity, and presumption. They were invisible to those who were carried away by the enthusiasm of religious fervour; they could easily be pardoned by all who felt that such evils were superficial and insignificant, as compared with results which to thousands of souls were nothing less than light out of darkness, and a turning unto godliness from sin. But when such facts were detached from the fervent surroundings which did so much to excuse them— when they were marshalled out in long array under the cold light of criticising reason—when they were confronted, so to say, with a wholly unsympathetic audience, and encountered by the wit and learning of a counsel who had studied the case with the one purpose of bringing it into discredit and ridicule, it can be well understood that to

[1] *Doctrine of Grace*, Pt. II. ch. i., iv. 595.
[2] Wesley's *Works*, ix. 151.   [3] *Qu. Review*, vii. 407.

many minds the exposure seemed convincing and complete. Looking back on Lavington's work with a better knowledge than he could have of what Methodism has been able to achieve, his treatise does little honour to his memory. Whatever were the faults of Methodism, it seems intolerable that it should be treated in so flippant and contemptuous a way. Yet the bishop was a man of much worth. It is said of him that he was a faithful and vigilant pastor and an awakening preacher,[1] and that he died with words of joy upon his lips—'Δόξα τῷ Θεῷ.'[2] Only, like Warburton, he was utterly unable to understand the best points of Methodism. He thought it a revival of the fanatic excesses which the preceding century had seen so much of, or of the wild vagaries which, some thirty years before, the 'French Prophets' had introduced into England. It is a curious study to read side by side, and section with section, the charges advanced by Lavington, and the detailed justification which John Wesley wrote in reply. Often Wesley argues against his opponent, and explains; often he indignantly remonstrates; but often, and especially on such points as were common between Wesley and the mystics, he avows that it is no longer a question of argument, but of feelings which the other had no capacity of understanding. 'Far out of your depth,' he exclaims, speaking of conflict with powers of evil; and presently, when the subject is spiritual loneliness, 'Equally out of your element!' Or, again, when Lavington had been quoting what seemed to him foolish and extravagant sayings about vicissitudes of faith, torments and scruples, doubts and fears, relapsings and despairs—'I cannot,' writes Wesley, 'prevail upon myself to prostitute this awful subject by entering into any debate concerning it with one who is so innocent of the

---

[1] Polwhele's *History of Devonshire*, p. 513.
[2] Polwhele's introd. to Lavington's *Enthusiasm of Methodists*, &c., lxxx.

whole affair.'[1] Some have said that Lavington in later life regretted the violence of his attack. Polwhele denies this; but in any case there were many good men who were no less impatient of Methodism than he; and it must be remembered that the violent language in which Whitefield sometimes indulged made it only too likely that those who disliked Methodism would be as keen-sighted to its defects as they would be disinclined to understand its merits.

Bishop Douglas of Carlisle (1787–91) was an acute observer and a skilled critic; but his work against the Methodists, entitled 'The Criterion,' is perhaps chiefly noticeable for the instance it gives that even great natural powers of discernment may be wholly at fault in judging of movements which are guided rather by feeling than by reason. 'The journals,' he writes, 'and other works of Wesley and Whitefield furnish an inconceivable number of most curious instances of this kind amongst their misled followers. But as the writings of these gentlemen, already almost as much forgot as if they had never been published, may be difficult to be met with, the reader will have full satisfaction by consulting that excellent treatise, 'The Enthusiasm of Methodists and Papists compared,' in which the folly and absurdity of Methodism are so clearly pointed out, that it is amazing so many who would neither be thought deficient in sense, nor mistaken in their notion of religion, should still continue in this state of superstitious enchantment.'[2] Douglas lived long enough into this century to know that the flame which Wesley and Whitefield had kindled was not thus lightly to be snuffed out.

It has seemed desirable to give some general account of the action of the bishops in regard of Methodism. Their attitude in the matter is illustrative both of the men and of

[1] Wesley's Answer to Lavington, *Works*, ix. 28.
[2] Douglas's *Criterion*, p. 170.

their times. On no one point is there a greater change for the better in the Episcopate of our own days than in their greatly increased sympathy in the feelings and interests of the masses. Eighteenth-century bishops seem to have had very little in common with the general bulk of the population. The clergy, whatever might be their faults, at all events lived among the people, and were a part of them. The bishops, even those of them who had risen quite out of the ranks, lived for the most part in quite a different world. They made, in somewhat formal and ceremonial manner, their confirmation tours; but otherwise they seem to have associated almost exclusively with the upper classes of society, with the superior clergy, and with men of study and letters. They preached far less than now before large popular assemblies; the public meeting and the busy committee-room were almost unknown to them; they troubled themselves (speaking of the great majority) but very little with wide plans for improving the condition of the people, and for instituting and organising new forms of spiritual machinery. Their official work completed, they retired with a thoroughly satisfied conscience to fill up the long remainder of the day in the quiet employments of study or of society, of friendship or of hospitality. The graver and more serious had abundant time for theological reading, and of devoting as much labour as they chose to the work of meeting the arguments of the Deist or the Arian, the Roman Catholic or the Methodist. Those who preferred other studies could follow out without blame or compunction their classical, or literary, or scientific, or antiquarian tastes. Some, no doubt, took great interest in various charitable institutions; but, with rare exceptions, there was sadly little in common between them and the multitude whose irreligion they deplored, or who hung with pangs of awakened conscience upon the impassioned lips of

Whitefield. Enthusiasm, which to their minds was synonymous with gross fanaticism, seemed scarcely less formidable to them than infidelity itself. In one sense it was almost more alarming. For unbelief, or what was generally held to be such, was a familiar enemy, against whom the more learned of them were trained, equipped, and prepared. Enthusiasm was a new opponent, or rather it might be the re-quickening into life of a power which a century before had dashed to the ground crowns and mitres, churches and constitutions. They knew not what it might be, or how far, if it gained head, it might corrupt all pure and reasonable religion. Little or nothing of it came before their actual sight and hearing, but they were informed to some extent of its excitements and irregularities. The dim and scarcely intelligible murmur of it reached them in their cathedrals and their studies; and now and then they were perplexed with questions from incumbents who knew no better than themselves what to make of these new lights. Moreover, they had tasted to the full the sweets of tranquillity and peace. A sort of cultivated indolence, not unliterary and not altogether undevout, had stolen over them. But now these wandering preachers must have awakened in them some uneasy thoughts. Their dignified leisure did not stand out in very favourable contrast with the unwearied activity of many among these itinerants. Nor were such reflections left to themselves only to make. Many of the preachers, even while they yet claimed to be true members of the National Church, were very unsparing in their censures of the slackness which they asserted to be everywhere common both among bishops and clergy. While, therefore, the majority of the Episcopate were inclined to condemn the Methodists, as doing more harm by their excesses than they did good by their zeal, we can scarcely doubt that this mistrust of the movement was generally blended with something of more personal feeling. In the end the stimulus of the Methodist revival was scarcely less beneficial than that of the Evangelicals in reawakening the energies of the Church; but, for the time, both in their merits and defects, the average bishop and the average Methodist were as opposite to one another in thought and sympathy as worthy Christian men well could be.

In the course of these pages there will be abundant opportunity of referring to the views entertained by this or that bishop upon various questions of the day. It would be needless, therefore, to lengthen out a chapter on the Episcopate collectively. Mere generalities have very little interest. It is pleasanter also, in this case, to write of the individual rather than of the class. As a class, the bishops of the greater part of the eighteenth century were undoubtedly deficient, although not so much by their own fault as by the general circumstances of the age. As individuals, there were a number of excellent men who, in times when the general standard of episcopal duty was higher, would doubtless have been as exemplary as bishops as they were estimable in their private and personal capacity. Nor, indeed, was the age, even as it was, altogether wanting in excellent prelates who discharged their offices in a manner worth of any time.

END OF THE FIRST VOLUME.

Spottiswoode & Co. Printers, New-street Square, London.

www.ingramcontent.com/pod-product-compliance
Lightning Source LLC
Chambersburg PA
CBHW022116290426
44112CB00008B/690